THE INSIDE TEXT

T0135033

The Kluwer International Series on Computer Supported Cooperative Work

---

Volume 4

---

ecord for this book is available from the Library of Congress.

-6780-7 (PB)
)-3060-4 (e-book)

inger,
0 AA Dordrecht, The Netherlands.

ted in North, Central and South America

, Norwell, MA 02061, U.S.A.

tries, sold and distributed

300 AH Dordrecht, The Netherlands.

d-free paper

The Inside Te

Social, Cultural and D
on SMS

Edited by

R. HARPER

Microsoft Research,
Cambridge, U.K.

L. PALEN

University of Colorado,
Boulder, CO, U.S.A.

and

A. TAYLOR

Microsoft Research,
Cambridge, U.K.

 Springer

A C.I.P. Catalogue

ISBN 978-90-48
ISBN 978-1-402

Published by Spr
P.O. Box 17, 330

Sold and distribu
by Springer,
101 Philip Driv

In all other cou
by Springer
P.O. Box 322, 3

Printed on ac

For Lilja

(who came into this world when this book was being written)

Table of Contents

Section Two: Texting and the Moral Order of Place

Section Three: Designers' Text

Contributors

Frøydis Bakken, University of Oslo, Norway

Sara Berg, Umea University, Sweden

Keith Cheverst, University of Lancaster, England

Bella Ellwood-Clayton, University of Melbourne, Australia

Shelly Farnham, Microsoft Research, Redmond, USA

Dan Fitton, University of Lancaster, England

Julian Gebhardt, University of Erfurt, Germany

Ylva Hard af Segerstad, Goteborg University, Sweden

Richard Harper, Social Shaping Research and Microsoft Research, England

Joachim Höflich, University of Erfurt, Germany

Mimi Ito, University of Southern California and Keio University, Japan

Scott Jenson, Jenson Design, Minneapolis, USA

Tom Julsrud, Telenor, Norway

Pedram Keyani, Microsoft Research, Redmond, USA

Timo Kopomaa, University of Helsinki, Finland

Ditte Laursen, University of Southern Denmark

Christian Licoppe, France Telecom, France

Rich Ling, Telenor, Norway

Daisuke Okabe, Yokohama National University, Japan

Sarah Olofsson, Blekinge Institute of Technology, Ronneby, Sweden

Leysia Palen, University of Colorado, USA

Mårten Pettersson, Blekinge Institute of Technology, Ronneby, Sweden

Carole Anne Rivière, France Telecom, France

Mark Rouncefield, University of Lancaster, England

Matthias Schneider-Hufschmidt, Siemens, Munich, Germany

Alex Taylor, Social Shaping Research and Microsoft Research, England

Birgitte Yttri, Telenor, Norway

Inside Text: an introduction

Richard Harper, Leysia Palen and Alex Taylor

Mobile phones and the short-text messaging service (SMS or "text") in particular are new social phenomena, much marvelled at and much commented upon (See Brown et al, 2002; Katz & Aakhus, 2002; Ling, 2004). This success is said to be because mobiles allow new levels of micromanagement in an age of fraught and tight deadlines (Plant, 2002), or because they allow communities to create and sustain their own language networks (Sandor, 2003: 71-81); but for some commentators, mobiles are making teenagers inarticulate (Gergen, 2003, pp227-41); they are a distraction from true engagement with people at a face to face level (Katz, 2003, pp21-33), and, along with other technologies, they are leading to a dissolution of the 'civic' society (cf Sennet. For a sample of papers on these topics see: Nyiri, 2003).

What is certain is that mobile communication, whether it be fully duplex telephony or SMS traffic, is at once 'merely' people communicating, undertaking the prosaic activity of chit-chat within the frame of a particular medium, yet at the same time, many other things too: talking is after all not always merely chit-chat: it is made up of very many different goals, functions, and content. Indeed one might argue that what one finds when one looks at texting is a microcosm of society at large, as Harvey Sack's taught us long ago about everyday conversations (Sacks, 1992).

Insofar as mobile communication is thus a reflection of the society of which it is part and a technology helping society evolve, it is a wonderful topic for inquiry, both technological and social. It is, also, an opportunity to do good research and to do bad. For example, the sociological research on texting (certainly what has been published in the past four or five years), attests not only to the insights that sociological explorations can provide but also to the limits of sociology when it is done poorly. To capture and explore just how society is writ large in these little alphanumeric messages known as texts requires a sensitivity as well as a delicacy of understanding that is not always present. It is all too easy for the precise meaning of a text message to become obscured in the sociological efforts to prise open society; and on the other hand in focusing on the meaning, the sociological analysis can result in society itself disappearing from view (See Harper & Gosset, forthcoming).

Richard Harper, Leysia Palen and Alex Taylor (Eds), The Inside Text: Social, Cultural and Design Perspectives on SMS, 1–6.

The technological research, too, is at times wonderfully insightful, offering new designs and opportunities for use that Nokia had no inkling of when they put the SMS protocol to the GSM standards committee all those years ago. But some technical research shows very little insight into the unique properties of texting or how new technologies might enhance those properties. All too often texting is seen as merely a halfway point on the path to a future where fully duplex video-telephony will kill off any need for text (See Jenson, chapter 15 of this book).

It is in light of this mix of good and bad, of well reasoned and creative, that this book has been brought together. And key to the success or otherwise of the book is not simply that we have selected chapters that we think have merit, but we have sought to bring together a range of perspectives on SMS that enable one to see clearly the relative merits and limitations of any one perspective. No one discipline can explore every aspect of what texting means to those who do it, nor is there any one design that would answer all that users would want in the future. Of course, this holds true for any subject matter: texting is no different in this. But our concern is not to debunk disciplinary differences; ours is related to the interdisciplinary area known as computer supported cooperative work or CSCW. Now, this interdisciplinary area entails bringing together the social and the technological to create new insights and perspectives on how to understand the social shaping of technology, the evolution of social practice and how to design in ways that produces greater richness and opportunity for users. In sum, the book deliberately brings together different perspectives, different research paradigms and different orders of social and technological inquiry to create a space for thinking about text.

The book is divided into three sections. The first consists of chapters that attempt to locate texting (and mobile communications more generally) within a larger frame of understanding. Thus Höflich & Gebhardt explore the relationship between the unique and common properties of text and other communications media when considered as part of a culture of widespread and multifarious communicative practice. From their view, texting needs to be understood both for what it is and what it is not, and this is in part determined by analysis of the broader culture of communication of which texting is a part. Their chapter also has the great merit of introducing more of the German research on communications which is sadly unknown in the Anglo Saxon research world.

In *Language and SMS*, Ylva Hård af Segerstad explores some of the specifics of texting from a linguistic point of view, where the goal is to highlight language use in the general, and in particular how its general grammatical and lexical forms are adapted and transformed in texting. Though her evidence is taken from one county, it would seem reasonable to assume that similar linguistic transformations occur in other languages: and this is why it is in the first section of the book, *Text versus Talk.*

The next chapter looks at another aspect of rules as manifest in communication, this time in the rule that texts, like turns-at-talk in ordinary face to face conversation, should be replied to. Applying insights from conversations analysis, Laursen shows how texting has turn-taking qualities which impose a certain order or moral implicativeness on participants. In this, as with Hård af Segerstad's work, the claim is made that there are some general properties of texting that are worth mapping out.

Clearly, there are likely to be other properties that these two chapters don't deal with; but they have expanded the territory that others can explore. It is unlikely that such endeavours will ever produce a fully blown taxonomy of texting since the dynamics of user behaviour and technological change will render that all but impossible. Still, there are certain tasks that need to be done, even in light of this constant change and one is sketching the genres of texting. This is the task that Ling, Jarlsule & Yttri attempt in chapter 4. The authors look forward, too, to the prospect of multimedia messaging and its particular genres. Ling et al consider how one might gather and generate evidence, and how one might sort it with this task in mind. Doing so entails drawing parallels with other communications media: thus we are returned to the opening chapter that locates texting as one genre within a larger frame that includes not only texting but letter writing, email and, of course, talk.

The next set of chapters seek to specify the particular social, political and emotional contexts in which texting occurs. If the first section seeks to delineate the common properties of texting as one species of communicative act, then the chapters in this section seek to define how cultural variation and localised practice are determinative of what text gets used for in particular places: hence this section is called *Texting and the Moral Order of Place*. The first chapter in this section, by Riviere & Licoppe reports on a comparative study of texting in France and Japan. In the former country, texting is used to avoid the emotional possibilities of close contact whereas in the latter country texting is used to negotiate subtle rules about interpersonal access rights. Put another way, in France, couples use text to avoid certain possibilities relating to emotional expression; in Japan, to achieve a formality of address and social propriety through using text to avoid interrupting those they have no right to. In the following chapter, Ito & Okabe report on their own studies of Japan, focusing in particular on how teenagers try and use texting and mobile telephony more generally to alter the spatial and social geometries they exist within. Whereas before, their bedrooms, their classrooms and so forth were places that caught and restrained teenagers, now, with texting, these bonds of place seem weaker.

These two chapters report on contemporary activity; the next takes a look back at the emergence of texting in Finland. Kopomaa was one of the first sociologists to report on texting in large part because of his location: in the country in which texting was invented: Finland. The benefits that texting provided then and which motivated its widespread adoption thereafter do not seem to have changed greatly, though certainly we are beginning to recognise much more cultural variation in how these benefits are utilised. For example, in Norway, deaf teenagers find texting a real benefit, the benefits of doing so being at once obvious and more subtle than one might imagine. It takes no wit to appreciate that texting is an easy medium for those who cannot hear; but texting is also asynchronous in nature. It can also help people bond. This is the thesis of Bakken in chapter 8. Using Granovetter's network theory approach to social relations (Granovetter, 1973), she is able to show how these bonds are sustained with texting, as well as provide some indices of their strength.

Continuing our concern with Scandinavia and unusual social groups, Ling reports on the relationship between texting and deviance in Norway. He finds that there is indeed a relationship between deviance and texting, though it is not clear that there is any causal link. Villainy may require communication; that is all. Ellwood-Clayton takes us a long way from this and concerns herself with romance in the Philippines. She finds that Filippino girls exploit the anonymity and discreteness of texting to cultivate multiple relationships with boys and men, and, further, stretch those relationships to include the most passing and ephemeral to the most erotic, from the short lived to those which become almost permanent. The evidence suggests that here in this vast archipelago one will find a new form of blind dating, this time on a truely enormous scale. Whether this is just a passing fad or something that texting will afford in the future waits to be seen.

Whether this will be so of course depends upon the willingness of technology designers to ensure that some of the affordances that make texting so usable remain embedded in mobile devices. There is no guarantee that they will do so. Thus it is that we come to the third section of the book, *Designers' Text*. The selection of chapters here commence with one that reports on the history of research in to text input on mobile devices and shows that, though it might seem obvious to the layman that text entry is not altogether easy, other ways of entering text are not any better. Schneider-Hufschmidt has been in the thick of research in this area since more or less the beginning of the mobile age, working within one of half a dozen or so technology providers that helped define the GSM standard.

Olofsson & Pettersson treat text entry in quite a different way, exploring how machines might produce automatic text messages dependant upon certain types of systems' state rules. Taking the example of distributed support for house heating systems, they suggest that texting could be one of the ways that machines communicate to roving workers. Texting affords a discrete way of doing so with little interactional overhead for the user. Texting in this regard offers a lightweight solution to machine person connectivity, avoiding thereby the dilemmas of designing for complex information exchange. In particular the Olofsson & Pettersson solution consists of place-to-person connectivity; in contrast, Cheverst, Fitton & Rouncefield's chapter reports on an application that allows persons to text-a-place. In this case the place is an office door within a computer science department or a range of places in a charitable organisation. In both cases, the benefits of text to place were clear but these need to be seen as additional rather than substitutive of other communicative practise (like phone calls and email).

The same argument is put forward in Berg, Taylor & Harper's *Gift of the Gab*. This holds that people use text messages to create systems of give and take that help sustain already existing social bonds. But the values of such texts – gifting as they call it – are such that it suggests to Berg et al how technology might be designed to support and exploit these social practices. The most obvious of these implications has to do with the design of text storage on devices, but these implications can be developed to help design the interface for a host of applications, most particular the address book.

The idea of social connectivity motivates Keyani & Farnham's SWARM: an application that is designed to use SMS as a communications channel for distributed groups of friends and colleagues. Rather than confining themselves to the mobile device, as do Berg et al, these researchers develop an application running on a web server which mobile users log into when wishing to send, store and learn about others' activities. Though trials of the application demonstrated that users found interacting with the remote server difficult, the basic benefits of SWARM were clear.

Designing for mobile phones is perhaps one of the most underestimated and yet difficult tasks of the current period: a period one might call the mobile age. Designing for mobiles is not a question of shrinking down applications and programmes designed for the PC: such solutions are hardly solutions at all since they make mobile devices almost impossible to use (for discussion of the issues here see Lindholm et al, 2003). The failure in the mobile marketplace of those manufacturers who persists in this view is testament to this. The problems of mobile design, and the ways in which those problems can be avoided is the task of the last chapter of the book by Scott Jenson. In *Default thinking: Why consumer products fail,* Jenson explores how texting has succeeded in part because of its apparent ease of use, at least given the values (what one might call the social values) it affords. Jenson contrasts this with how much more difficult multi-media messaging is to undertake, all the more so when the values thus afforded do not seem any greater that those provided by SMS. He does not confine himself to critique, however, but outlines how careful thought about what texting enables can be used to define possibilities for future services: these include the 'text tap' and 'voiceSMS'.

Whether these possibilities will show themselves in the next few years is of course another matter, but Jenson's chapter brings us back to the Höflich & Gebhardt arguments in the first: both concur in believing that human action is at once framed by and framing of the technologies that are designed to support it. These technologies, whatever they are, offer discrete and particular benefits and are rarely substitutive of one another: just as the written letter is different from the spoken word, so texting is different from either. These differences are the frames in which we operate in our everyday lives; these are also the constraints with which the sociologist, the linguist and the designer have to explore and operate. This text, this book, is itself a small frame in which explorations of these constraints are presented. Whether they are conclusive, comprehensive or accurate is of course a judgement that the reader must make. Welcome to the Inside Text.

References

Brown, B. Green, N & Harper, R. (Eds) (2002) *Wireless World: Social and Interactional Aspects of the Mobile Age*, Springer, Godalming.

Ellwood-Clayton, B. (2003) 'Virtual Strangers: Young Love and Texting in the Filipino Archipelego of Cyberspace,' in Nyiri, K (Ed) *Mobile Democracy*, Passengen Verlag, Vienna, pp225-239.

Gergen, K., (2002), 'The challenge of absent presence' in Katz, J. & Aakhus, M, *Perpetual Contact. Mobile Communication, Private Talk, Public Performance,* Cambridge University Press, Cambridge and New York, pp 227-241.

Granovetter, Mark S. 1973 "The Strength of Weak Ties", American *Journal of Sociology*, Volume 78, Issue 6 (May, 1973), 1360-1380.

Grinter, R. E., & Eldridge, M. A. (2001), 'Y Do Tngrs Luv 2 Txt Msg?' in *Seventh European Conference on Computer Supported Cooperative Work.* Bonn, Germany, 18–20 September, 2001.

Harper, R. & Gosset, P. (Forthcoming), The Moral Order of Text, in Hoflich, J. & Gebhardt, J. (Eds) *Mobile Communication: Current Trends in Research*, Peter Lang, GmbH-Europaischer Verlag der Wissenschften, Berlin.

Hoflich, J. & Gebhardt, J. (2003) *Vermittlungskulturen im Wandel: Brief – E-mail – SMS*, Lang, Frankfurt am Main.

Ito, M. (2003) 'Mobile Phones, Japanese Youth, and the Replacement of Social Contact', in *Proceedings of Frontstage-back stage: Mobile Communication and the Renegotiation of the Public Sphere,* Ling & Pederson, (Ed), Telenor, Norway, Summer.

Kopomaa, T. (2000), *The City in your Pocket. Birth of the mobile information society*, Helsinki, Gaudeamus.

Katz, J. (2003) 'A Nation of Ghosts', in Nyiri, K (ed) *Mobile Democracy*, Passengen Verlag, Vienna, pp21-33.

Katz, J. & Aakhus, M, (2001), *Perpetual Contact. Mobile Communication, Private Talk, Public Performance,* Cambridge University Press, Cambridge and New York.

Kaseniemi, E. (2001) Mobile Message, Tampere University Press, Tampere, Finland.

Lindholm, C., Keinonen, T., & Kiljander, H. (2003) *Mobile Usability: How Nokia changed the face of the mobile phone*, McGraw-Hill New York.

Massey, D. (1994), *Space, Place and Gender*, University of Minneapolis Press, Minneapolis.

Ling, R. (2004) *The Mobile Connection: The Cell Phone's Impact on Society*, Morgan Kaufmann, New York.

Meyerwitz, J. (1985) *No Sense of Place*, Oxford University Press, Oxford.

Nyiri, K. (2003) *Mobile Democracy*, (Ed) Passengen Verlag, Vienna.

Plant, S. (2002), *On the Mobile: the effects of mobile telephones on social and individual life.* Report commissioned by Motorola.

Sacks, H. (1992) *Lectures on Conversation*, (ed. G. Jefferson). Blackwell, Oxford.

Sandor, K. (2003) 'The fall of linguistic aristocratism', in Nyiri, K (Ed), *Mobile Communication,* Passengen Verlag, Vienna, pp71-81.

Section One: Text versus Talk

1 Changing Cultures of Written Communication: Letter – E-mail – SMS

Joachim R. Höflich and Julian Gebhardt

Introduction

The eighteenth and nineteenth centuries are regarded as the heyday of a German culture of letter writing. The letter was released from the constraints of a restrictive formal language style (*Kanzleistil*) and was now written in German instead of Latin. The letter had always been considered a speech substitute as well as a 'written conversation' and so the orientation to the conversation even became the new guideline of letter-writing. Write as you speak, this was effectively the instruction that is associated with the name Christian Fürchtegott Gellert (1715-1769). It may be an overstatement, but you could consider Gellert a prophet of electronic mail, which is released from all formal constraints and indeed is written much like one speaks. Gellert would not necessarily be pleased by this. For him, it was not about writing as one speaks, but rather: "When I write: I do it only, as if I were speaking, and I must not drive the natural to the revolting" (Gellert 1989: 113). In contrast to the unwieldy and often obsequious official writing style, the ideal style of writing was now naturalness and ease. The letter was rational, plain and clear. When one thinks of the circumstances of the German letter culture, one thinks mainly of the sentimental and effusive personal letter, which was understood to be not just a mere written exchange but rather a visit to the soul, carrying a sometimes excessive intimacy (*Inniglichkeit*), of affairs of the heart, ideas of friendship, of questions of spirit, of culture, philosophy and education.

At the same time, a conversation through letters was not easy. Letters very often had an impressive scope and the cost of sending a letter was so considerable that a criterion of exclusivity existed. However with the introduction of the stamp, a standard and low rate of postage (regardless of distance and season) the costs declined (see Siegert 1996). In general, the postal service improved, although insignia which are so familiar today, such as the letterbox and the postman did not appear until the 19th century (see Fontius 1988: 277). Despite this, it seems that today one do not want to take the trouble of composing letters and certainly not long ones. Over one hundred years ago, in his history of the German Letter, Georg Steinhausen had already seen the decline of the letter culture coming, in face of the

9

Richard Harper, Leysia Palen and Alex Taylor (Eds), The Inside Text: Social, Cultural and Design Perspectives on SMS, 9–31.
© 2005 *Springer. Printed in the Netherlands.*

postcard and particularly the telegram "because", he wrote about the letter, "its true history is behind us and it looks as if its further development is over anyhow" (Steinhausen 1889: 410). Steinhausen's description of the situation is still relevant. Even then, he realized that the period was characterized by brevity and convenience, to the point that the 'valuable' characteristics and formalities that make up the letter would be more and more rejected. A distinctive pessimism with regard to the future of the letter has persisted ever since (see Hess-Lüttich 1997: 225f.). This applies more than ever as the medial competitors have increased dramatically in contemporary media societies.

In the meantime, there are more medial alternatives than ever available to get in contact with others. A letter culture is being expanded if not replaced by a plurality of communication cultures – although the internet and mobile communication are not the first to do so[1]. After all, besides the letter – one could speak of a telephone-, fax-, e-mail-, cellphone-, or SMS-culture. Culture here refers to different ways of dealing with a medium. Speaking of culture in this context means culture in a broad sense – as an expression of "meaningful practices and experiences that can be found in a given social world" (Hörning 2001: 157). Cultures of communication understood in this way are meaningful (*sinnhaft*) communicative practices for dealing with interpersonal communications media. However these practices are in no way uniform; behind the use of a medium there exists a multitude of practices. Seen as such, cultures of communication are not based solely upon the practices of an isolated use of a singular medium, but rather in the use of extensive, communicative and especially medial activities: "Whoever (...) wants to take a meaningful look at the use of media must contemplate different media, must take into account the ensemble of media that people have to deal with today" (Bausinger 1983: 32/33). With regard to Friedrich Krotz (2001: 33) one can speak of an ongoing process of "mediatisation" (*Mediatisierung*), meaning that in the course of history "new communication media were always developed and found and find use in many ways. Consequently, ever more complex medial forms of communication are developing, and communication takes place more regularly, for longer and in many more areas of life and is related to more themes regarding media."

As part of these extensive mediatisation processes also "telematisation" (*Telematisierung*) should be understood, whereby the term telematisation expressly emphasizes that everyday life is penetrated by long-distance communication media. This extends from household multi-media equipment such as the telephone, fax, answering machine, internet and e-mail to the omnipresence of medial communication through mobile equipments. At the same time, at least passing similarities to the Flusserian term *telematic* can be seen, if one understands this to mean a technology "thanks to which we come closer to each other" (Flusser 1998: 18), without having to agree with him that this is a technology "which transmits the

---

[1] Nonetheless, at least before the telegraph, the letter was without competition. In this sense, in his 1857 treatise on the telegram as a means of transport, Karl Knies (1996: 75) wrote: "As different as the forms and modes of transport of communication are, until the use of the telegraph, when this was mentioned one thought only of the letter and the letter post which carries newspaper sheets."

establishment of a society for the realisation of one thing into another, from the utopian to the possible".

Even if things will be different in the future, for the moment the new media are being used mainly as media for written communication. Although the heyday of the letter culture also demonstrated that the desire to communicate was almost impossible to suppress (Nickisch 1991: 45), at the moment people are writing more than ever before. People meet through the internet for ongoing written (synchronic) conversations conducted via the computer keyboard – the online-chat – and they post their written thoughts and opinions in public forums. The dominant use of the internet – sending e-mails – should also be mentioned. Although a slight declining tendency has been noted recently, the use of e-mail is still *the* dominant form of internet use (see Eimeren et al. 2003: 347). Having been around for 30 years now, the e-mail is already an 'old' medium. In contrast, a relatively new medium is the Short Message Service (SMS) which offers the opportunity to send and receive short (until recently only up to 160 characters) text messages over a cell phone. The use of text messaging spread very quickly in a short period of time and is a particularly popular use of the cell phone among teenagers.

In the following the letter especially together with the e-mail and Short Message Service will be focused. It will be investigated whether this arrival of new forms of written communication really can be seen as a manifestation of a 'letter culture' (albeit one in the process of change) and if this constitutes a new electronically based epistolary practice. Uka (1994: 108) suggested the following definition for the letter: "In communication theory, the letter is a communication written on a piece of paper and targeted to an address (one-way if the contained message is informative and commanding, two-way if an answer is expected), delivered by a person or an organisation (the postal service)".

If one accepts this definition, the aforementioned media – e-mail and SMS – would have nothing in common with the letter. Even if you hesitate to see these media as 'letters' they could still be considered as forms of 'letter-like' communication, which are associated with the same functions as they are performed by the universal medium of the letter. This would be agreeable if one accepts Nickisch's recommended definition of the letter on the basis of its basic functions. The invariant communicative possibilities of the letter are highlighted by transmission of information, request and self-expression. In Nickisch's words (1991: 12): "Because the letter functions as a conversation substitute with the goal of a dialogue exchange, like each communicative act, it shows a corresponding feature to be dominant: it informs (factually-oriented), appeals (partner-oriented) or demonstrates (self-oriented)". A further commonality among the letter, e-mail, and SMS is that they are all written communication media which operate under the condition of a temporal phase delay (although with transmission and receipt of text messages, this delay is quite short). It is precisely this phase delay which differentiates these media from the online-chat for example, which also takes place in written form but temporal synchronised. In addition, it is the personal letter that is of interest here and therefore online-forums are not considered in this study, although they indeed could also be considered as forms of public letters.

With regard to the analysis of a changing culture of written communication a functional approach could be considered. A related question to this is: which functions are assigned to these media in the context of a common communicative practice? Such a change demonstrates in particular that new medial possibilities are related to specific intended usages (functions), which disassociate these from other medial alternatives, especially the 'classic' letter. After all, also the old media will always be affected by the new media. It is not just new media that arrive and (have to) find their place in the structure of communicative practices; the previous media also change "in that they are used for new purposes, their area of application expands or is reduced and becomes specialized" (Krotz 2001: 19). This emphasizes the necessity of investigating media in their entirety of (medial as well as non-medial) communicative everyday activities. In turn, the empirical methods should correspond to this.

Forms and functions of 'letter-like' communication – empirical findings

The status of the 'letter-like' media can only be investigated in a broad research context. Here the analysis of changing cultures of communication, as exemplified by the media of written communication, is integrated into an extensive communication research project. Within this framework, various qualitative as well as quantitative studies were conducted.

Subsequently most and for all the findings of the written survey conducted in July and August of 2001 with 367 adults about their media choice behaviours and media usage especially with regard to the letter and new communication technologies will be concerned. This study was by no means representative although we did try to attain a wide variety of respondents through quota-settings (e.g. age, sex, family status, children in the household, media equipment).[2]

---

[2] The average age of the respondents was approximately 37 years old; roughly 57% were male and 43% female. About 30% of the study subjects had a post-secondary education, 40% an advanced high school diploma, 20% a middle-level high school diploma, and 7% had a junior high school diploma. The majority of the participants (approx. 80%) lived in a household of two or more people; of these about 44% indicated that they were married and slightly more than 54% that they had children. Furthermore, the sample contained many people who lived in households that are technically well-equipped. Over 80% have use of a cell phone and personal computer, almost 65% have their own internet connection and 77% have cable or satellite reception.

The meaning of 'letter-like' communication in everyday media practices of adolescents	1.)	Written survey of 204 adolescents about the use of new communication technologies, particularly the Short Message Service (in July 2000).
	2.)	19 qualitative group discussions with adolescents about their media usage in general and the letter in particular (from July 2000 to January 2001).
The meaning of 'letter-like' communication in everyday media practices of adults	3.)	Self-administered questionnaires with 367 adults focusing media choice behaviours with a special consideration of the letter and new communication technologies (from July to August 2001).
	4.)	15 qualitative in-depth interviews with adults about the perception and usage of the letter in comparison with electronic media for interpersonal communication (from December 2001 to March 2002).
	5.)	Internationally comparative written survey (self-administered questionnaires) of 400 adults from four European countries (Finland, Spain, Italy and Germany) with special consideration of media usage and media-related attitudes (from December 2002 to March 2003).

Figure 1: Overview of different case studies

The results cited here must be seen in the context of its multi-methodical approach. They are exemplary in so far as the results of the preceding explorative qualitative orientated pre-studies reflect them and therefore are particularly suited to more clearly portray the selected findings regarding the changes of written cultures of communication. More than the other parts of the study, this survey focussed concretely on the functionalities of media of interpersonal communication. The starting point for the further considerations is the assumption that such functionalities are connected to fundamental media orientations, and with these, particular media affinities (of interest here: specific affinities to media of written communication) are expressed. Ideally, medial orientations correspond to their use. It is assumed, for example, that writing and reading based orientations go together with a more intensive reading of books and also an increased letter-writing. Media related orientations can be understood as analogous to reasons or motives for media usage. However, as could be learned especially in connection with the Uses-And-Gratifications Approach with its origins in mass communication research, the gratifications associated with media usage can only serve as limited predictors of media related behaviours. This is seen even more so with regard to media orientated attitudes and appraisals of media concerned 'images'. Also media orientations can be understood in this sense, if one assumes that these orientations are rather formed by certain group specific (i.e. dependent upon education or gender) variables than by mere individualistic or idiosyncratic features. Already the group discussions showed that there are really clear ratings concerning the estimated importance of media whereby the letter stands out here by an impressive measure. Accordingly in a very concrete and profane sense the respondents were asked to assess the importance and credibility of different media. Figure 2 illustrates the responses to the question about the importance of particular media of interpersonal communication.

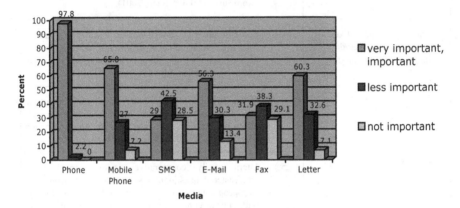

Figure 2: Importance of media

Face-to-face communication is not included in this figure. It should be noted that face-to-face communication is nearly universally – and also in accordance with other studies (see e.g. Katz et al. 1973) – of central significance and also preferred over almost all forms of medial communication. By no means unexpected was that the domestic telephone, which ranks next, followed at any rate by its mobile counterpart, the cell phone. In this case, the cell phone is differentiated from the household telephone because even though you can make calls with it, it is more than just a portable telephone. It is becoming more of a multiple functions device that can be drawn upon to call up information (in the sense of a "call up"- and "information"-medium) and recently also to send pictures and sounds (MMS) as well as sending written short text messages. In order to emphasize this special possibility, the sending of SMS messages is in turn showcased as its own medial quality. As the following diagram also shows, for 60% of the respondents the letter, closely followed by the e-mail, is regarded as a very important or important medium. According to Harper et al. (2002), social benefits are associated with the letter, which other media lack. A Finnish study came to a similar conclusion: it stressed the emotional value of the letter and emphasized that it is the handwritten letter that is particularly held in high regard (see Leppännen 2001: 53).[3]

A medium is not only a mere (neutral) vehicle for the transmission of messages. It always has a meta-communicative meaning that has an effect on the communicated

---

[3] The group discussions conducted within the framework of our research project with adolescent and adult user groups also refer to the special meaning of the handwritten letter. Above all, a 'proper' letter is considered to be one which is written by hand.

content. It is therefore significant which medium is used to distribute a message. After all, in the end the importance of a medium is connected with how credible the message transported by it is rated (see Figure 3).

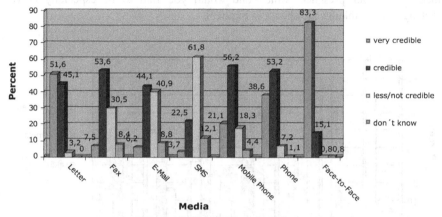

Media

Figure 3: Credibility of media

Face-to-face conversation was considered very credible, followed by the letter and then the telephone. People seem to be more skeptical towards new media: SMS, e-mail and the cell phone are regarded as less and not credible. Concerning importance as well as credibility, it appears that the appraisal of media is based more upon familiarity than actual use. Although the letter does not occupy the top spot in terms of usage preferences, it is evaluated as more important and more credible than the new medial alternatives. The following quote is taken from the aforementioned Finnish study: "Paper is considered a reliable method of communication. Something that has been said on paper (black on white) is true to the receiver in a different way than an electronic message could make it. It is something concrete. Of course, one could make a printout of an electronic message, but it is not the same thing. One might accidentally delete an electronic message, or an important message could be lost among the other e-mail messages. A paper message is considered a document (an official paper, proof)" (Leppännen 2001: 53).[4] Above all, a particular feature of the letter based correspondences must not be forgotten: the secrecy of letters (*Briefgeheimnis*). Concerning this the group discussions conducted with adolescences clearly showed that this secrecy of letters is very highly prized – a special quality which other media do not have.[5]

Mediatisation also means an omnipresence of media. However, this can constitute problems as there are rarely media-free spaces – you just can't get away from it.

---

[4] How quickly moments of credibility can change was demonstrated in the aftermath of the terror attacks of September 11, 2001: How can one trust a letter, if its contents may contain anthrax?

[5] Here, one nevertheless runs into cultural differences, as demonstrated by the study from Harper et al. (2002). While the secrecy of the letter is of great importance in Germany, according to this study, in England it is often considered a matter that concerns the entire family.

This speaks to the obtrusiveness of media; they can 'get on your nerves' and be considered as irritating. Regarding this, we asked the following question: "Sometimes certain media can be annoying. If someone is using a particular medium in your presence, which one would you find to be especially nerve racking?" The rankings are shown in Figure 4.

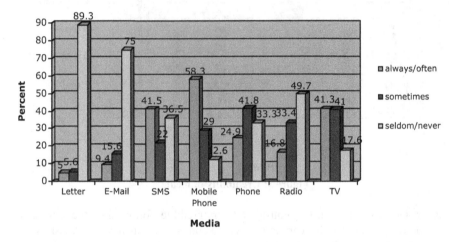

Figure 4: Obtrusiveness of media

Trouble maker number one is the cell phone: nowadays cell phones are all over the place, people everywhere are being annoyed by their "inappropriate sound" (see Ling 1998a: 70). Without having sought it, people become an involuntary audience, having to listen to someone else's private conversation conducted in public.[6] These data do not stand on their own. Other studies also show that about two thirds of respondents feel annoyed by the cell phone (see Ling 2003). In the ranking of obtrusive media, it is not the telephone that comes next but rather the television, which is apparently annoying more and more people. Contrary to expectations, the assumedly unobtrusive Short Message Service was rated the same as the television – albeit by all means ambivalent. In this case, it was not the reception of messages that was considered irritating but rather the act of typing in the messages and together with this the breakdown of familiar rules of personal face-to-face communication. It was hardly surprising that the letter was deemed to be *the* most unobtrusive medium[7] followed by the e-mail. Amazingly, as an aside, half the

[6] "Mobile phone conversations are still regarded as annoying, but perhaps no longer because they are personal but because they exclude the persons who overhear it and, paradoxically, impose the presence of the speaker on them, forcing them to adopt evasive behaviour" (Kopomaa 2000: 96).

[7] Although there might also be people who find it obtrusive to receive unwanted post. For instance, the philosopher Friedrich Nietzsche: "The letter is an unannounced visit, the mailman a mediator of impolite invasions. Every eight days one should take an hour of reading the received letters and then take a bath" (quoted in Seitz 1999: 9).

respondents found the radio rarely or never irritating. It is quite evident that people have become accustomed to this medium as a constant companion of everyday life and it does not appear to be a disturbance.

Everything speaks in favour of the letter: it is considered important, regarded as credible, and (in contrast to the electronic media) is deemed unobtrusive. This positive appraisal of the letter is quite astounding when one considers that almost one third of the respondents never write letters and approximately another third do so very seldom (i.e. less than once a month).[8] This situation appears paradoxical in so far as it is generally the rule that the importance of a medium results from its usage. However in this case, an important meaningful dimension of the letter is revealed despite the fact that this medium is seldom or never used.

With respect to medial orientations we looked in particular at the influences of education, gender and age. Education had less of an effect than was expected. However the study concerns the subject of writing and one thing cannot be ignored: the gender factor. *Women write more letters.* This is shown in Figure 5.

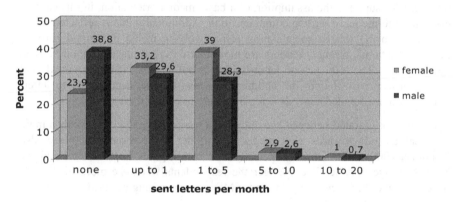

Figure 5: Gender and letters

This affinity to literally forms of communication also extends beyond just writing letters.[9] The data clearly show that women also write more SMS messages. With e-mails we found a more heterogeneous picture. E-mail still seems to be very much a masculine domain. Although it is recognized that here too women are playing an ever increasing role. After all, forms of letter-like communications – from the letter to acquaintances to holiday postcards – have a household related integrative function (see Di Leonardo 1987: 448) and taking care of this is generally a woman's responsibility. This is also reflected in the fact that among housewives

---

[8] It appears that people are more to expect a letter than to write one themselves. Only 16% replied that they do not receive any letters.

[9] For more in relation to the e-mail see e.g. the work of Boneva et al. (2003); for SMS see: Höflich/Rössler (2001) as well as Ling (2001).

one can find the smallest number of respondents who do not write any letters at all. In this context, one has to emphasize that media behaviour – in particular the affinity to speech and writing – must be investigated in the context of gender roles. In regards to the letter, Barton gets right to the point in the following quote (1991: 9): "Wives write Xmas cards (...) Husbands write checks". He expands on this: "In couples, often women write in the personal sphere, keeping in contact with friends and relations, while men deal with the business world. These roles can be followed to the extent that men are unable to write personal letters and women do not know how to write a check".

Media socialization and gender socialization are related. Women have a greater affinity for books than men do, at least when it comes to reading for pleasure. Accordingly to the Media Analysis 2001, 42.1% of women read books more than once during the week, while this is only the case for 25.5% of the men.[10] Our study revealed an interesting connection between reading books and writing letters. The more time a person spends reading books, the more often he or she will write letters. Those who do not read also do not write letters (here: almost three quarters of the non-readers do not value letter-writing), which meanwhile does not apply in reverse. This supports the assumption of a basic medial orientation, in this case an orientation to media of written communication. Additionally this is reflected in the context of media related socialization respectively in media concerned parental education patterns: frequent readers are more likely to recommend a good book to their children. The influence on letter-writing is not as clear. If the parents do not read books or write letters the children will also be less accustomed to letter-writing. A more detailed analysis is required here to clarify these tendencies.

A further link is found between age and media usage. In general, it reveals a more skeptical attitude towards new media among the older respondents (see also Kopomaa 2000: 107). This is especially true with regards to the e-mail and the Short Message Service. The younger the respondents were, the more likely they were to have had sent e-mails and SMS messages. Figure 6 depicting text messaging exemplifies this.

---

[10] Available under: www.ard.de/ard_intern/mediendaten/index.phtml/4_2 (here compare as well: Saxer/ Langenbucher/Fritz 1998: 49).

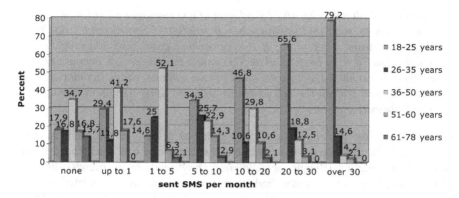

Figure 6: Age and SMS

At this point, we would like to take a closer look at the cell phone usage among adolescents (see Kasesniemi 2003; Kasesniemi/Rautiainen 2003; Ito 2003; Ito/Okabe 2003, chapter 6; Green 2003; Höflich/Gebhardt 2003; Höflich/Rössler 2002; Höflich 2001; Karvinen 2001; Ling 2001). For them, the Short Message Service is more important than the telephone function of a cell phone. It is shown that the cell phone in general and the Short Message Service in particular are used by urban youth to organize their everyday lives – i.e. mostly for making plans to meet and for reassurance ('how are you? I am fine'). In this context, the letter is quite obviously out of place. The cell phone in contrast meets distinctive peer-group orientations (see Ling 2000). For younger people it is a matter of course to always (and on short notice) be able to reach their friends and acquaintances with this medium. This is demonstrated by one of the group discussions conducted within our study[11]:

> *Interviewer: When you compare letter-writing to the various new communications media, for example SMS, e-mail, fax or the telephone, is there a particular preference for certain purposes for each medium?*
>
> *Anette: Yes, when I'd like to meet someone or quickly send a message, then I usually use the SMS. If I want to meet someone in an hour then I obviously can't send a letter. A SMS can even be written quickly in the tram. That's just the advantage of the SMS over the letter (...) letters mean just one thing: waiting!*

---

[11] The single discussion groups generally consisted of 6 to 8 participants (differentiated by age and educational level) who were, with a few exceptions, between the ages of 14 to 18. Approximately two thirds of the interviewed youth were male and lived in a four-person household, for the most part in communities of 100,000 to 500,000 inhabitants. On average, the interviewed adolescents had 150 up to 250 Euro to spend each month, although at least a third of the participants had less than 50 Euro per month. Well over three quarters owned a cell phone (mostly financed with a 'pre-paid card contract') and had access to a personal computer, of whom only about half were equipped with an internet connection.

Wolfgang: Yeah and otherwise I send a lot of text messages when I'd like to make plans to meet and always when it needs to be quick and I don't necessarily want a reply. So, if I were making plans with someone for tonight than I'd more likely send an SMS rather than an e-mail, because for me there is too much risk that the other person will not read it. In that case, I'd rather just call on the cell phone or write an SMS. (Group discussion with University students)

In this context, the perception of the cell phone as a 'personal medium' is very important. With the help of this mobile technology, one can reach the desired conversational partner (friends, acquaintances, boyfriends or girlfriends) directly without involving the parents and therefore without the associated social standardizations that were previously the norm with the household telephone (e.g. calling only within 'acceptable' hours; see also: Licoppe 2003; Ito/Okabe 2003; Ling/Yttri 2002). The following transcription of a group discussion concerning the flirting behaviour with the mobile phone makes reference to this:

Interviewer: Is the cell phone a flirt machine?

Andrea: Sure, a bit. For example, if you meet someone than you'll write to each other now and then.

Carsten: Yeah it's much easier to say something to someone over the mobile. You don't say it directly to their face, but rather over the phone.

Interviewer: Do you mean by telephone or with SMS?

Carsten: It's easier with SMS.

Bernd: It's just generally easier with the cell phone (...) in the past you got the home phone number but you didn't want to be calling there a hundred times. Today you just punch in the number on the cell phone and you can directly reach the person you want to speak to. (Group discussion with vocational school students)[12]

In connection with the usage of SMS, it also stands out that girls not only send more and longer messages but that they also write more letters than their male counterparts. For them, SMS is not really a substitute for the letter but more of a postcard-replacement, although this is not quite an exact description either. In fact, the Short Message Service can best be compared to the classroom notes that pupils pass around under the desk (see Cherubim 1981). Nevertheless these studies already showed that despite – or precisely because of – the medial alternatives, the letter still enjoys a remarkable appreciation and this leads to "(...) that an awareness of character of letter correspondence has developed, that is not actually depleted by

---

[12] At this point it should be mentioned that the cell phone and the SMS respectively are often used for flirting or delivering a 'love note' but adolescents (especially girls) vehemently maintain that a SMS cannot come close to the sentimental-emotional quality of a hand written love-letter.

the technically slower mode of transmission, but rather makes a sort of exchange of feelings and thoughts possible" (Baier 2000: 70). The letter is still regarded as a medium to communicate personal and confidential information.

But the letter also serves to demonstrate that someone is thinking of another person and, not least of all, letters are written on certain occasions (like Christmas) to keep in contact. And despite SMS and e-mail, adolescents are still writing letters and especially love letters. If anything, Bausinger was right when he asserted that in a few years the grandchildren of today's adolescents will also probably find the collected works of their grandparents one day. On the other hand, it is certain "that the back and forth of planning to meet, agreeing on meeting places, and the simple questions about the feelings of the other person (in earlier letter exchanges between lovers this was the real foundation of emotion!) today are more likely entrusted to another medium: the telephone" (Bausinger 1996: 297)[13] – or the cell phone and SMS, one could add. At least to that effect, one can agree with Bausinger when he maintains that letters are regarded almost automatically as a sign of devotion; this is in contrast to telephone calls which require much less effort. In this respect, e-mail and SMS are even rated lower. And further: e-mail and SMS appear to be functional equivalents of the telephone communication, even if they are less valued than the telephone in every realm.

This is suggested in the next table which portrays the rating of different media (in this case: letter, e-mail and SMS in comparison with the household telephone) on the basis of predetermined motives of usage.[14] In this sense a functional equivalence would exist if the motives for use largely correspond to each other, or in other words, if the curves overlapped. A tendency toward a functional equivalence can be assumed even if the estimations are not congruent but run analogous in their characteristics (as shown by the comparison of e-mail, SMS and telephone). In a partial equivalence there are deviations with respect to specific motives for usage. In the case of the letter this is true for the possibility of reassurance ('seeing how others are doing') and of making plans to meet. Here something like a niche exists which offers other media an advantage in the sense that more gratifications can be obtained – to speak in terms of a Uses-And-

---

[13] Yet it is also evident that people do not necessarily go back to the letter in the case of a temporarily absence of the telephone. At least this is suggested by the study of Wurtzel and Turner (1979). After a failure at the New Yorker Telephone Company in February 1975, people were without telephone service for 23 days. However, during this time people did not really switch to other media (certainly not the letter), with the exception that the passive reception of mass media became more popular. This is of course different in the case of a long-term media withdrawal. Studies about the usage of the letter by death-row inmates showed that here the letter takes over the functions of the telephone again (on this, see: Maybin 1999).

[14] In this particular case, the following statements were used: to get in touch on certain occasions (e.g. Christmas), to show that I am thinking of someone, to know what my friends, partner or child is doing/how they are doing, to communicate something personal or confidential, to seek comfort or be comforted when worried, to deal with a conflict (e.g. an argument) with others, to convey 'bad' news to someone, to kill time when I am bored, to make plans to meet or set an appointment, to take care of official/business matters (e.g. to order something).

Gratifications perspective (see Dimmick et al. 2000). When something personal or confidential needs to be communicated, then the letter is equal to the telephone. And if one wants to show that he or she is thinking of someone else than this medium at least comes very close. E-mail and SMS are achieving an ever-greater status in day-to-day communication. However, they are quite far (more so because they are still new) from encroaching upon the domain of personal communication occupied by the telephone – not to mention that of face-to-face communication.[15]

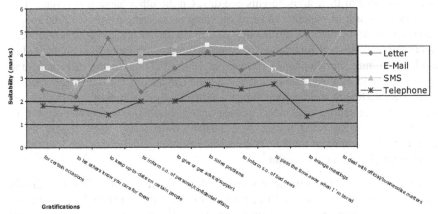

Figure 7: Letter, e-mail, SMS and telephone in comparison

The changing of medial practices – some theoretical reflections

Medial innovations are bringing about a change in the media ecology. Although such changes could not be investigated in a procedural sense of a longitudinal study here, changes were nevertheless apparent. Here the central research question was which status letter-like communication media as well as what functions these media show in a telematic society. A change in the existing cultures of mediation can be seen – as was already mentioned – in the fact that new media are added to the previous media repertoire leading to a functional differentiation straight to the point that they overtake functions which earlier media had to take simply for lack of alternatives. Within these processes, the communicative functions of earlier media can change even to the point that they will finally loose their cultural relevancy – extremely spoken. A good example for this is the telegram service of the German Postal Service (Deutsche Post AG) which meanwhile has been discontinued.

It is often assumed that the functions assigned to media are related to general media orientations coming into effect in certain situations but showing an affinity to

---

[15] Notice: In the following table we used the German school mark system for rating the suitability of the listed media. This means that 1 stands for very suitable whereas 6 means not suitable at all.

certain media anyhow. Such a media related orientation – here to media of written communication – is linked especially to gender but also to certain age groups. The close relationship between gender and letters has existed since the heyday of a culture of letter writing. Steinhausen (1889: 287) described letter writing as something like a 'pouring out ones heart into an envelope' (*'Herzblut im Briefcouvert'*) whereby the sensitive and sentimental qualities of the letter were associated with a particularly female ability.[16] This appears to have remained consistent until today. A psychological study rating the communication qualities of different media demonstrated that women have a significantly better idea than men do of their ability to communicate their own feelings as well as interpret those of others – whether the medium be telephone, e-mail, online chat or letter (see Hartig et al. 1999).

However, it is the linkage between the division of gender-specific roles and media behaviour in general (and letter-writing in particular) that really stands out. In addition to this stands the telephone usage of women, which practically emphasizes the role aspect. Women also telephone more often than men (see e.g. Höflich 1989: 210). As stated before, it is primarily women who take on the family's external social contacts and the task of maintaining a solid social network. Expanding Ling (1998), one could say that the study of social networks is virtually the same as the study of the special communicative contribution of women. Since gender socialization is always connected with media socialization than it can absolutely be expected that a modification in gender specific role patterns is accompanied by a changing of cultures of mediation.

Meanwhile, a supplementary annotation is necessary. Media related orientations can explain media usages only inadequately. Not every form of written communication is in competition with the letter. Although e-mail and SMS are both forms of written communication, they share a greater similarity to the telephone. This can be shown by the fact that every medium creates its own spectrum of use. This means that an e-mail or an SMS can sometimes be more like a letter and sometimes more like a telephone call. On the one hand, we have the idea of a 'medial dimension', derived from the work of Koch and Oesterreicher (1994), which is connected to the aforementioned orientations (meaning the choice between a more spoken- or a more written-like medium). On the other hand, a continuum of a conceptual 'literal' and a conceptual 'oral' form of communication can be distinguished here both expressing basic characteristics of the communicative situation (i.e. distance and proximity). So for example, an e-mail can take the form of a formal letter (conceptually literal). In the extreme, a formal letter can be delivered as an attachment via e-mail. It can also appear in an informal spoken

---

[16] This was particularly emphasized by Gellert (1998: 136): "Who can choose, under many ideas, with the help of a delicate and fortunate feeling the lightest, finest and most necessary and can observe a certain prosperity in its connection, will definitely write good letters. For this reason, one can discern why it is that women often write more natural letters than men. The feelings of women are more delicate and lively than ours. They are touched by many little conditions that do not make any impression on us."

language (in this sense: conceptually oral) to the point where it resembles a dialogue. As it is supported by the findings of other studies (see, for example, Androutsopoulos/Schmidt 2002; Dürscheid 1999; Günther/Wyss 1996) one can assume that e-mail and SMS – as relationship orientated communication media – fall on the conceptually oral side – which explains their functional similarity to the telephone communication. However, as has been demonstrated in our results, this does not rule out that on certain occasions the letter is able to communicate a personal closeness better than any other media will do.

We have already referred to a paradox: it appears that the letter is well past its prime but is nevertheless still held in high regard. William Ogburn (1969: 134) writes about a "cultural lag" which occurs "when one of two related cultural elements changes sooner or more drastically than the other so that the degree of conformity between the two elements is smaller than before". With the diffusion of new media, such a lag manifests itself when the behavior standards associated with a medium at first lag behind its development. It can also be assumed that existing lags decrease or disappear over time. Concerning such phase shifts or cultural lags the importance of the letter still can be understood despite of its non-usage demonstrating rather increasing but decreasing lags. In this context, Leppännen writes: "People have a tendency to regard routines in an emotional way. Old habits die hard, even if new ways of doing things might be easier and more useful. People view old habits with certain nostalgia, which can also be seen when investigating common attitudes towards mail". Positively interpreted, this could mean that the letter has ingrained itself as a cultural asset in the collective consciousness and is therefore appreciated, even by those who do not write letters. There is also a negative interpretation to this: what we are witnessing now is the last flare of a dying star meaning that sooner or later the symbolic value of the letter will decline.

With respect to the functions and meanings of media in the context of communicative practices, the term of a 'functional image' indicated by Flanagin and Metzger (2001) can be used here to express central media related qualities and ways of their usage. Such functionalities of a certain medium, in the sense of 'collectively held notions of how a medium is used' (p. 159), on the one hand can be understood as ideas of available medial alternatives, i.e. whether similar needs could be met with other media as well. In this sense, especially media of letter-like communications have been examined here. Having this theoretical background in mind the aforementioned 'cultural lag' can be understood as existing media images which do not lead to dominant ways of usage. On the other hand, a 'normative image' goes along with the ideas about the functionalities of a medium. With this it is expressed that the perception of how a medium should be used is shared with others and therefore can be made expectable. Or, to phrase it differently: the normative side refers to the effectiveness of common rules, more precisely common media rules, which determine which media should be used for which purposes:

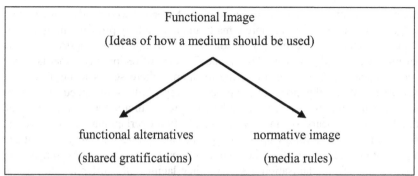

Figure 8: Functional image of media

The last mentioned aspect of the normative image of a medium should – although briefly – be examined further more. There are individual media preferences. However, the choice of a medium seems to be arbitrary only within certain limits, since it always reflects the relationship of the communication partners as well as certain role behaviour patterns and also specific lifestyle aspects.[17] Most notably: the practice of media usage is always a shared experience; media of interpersonal communication can only be used together with other communication partners, and not all what is possible will be supported by others. Who would appreciate friends calling at midnight to discuss the full particulars of their current feelings? As with every social and communicative act, there are rules underlying the practices of media usage, which determine whether the use of the medium is appropriate or inappropriate in a given situation. According to Clyne (1985: 13), in this context one can speak of specific channel or media related rules which prescribe whether a communication based on a particular purpose should happen face-to-face, via telephone or in letter form. A change in cultures of mediation manifests itself in a change of the normative basis. When new media appear a cultural phase shift takes place resulting – at least in the beginning – in a more or less rule-less or anomic state, where people do not always know which medium they should use for which purpose. Yet the question of what kind of rules for written communication will appear and to which extend will be consolidating seems to be open by any means. Regarding this it seems that a fundamental change in the norms of reciprocity is initiated, that indeed applies to the coexistence of media.

Reciprocity is regarded as a basic social and communicative category of interpersonal exchange. As a general principle of communication it can be paraphrased like this: when A acts, B is under constrain to do much the same (see Mortensen 1972: 264). In this sense reciprocity has a stabilizing influence on the communication process and if it is missing, the communication becomes one-sided and unstable. Simply put and this is also a result of our study: those who

---

[17] No more attention will be given to this here, even though it would be perfectly justified to ask the question to what extent socio-demographic indications would be sufficient for the discovery of media orientations or where lifestyle related aspects would be more useful instead.

communicate a lot also receive many replies. A person who sends a lot of text messages is also likely to write more e-mails and incidentally probably more letters. But this also applies in reverse: a person who receives a lot of messages is also under pressure to reply to many. On the medial level of reciprocity – that is, when the communication remains in the same medium – there seems to be a peculiar characteristic. While this norm of reciprocity is especially pronounced in the case of the paper based letter – a letter is to be answered with a letter – with electronic media this norm appears to vanish. Here we can find overlapping practices. A text message can be used to follow up to a telephone call or a personal meeting, but can also be sent as a reminder of a failed letter or even to replace one. Accompanying this process of mediatisation is an "interlacing of different forms of communication" (Krotz 2001: 19). Additionally and in particular in the case of the mobile phone and the Short Message Service, a process of expanding such media related barriers "takes place simultaneously in a spatial, temporal, social and meaningful (*sinnbezogen*) manner" (Krotz 2001: 21). Last but not least, these 'overlapping practices' signify a change in cultures of mediation under the conditions of a multiple media society – which does not necessarily mean that media practices become arbitrary nor that media become equalized in their meaning. In the words of Decker (1998: 234): "Whatever one's preferences, the concurrent existence of different orders of accessible epistolary media creates a situation in which practices overlap and interact and the choice of one medium over another is inherently meaningful. To write rather than call, to call rather than write, to write or not by e-mail are decisions made with respect to the time frame in which the message must be conveyed, the status of interpersonal relations, rhetorical advantages and disadvantages, and many other considerations more or less complicated."

Cultures of mediation are never static and not at all homogeneous. It is exactly the pluralisation of these cultures which is expressing their change so that at least generalized media rules are not likely to be expected under these conditions. Media, including media of written communication, have different meanings in different segments of society. After all, there are intercultural differences, as our internationally comparative study conducted in 2003 demonstrates.[18]

---

[18] In the following, we are referring to an internationally comparative questionnaire study conducted with 400 adults (n=400) from four different countries (Finland, Spain, Italy and Germany) from December 2002 to March 2003, concerning the use and importance of various media of interpersonal communication. The average age of the respondents was 34.2 years old, of whom 54% were female and 48% male. Approximately 35% had a post-secondary degree, 32% an advanced high school diploma, 16% a middle-level high school diploma, and 4% had a junior high school diploma. About 14% of the study participants declared that they had no diploma or degree. The majority of the survey participants (85%) lived in a household of 2 or more persons, while of those 70% indicated they were living in a steady relationship and slightly less than half (42%) of them had children. Furthermore those surveyed were distinguished by their very high rate of ownership of new communication media: over 95% are having their own cell phone and approximately two-thirds (70.3%) have a personal computer, whereas barely three-quarters of computer owners (73.5%) also have an internet connection.

For example, while the letter is generally perceived as a medium well suited for personal communications purposes, this applies more so for the German respondents. More than respondents from the other countries, it is the Germans who associate the letter with a special distinctive 'leap of faith'. As previous results have also suggested, it appears to be the secrecy of letters (*Briefgeheimnis)* that is the basis of such a positive evaluation. Accordingly the letter is well appreciated as a medium for personal and confidential messages. Based on this, it was shown that the majority of survey participants in Germany, Finland and Spain categorized the letter as a particularly trustworthy communication medium and this especially in comparison to electronic media of interpersonal communication, whereas the majority of the Italian participants found the letter to be a more insecure medium.

Amazingly for the Italian and Spanish participants and this much more than for other respondents, the letter seems to be a medium 'to flirt with someone'. Although the Italian respondents found the letter somewhat less suited 'in order to confess your love to someone'. In this regard, again the letter was rated positively especially by the German as well as the Finnish survey participants.

Concerning the suitability of the letter to 'deal with a conflict with someone', it was not collectively regarded as a particularly suitable medium for conflict. While this was especially true for the German and Finnish participants, the letter nevertheless appeared to be seen by the Spanish and Italian respondents as a medium 'to deal with a conflict (e.g. an argument) with others'. In comparison, Germans are more likely (especially compared to Spaniards) to write a letter 'in order to convey bad news to someone'. From these findings, the letter seems to be a 'shield' (although used differently in each country) with whose 'protection' unpleasant news can be delivered to another person.

Quantitative studies, like the one conducted here, have their limits and it is precisely due to the explorative nature of this study that only a preliminary investigation of the problem could be achieved. Furthermore, the letter related estimations are still very general. Nevertheless differences as well as similarities can be read out, but it particularly stands out that it is especially the German respondents who instill in the letter a remarkable amount of trust and credibility. At this point, further studies are necessary – not only more widely applied (keyword: representative studies) but also deeper in their qualitative investigations. As well, with the globalization of media developments, internationally comparative studies appear to be of urgent necessity (on this see also: Fortunati 2001; Ling, Haddon and Klamer 2000). It is only when one adds the perspective of intercultural communication with regard to the changing cultures of mediation that the need for further research activities becomes evident.

References

Androutsopoulos, Jannis/Schmidt, Gurly (2002): *SMS-Kommunikation: Ethnographische Gattungsanalyse am Beispiel einer Kleingruppe*. In: Zeitschrift für Angewandte Linguistik (ZfAL), 36, 2002, 49-80.

Baier, Lothar (2000): *Keine Zeit! 18 Versuche über die Beschleunigung*. München: Kunstmann.

Barton, David (1991): The Social Nature of Writing. In: Barton, David/Ivanic, Roz (Eds.): *Writing in the Community*. Newbury Park, London, New Delhi: Sage Publication, 1-13.

Bausinger, Hermann: Alltag, Technik, Medien (1983). In: Pross, Harry/Rath, Klaus-Dieter (Hrsg.): *Rituale der Medienkommunikation*. Gänge durch den Medienalltag. Berlin, Marburg: Guttandin & Hoppe, 24-37.

Bausinger, Hermann (1996): Die alltägliche Korrespondenz. In: Beyrer, Klaus/Täubrich, Hans-Christian (Hrsg.): *Der Brief. Eine Kulturgeschichte der schriftlichen Kommunikation*. Heidelberg: Edition Braus, 294-303.

Cherubim, Dieter (1981): Schülerbriefchen. In: Baumann, Jürgen/Cherubim, Dieter/Rehbock, Helmut (Hrsg.): *Neben-Kommunikationen*. Braunschweig: Westermann, 107-168.

Clyne, Michael (1985): Beyond Grammar: Some Thoughts of Communication Rules in Our Multicultural Society. In: Pride, John B. (Ed.): *Cross-Cultural Encounters: Communication and Mis-Communication*. Melbourne, 12-23.

Decker, William M. (1998): *Epistolary Practices. Letter Writing in America before Telecommunications*. Chapel Hill and London: University of North Carolina Press.

Di Leonardo, Micaela (1987): The Female World of Cards and Holidays: Women, Families, and the work of Kinship. In: *Journal of Women in Culture and Society*, 12, 1987, 440-452.

Dimmick, John/Kline, Susan/Stafford, Laura (2000): The Gratification Niches of Personal E-mail and the Telephone. Competition, Displacement, and Complementarity. In: *Communication Research*, 27, 2000, 227-248.

Döring, Nicola (2002): „1xBrot, Wurst, 5Sack Äpfel I.L.D." Kommunikative Funktionen von Kurzmitteilungen (SMS). In: *Zeitschrift für Medienpsychologie* 2002, 14(3), 118-128.

Dürrscheid, Christa (1999): Zwischen Mündlichkeit und Schriftlichkeit: die Kommunikation im Internet. In: *Papiere zur Linguistik*, 60, 1, 1999, 17-30.

Eimeren, Birgit van/Gerhard, Heinz/Frees, Beate (2003): ARD/ZDF-Online-Studie 2003: Internetverbreitung in *Deutschland: unerwartet hoher Zuwachs*. In: Media Perspektiven 8/2003, S. 338-358.

Flanagin, Andrew/Metzger, Miriam J. (2001): Internet Use in the Contemporary Media Environment. In: *Human Communication Research*, 27, 2001, 153-181.

Flusser, Vilém (1998): Verbündelungen oder Vernetzungen. In: Bollmann, Stefan (Hrsg.): Kursbuch Neue Medien. *Trends in Wirtschaft und Politik, Wissenschaft und Kultur*. Reinbek bei Hamburg: Rowohlt, 15-23.

Fontius, Martin (1988): Post und Brief. In: Gumbrecht, Hans Ulrich/Pfeiffer, Ludwig K. (Hrsg.): *Materialität der Kommunikation*. Frankfurt/Main: Suhrkamp, 167-279.

Fortunati, Leopoldina (2001): Italy: Stereotypes, True and False. In: Katz,J. and Aakhus, R. (eds.): *Perpetual Contact: Mobile Communication, Private Talk, Public Performance*. Cambridge: Cambridge University Press, 42-62.

Gellert, Christian Fürchtegott (1989): Praktische Abhandlung von dem guten Geschmacke in Briefen. In: Witte, Bernd (Hrsg.): Christian Fürchtegott Gellert. Gesammelte Schriften. Kritische Kommentierte Ausgabe. *Band IV: Roman, Briefsteller*. Berlin, New York: de Gruyter, 111-152.

Green, Nicola (2003): Outwardly Mobile: Young People and Mobile Technologies. In: Katz, J. (ed): *Machines that Becomes Us: The Social Context of Personal Communication Technology*. New Brunswick: Transaction Publishers.

Günther, Ulla/Wyss, Eva Lia (1996): E-Mail-Briefe – eine neue Textsorte zwischen Mündlichkeit und Schriftlichkeit. In: Hess-Lüttich, Ernest W.B. (Hrsg.): *Textstrukturen im Medienwandel*. Frankfurt a. M.: Lang, 61-86.

Harper, Richard et al. (2002): *Paper-mail in the Home of the 21st Century: An Analysis of the Future of Paper-mail and implications for the Design of Electronic Alternatives*. Digital World Research Centre, School of Human Sciences, University of Surrey, Guildford Surrey.

Hartig, Johannes/Jude, Nina/Moosbrugger, Helfried (1999): Mittelbarkeit von Emotionen in computervermittelter Kommunikation. In: Reips, Ulrich-Dietrich et al. (Hrsg.): Current Internet Science. Trends, Techniques, Results/Aktuelle Online-Forschung. Trends, Techniken, Ergebnisse. Deutsche Gesellschaft für Online-Forschung. e.V. Zürich. URL: http://www.dgof.de/tband99/

Hess-Lüttich, Ernest W.B. (1997): E-Epistolographie: Briefkultur im Medienwandel. In: Hepp, Andreas/Winter, Rainer (Hrsg.): Kultur – Medien – Macht. *Cultural Studies und Mediananalyse*. Opladen: Westdeutscher Verlag, 226-246.

Höflich, Joachim R. (1989): Telefon und interpersonale Kommunikation. Vermittelte Kommunikation aus einer regelorientierten Kommunikationsperspektive. In: *Forschungsgruppe Telefonkommunikation (Hrsg.):* Telefon und Gesellschaft. Bd. 1: Beiträge zu einer Soziologie der Telefonkommunikation. Berlin: Spiess, 197-220.

Höflich, Joachim R. (2001): Das Handy als „persönliches Medium". Die Aneignung des Short Message Service (SMS) durch Jugendliche. In: *kommunikation@gesellschaft 2*, 2001. Electronic publication, URL: http://www.kommunikation gesellschaft.de.

Höflich, Joachim R./Rössler, Patrick (2001): Mobile schriftliche Kommunikation – oder: E-Mail für das Handy. Die Bedeutung elektronischer Kurznachrichten (Short Message Service) am Beispiel jugendlicher Handynutzer. In: *Medien & Kommunikations-wissenschaft*, 49, 2001, 437-461.

Höflich, Joachim R./Rössler, Patrick (2002): More than JUST a telephone: The Mobile Phone and Use of the Short Message Service (SMS) by German Adolescents: Results from a Pilot Study. In: *Juvenas y los teléfonos móviles. Revista de la Juventud. No.57.* Electronic publication, URL: http://www.mtas.es/injuve/biblio/revistas/Pdfs/numero57ingles.pdf.

Höflich, Jochim R./Gebhardt, Julian (Hrsg.) (2003): Vermittlungskulturen im Wandel: Brief – E-Mail – SMS. Frankfurt am Main: Lang.

Hörning, Karl H. (2001): Experten des Alltags. Die Wiederentdeckung des praktischen Wissens. Weilerswist: Velbrück Wissenschaft.

Ito, Mizuko/Oktabe, Daisuke (2003): *Mobile Phones, Japanese Youth, and the Re-Placement of Social Contact. Front Stage – Back Stage: Mobile Communication and the Renegotiation of the Social Sphere*. Paper presented in Grimstad, Norway, June 22-24. Electronic publication, http://www.itofisher.com/PEOPLE/mito/mobileyouth. pdf.

Karvinen, Timo (2001): *The Use of SMS Service. In: Digital Media Institute (Ed.): Case Study: Mobile Services and Young Consumers*. Consumer Research Project. Tampere, November 2001, 17-22.

Kasesniemi, Eija Liisa/Rautiainen, Pirjio (2003): Das Leben in 160 Zeichen. Zur SMS Kultur finnischer Jugendlicher. In: Höflich, Jochim R./Gebhardt, Julian (Hrsg.): *Vermittlungskulturen im Wandel: Brief – E-Mail – SMS*. Frankfurt am Main u.a: Lang, 291-313.

Kasesniemi, Eija Liisa (2003): *Mobile Messages: Young People and a New Communication Culture*. Tampere: Tampere University Press.

Katz, Elihu/Gurevitch, Michael/Haas, Hadassah (1973): On the Use of the Mass Media for Important Things. In: *American Sociological Review*, 38, 1973, 164-181.

Katz, James (2003): *Machines that Become Us: The Social Context of Personal Communication Technology*. New Brunswick: Transaction Publishers.

Knies, Karl (1996): Der Telegraph als Verkehrsmittel. *Über den Nachrichtenverkehr überhaupt. Faksimile Nachdruck der Ausgabe von 1857*. München: Fischer.

Koch, Peter/Oesterreicher, Wulf (1994): Funktionale Aspekte der Schriftkultur. In: Günther, Hartmut/Ludwig, Otto (Hrsg.): *Schrift und Schriftlichkeit. Ein interdisziplinäres Handbuch internationaler Forschung, Bd. 1*. Berlin: de Gruyter, 587-604.

Kopomaa, Timo (2000): *The City in your Pocket. Birth of the Mobile Information Society*. Helsinki: Gaudeamus.

Krotz, Friedrich (2001): *Die Mediatisierung kommunikativen Handelns. Der Wandel von Alltag und sozialen Beziehungen, Kultur und Gesellschaft durch die Medien*. Wiesbaden: Westdeutscher Verlag.

Leppänen, Sanne (2001): The Relationship between Electronic Mail and Paper Mail. In: Digital Media Institute (Ed.): *Case Study: Changes in Postal Services – Paper or Bytes? The Consumer Research Project*. Tampere, September 2001, 51-80.

Licoppe, Christian (2003): Two Modes of Maintaining Interpersonal Relationships through Telephone: From the Domestic to the Mobile Phone. In: Katz, J. (ed): *Machines that Become Us: The Social Context of Personal Communication Technology*. New Brunswick: Transaction Publishers, 171-187.

Ling, Rich (1998a): "One can talk about common manners!" The use of mobile telephones in inappropriate situations. In: *Telektronikk 94*, 1998, 65-76.

Ling, Rich (1998b): *"She calls, (but) it's for both of us you know": The Use of Traditional fixed and Mobile Telephony for Social Networking among Norwegians Parents*. Kjeller, Telenor Research and Development, 1998 (R&D Report 33/1998).

Ling, Rich (2000): "We will be reached": The Use of Mobile Telephony among Norwegian youth. In: *Information Technology and People*, Vol. 13, No.2, 102-120.

Ling, Rich (2001): *Adolescent Girls and Young Adult Men: Two Subcultures of the Mobile Phone*. Kjeller, Telenor Research and Development (R&D Report 34/2001).

Ling, Rich (2002): *The Social Juxtaposition of Mobile Telephone Conversations and Public Spaces*. Kjeller, Telenor Research and Development (R&D Report 45/2001).

Ling, Rich, Haddon, Leslie and Klamer, Lajla (2000): The understanding and Use of the Internet and the Mobile Telephone among Contemporary Europeans. Paper presented at the conference *'e-Usages'*, Paris, 12-14th June. Electronic publication, http://www.mot.chalmers.se/dept/tso/haddon/ICUSTjoint.pdf.

Maybin, Janet (1999): Death Row Penfriends: Some Effects of Letter Writing on Identity and Relationsships. In: Barton, David/Hall, Nigel (Eds.): *Letter Writing as a Social Practice*. Amerstam/Philadelphia: Benjamins, 151-177.

Mortensen, David C. (1972): *Communication. The Study of Human Interaction*. New York: McGraw-Hill.

Nickisch, Reinhard, M.G. (1991): *Brief*. Stuttgart: Metzler.

Ogburn William F. (1969): *Kultur und sozialer Wandel*. Berlin: Luchterhand.

Saxer, Ulrich/Langenbucher, Wolfgang/Fritz, Angela (1998): Kommunikationsverhalten und Medien. Lesen in der modernen Gesellschaft. *Eine Studie der Bertelsmann Stiftung*. Gütersloh: Verl. Bertelsmann Stiftung.

Seitz, Helmut (1999): Vom „Breve scriptum" zum E-Mail. Briefkultur einst und heute. Manuskript zur Radionsendung im Rahmen der Reihe Diese unsere Welt". *Bayern 2 Radio*, Sonntag, 3. Oktober 1999.

Siegert, Bernhard (1996): Verschmähte Majestät. Die Erfindung der Briefmarke. In: Beyrer, Klaus/Täubrich, Hans-Christian: *Der Brief. Eine Kulturgeschichte der schriftlichen Kommunikation.* Heidelberg: Ed. Braus, 68-77.

Steinhausen, Georg (1889): *Geschichte des deutschen Briefes. Zur Kulturgeschichte des deutschen Volkes.* Berlin: Weidmann.

Uka, Walter (1994): Brief. In: Faulstich, Werner (Hrsg.): *Grundwissen Medien.* München: Fink, 108-125.

Wurtzel, Alan H./Turner, Colin (1977): What Missing the Telephone Means. In: *Journal of Communication,* 27, 1977, 48-57.

2   Language in SMS –
a socio-linguistic view

Ylva Hård af Segerstad

Introduction

Text-based communications in many forms are abound in the lives of most people in computer literate societies today. The introduction and popularity of mobile phones and mobile text messaging has come to evoke excessive hype and hysteria about the kinds of cultural, social and psychological impacts that the new technology is likely to have, just as with many earlier communication technologies (Turkle 1995). Central to the hype of popular media representations about new communication technologies are concerns about the way that standard varieties and conventional linguistic and communicative practices are affected (Thurlow 2003). Doing research in Finland, which has a high population of mobile phone and SMS users, Kasesniemi (2003) observes that "the wider the phenomenon has spread, the more discussion it has aroused in the Finnish media concerning its influence on the language and, most notably, the written expression of teenagers." Similar populist concerns and a 'moral panic' about language use and language change are found in the Swedish media.

This chapter presents some of the findings of a linguistic analysis of SMS messages written by Swedish users. The study was part of a doctoral dissertation which analyzed and compared data from email, web chat, instant messaging and SMS (Hård af Segerstad 2002). The main focus of the study was on factors that influence written language in these particular settings; what characteristics the resulting texts show in comparison with traditionally written language and spoken language.

The chapter begins by presenting the research questions and aim of the study, followed by a brief account of the communicative setting of mobile text messaging, language in SMS and findings from previous studies. A description of the data and methods follow. Results are then presented and examples of language use found in the Swedish corpus are given. The chapter ends with a discussion of the results. The terms *SMS*, *mobile text messaging* and *texting* are used interchangeably.

Richard Harper, Leysia Palen and Alex Taylor (Eds), The Inside Text: Social, Cultural and Design Perspectives on SMS, 33–51.
© 2005 *Springer. Printed in the Netherlands.*

Research questions and aims

The aim of this study was to analyze SMS messages in order to answer the following main questions: How is Swedish written language actually used in SMS? What are the conditions that influence mobile text messaging? How is written language adapted to suit the conditions of text messaging? Are syntactical and lexical reductions used? Are these reductions and short forms based on Swedish or any other language? This chapter will focus on the linguistic features, rather than on the communicative function of the text message.

The communicative setting of mobile text messaging

SMS is an asynchronous mode of communication, i.e. it does not require the communicators to be online simultaneously. As it employs writing as means of expression, it is monomodal and thus can only take advantage of what can be conveyed through the single channel of the visible writing system. On the other hand, the asynchronicity allows the writers time to compose and edit messages before sending them, and the communication does not require immediate response like spoken interaction. Studies have shown that most messages are sent between friends who share considerable amounts of background knowledge (Hård af Segerstad 2002; Telia/Temo 2002; Ling 2003). Compared to other modes of CMC, e.g. instant messaging and web chat, text communication via mobile phones is more constrained vis-à-vis production and perception conditions. Most commonly, messages are produced on the tiny keypad of the phone and are limited to 160 characters in length. They may also be typed on a computer keyboard when sending messages from one of a multitude of web-based SMS-services. Messages are read on the small screen of the phone, and must often be scrolled through to read the entire message.

Typing on the phone is achieved either by using "multi-tap", or some form of predictive text entry. Each key on the keypad holds several letters and symbols. With the multi-tap method, the user presses each key one or more times to specify the input character. For example, the 2 key is pressed once for the character *A*, twice for *B*, three times for *C*, four times for figure *2*, five times for the Swedish vowel *Å*, and six times for the Swedish vowel *Ä*. Multi-tap suffers from the problem of segmentation when a character is on the same key as the previous character (e.g., the word "ON" because both O and N are on the 6 key).

With predictive text input, linguistic knowledge is added to the system. MacKenzie and Soukoreff (2002) call this technique *one-key with disambiguation*. An example of software for predictive text input is *T9* by Tegic Communications, Inc. (Seattle, WA; http://www.tegic.com/). The user needs to press each number key only once for each letter. The phone will try to identify what the user intends to write based on a dictionary stored in the phone's memory. The predictive text input system does not accept slang or different dialects unless taught by the user. It is possible to type in new words using the multi-tap technique to input them into the memory of the phone (in the *user dictionary*). As Kasesniemi and Rautiainen (2002) argue, the mobile of a "lazy" user "speaks" only standard language with no personal tones. Multiple words may have the same key sequence, which makes disambiguation difficult. In these cases the most frequent word is the default[1].

In short, compared to speaking or typing on a keyboard, texting is rather cumbersome and time consuming. The sender has to consider the limited number of characters per message, software-driven spelling problems as well as the asynchronicity of the medium when producing messages. One could expect to find strategies to save time, effort and space in a corpus of SMS messages.

Written or spoken language in mobile text messaging?

Many scholars of computer-mediated communication (CMC) have been concerned with the question of whether the language of CMC is to be regarded as spoken, written or a kind of hybrid between the two. Early CMC research seems to have generalized language use, even though the many forms of CMC vary in communicative settings and functions (cf. 'interactive written discourse', in Ferrara, Brunner et al. (1991)). The same generalizing view is found in Crystal. Crystal coined the term *Netspeak*, which he claimed to be neither speaking nor writing, but a new medium of linguistic communication. This view is also taken with regards to language use in the particular setting of SMS by Schlobinski et al (2001). Ling (2003) observes that at the linguistic level, language in SMS seems to be a kind of *trans-linguistic dragqueen*. It has features that are characteristic of both spoken and written communication. Among several elements, he points out that SMS is more like speaking than writing because one often finds immediacy and informality in the communications: messages are often produced in first person present tense and there is generally a lack of ceremony. Furthermore, messages are addressed to specific individuals with a high degree of personal disclosure in the SMS messages. That is, the sender and receiver have a high degree of insight into each other's lives. The vast majority of SMS messages are written with the intention of sending them to a single individual. Ling further claims that SMS messaging is like writing in that it does not assume that the interlocutors are physically coproximate. Thurlow (2003), on the other hand, prefers to view the language of SMS in its own terms.

Whatever view of language one chooses to advocate, language use is influenced by a complex weave of interacting variables. Humans have the ability to adapt their behaviour, including linguistic behaviour or language use, according to the factors that condition a situation (Hård af Segerstad 2002). Whatever formal similarities language use may have with other types of computer-mediated discourse, the linguistic and communicative practices of text-messages emerge from a particular combination of technological affordances, contextual variables and interpersonal priorities (cf. Thurlow 2003; Herring Forthcoming).

---

[1] Which word is the most frequent naturally depends on what kind of language corpus the frequency statistics is based on. The corpus might be more or less suited for the task in which the language tool is being used.

Most people master several styles, registers, and variations of linguistic and communicative behaviour. One form of language use does not necessarily exclude the other. Apropos the popular presumption that CMC and SMS follow a certain fixed formula, Kasesniemi points out that "most teenagers [are] in possession of several different repertoires" (Kasesniemi 2003:208). People draw upon their knowledge and experience from their previous communication through various channels and for various purposes, and use their language in a manner suitable to the conditions of communication, intent and purpose of communication, etc. As Thurlow (2003) points out, it is not really possible to imagine communicative practices breaking completely, or that dramatically, with long-standing patterns of interaction and language use. Furthermore, he argues that what is evident from his study of language use in SMS is just how blurred the boundary between computer-mediated communication and face-to-face communication really is. For SMS users, there certainly seems to be little sense in which their text messaging necessarily *replaces* face-to-face communication or whether it is like written or spoken language. New linguistic practices are always adaptive and additive rather than subtractive. Thurlow found that conventional linguistic practices are manipulated with creativity and humour in pursuit of intimacy and social intercourse.

Previous studies of mobile text messaging

Of the few studies that have been published on text messaging, most have centred on the use and function of texting and only a small proportion on language use in SMS. Schlobinski et al. (2001) regarded language use in their corpus to be a hybridization of written and spoken language, judging from its use of colloquial expressions, reductions and assimilations. They also remarked on unconventional ways of writing, such as writing consequently in lower-case. They argued that syntactical reductions are caused by the medium, and that abbreviations and short forms of words were frequently used. Eldridge and Grinter (2001; Grinter and Eldridge 2001) report that the reasons for teenagers preferring to text one another are that it is *quicker, cheaper, easy to use/more convenient than other commun-icative methods.* They found minimal use of predictive typing technologies. The teenagers' common use of abbreviations and shorthand made it barely usable in practice. Kasesniemi reports that teenagers have been slower than adults in adopting the predictive text input. Teenagers are not willing to write dictionary language (2003:206). Döring (2002) analyzed types, frequencies, and functions of short forms in text messages using a corpus of N=1000 authentic text messages and questionnaire data. Like Thurlow (2003), she found that the widespread claims about the linguistic exclusivity appear greatly exaggerated. Döring found almost no SMS-specific short forms exist, which could manifest a collective identity. Furthermore, abbreviations and acronyms were found to play an unexpectedly small part – out of 1000 words, only 30 were abbreviations or acronyms – and were thus not as common as popular hype and fear suggest. Döring's (2002) findings of syntactical reductions confirms the findings of Androutsopoulos and Schmidt (2001) and Schlobinski et al. (2001), the most common were found to be:

- Deletion of subject (especially subject pronoun)

- Deletion of preposition, article and possessive pronoun

- Deletion of copula-, auxiliary- or modal verbs (+XP)

- Deletion of Verb and Subject pronoun; Telegram style

Thurlow (2003), Bodomo and Lee (2002) and Kasesniemi (2003) all report similar findings of linguistic features that are characteristic to language in SMS, as well as various ways in which language is reduced and shortened:

- Shortenings, contractions and G-clippings and other clippings

- Acronyms and initialisms

- Letter/number homophones

- 'Misspellings' and typos

- Non-conventional spellings

- Accent stylizations

- Omission of punctuation and word spacing

- Exclamation marks and question marks

- Emoticons (or smileys)

- Capitals or small letters only (whole messages)

- Inflectional endings reduced

- Substitute long words in native language with foreign shorter ones

These, and other, linguistic features and strategies to reduce and shorten messages were also found in the Swedish SMS corpus, and examples will be given below in the Results section.

Eldridge and Grinter (2001; Grinter and Eldridge 2001) argue that texting allows teenagers to forego conversational conventions and makes the communication quicker by reducing the overall time spent on interaction. This was also supported by Döring (2002), who concluded that one may make oneself brief without fear of being perceived as short-spoken. One has to be brief not to go beyond the scope of the limited number of characters per message, because each message sent is charged at a relatively expensive rate. Döring also suggested that, in the long run, one is brief because the text input is so cumbersome. However, it seems that this view might be too general. Despite the supposed awkwardness of text input, people seem to be quite willing to invest time and effort in creating messages and sharing content. Also, the experience of text input as an awkward manoeuvre is far from universal. Some users report a mastering of the interface and have adapted their language use to what they know it can or cannot do. These users do not find the text input laborious and do not consider the interface to hamper their expression (cf.

Hård af Segerstad 2002). Indeed, as shown by Taylor and Harper (2003), teenagers can use the limitations of texting to express themselves in ways that sustain and invigorate their social networks. Texting, as one of several ways of using the mobile phone technology, acts to mediate the social relationships of teenagers. Thus, the social element of maintaining and mediating relationships may often exert greater impact than the mere physical effort of typing. Nevertheless, because most SMS communication is interpersonal communication between people who know each other, one may be brief when relying on pragmatic and shared background knowledge. The character limit of the messages themselves makes this terse and otherwise rude behaviour completely acceptable. Text messaging can prevent the other person going "off topic" and making a conversation longer than planned. The character limit forces both sender and respondent to stick to the topic.

In sum, studies have shown that text messaging is mainly used for maintaining relations between people and for coordinating social activities (cf. for example Eldridge and Grinter 2001; Ling 2003; Berg, et al, chapter 13; Thurlow 2003). It is used foremost for private communication between partners, friends, family and loved ones. Studies have shown that teenagers find SMS to be quicker, cheaper and more convenient to use than other modes of communication. Judging from the factors illustrated by, for example, Döring, production and perception conditions in combination with situational parameters (the technical restriction of 160 characters per message, each message sent is charged, text input is so cumbersome, interpersonal communication) both permit and force people to express themselves concisely in mobile text messaging. Previous studies have shown that there is frequent use of lexical short forms and syntactic reductions that save keystrokes compared to longhand forms.

Data and Methods

Three methods for collecting data were used in the present study: a web-based questionnaire; user diaries and forwarding methods; as well as messages gathered from the researcher's friends and family. Each method has its merits and drawbacks so the aim was that they should complement each other. Despite the popularity of mobile text messaging, it proved difficult to gather data. Possible reasons for this will be discussed in the concluding section. The resulting corpus is large enough, however, to give interesting insights into how written language may be used in SMS. It consists of 1,152 messages and a total of 17,024 words. The data was analyzed using both quantitative, automatic methods as well as qualitative, manual methods.

Data collection

Web based questionnaire

A web page consisting of a questionnaire was constructed, which informants accessed to answer questions and share a text message that they themselves had sent either by mobile phone or a web site offering the SMS service. The messages were copied character-by-character exactly as typed in the original. The data from this web-based form were entered automatically into a database. The informants were recruited and invited to join the study through daily newspapers in which the researcher was interviewed, as well as through a link on the researcher's web site. All entries in the web-based data questionnaire were anonymous and all informants remained completely anonymous to the researcher.

There are pitfalls of copying and of selection. Copying requires retyping on a keyboard a text that is read on the small screen of a mobile phone. Caveats in the case of copying are that it is very easy to make typos or to simply copy the original incorrectly. The informants selected a message that they wanted to share, which might result in a biased corpus for various reasons.

User diaries

Four informants (two male and two female, between 12 and 25 years of age) were recruited to participate in the research project. They were asked to keep a user diary in which they recorded information about each text message that they sent and received during a period of one week (or longer if they wished), as well as to forward messages straight to the researcher's mobile phone. The messages were transferred into a database on a computer by connecting the mobile phone to the computer by a serial cable along with the use of software, so as to eliminate further copying and thus possible typos by the researcher. The informants were interviewed individually when they considered the forwarding and diary-keeping period finished. It was pointed out that the messages that were forwarded, and everything that informants told the researcher in the interviews or wrote in the diaries was to be dealt with the strictest confidentiality, and that they would remain anonymous to everyone but the researcher. The selection problem remained, but could be discussed in the interviews.

Friends and family

The third method of data collection was to ask friends and family to part with their messages during a period of time. Sixteen informants (8 female, 8 male) contributed to the corpus by sending 788 messages. Messages were either sent directly to the researcher's mobile phone, or copied character-by-character into a text document in a word processor. Messages that concerned the researcher directly were omitted.

All in all, the three methods of data collection resulted in a corpus consisting of 1,152 messages with 17,024 tokens (4,045 types). Table 1 below shows the distribution of messages from the different categories of informants.

Table 1: Number of messages and number of words from each method of collection.

	Web based questionnaire	Informants' forwarded messages	Friends and family
No. messages	112	252	788
No. words	1,457	2,512	13,055

Methods of analysis

The corpus was stored in machine-readable format, and analyzed automatically with the help of a software tool, TraSA (Transcription Statistics with Automation)[2]. TraSA is a computer tool used in corpus linguistics to calculate measurements like the number of *Tokens, Utterances, Turns, Pauses, Overlaps, Vocabulary Richness,* and *Word frequency lists.*

The frequency lists were manually checked for occurrence of abbreviations (both established and new), complex punctuation expressions, emoticons, asterisks and ASCII-art.

The corpus of messages was checked manually for occurrences of syntactical and lexical reductions such as deletion of subject pronoun, deletion of verb phrase (e.g. auxiliary verb, copula verb, subject pronoun), features that are typically associated with spoken interaction. The present chapter presents results from qualitative and manual analyses.

Results

The aim of this study was to analyze how Swedish written language is used in SMS. Strategies to save time, effort and space seem to have been developed to suit the conditions of text messaging, such as production and perception conditions. The analysis of messages collected for the present study reveal that Swedish SMS communicators use the same basic types of syntactical and lexical reductions as were found in the studies of Döring (2002), Schlobinski et al. (2001), Thurlow (2003) and Kasesniemi (2003). Linguistic features that were found to be used frequently are listed in Table 2, and will be exemplified and discussed below.

Linguistic features of SMS

The present chapter is limited in size and does not allow for extended illustration of all categories, and thus a selection of them will be presented and exemplified below. For an extended discussion, see Hård af Segerstad (2002)[3].

---

[2] TraSA was developed by Leif Grönqvist at the Department of Linguistics, Göteborg University, Sweden (cf. Grönqvist 2000).

[3] The entire dissertation can be downloaded as a pdf-file at <http://www.ling.gu.se/~ylva/documents/ylva_diss.pdf>.

Table 2: Categories of linguistic features of SMS

Category	Feature
Punctuation	
	Omission of punctuation
	Unconventional punctuation
	Omission of word spacing
Spelling	
	Mispredictions
	Spoken-like spelling
	Split compounds
	Consonant writing
	Conventional abbreviations
	Unconventional use of conventional abbreviations
	Unconventional abbreviations
	Either all capitals or all lower-case
	Exchange long words for shorter
Grammar	
	Omission of Subject pronoun
	Omission of VP (copula, auxiliary, or modal verb + preposition)
	Omission of Article, Preposition, Possessive pronoun
	Reduction of inflectional endings
Graphical (non-alphabetical) means	Emoticons
	Asterisks
	Symbol replacing word

Punctuation

Omission of punctuation

By omitting punctuation a user saves the time and effort it takes to type those characters (period, comma, etc). Omitting punctuation also saves keystrokes, which could be important when the message size is restricted by technical limitations. Results show that the strategy of saving space and effort by omitting punctuation may also be used in messages that are short enough not to threaten to exceed the restricted number of characters. Example 1 below gives an illustration of such a case.

> *Ge mig ditt nummer har det inte längre så ringer ja ikväll ska spela fotboll*
> [Give me your number don't have it anymore then I call tonight will play football]

Omission of word spacing

Similar to the strategy to omit punctuation, by omitting space between words the user saves keystrokes as well as time and effort. In some cases it was not necessary to save space, but omitting it renders a personal tone to the message. Example 2 below was typed on the keypad of a mobile phone.

BANKOMATJÄVELNFUNKAINTESOMVNLITKOMMERSENARE
[THEDAMNCASHMASHINEDIDNTWORKASUSALWILLBELATE]

Example 3 was typed on a computer keyboard and sent via a web-based SMS service. The latter utilized all 160 characters, and seems to be a good example of linguistic awareness: by capitalizing each word readability was increased. Moreover, given its content, it seems to render a sort of pleading touch to the message. This technique to produce text would be very difficult and time consuming if typed on a mobile phone, and no equivalents were found that were produced on a keypad.

> *UtanBaraÖkatOchJagÄlskarDigMer&MerFastänDuÄrSurPåMig.MenVillD*
> *uInteHaMigSå..SåBlirJagJätteledsen.DuBehöverInteFlyttaUppHitKäraVän.*
> *DuÄrNogBaraRädd.*
> [ButJustExpandedAndILoveYouMore&MoreEvenThoughYouAreMadAtM
> e.ButIfYouDon'tWantMeThen..ThenI'llBeVerySad.YouDon'tHaveToMove
> UppHereMyDear.You'reProbablyJustAfraid.]

Spelling

Mispredictions and typos

Spelling in mobile text messaging seemed to be very much dependent on whether the sender used predictive text entry or not. However, in many cases it was not stated whether the phone had this software or whether it was actually employed. As touched upon above, predictive text entry compares the entered sequence of characters with a lexicon stored in the software. It predicts the most likely word or words with that particular sequence, and unless checked, the most frequent word will be the one that appears on the screen. The software does not consider syntactical or semantic context, and is not tailored to suit the everyday informal type of conversation, which results prove to be the most common. Thus, many strange technology-driven "typos" may appear in mobile text messaging. Example 4 illustrates a misprediction in which the predictive software judged räknar [counts] to be more frequent than saknar [misses]. The receiver may figure out the intended meaning from pragmatic knowledge, such as who sent the message, as well as from computing what other letter combinations the particular sequence allows for.

> *Jag **räknar** [saknar] dig.*
> *[Mispredicted output: I **count** you*
> *Intended output: I **miss** you]*

Example 5 below is an illustration of a misprediction of a colloquial phrase "*Gott mos*", the literal meaning of which is "*Good mash*" and the intended meaning is something like "*Good stuff*"). Strangely enough, the predictive software appears to judge the following to be more likely and frequent:

> *Gott **öms***

The word *"Öms"* does not really mean anything in Swedish, which renders it somewhat untranslatable. Anecdotal evidence from the informants suggested that as a result of mispredictions of a common phrase such as found in both examples 4 and 5, as a joke people start using the misprediction literally both in speech and writing, instead of the original. This phenomenon was also noted by Kasesniemi, who observes that "the expression is connected to the device in other ways, too. A mistake in one letter, a typing error, may produce a new term of endearment that may remain in the language of text messages either briefly or permanently" (2003:205).

Spoken-like, or unconventional spelling

In many cases unconventional spelling, or spelling which imitates the phonetic value of speech, saves keystrokes and time and effort. One does not have to be as explicit and careful in spoken interaction as in writing. Sometimes, though, unconventional spelling results in the same number of keystrokes as the normative spelling, sometimes in even more keystrokes or more effort spent. This proves that the economy principle is not absolute and that what is considered rational behaviour is instrumental, it is rational for the purpose it serves (cf. Allwood 2000). The word *strumper* [strumpor=socks], in example 6, did not save any keystrokes, but rendered the word a spoken-like feel. Given the rather delicate request of the message (asking someone to wash your old socks!), the informal and friendly tone might be seen as a politeness strategy. The abbreviated word *ngnstans* [någonstans=somewhere] saved two keystrokes compared with standard spelling. At the same time, it also helps bring an informal and friendly tone to the message.

> *det finns en påse **me**[med] **klär**[kläder] kan du tvätta dem? ligger ngnstans*
> *i rummet,mest **strumper**[strumpor] **å**[och] sånt*
> [there's a bag **of clothes** can you wash them? somewhere in the room,mostly
> **socks and** such]

Colloquial words and dialectal pronunciation are often spelled out in SMS texts. Choice of words and how to render them in writing seems to be strongly dependent on the relationship between communicators. It possibly acts as in-group markers and connects with the interlocutor's shared background knowledge. It might also function as a pragmatic strategy. The message in example 7 might well be interpreted as a way of reminding the receiver that he or she ought to get back with some information soon.

> ***Höllö höllö** [hallå hallå]! **Bler** [blir=going to be] det **nön** [någon=any]*
> *beachvolley **elle** [eller=or]?*
> [**Hullo Hullo**[Hello Hello]! Is there **gunna** [going to be] be **any** beach
> volley or what?]

Another type of unconventional spelling, or rather a feature that is unconventional to spell out in writing in the first place, is found when "Own Communication Management", or OCM, features, such as eh, öh, hmm (Allwood 2000), from spoken language appear in mobile text messaging. Results from web chat and IM also show these features (Hård af Segerstad 2002).

Hmm, kanske det!? Vi hörs i morr'n [morgon=morning] :-)
[**Hmm**, may be!? Let's get in touch tmorro (tomorrow) :-)]

Example 8 was opened with an OCM feature and closed with a conscious marking of a word rendered in its spoken form.

Split compounds

The SMS log showed a few cases where the predictive text entry software seemed to be responsible for splitting compound words. Splitting compound nouns is a tendency emerging in Swedish which, similar to so many other changes, has started a public discussion[4]. Whether the presence of split compounds in SMS might expedite the changes in Swedish remains to be seen. Splitting compounds in many cases entails a semantic change, but the example below is not as severe.

*HAJ! JAG HAR KÖPT ENA NY LUR. **JÄTTEROLIG!***
[HI! I'VE BOUGHT A NEW PHONE. **REALLY GREAT!**]

Exchanging longer words for shorter alternatives

Yet another strategy to save space was to exchange a long word for a shorter alternative, even though the shorter word may not be in common usage. For example the word *ej* has a slightly archaic stylistic tone, and is not used as often as the everyday *inte*. Both are equivalents to the English *not*.

*japp men det syns **ej** [inte=not] vem det är ifrån. X*
[yepp but it does**n't** show who sent it. X]

If there is a shorter word to be found in another language, in the gathered corpus it was always English, it could just as well be used. It then serves the double function of an informality marker and a saver of time, effort and space. Perhaps it just exhibits word play in general. Judging from conversations that can sometimes be overheard on the bus and the like, it seems that English words are commonly used in this way in young people's interaction.

*KATTEN HAR FÅTT **KIDS** [ungar]*
[THE CAT GOT **KIDS**]

Consonant writing

By sometimes omitting vowels, the message appeared to be almost like consonant writing. The intended meaning seems to come through even without them. The

---

[4] See, for example, the popular TV show on language: *Värsta Språket (=the Worst Language*, meaning *cool language* or something like it) (www.svt.se). There is also a web community, *Skrivihop.nu*, dedicated to fighting the splitting of compounds (http://www.skrivihop.nu/). The web address means in translation "write together.now" or "compound.now".

examples below did not have to be shortened in order to save space, but, rather, appear to be expressions of language play.

> *Har du **prgmrt** [programmerat=programmed] videon?*
> [Have you **prgrmd** the video?]

The "consonant written" word *SVNGLSKA* in example 13 illustrates linguistic awareness by indicating consciousness of the "Swenglish" construction *blada*, which is a shortened form of an English loan word (*roller blading*), adapted according to the Swedish inflectional system.

> *BLADA? **SVNGLSKA** [SVENGELSKA=swenglish]!*
> [BLADING? **SWNGLSH**!]

Unconventional abbreviations

Conventional, or established, abbreviations were found in the SMS corpus. They are used for the same reasons as they are used in other contexts of written communication: saving time and space. Results from the other studies (email, webchat, instant messaging) in a wider investigation (Hård af Segerstad 2002) all showed use of unconventional abbreviations. This was also the case in the SMS corpus. Conventional methods of abbreviation may be used unconventionally which would require additional explicit information if it had occurred in an autonomous text. The first letter in a word may stand for the whole word, as in example 14.

> *SKITSNACK! VILKEN **T** [tid]?*
> [BULLSHIT! WHAT **T** (TIME)?]

Messages illustrated in example 15 and 16 show innovative new types of abbreviations based on Swedish words. The abbreviations are unconventional and not yet established in more formal types of written communication. Time will tell whether they will be established and accepted.

> *hallå x, hur **e**[är] **d**[et]? vad händer i helgen. ska vi ta en fika? ha **d**[et]*
> *bra! Vi **cs**[ses]. **p&k** [puss och kram]/y*
> [hello x, how's things? what happens this weekend. wanna go for a coffe? take care! **cs** [see you]. **k&h** [kiss and hug]/y!]

> *Va **QL**[kul] det ska bli på LÖR!*
> [How **FN** [fun] it'll be on SAT!]

Abbreviations based on non-Swedish words were found in the SMS data. Words and whole phrases in English may appear in the midst of a Swedish conversation. These might be in the form of snippets of song lyrics to popular songs, poems or fixed phrases. Examples of the latter are illustrated in examples 17 and 18. It seems likely that this usage has been observed and picked up from chat room norms.

> *YES YES, MASTER OF BARBECUE RETURNS... **BTW** [by the way = förresten]: LYCKADES INTE FÅ MED EXPEDITEN PÅ SYSTEMET...*
> [YES YES, MASTER OF BARBECUE RETURNS... **BTW** [by the way =

förresten]: DIDN'T MANAGE TO BRING THE SALES PERSON AT
THE LIQUOR STORE WITH ME...]

Det var ju inte ett kryptisk meddelande... man skulle kunna tro att du hade
*X. på besök:) Lev Väl! Miss **U** [you=du]!*
[As if that wasn't a cryptic message... one could well believe that you had x.
visiting:) Take care! Miss **U** [you=du]!]

Grammar

Grammatical reductions were found to be used in mobile text messaging in order to
save time, effort and space. Results suggest that written language in SMS show
characteristics of informal spoken interaction. As most messages are sent between
people who know each other already, senders were able to rely on the receiver's
ability to pragmatic inference when decoding the message. This allowed senders to
omit elements that the message could be interpreted without. In this way, SMS
texting does not have to be as explicit and autonomous as traditional writing has to
be.

Subject pronoun

Supporting the findings of Döring's study (2002), the subject pronoun was found to
be omitted frequently. One reason for this can be if the sender's phone number is
stored in the receiver's phone book. In this context, the sender's name appears
above the message on the screen so it is obvious who sent the message. As
illustrated in example 19, it is thus obvious to the receiver whom the deictic
expression *jag [I]* refers to, and it may just as well be left out.

[Jag] kan inte ikväll. [Jag] måste jobba. [Jag] gillar dig i alla fall. KRAM
x
[I] can't tonight. [Jag] have to work. [Jag] like you anyway. HUGS x

The omission of subject pronoun is a feature that is normally characteristic of
spoken informal interaction, and is not associated with traditional writing.

Verb phrase

Other grammatical reductions may save time and space. Leaving out the copula,
auxiliary or modal verb sometimes in combination with a preposition may save
several keystrokes. Several interpretations of the message in 20 are possible (e.g.
blir det på...[is it going to be at...], sa vi på...[did we say at...]), but the receiver
who had all the necessary background information presumably had no trouble
decoding it.

[Ska vi ses på] cafe japan [kl] 19?
[Can we meet at] cafe japan [at] 19 [o'clock]?]

Reduction of inflectional endings

Inflectional verb endings are not always articulated in spoken interaction. This is
also reflected in the spoken-like rendering of words in SMS. Messages in which the

verb endings have been reduced were found in the SMS corpus, which is illustrated in example 21.

Din syrra skrev att du blev arg då å då skrev jag att det var töntigt. Jag svara[de] ju å då prata[de] ja[g] ju ja[g] sa ju nej.
[Your sister wrote that you got angry then and then I wrote it was silly. I answer[ed] and then talk[ed] I did say no.]

Graphical (non-alphabetic) means

Emoticons

Emoticons, or smileys, are used to enhance alphabetic writing by conveying moods or emotions that are normally expressed with extralinguistic cues such as facial expressions and tone of voice in spoken interaction. Symbols in imitation of facial expressions in a monomodal written means of expression may help to make it easier to interpret text-only communication. The experienced communicator seems to know that some messages might need additional information to disambiguate text-only communication.

Inserting non-alphabetic symbols in mobile text messages may be somewhat troublesome on most types of mobile phones, due to the limited keypad. Some phone models are targeted and marketed for teenagers. As it seems that the mobile phone market assumes teenagers are the stereotypical users of emoticons, some phones have the most common emoticons (i.e. the happy face [:-)], the sad [:-( ] and the winking emoticon [;-)]) preformatted. These do not require insertion of three separate symbols, but the whole emoticon may be selected and inserted as one. The economy principle does not always hold, as mentioned above, and people seem willing to spend the time and effort it takes to insert emoticons to enhance their messages. Example 22 below was typed on a mobile phone that did not have any preformatted emoticons.

HEJ X, har sträckt ryggen & har ont i halsen. Vi får träna tillsammans ngn annan dag :-(X
[HI X, have strained my back & a sore throat. We'll have to workout together another day :-(X]

Asterisks

As has been shown in studies of web chat and instant messaging, asterisks to frame words or phrases often serve the same purpose as emoticons. Compared to the use of emoticins, by adding explicit words the message is rendered even more unambiguous. Actions described explicitly in words, such as the one illustrated in example 23 below, may also be marked to resemble additional prosodic features by the repetition of letters.

No information was given of how example 23 was created. It seems likely, though, that it was typed on a computer keyboard as it includes both emoticons and asterisks. Situational variables such as relationship between communicators and the goal that the sender wishes to reach may exert more powerful influence than economy, though.

pet i sidan Hur vågar du ha upptaget när goa pågen ringer..!? *peta lite till* ;o) Hör av dej när linjenär öppen! *Cjamiz* /Förnamn.
[*poke* How dare you keep the line busy when the nice boy calls..!? *poke again* ;o) Call me when the lineis open again! *Hugz*/First name.]

Example 24 illustrates a feature that is most often associated with spoken interaction (see *Spoken-like, or unconventional spelling*, above). Extralinguistic cues, such as laughter and gestures, are normally not spelled out in writing. By adding asterisks around the typed version of laughter, it is marked explicitly as an action and most probably also as an indicator of how it was supposed to be interpreted.

ello babe.. va görs?? spanar du på kalle eller..? :p *haha* [skratt] keep rockin' //x.
[ello babe.. what are you doin?? Looking for kalle..? :p *haha* [laughter] keep rockin' //x.]

Symbols replacing words

By replacing a word with a symbol that stands for the word, several keystrokes may be saved. Example 25 utilizes the maximum character limit. The last word was misspelled by leaving out the last letter, had it conformed to standard spelling: *[kväl –> kväll=evening]*. This misspelling does not seem to pose any difficulties in interpretation. People add and subtract information, and use their experience and pragmatic knowledge to get to the most likely and relevant interpretation (cf. Sperber and Wilson 1986). By using symbols instead of words, 7 keystrokes were saved in this particular message. Additionally, abbreviations were used to save space *[gbg->Göteborg=Gothenburg, ngt->något=something]*.

Jo, är i gbg sen 1 [en=a, one] vecka. men har gjort ngt idiotiskt. skaffat ett 2 [två=two] veckors städjobb i hamnen. måste upp 5 [fem=five] på morron & [och=and] är DÖD när jag kommer hem.. Ringer i kväl
[Well, been in gbg 1 week. but have done something stupid. got myself a 2 week cleaning job in the harbour. have to get up at 5 in the morning & am DEAD when I get home.. will call tonigh]

In example 26 an emoticon was employed to stand not just for an emotion, but actually also for the word *glad [happy]* itself. The message is a fixed expression common in Sweden for happy wishes around midsummer.

:-) [glad] midsommar!
[:-) [happy] midsummer!]

Conclusions

This chapter presented some of the findings of a linguistic analysis of SMS messages sent by Swedish users. Language use in mobile text messaging was found to be adapted to the constraints of production and perception conditions due to the means of expression, as well as situational parameters. It revealed a number of interesting strategies to adapt language use to the conditions of mobile text messaging. Different types of syntactical and lexical reductions to save time, effort and space were found, many of which correspond to the findings from studies of SMS written in Germany (Androutsopoulos and Schmidt 2001; Schlobinski, Fortmann et al. 2001; Döring 2002), Finland (Kasesniemi 2003), Hong Kong (Bodomo and Lee 2002), and Wales (Thurlow 2003). Syntactical reductions by omitting subject pronoun or even whole verb phrases were common. Creative lexical reductions in the form of unconventional and not yet established abbreviations were frequently used. Many of these were found to be based on Swedish words, but some were also transferred from norms in other modes of CMC, e.g. web chat, and thus most of the time based on English words. Language use in SMS showed many features associated with spoken language, omission of subject pronoun, verbalization of "Own Communication Management", hesitation sounds and laughter. Spelling reminiscent of spoken interaction served to save time, effort and space, and to render an informal touch and serve as in-group markers. Given these findings it would seem the use and adaptation of written language in mobile text messaging is to be regarded as a variant of language use, creatively and effectively suited to the conditions of SMS and the aims for which it is used.

Technology driven language use

Popular concerns about the way that standard varieties and conventional linguistic and communicative practices are affected have been noted in several studies of SMS (cf. Kasesniemi 2003; Thurlow 2003). The human ability to adapt linguistic behaviour can be witnessed in SMS language. As Thurlow (2003) suggests, text-messaging is in fact yet another example of how the human need for social intercourse – a kind of 'communication imperative' – bends and ultimately co-opts technology to suit its own ends, regardless of whatever original ambition the developers had for the technology. Many users do indeed explore and develop imaginative ways of making the technology work best for them. The creative ability of humans should not be ignored or underestimated. As Taylor and Harper (2003) and Berg, et al, (chapter 13) point out, technologies often end up being used in unexpected ways. When technologies are adopted they become part of an already established social context as well as social behavioural patterns and experience. These often shape they way the technology is used.

Gutowitz (2003) argues that users adapt their behaviour to the shortcomings of existing predictive text input systems, either by ignoring the problem or employing different types of work-arounds (See also Schneider-Hufschmidt, chapter 10).

Users have identified that the dictionary-based system has problems with compound, slang and shortened words. Gutowitz claims that users have the ability to anticipate, before a word is typed, whether the word is likely to be in the dictionary or not. This involves a higher-level classification of words into types that are likely to be accepted by the system, and types that are not. This requires a fairly sophisticated linguistic knowledge that takes time and motivation to acquire.

Predictive input technologies have the capacity to significantly reduce the effort required to enter text – if the prediction is good. As MacKenzie and Soukoreff (2002) point out, there are a few caveats to consider in basing a language model on a standard corpus. The corpus may not be representative of the user language, the corpus does not reflect the editing process, and the corpus does not reflect input modalities. There seems to be a tendency to split Swedish compound words. Theories as to the reasons for this vary; one of them is the influence that the English norms of writing have had. The difficulty that predictive text entry software has in accepting compound words makes it easier to split compounds rather than to manually enter the word in the memory of the phone. Whether all split compounds are due to software mispredictions or the senders' own tendency to split compounds is not always evident.

Texting is often used in a context for mediating and maintaining social relationships. The language in those exchanges are most often characterised by being informal everyday talk. The text entry systems of mobile phones might be made more effective and more attractive to use by considering messaging in this context and recognising the interplay between the technological, social and linguistic.

References

Allwood, J. (2000). An Activity Based Approach to Pragmatics. *Abduction, Belief and Context in Dialogue: Studies in Computational Pragmatics*. H. B. Bunt, B. Amsterdam, John Benjamins: 47-80.

Androutsopoulos, J. and G. Schmidt (2001). "SMS-Kommunikation: Etnografische Gattungsanalyse am Beispiel einer Kleingruppe." *Zeitschrift für Angewandte Linguistik*.

Bodomo, A. B. and C. K. M. Lee (2002). "Changing forms of language and literacy: technobabble and mobile phone communication." *Literacy and Numeracy Studies* 12(1): 23-44.

Döring, N. (2002). ""Kurzm. wird gesendet" – Abkürzungen und Akronyme in der SMS-Kommunikation." *Muttersprache. Vierteljahresschrift für deutsche Sprache* 2.

Eldridge, M. and R. Grinter (2001). *Studying text messaging in teenagers*. CHI 2001 Workshop #1: mobile Communications: Understanding User, Adoption and Design, Philadelphia, USA.

Ferrara, K., H. Brunner, et al. (1991). "Interactive Written Discourse as an Emergent Register." *Written Communication* 8(1): 8-34.

Grinter, R. E. and M. A. Eldridge (2001). *y do tngrs luv 2 txt msg*. ECSCW2001, Bonn, Germany.

Grönqvist, L. (2000). *The TraSA v0.8 User's Manual. A user friendly graphical tool for automatic transcription statistics*. Dept. of Linguistics, Göteborg University.

Gutowitz, H. (2003). 'Barriers to Adoption of Dictionary-Based Text-Entry Methods: A Field Study'. *10th Conference of the European Chapter of the Association for Computational Linguistics*, Budapest, Hungary.

Herring, S. C. (Forthcoming). "A Classification Scheme for Computer-Mediated Discourse."

Hård af Segerstad, Y. (2002). Use and Adaptation of Written Language to the Conditions of Computer-Mediated Communication. *Department of Linguistics*. Göteborg, Göteborg University.

Kasesniemi, E.-L. (2003). *Mobile Messages. Young People and a New Communication Culture*. Tampere, Tampere University Press.

Kasesniemi, E.-L. and P. Rautiainen (2002). Mobile Culture of Children and Teenagers in Finland. *Perceptual Contact – Mobile Communication, Private Talk, Public Performance*. J. E. Katz and M. Aakhus. Cambridge, Cambridge University Press: 170-192.

Ling, R. (2003). 'The socio-linguistics of SMS: An analysis of SMS use by a random sample of Norwegians.' *Front Stage-Back Stage. Mobile communication and the renegotiation of the social sphere*, Grimstad, Norway.

MacKenzie, I. S. and R. W. Soukoreff (2002). "Text entry for mobile computing: Models and methods, theory and practice." *Human-Computer Interaction* 17: 147-198.

Schlobinski, P., N. Fortmann, et al. (2001). *Simsen. Eine Pilotstudie zu sprachlichen und kommunikativen Aspekten in der SMS-Kommunikation*. Hannover, Networx Nr. 22.

Sperber, D. and D. Wilson (1986). *Relevance: Communication and Cognition*. Oxford, Blackwell.

Taylor, A. S., & Harper, R. (2003). "The gift of the gab?: a design oriented sociology of young people's use of mobiles." *Journal of Computer Supported Cooperative Work (CSCW), 12(3)*, 267-296.

Telia/Temo (2002). *SMS-undersökning*.

Thurlow, C. (2003). "Generation Txt? Exposing the sociolinguistics of young people's text messaging." *Discourse Analysis Online 1*(1).

Turkle, S. (1995). *å*. New York, Simon & Schuster.

3 Please reply! The replying norm in adolescent SMS communication

Ditte Laursen

Introduction

Text analyses of SMS communication have investigated their linguistic form – shortening strategies, colloquial features, creativity – and their communicative function, but have studied messages as single entities (Androutsopoulos and Schmidt, 2002; Döring, 2002a, 2002b; Hård af Segerstad, 2002; Kasesniemi and Rautiainen, 2002; Ling, 2003; Schlobinski, 2001; Thurlow, 2002). This article, on the other hand, reports on research that examines SMS communication as an interaction by beginning with the observation, as also found in previous studies (Androutsopoulos and Schmidt, 2002, p.15-19; Kasesniemi and Rautiainen,2002, p. 187), that SMS communication is dialogic. Furthermore, this research looks at communication sequences where SMSs and mobile telephone conversations interact.

The sociological method used is *conversation analysis*. This method is built upon concrete occurrences in the data, and attempts to find patterns that can be formulated as normative behaviors. Adolescents' SMS communication is constituted of an exchange where the parties take turns communicating, just like spoken interaction. It is in these exchanges that the participants orientate themselves toward the norms. Conversation analysts can gain insight into these norms by studying how a turn is constructed to achieve particular actions, and how these actions are a reaction to the previous turn.

In this article, I will show that, among adolescent mobile users, there is a dominating norm that dictates that an SMS receives a response. This reply norm is a practice that has been suggested in previous studies. Taylor and Harper (2003) have identified an "obligation to reciprocate" in adolescents' SMS usage. Also, Kasesniemi and Rautiainen (2002) state that "Leaving an SMS message unanswered is almost without exception interpreted as rudeness" (p. 186). The research presented here studies the precise manifestation of the reply norm in adolescents' SMS communication, and will be looking at the interactional and relational consequences for the parties when this norm is broken.

Richard Harper, Leysia Palen and Alex Taylor (Eds), The Inside Text: Social, Cultural and Design Perspectives on SMS, 53–73.

The data presented in this paper will be in an alternating A-B sequence, where A stands for an SMS from the initiator of the SMS communication sequence, and B stands for the reply SMS from the recipient. An A-B sequence may or may not continue (A-B-A-...). Therefore, the norm that binds the participants can be formulated as follows: *The initiating message must receive a responding message.* In other words, an initiating A requires a B.There are three main analytical sections in the article: The first section focuses on the typical A-B sequence and shows how deviances from the sequence actually confirms the norm. The second section presents the occurrences where the first A does not receive a response in the form of an SMS, but instead as a telephone call. Finally, the third section will discuss the kind of A messages that do not require a response: chain messages, night time messages and messages that occur as a continuation of a conversation.

The data set is based on 511[1] text messages and 287[2] mobile conversations of three 14 year old girls and three 14 year old boys. The six participants are all from the same 8th grade class and are all friends. Participants' mobile phone communication was collected over a period of one week each and took place during six weeks in 2001-2002. Recordings of calls and computer logs of messages were made in collaboration with the telecommunications company TDC Mobil. This is part of a series of ethnographic observations and interviews, which act as the data set for the Ph.D. project "Mobile Spaces of Communication" (Laursen, in prep.).

The reply obligation to the initiating SMS

The following section will present the typical A-B sequence. The deviances from the sequence will be analysed with reference to the interactional and relational consequences experienced by the parties when the replying norm is broken and will show how the deviances from the sequence actually confirms the norm.

The canonical sequence

In the dataset, the typical and unmarked SMS interaction is an exchange between A's and B's. Here's an example of the beginning of such an exchange:

(Example 1)[3]

Daniel   11:30 am   Should we walk together from school today...

---

[1] Automatically generated messages of the type, "*Mobile text to XXXXXXXX sent 01.12.01, at 15:03:10 was received at 15:03:17*" were deducted from this total.

[2] Voice mail calls and zero-phone calls are also deducted from this total. Zero-phone calls will be dealt with later.

[3] Typing and spelling errors, abbreviations, and fluctuation in the use of capitals and lower-case lettering have been reproduced in the translation from Danish. The number of characters utilized varies between the original messages and their translations. Names and places have been changed in order to secure the anonymity of the persons involved.

Rune	11:30 am	*I have to get home and sleep...but you're welcome to come with me.....*

This A-B sequence can be termed a *paired sequence* (Schegloff and Sacks, 1973) with Daniel's initating question as the 'first pair part' (i.e., first part of pair) and Rune's answer as the second pair part. The paired sequence refers to a two-part sequence of turns whereby the utterance of a first turn, or pair-part, provides a 'slot' for a second turn which is precipitated by the form of the first turn. 'Question-answer', 'greeting-greeting', 'offer-acceptance/refusal' are instances of pair types. Paired sequences like example 1 are frequent in the data, however, even though they do not contradict the normative rule that *the initiating message must receive a responding message*, they do not provide evidence for it.

Exchanges like example 2 will be the first evidence of the replying rule. Here the message gets a reply even if it is not sequentially relevant:

(Example 2)

Daniel	11:02 am	*Hi trine. i'm done with church now and I'm totally worn out. Pretty soon I'm gonna go out and buy gifts for rune and jonas. See you.*
Katrine	11:03 am	*Yes we certainly will ! Kisses me!*

Daniel's SMS has not first pair part status, i.e. is not designed as something that demands a response from the receiver. His SMS is a sort of situational report that could have easily stood as a single entity; a little electronic postcard that pleased the recipient, but did not lead to further communication. However, Katrine responds immediately with an SMS. Adjacent positioning, where an SMS gets a reply even though the reply is not called for, is used throughout the data set. What two messages produced by different speakers can do that one utterance cannot do is this: by a B reply, the recipient of A can show not only that A has been received, but also that he understood what A aimed at, and how he is willing to go along with that. Also, by virtue of B, the initiator of A can ascertain how his message was understood, and in what way it was accepted. Thus, the reply rule confirms and strengthens the interaction between the two parties. Furthermore, the reciprocal principle is a tangible point for social exchange and confirmation as it ratifies and develops the relationship between the parties. In some cases, the exchange is primarily a social act with the purpose of communicating and nurturing the mutual connection:

(Example 3)

| *Sara* | *2:53 pm* | *Forest Haha* |
| *Malene* | *2:54 pm* | *No OAK TREE!!!!* |

The content of this exchange is not easily accessible to an outsider but the content itself is presumably not what holds meaning either. In cases like this, the exchange seems most of all to be a ritual act that ensures contact and serves to build and maintain relationships.

Exchanges like example 2 and 3 will be the first evidence of the normative rule *the initiating message must receive a responding message*. Before I turn to further evidence of the replying norm, I will briefly discuss the response time between the initiating message and the responding message in the canonical sequence.

The response time for a typical and unmarked B-answer is dependent on the relationship of the communicating parties[4]. For couples and best friends, the average response time is under three minutes (cf. ex. 1-3), but this time can increase in more distant relationships:

(Example 4)

| *Michael* | *9:06 am* | *Hi beautiful ninja nini. what are you up to at the moment. when are you coming to denmark` hope too hear from you. your friend michael-matros* |
| *Nete* | *10:55 am* | *HI MICKEY! I'M FINE. HOW ABOUT YOU HOW IS THE LOVE GOING? K NETE* |

Michael and Nete are not close friends, and there is a lapse of nearly two hours between the moment when Michael sends his SMS and Nete replies. The long response time, however, is not problematic for either party.

The response time is of great importance for the reply rule. Not only must the initiating message receive a reply, it must also be in due time. The next section will deal with cases where the reply is not produced in due time and where the reply norm is consequentially broken.

---

[4] This is somewhat different from Kasesniemi's statement that a message "should be responded to as quickly as possible" (2003, p. 197).

The deviating sequence

The strong relationship between the A-B sequence's first two parts manifests itself not only in the many examples where an A doesn't require any answer, but nevertheless receives one. The norm is also visible in the occurrences where it is not respected: if a B reply is not produced as the norm prescribes, then it will be treated as a 'noticeable absence' (Sacks 1992) and the producer of the first A will send a reminder and/or the recipient of the first A will send an excuse for not replying in good time. Paradoxically, it is consideration of these 'deviant cases' (Heritage, 1984) in which the A-B sequence is not implemented fully or is otherwise problematic that provides the strongest evidence for the normative character of the reply rule.

In this section, I will show how the sender of the initiating A will treat a missing B reply and makes sense of it in terms of possible problems with the delivery of A. Thus, when a B reply is not provided in due time, the sender of the initiating A will construct his reminder as a solution to what could have gone wrong since the receiver has not replied. Transmission problems, recipient problems, content problems, and relationship problems are the four problem types that the adolescents in this data are attempting to solve with their reminders.

Transmission problems

If the sender of an A message does not get a reply as normatively expected, he will most often treat the missing reply as a transmission problem. This is visible in the way he deals with the missing reply, which is to send the same SMS one more time:

(Example 5)

Morten	3:04 pm	Hmmm Vanlose... Damn long time since I've been to this station...
Maja	–	–
Morten	3:11 pm	Hmmm Vanlose... Damn long time since I've been to this station...
Maja	3:13 pm	What are you doing by vanlose st....?

The minutes that pass after Morten has sent his first SMS give him reason to consider that there might be a problem with his message since he did not receive a reply. Then, he decides to send the exact same SMS one more time.

The transmission problem is normatively minor and can be solved easily and quickly. First of all, it is an easy matter for the sender to verify the transmission in sending the same SMS once more, especially if he has saved the message in his outbox. Secondly, it is simple for the recipient to confirm that the transmission is functioning. The interaction can then follow its normal course without the parties dwelling on the confusion there might have been. Finally, the transmission problem is socially and interactionally uncomplicated because it is technological and therefore not considered to be a reflection of the relationship between the parties.

The fact that the sender of the first A most frequently assumes there is a transmission problem when a B reply is not produced could have two explanations. The first might be that if there is some question as to why the recipient has not responded, the sender of the initiating A may try the least complicated and costly remedy first, just as a television repairman will first check if the television is even plugged in (cf. also Pomerantz 1984, p. 156). Secondly, the transmission problem gives the possibility to send a reminder that does not reflect character or relationship deficiencies. In this case, it is worth noting that there are not any examples of true transmission problems[5] throughout the data. One can therefore assume that the transmission problem is a pretext that is used in order to construct a risk-free reminder.

Recipient problems

Recipient problems can be another explanation of what might have gone wrong when an initial A message doesn't receive a reply. It is investigated and resolved by sending a new SMS, which explicitly asks for a reply:

(Example 6)

Henrik	9:11 am	HI Dorte could you please tell grete that i'm ill?
Dorte	–	–
Henrik	10:18 am	HELLO?
Dorte	10:52 am	I have told it grete and ther's porno between anders and maja! It's really funny! What r u doing? Hugzz..

In this example, Henrik is asking his classmate, Dorte to let their teacher, Grete know that he is ill. After a good hour, he sends her a reminder with his *HELLO?* This reminder takes for granted the fact that Dorte has technically received the first message, and is also "yelling", with the use of capital letters, that there should have been a response. The capital letters signify impatience and disappointment and

---

[5] True channel problems can, however, occur; for example the mobile networks broke down in several countries under the pressure of Christmas and New Year's messages in 2002 (www.mobil.nu 08-01-2003).

thereby intensify the potential conflict that can ensue since Dorte has not yet answered. In other words, Henrik is showing with his *HELLO?* that he has identified a problem, and that this problem lies with the recipient. Dorte also writes something in her reply that can be seen as an explanation of what had been distracting her: *ther's porno between anders and maja!*.

Recipient problems are a little more complicated and demand some more interactional work than the channel problems. First of all, the sender has to construct an entirely new SMS in order for it to be manifested as a reminder, while also remaining open for an explanation for the missing reply. Furthermore, the recipient does not only have to confirm or deny that she actually has received the first SMS, but she also has to respond to it and, in addition, alleviate the potential conflict created by the fact that she might have had more important things to do. Finally, the recipient problems are a latent threat to the interaction and the social relationship, and could lead to explicit treatment of relationship matters.

Content problems

Content problems are a third possibility, from the sender's point of view, of what might have gone wrong in the case of a missing reply. The problem is investigated and resolved by sending a new SMS which modifies what has been said in the first SMS (example 7) or deletes it (example 8):

(Example 7)

Maja	3:05 pm	*I have just sat and read something..... It fit you a little..... "why kiss boys' cheeks? When the cock is of the same skin....! Pretty funny heh? Hugs maja...*
Katrine	–	–
Maja	3:30 pm	*Oh ok sorry!!! I'm just having a little fun with it......! You're more porno than any other ok maybe not markus but otherwise....! Ha ha....=:)*
Katrine	4:33 pm	**Katrine calls Maja**

Maja's reminder presupposes that Katrine has received the message and changes the potentially offending content of the first SMS. The change is mostly about showing Katrine how the first SMS is to be understood: that it was not negatively meant, but rather, with the use of *You're more porno than any other*, a kind of compliment. In addition, the change clarified that it had been sent to tease and was to be understood as fun: *Ha ha....* The smiley at the end of the SMS functions as a sender's signature (Maja's hairstyle has bangs), but it also is also intended perhaps to redeem Maja and eliminate possible offense a second time. It is also important to note that Maja, with her apology, *Oh ok sorry!!!* and its three energetic and genuine exclamation marks, shows that she takes responsibility for the problem that might have occurred. In spite of Maja's persistence, the time gap between 3:30 pm and 4:33 pm suggests that she did not succeed in eliminating the problem that occurred with her first SMS. And when Katrine finally calls Maja, they do treat the two SMS's with great caution, and it slowly appears that the problem has a much more serious character: Katrine does not at all feel sexy, especially now that her boyfriend, with whom she should have been spending the afternoon, is with his best friend instead.

In a more radical case, the sender of the first SMS can change the content of her SMS by 'withdrawing' it. This is done by sending a completely new SMS, which 'erases' the first one:

(Example 8)

Katrine	9:51 am	When do are you free on wednesday? Hugzz me!
Rune	–	–
Katrine	11:05 am	Hey there.... Can we meet quarter to four at vanløse st. So I can get home first? Write back...!
Rune	11:06 am	Yeah yeah... sweetie...

In this example, Katrine is attempting, on a Monday, to find out if her boyfriend is free on the following Wednesday. He does not answer, and she then sends him a new SMS dealing with the appointment they already have on that same afternoon. This SMS is not explicitly constructed as a reminder.

Unlike Maja's first SMS (example 7), the problem with the content of Katrine's SMS is not obvious. The only obvious thing that could be wrong is that Rune does not wish to be with her on Wednesday. Instead of addressing the possible problem with the content of her first SMS, Katrine 'erases' her first SMS by sending a new SMS which is, with its *Hey there*, constructed as a first SMS often would be. Accordingly, Rune's SMS does not address Katrine's first SMS. However, there are small signs suggesting that they are orienting toward the norm that there should have been a response: *Write back...!* is not something one usually writes in SMS, so it is probable that it is reflecting Rune's lack of an answer to the first SMS, and is also a move to ensure that he'll reply to the new SMS. Rune's *yeah yeah* is in turn subtly teasing Katrine's impatience, and his *sweetie* softens his lack of answer and ensures that there are no negative consequences in their relationship. In this way, they are both pretending that the first SMS did not take place, agreeing that it does not have to be dealt with at this particular moment. The question in the first SMS nevertheless still remains, and presumably, it is only when Rune will respond to it that the tension between them will be resolved.

The content problems are issues that demand a lot of interactional work from the parties involved. The sender must first go through the sent message to identify what the content problem is. She then has to construct a whole new SMS to eliminate the problem and maybe also apologize for a mistake. The recipient has, for his part, to accept the reminder as such, confirm that there isn't a problem (anymore) and send a response for the interaction can follow its course. The content problems are a latent threat to the interaction and social relations and can also lead to an explicit treatment of the relationship matters.

Relationship problems

Relationship problems are the fourth and last possibility, from the sender's point of view, of what could have gone wrong when a reply is not received. The problem is investigated and resolved by sending a new SMS which explicitly addresses the relationship between the parties:

(Example 9)

Michael	13:03 pm	*What's up beautiful are you coming over to my place by my mother. morten and I can't be bothered to go to training. Michael*
Susanne	–	–
Michael	16:28 pm	*Heydi/hey there. are you doing something on friday. now we haten't seen each other in a long time.. I thourght you had plenty time when we started going out but ->*
		<- I was maybe wrong... I don't know can you answer me. miss you michael
Susanne	16:59	*Hey Mick! I just got back from school.. Did you think I had more time?? Im a busy train train girl.. Hey r you upset about it? What are you doing? *Your Girlfriend**

Michael and Susanne are dating, and Michael tries in his first SMS to make an appointment. Susanne does not answer, and the amount of time of over three hours since Michael sent his SMS is reflected in the serious character of his reminder.

After having proposed a new meeting time, thereby withdrawing the current appointment that is no longer relevant, Michael addresses their relationship: *now we haten't seen each other in a long time.. I thourght you had plenty time when we started going out but I was maybe wrong... I don't know.*[6] He then marks the lack of response to his first SMS with *can you answer me* which is constructed to better ensure that Susanne will reply to the new SMS. Finally, he shows with his *miss you* that the relationship is important to him. All at once, his reminder SMS reflects openness and vulnerability. Susanne's reply presents in turn something that can be interpreted as an apology and an explanation of why she did not respond to the first message, and only now responds to the second: *I just got back from school.* She furthermore treats Michael's complaint in the following way: *Did you think I had more time?? I am a busy train train girl.* Susanne's response to Michael's SMS only treats his complaint superficially. It does not address Michael's attempt to make an appointment, and his statement about them not having seen each other in a long time is turned into a question about how busy Susanne is. In addition, she implies with *r you upset about it?* that Michael is the one who is wrong, and with *What are you doing?* and **Your Girlfriend** that everything is as it should be. In other words, Susanne acts surprised and innocent, and denies that there should be anything wrong with their relationship.

Supposed problems with the relationship demand a lot of interactional work from the parties involved. The sender has to review his first message to rule out any other type of problem. Then, he has to construct a whole new SMS that will address the relationship without threatening it, and that will maintain the possibility of further communication. The recipient must for her part accept the reminder and give an account for the reason why the reply did not come in due time. Furthermore, she has to confirm or deny that there is something wrong with the relationship in accounting for her own position. Problems with the relationship are a direct threat to interaction and social relations, in that they ultimately can lead to a rift between the parties.

Secondary problem: reminders by telephone call

We have now reviewed the different forms of reminders that the initiator of the first SMS can send via SMS. The sender of the first SMS has, however, other options for sending a reminder. In the data, reminders for a response are also sent by calling the recipient by telephone. In the next example, Katrine sends an SMS to Karsten, to which he does not reply. The following day, she telephones him:

---

[6] The two arrows indicate that Michael's message takes two SMS's, which also reflects the extent of the interactional work he is performing.

(Example 10a)

Katrine	10:01	*Hi lowsy.... I need my money...sorry...*
		Could you bring it tomorrow and go
		down to joshi with it? Hugs katrine!
Karsten	–	–

(Example 10b)[7]

The following day at 11:47

Kar: yes hello this is ↑Karsten

Pause:(0.4)

Kat: >hi this is Katrine where are you<

Ps: (0.4)

Kar: I'm at my school

Ps: (0.6)

Kat: could I get my mo:ney soon

Kar: SU:RE but I don't have any fucking ATM card and I >also owe my dad a hundred crowns or something you're gonna get your fucking money the first<

    [...]

Researcher field notes on the same day as the phone call, between 11:30 am and 12:00 pm, further elaborate:

It is lunch break and I have asked Katrine if she minds that I accompany her and her friends from school when they leave. She doesn't, so we walk a couple hundred meters to a store called Joshi. I think we are going inside to shop, but everybody stands outside. A couple more people come from school, and some are standing smoking and chatting. Katrine asks if I know the senior high school that is nearby, and I say that I have heard of it and ask if that's where she will be going. She answers that it is a bit too junior-highish and names two other senior high schools that she would rather go

---

[7] Transcription symbols and conventions are adopted from Gail Jefferson's transcript notation, as related explained in Atkinson and Heritage (1984).

to. After having stood there for about five minutes, Katrine and the others
decide that we should leave. On the way back from there, Katrine phones
someone that owes her money.

In her SMS, Katrine asks Karsten to come down to Joshi on the following day with
the money that he owes her. Joshi is the grocer situated halfway between Katrine's
school and Karsten's school, and they often meet there with their common friends
during lunch break as the field notes illustrate. Karsten nevertheless does not reply
to the SMS, and Katrine phones him the exact place where she had asked him to
meet her, but where he did not show up. (In the field notes, there is an indication
that she is waiting for Karsten during these minutes, as she talks about his school).

In the telephone conversation, Katrine's first question is *where are you*. Such a
question about the recipient's geographic location is routinely used in mobile
conversations (Arminen and Leinonen, 2003; Laurier, 1999), and when it occurs
during the opening sequence, it is often expressing an orientation towards the
recipient's interactional availability (Arminen/Leinonen, 2003, p. 2, also cf.
Schegloff and Sacks, 1973, p. 316). Karsten's answer, *I'm at my school*, is
interpreted by Katrine as a sign that Karsten is interactionally available since she
does not propose to postpone the conversation, but instead carries on with her
reason for the call: *could I get my money soon*. But Katrine's question also gives
Karsten the possibility to explain why he is not where Katrine had asked him to be
in her SMS. The 0.6 second pause can therefore be seen as the place where Karsten
chooses to not explain himself, and where Katrine chooses to not pursue Karsten's
failure to appear. It is also worth noticing that Katrine's *could I get my money soon*
is not constructed as a reminder.

The sender of the first SMS who chooses to send a reminder via a telephone call
seems to be less oriented toward the reason why the SMS hasn't been answered
than the one who sends a reminder via SMS. The caller does not investigate the
reason for the lack of response, but is rather interested in the response itself. The
fact that the people sending a reminder through a telephone call are less interested
in the reason why there was no answer and are more interested in getting the answer
might be related to the fact that the telephone call seems to be triggered by a
change of situation/circumstance which (re)makes an answer from the recipient
relevant. The mitigation of the fact that a norm has been broken can also be related
to the fact that a phone call in that context is a confrontation of the problem itself.

The continuing sequence

The A-B sequence is the standard sequence, but it can carry on in a continuing
exchange: A-B-A-.... . In this data set, the longest exchange is of 28 messages. Two
messages *can* be sent in a row by the same person, but they are then specifically
built to be a single unit (cf. example 9). It is only the first A that binds to a B-
answer, while the first B, second A, second B, etc. do not necessarily bind to any
response (but can very well be constructed as such, as in for example the form of a
question). If a first B, second A, second B are designed to be answered to and do

not receive any response, it will give rise to reminders of the type that we have seen in the above examples.

A sequence that continues after the standard exchange A-B can be terminated with the parties explicitly closing the exchange. In most cases, nevertheless, the exchange has an open ending:

(Example 11)

Daniel	2:16 pm	*Is it okay if me and trine come by when we're finished in church? We're at the nativity show...*
Rune	2:17 pm	*I have to do tons of homework so I'm probably not so fun to b with*
Daniel	2:18 pm	*I'll check with trine and call you later... Then we might come by*

Daniel's last message is open in the way that Rune can answer it if he wishes to, but he can also choose not to. As Rune chooses not to answer, Daniel's message becomes, ex post facto, the one that closes the exchange. In this way, the example illustrates that whether an SMS (which is not a first SMS, and which is not designed to be answered to) will be closing a sequence or not is a question that primarily the recipient of that SMS decides. In addition, the example demonstrates that SMS communication within a group of friends is a running connection, where it is often unnecessary to formally open and close dialogues.

Alternative replying options: when the SMS is responded to with a telephone call

The first A does not always get responded to with an SMS; the answer can also come as a telephone call. If the initiator of the first A wishes to get her response with a telephone call, she will typically make this wish explicit by writing "call me":

(Example 12)

| Katrine | 4:44 pm | *Hi rune and daniel..... One of you.... Call me as soon as you're finished THANKS!* |

In the example, Katrine is addressing Rune and Daniel, whom she seemingly assumes are together. She nevertheless only sends the message to Daniel, and he is also the one who calls her in return.

In other cases, the receiver of the first A calls on her own initiative. In the following, Malene sends an SMS to Sara, her best friend, on a Sunday morning. One and a half hours later, Sara telephones Malene:

(Example 13a)

Malene   *10:59 am*   *Hey! What are you doing was it fun yesterday?*

(Example 13b)

at 12:29 pm

Ma: >this is Malene<

Pause:(0.2)

Sa: *he*llo::

Ps: (1.6)

Ma: hello:

Ps: (0.6)

Sa: ey you sl*ept*- ey you woke up early *man* £.hh I was

ju[st laying and <u>sno</u>ring when your message

Ma: [°hen°

Sa: arrived I was just like a::a:a:<u>argh</u>£ h

Ps: (.)

Ma: hm<u>um</u>

Ps: (0.4)

Ma: °°what *are you talking about*°° (.) anyway- .hhh big laugh (.) what::
what did you do yesterday

[...]

In example 13b, the SMS is, after the opening identification and greetings, the first topic to be addressed in the telephone call. In lines 7-8 and 10, Sara makes a reference to Malene's SMS by commenting on how early it arrived, and explaining why she was unable to answer it at the time she received it. It also seems that she, in the same turn, treats Malene's question *was it fun yesterday?* by implying that she came home late. In a telephone call reply to an SMS, the SMS will, just as in this case, be treated as one of the first topics. This SMS-conversation relationship is elaborated elsewhere (Laursen, in prep.); here only examples 12 and 13 are presented as evidence that an SMS message can sometimes receive a telephone conversation in reply instead of an SMS.

A particular type of telephone call can also function as a response to a first SMS message: the zero-phone call. I define zero-phone calls as the occurrences where the caller hangs up immediately after the telephone has rung once.[8] The recipient does not manage to pick up the telephone, but can see who has called on the display. Among adolescent mobile users, such a phone call is used to let the recipient know that he should call the caller back. The recipient will then – if he agrees to call back – be responsible for the call's charges. The adolescent mobile users can for example use the zero-phone call if their pre-paid phone cards are about to run out of credit, or if they know that the recipient is at home and able to call from the parents' home phone:

(Example 14)

| Malene | 10:49 pm | *Hey Trine! Can't come with you on friday after all.... Forgot I have to meet with Dorte....! See you tomorrow! Malene....* |

In the above example, Malene writes to Trine on Wednesday evening to cancel their appointment on the following Friday evening. Malene is at home, and a minute later, she receives a zero-phone call from Trine. I cannot, from my data, know with certainty that Trine's zero-phone call is a reaction to Malene's SMS, because I do not have any recording of Malene's following phone call (which probably was made using her parents' home telephone). But it is most probably not a coincidence that Trine's zero-phone call occurs within a minute following Malene's SMS.

---

[8] Oksman and Rautiainen (2003) call these types of telephone calls bomb calls, but I haven't come across this designation elsewhere. I have chosen to name these calls zero-phone calls, because, in the telecommunications company TDC Mobil's itemized records, the talk time is recorded as 0:00. No designation exists for this type of phone call among Danish mobile users. It is not something they talk about; they just do it.

Kasesniemi and Rautiainen (2002) mention in their work that Finnish teenagers can respond to an SMS by using the zero-phone call as an "acknowledgement call" (p. 186), which does not tell the recipient to return the call, but simply confirms that his SMS has been received. This practice however, does not seem to have found its way into the circles of Danish teenagers.

SMS messages which do not require a response

In certain circumstances, an initiating A will not receive any reply, and there are no normative expectations that have sequential implications in obliging the recipient to reply. Thus, the sender of the initiating A does not send any reminder for a response, and the recipient does not excuse oneself for not having replied. These types of initiating A's appear to be of three different kinds: when the initiating A is a chain message, when the initiating A is a night time message, or when the initiating A follows a conversation.

Chain messages

Chain messages do not demand an answer. They can take the form of jokes, images, voice messages and short poems, or they can resemble the traditional chain letters that promise love and happiness:

(Example 15)

?	11:07	*<3 <3 <3 <3 <3 <3 send these 6 hearts to 6 of your FRIENDS & the one you love will love you during the whole year 2002 if you break the chain the person will disappear from your life!*
Daniel	–	–

The idea behind a chain message is not to respond to it, but to forward it to someone else than the one it was received from. When the chain message circulates within a group of friends, it ties the group together around a common experience and thereby creates a solidarity on which further interaction can be based. In this example, Daniel does not forward the message, and generally speaking, chain messages are not very widespread in the data: they are rare and do not get forwarded. Kasesniemi and Rautiainen (2003) write about Finnish teenagers' mobile culture that chain messages seem to be more popular with the younger teenagers than the older ones, and it might be the case in this data that Daniel and his friends are too old to be interested in chain messages. Nevertheless, the claim can still be made that chain messages are a type of initiating A's that do not and should not receive a B.

Night time messages

Another exception from the otherwise standard A-B sequence are the messages being sent late at night. I will be referring to them here as night time messages. Night time messages are often messages wishing good night, and particularly around bed time, the message activity between friends and couples is very high. The SMS function of the mobile telephone seems to be perfect for late hours where one does not wish to wake the recipient or his family. Night time messages often get a response, but not always:

(Example 16)

Daniel	*11:25 pm*	*Goodnight... I love you... Daniel.*
Katrine	–	–

(Example 17)

Henrik	*11:27 pm*	*HELLO HELLO DO WE HAVE TO DO SOMETHING FOR TOMORROW?*
Dorte	–	–

In these two examples, the initiating A does not get a response – but it is not treated as problematic by either party. The initiator of the first A does not send a reminder, the recipient does not subsequently apologize for the lack of response. It therefore seems that the normative replying rule does not apply to night time messages. The initiator of the first A knows that the recipient might already be in bed sleeping, and the following morning, when the content of the night time message is no longer relevant, both parties let the message be.

Messages as a P.S. to a telephone call

The last situation where an initiating A does not require a response is when the A is following a conversation:

(Example 18a)

at 2:19 pm

Ka: *£hi Maja£*

Pause: *(0.5)*

Ma: *hi: >where are you<*

Ps: *(0.3)*

Ka: *I'm at °school°*

Ps: *(0.6)*

Ma: *are you inside school*

Ka: <u>*yem*</u>

Ps: *(0.5)*

Ma: *could you bring my cap to catechism*

Ps: *(0.9)*

Ka: *are you going to catechism*

Ps: *(0.5)*

Ma: *>m I don't know I c- wha- I'll drop b<u>y</u> anyway*

          so can you just take it<

Ps: *(0.2)*

Ka: *yeah if I can find it*

Ps: *(0.8)*

Ma: *It <u>is</u>- >it must be somewhere around my seat<*

          °okay°?

Ps: *(0.3)*

Ka: *>yeah oka[y<*

Ma: *[bye*

Ka: *bye*

(Example 18b)

Maja   15:44   Hi trine... Now I forgot my cap.... But
                                     I'll call you later... Hugs maja...

In example 18a, Maja calls Katrine to ask her to bring her cap to catechism. After catechism, Maja writes that she has forgotten her cap, but Katrine does not respond. Presumably the A must not, in cases like this, be considered as an initiating A, but an A that comes in the continuation of a dialogue between the two parties. The dialogue about the cap has happened over the telephone, and maybe also during catechism, so the A that Maja is sending is the continuation of this communication sequence. So what appears to be an exception to the normative rule that *the initiating message must receive a responding message* actually is not because the A in question is not an initiating message.

Conclusion

I have now shown how the replying norm is enacted throughout my data. The norm is not a rule that absolutely must be respected; rather, the sender of the initiating A and its recipient are orienting themselves with the norm by following it or sending a reminder and excuse when it is not respected. The initiating A messages are most frequently replied to by using the same medium, a text message, but they can also be made by telephone calls. Two types of initiating A messages elude the reply norm: chain messages and night time messages.

Although the SMS sequences in the dataset are indeed frequently organised in ways that the replying norm prescribes, some of the more significant and characteristic aspects of the nature and workings of the replying norm come to light when the expected pattern is breached. The analysis of the breaches of the norm show that the senders design the reminders to be a candidate understanding of and a solution to what could have gone wrong since the receiver has not replied. The reminders are constructed according to four problem types which the recipient can acknowledge, reject, or rephrase: Transmission problems, recipient problems, content problems, and relationship problems.

The reminders can be seen as instances of *repair work*, i.e. organized ways of dealing with various kinds of trouble in the interaction's progress (Schegloff, Jefferson and Sacks, 1977). Explicit other-repair in this manner can be a sensitive issue: to remind another person is to draw attention to an error or lapse in performance on their part, which in turn may undermine the harmony or accord of the exchange. Repair of others' actions, then, has potential implications for the coordination of the interpersonal relations of the relevant parties. The analysis of the reminders and the work that they generate has shown that the four types of reminders are more or less serious to the interactants and their relationship.

The time factor plays an important role when the adolescents are producing their SMS messages. First of all, it appears that, just as in face-to-face interactions, a maximum standard is reflected in the parties' tolerance towards silence. While this seems to be universal in face-to-face conversations (Jefferson, 1983), it depends, in the case of SMS interaction, on the relationship of the parties: best friends and couples must answer within a few minutes; more distant relationships can have an extended delay of some hours. The reply time therefore reflects the relationship between the parties, and is negotiated in the way that particular relationship usually is. Secondly, there is a relationship between the time gap from the initiating A to the reminder that is produced if a B-reply has not arrived in due time, and the type of the reminder: the longer the time gap, the more serious the reminder. A transmission problem reminder can be sent as soon as 7 minutes following the initiating A (cf. example 5), but a relationship reminder will occur after several hours (cf. example 9).

The A-B sequence is controlled by a dialogic principle where one alternates between sending and receiving. The reciprocity in the exchange is binding, but also rewarding: the sender of A receives attention and reward in the form of B, and the recipient of A receives attention and, through answering B, creates a balance in the relationship which leaves each party equal. The maintenance of the ritual contributes to the cultivation and the strength of the relationship. However, if the unwritten contract is not respected, it is a threat to the interaction and the social relationship.

Acknowledgements

An earlier version of this chapter was presented during the 16th Nordic Media Conference in Kristianssand, Norway, 15-17 August, 2003.

References

Androutsopoulos, Jannis and Gurly Schmidt (2002): SMS-Kommunikation: Ethnografische Gattungsanalyse am Beispiel einer Kleingruppe. *Zeitschrift für Angewandte Linguistik* 36, p. 49-80

Arminen, Ilkka and Minna Leinonen (2003): Mobile phone calls – reflecting a new type of openings as an emergence of a new genre of talk-in-interaction? Paper presented at the *8th International Pragmatics Conference*

Atkinson, J. Maxwell and John Heritage (1984): *Structures of Social Action. Studies in Conversation Analysis.* Cambridge University Press

Döring, Nicola (2002a): "1x Brot, Wurst, 5Sack Äpfel I.L.D." – Kommunikative Funktionen von Kurzmitteilungen (SMS). *Zeitschrift für Medienpsychologie* 3

Döring, Nicola (2002b): "Kurzm. wird gesendet" – Abkürzungen und Akronyme in der SMS-Kommunikation, *Muttersprache. Vierteljahresschrift für deutsche Sprache*, Heft 2

Haard af Segerstad, Ylva (2002): *Use and Adaptation of Written Language to the Conditions of Computer-Mediated Communication*, unpublised Ph.D. Thesis

Heritage, John (1984): *Garfinkel and Ethnomethodology*, Polity Press.

Jefferson, Gail (1983): Notes on a Possible Metric which Provides for a 'Standard Maximum' Silence of Approximately One Second in Conversation. *Tilburg papers in language and literature* 42, Tilburg.

Kasesniemi, Eija-Liisa (2003): *Mobile messages. Young People and a New Communication Culture*, Tampere University Press.

Kasesniemi, Eija-Liisa and Pirjo Rautiainen (2002): Mobile culture of children and teenagers in Finland. In: James E. Katz og Mark Aakhus (red.): *Perpetual Contact. Mobile Communication, Private Talk, Public Performance*, Cambridge University Press.

Laurier, Eric (1999): Why people say where they are during mobile-phone calls. http://www.receiver.vodafone.com/07/articles/pdf/07.pdf [16.10.03].

Laursen, Ditte (in prep.): *Mobile Spaces of Communication. The interactional and social patterns of adolescents' mobile phone communication*, Ph.D. Thesis, University of Southern Denmark.

Ling, Rich (2003): The socio-linguistics of SMS: An analysis of SMS use by a random sample of Norwegians. In: Rich Ling and Per Pedersen (eds.) (in prep.): *Front Stage – Back Stage: Mobile communication and the renegotiation of the social sphere.*

Oksman, Virpi and Rautiainen, P. (2003): "Perhaps It Is a Body Part". How the Mobile Phone Became an Organic Part of the Everyday Lives of Children and Adolescents. A Case Study of Finland. In Katz, James (ed): *Machines That Become Us. The Social Context of Personal Communication Technology*, Transaction Pub.

Pomerantz, Anita (1984): Persuing a response. In: J. Maxwell Atkinson and John Heritage: *Structures of Social Action. Studies in Conversation Analysis.* Cambridge University Press.

Sacks, Harvey (1992): *Lectures on Conversation*, Oxford UK/Cambridge USA: Blackwell.

Schegloff, Emanuel A. and Sacks, H. (1973): Opening up closings. In: *Semiotica* 7.

Schegloff, Emanuel A., Jefferson, G. and Sacks, H. (1977): The preference for self-correction in the organisation of repair in conversation. *Language*, 53.

Schlobinski, Peter (2001): Simsen. Eine Pilotstudie zu sprachlichen und kommunikativen Aspekten in der SMS-Kommunikation http://www.mediensprache.net/networx/ networx-22.pdf [05.01.04]

Taylor, A. S., and Harper, R. (2003). The gift of the gab: a design oriented sociology of young people's use of mobiles. *Journal of Computer Supported Cooperative Work (CSCW)*, 12(3), 267-296.

Thurlow, Crispin (2002): Generation Txt? Exposing the sociolinguistics of young people's text-messaging, *Discourse Analysis Online*

4 Nascent Communication Genres within SMS and MMS

Richard Ling, Tom Julsrud and Birgitte Yttri

Introduction

In the world of mobile telephony, SMS represented a major shift in the way we communicate in many parts of the world. Instead of synchronous voice communications, SMS allowed asynchronous text based interaction. SMS was conceived as a way of sending automatically generated messages to users – such as notification of voice mail, a function that it still serves in many cases – it has also developed into a form of interpersonal communication. SMS is now used in a broad variety of situations. It is used to coordinate group interactions, to send greetings, to ask and answer questions, to find out where others are, to send jokes and to communicate personal news. In many cases, it has developed its own linguistic form (Grinter and Eldridge 2001; Hård af Segerstaad 2003; Ling 2003). In this chapter we will contrast the development of SMS with the more recently developed Multi-media Messaging Service (MMS).

Material from around the world shows that SMS, or texting, has become one of the run-away successes of mobile telephony. In many cases, texting has become a central post in the lives of teens. According to the Norwegian Post and Telecommunications authority, subscribers in Norway sent almost 70 messages a month during the first half of 2003 (PT 2003). Many of these were sent by teens who make up a large portion of the mobile communications market. While other groups in society use SMS, it is often the teens who are the most intense users of the system. Teens have been reported to be a major user group in Italy, Finland, Japan, Korea and the Philippines (Hashimoto 2002; Ito 2001; Ling 2004; Mante-Meijer and al. 2001; Paragas 2000; Rautiainen and Kasesniemi 2000). Indeed it is teens that, in many respects, set the style when it comes to the use of SMS.

One can argue, as we will here, that SMS messages have developed into several genres of communication, albeit genres that are heavily influenced by their technical heritage. That is to say that SMS users have developed typologies of messages. These typologies inform one as to the expectations associated with the SMS messages and how the receiver should or might interpret those they receive.

Richard Harper, Leysia Palen and Alex Taylor (Eds), The Inside Text: Social, Cultural and Design Perspectives on SMS, 75–100.

It is clear that SMS has made its mark on society. However, as has often happened in the telecommunications world, developments make alternative forms of communication possible. MMS is now arriving on the scene. This is a method of creating, sending and receiving graphics, video clips, photographs, sound files and short text messages via wireless networks. MMS also supports e-mail addressing such that one can send a message from a mobile telephone to an e-mail address.

Many see MMS as the next generation of asynchronous mobile messaging. Where SMS is limited to 160 characters of text, MMS is much more generous. Where SMS is limited to only text, MMS offers one a variety of communication forms including text, sound but most often photographs taken with the "camera phone" of the sender. Finally, where SMS is relatively inexpensive, MMS usually costs more to use.

The question, of course, is whether MMS will establish itself to the same degree as SMS? Where SMS was a type of grass roots movement in many parts of the world, MMS is just starting to find a core use group, that is a group that uses the system and takes the lead in establishing the style and context of use. In this article, we examine this from the perspective of genre development. On the one hand it is possible to think of genre as a type of taxonomy, i.e. the genre of western films, murder mysteries or Italian opera. An alternative is to treat it more as socially grounded typifications of reoccurring situations (Miller 1984, 159). This approach is quite similar to the Berger and Luckmannian institution.

In the case of SMS, communications have become a reciprocal typification of habitual action (Berger and Luckmann 1967). That is, both the sender and the receiver have a general sense of what a communication should include, how it should be sent and received and the context into which they can place the communication event. They are able to fulfill each other's expectations as to when and how the communication is achieved. They are also in broad agreement as to how one interprets the message and how one reacts upon receiving a message. An institution (and, for that matter, a genre) in the sense used here is not one of the large-scale entities such as religion, the educational system or opera. Rather, it is an everyday routinized interaction that may only be shared by a small group of persons. Thus, the regular practice of a couple making coffee in the morning or the Friday afternoon beer shared by a group of workers at a building site can be seen in these terms.

In this chapter, we assert that SMS can be seen as having relatively well-established set of genres. At the same time, MMS is only in the process of developing this status. Further we argue that genre development is easier to accomplish in the textual based world of SMS than in the text/photo/sound world of MMS. This is because the intention of the sender and the interpretation of the receiver is more transparent in textual based communication than in pictorial based communication. This, however, is not always the case. In some situations pictorial information facilitates communication. One finds this particularly when communication is among those who have a strong pre-existing context within which intention and interpretation are closely matched.

SMS and MMS diffusion

SMS is a well-established communications channel. Indeed Norway seems to have a particularly high use of SMS when compared to other countries (Sandvin, Dagfinrud and Sæther 2002). In Norway there are approximately 8.8 million SMS messages sent every day – this in a country with only 4.5 million inhabitants. Simple math points out that each Norwegian man, woman and child would have to have send just under 2 messages a day to achieve this level of use. Clearly, however, some people are more active users than others. Our data indicates that it is teen girls who are the truly self-indulgent SMS users. According to data gathered in 2002, this group sends more than 9 messages a day (Ling 2003). Countries such as the UK, the Philippines and Japan also report extensive use of text messages. On a worldwide basis there were more than 366 billion messages sent in 2002. If one were to distribute this traffic evenly over the world's population, one finds that every sixth person would have to send a message a day in order to reach this sum.

Where SMS is a clearly established medium of communication, MMS is only starting to be adopted. During the first half of 2003, the average "SMS capable" Norwegian user sent about 68 SMS messages per month. Approximately 64 of these were interpersonal communications and the remaining were commercially based messages.[1] In contrast, the average "MMS capable" user sent somewhere around 3 MMS messages per month during a period when MMS use was free of charge. The difference in use represents an order of magnitude, both numerically and socially.[2]

There have been several technical and economic barriers to the use of MMS. These include the diffusion of MMS-capable terminals,[3] compatibility issues,[4] the complexity of setting up the terminals for use as an MMS device and pricing issues. The telecom operators have addressed these issues. In spite of this, MMS is only now arriving on the scene. This means that we can directly examine the social processes surrounding this development in real time. The question remains whether MMS genres will be established in the same way is occurring within SMS.

---

[1] These include ordering ringing sounds and icons, "voting" in various TV programs, ordering services such as additional access time for one's mobile telephone.

[2] This is not to say that Norwegians are ignoring the system. Telenor recently celebrated the 5 millionth MMS message sent through its system after only 6 months of commercially available service. The vast majority of mobile telephones sold since 2002 in Norway are MMS capable. This is not to say that they are camera telephones, but that they can receive MMS messages and also send messages that include downloaded pictures, drawings etc.

[3] The telephone terminal is the hand-set purchased by the user.

[4] Various terminals encode photographic material in different ways. Thus, it can be the case that a photograph taken by a Nokia terminal cannot be viewed on a Sony Ericsson terminal without an intervening step that recodes the material into an acceptable format.

What is a genre?

SMS has spawned several nascent genres including coordination messages, entertainment messages and information messages. To develop a niche for itself, MMS will also have to work itself into the everyday consciousness of our lives in the same way that SMS has.

There is the question, however, as to what constitutes a genre. There are two major directions when it comes to the investigation of genre. The first examines the development of more or less fixed taxonomy (Chandler 1997) and the second – the perspective that is adopted here – draws attention to the interactive development of loose typifications.

The word genre is related to genus and gender, that is, concepts used in the development of taxonomies, a seemingly innate human activity. Immense effort, for example, has been put into the organization of the Linnaean biological classification system and yet even biologists, botanists and zoologists are continually ending up in stews as to how one approaches categorization. Bryson describes the work of Colin Groves, an Australian taxonomist who spent four decades developing a relative definitive taxonomy of the 250 species of primates. His work involved untangling the competing discoveries and parallel research of various biologists and zoologists (Bryson 2003). There are, of course, hundreds of thousands of other plant and animal species that have not been given the same comprehensive treatment.

Beyond taking a lot of effort, the difficulty with taxonomies is the problem of insuring that the categories are mutually exclusive and comprehensive. To develop a successful taxonomy, a community must have a set of well-understood rules as to how one arranges the specific cases. Linnaeus, for example, relied on the classification of teeth and toes in the case of mammals and the shape of the beak in the case of birds. Before Linnaeus, animals were, for example, classified according to their degree of domestication, size, and perceived degree of nobility (Gould 1995, 421).

Taxonomic approaches to genre have been attempted (Chandler 1997). Indeed, the various systems of organizing library collections are based on the development of such taxonomies. According to the Encyclopedia Britannica, there are no less than six competing systems for keeping the books correctly sorted in the libraries. These include the Dewey Decimal, the Universal Decimal, the Library of Congress, the Colon, the Marxist and the endearingly named Bliss systems. Each of these has its adherents, conferences, journals and border wars.

There are also genre systems associated with film, television and art (Chandler 1997). Many of these have at the very least a quasi-commercial motivation in that they allow the producers of the film, book or artwork to guide potential customers into the correct cinema, section of the bookstore or the appropriate art gallery. Nonetheless, these categories are fuzzier and less precise than those associated with biological taxonomy. If one takes a further step and considers a taxonomy of interpersonal interactions, as is the case with SMS and MMS, the imposition of externally derived categories becomes even more problematic.

To be successful, the rules of classification need to cover all cases, and there cannot be cases that resist definition. One is reminded of Kenneth Boulding's taxonomy of birds that included "robins, seagulls and all the rest."[5] Boulding also wryly noted that "the trouble with taxonomic boxes is . . . that that they tend to be empty, however beautiful they are on the outside" (Boulding 1980, 75).

There are various systems for the classification of literary and artistic effort. Ideally, genre describes various types of efforts within the humanities such as film, literature, poetry, opera, etc. Looking at it in this way, genres can be seen as the humanities equivalent of biological taxonomy. One can also speak of genre of film, such as westerns, musicals, German post-war films and the like. Of more relevance to this article, however, one might speak of different types of interpersonal communication. There is the casual conversation, the love letter, the lecture, the post card, flirting, etc. To even a greater degree than with biological classification, the rules of placement are imprecise and the boundaries between genres are flexible and permeable. Thus, the potential for interbreeding of genre is always uncomfortably near at hand.

As noted above, there is a second approach to the issue genre, in particular the categorization of interpersonal communication. In this latter approach, the question is changed. Rather than the development of rules that allow one to build up mutually exclusive rules that are comprehensive, the question becomes what is the minimum degree of agreement needed by the communicating partners so that the interaction can succeed? In many ways, this approach is more suitable to the analysis of interpersonal communication. The point is that while categories help one to understand what he/she can expect from a specific type of situation, the boundaries around that must necessarily accept a certain ambiguity. Miller writes of this in her article on *Genre as social action:*

> *Thus, inaugurals, eulogies, courtroom speeches and the like have conventional forms because they arise in situations with similar structures and elements and because rhetors [speakers] respond in similar ways, having leaned from precedent what is appropriate and what effects their actions are likely to have on other people (Miller 1984, 152).*

When one speaks of a genre, one is saying that the expectations of both the communicator and the communicatee are in sync. In effect, those sending the communication and those receiving it are able to match their expectations as to the form, the content, the timing and the context of the communication (Orlikowski and

---

[5] The use of a catchall category is not unique to Boulding. Indeed Linnaeus' original categorization of the animal world included mammals, reptiles, birds, fishes, insets and vermes. The latter category originally included everything from common earthworms, lobsters and shrimp to anything else that showed up in the lab that could not be squeezed into one of the other categories. As it turns out, this was ponderous portion of the world's biological mass (Bryson 2003).

Yates 1998). The communicating parties have to have a set of mutually comprehensible categories that allow the communication to occur. There is always the possibility for misinterpretations, off-cue comments and *faux pas*. These, however, are nothing more than disagreements as to the context of the communication event.

Within this approach, one can immediately think of four alternative situations, only one of which includes a completely successful interaction. There is the situation where the intention of the person forming the communication is understood and interpreted correctly by those who receive it. In this case, the mutual expectations are in line. Both the communicator and the communicatee share enough of a common perspective so that a broad understanding can be assured. Alternatively, the specific intention of the person sending the message can be misunderstood by the receiver. As we will see, the opposite can also be true, namely that the interpretation system of the person receiving a communication can be more finely attuned than that of the person sending the message. That is, the person receiving the message can do a better job of interpreting the information than can the person sending it. These alternatives will be considered below. There is also the relatively absurd situation where neither the sender nor the receiver are clear as to the intentions, context or form of the interaction.

Turning this lens onto MMS and, for that matter, SMS at its same point in development, means that we are able witness the establishment of a practice. We can see the development of Berger and Luckmann's "reciprocal typifications" even as they are becoming habitualized (Berger and Luckmann 1967). That is, we can see the establishment of these institutions or, in the context of this chapter; we can see the establishment of what we judge to be genres. We endeavor to examine the hazy genres that are being developed in mundane practice. We look into those that have names and identities in everyday language. Thus, as we will see below, there are such genres as the "drunken SMS"[6] the chain message[7] and the like.

To be fair, there are several issues that play into these natural taxonomies. The most obvious, of course, is the mediating technology. An SMS is often produced, mediated, read via a completely different system than is e-mail. An instant mail message and a traditional hand-written letter are again mediated through quite different systems. From the perspective of the sender and the receiver, the technological dimension of SMS places heavy expectations and constraints as to the form of a particular communication. Indeed, we are surprised when one breaks

---

[6] In Scandinavia, many people have experienced either receiving, or sending an ill advised SMS message that was produced late on a particularly "wet" evening. The accessibility of the technology and the ability to impulsively send messages whenever and wherever means that things that might better be left unsaid are committed to text and transmitted. In many cases these are harmless, if rather indiscrete and are the cause of embarrassed jokes during the next days.

[7] That is messages that are usually humorous and not specifically authored by the sender. It will be more completely described below.

out of the expected form and, for example, writes SMS-based poetry, executes a contract or proposes marriage via the channel.[8]

In the case of film, etc. the encoding is highly commercialized and the transmission may also have a commercial dimension. In the case of SMS/MMS the encoding and interpretation is not usually commercialized but rather one sees the commercialization of the mediation.

The development of these forms of communication help to trace the domestication of a technology and a type of communication (Haddon 2001). We adopt various forms of interaction – i.e. SMS or MMS – in concert with our social networks. In order for the adoption to be successful, the communication, or for that matter the technology, must find a physical, temporal, utilitarian and expressive place in our lives. It is only after the mode of interaction has become domesticated that it can, in turn, become an element in our social profile.

The process is, however, never completely static. There is a tension between the formulaic use of a genre and the interpretation by the receiver of the communication. If the love missive is a poorly refitted version of a "canned" letter copied from a teen advice book, one can quickly end up with difficulties. That is, the writer has stayed too strictly within the genre. He or she has followed the rules too carefully. It is when one re-interprets the rules, and more importantly, when the receiver of the message is challenged and stimulated, that the message takes on a life of its own. Thus, we must be able to place a communication into a general context – an interoffice memo, a report, a letter from Grandma – however, within that context, the correspondence takes on a life when it tests the boundaries of the genre. Thus, there is a tension between the set of categories and their interpretation.

We develop progressively differentiated ideas as to the form and content of our communications. We go from simply sending an SMS or an MMS to sending an "SMS agreement," an "MMS post card" or the like. The early uses might be seen as a type of fumbling with the technology and with the composition of the content. Indeed Baron suggests that such a well-entrenched mediation system as e-mail is still searching for its final form (Baron 2000). Eventually, there is the progressive differentiation, even within the relative narrow constraints that are afforded by the technology. We gain a certain poise, self-confidence or bearing as we advance in the use of the communication channel. While early attempts may simply boil down to a fight with the technology, the experienced sender, as well as the experienced receiver, are able to apply a nuanced repertoire of devices in their encoding and decoding of the messages.

Communications sent via new mediation systems must necessarily draw on elements from existing established genre. The e-mail message often includes a

---

[8] Innovative uses of telecommunication technology have always been of note. Romances carried out via the telegraph (Standage 1998), and concerts have been "broadcast" via telephone (Fischer 1992). In each case the particular blending of medium and content have been seen as existing outside the traditional boundaries of the genre.

salutation ("Dear Ms. Simpson"), an informal introductory paragraph, the core of the message, a summary section and a closing ("Sincerely yours, W. Smithers"). The use of newer forms of mediation, however, opens up the options. Communications can adopt the portions of other genre and weave them into the communication. Thus, e-mail seems to be a combination of written and spoken traditions with unique elements of its own (emoticons, certain abbreviations, methods of broadcast, expectations as to responses etc). This underscores the notion that we need have elements of the existing repertoire and present our communications in a familiar form, even when the mediation is being carried out in a novel way and there are new elements being added to the communication.

This is not to say that the form will remain static as it moves from one form of mediation to another. New devices arise and come to characterize the communication form (Baron 2000). In the case of e-mail and later SMS, paralinguistic items such as emoticons could, in the early phases of a communication form, be seen as a liberating influence. They allowed users to express themselves in various unique ways.

As the communication form matures the use of such devices might be taken into over-enthusiastic use by, for example, teens, and thereafter be seen as a sign for shallow and un-reflected communication. To be a successful user of a communications channel, we need to have an updated sense of how we should formulate or interpret communication. We must have a sense of what is being offered if for no other reason to understand how it is that we should respond. Without these general concepts, one is continually being caught out. Thus, there is also a tension here as the genres grow, shift and change. On the one hand, there is the traditional canon of structures and formulations; on the other hand there is their more or less successful reinterpretation. We need to have a sense of the current state of the genres and at the same time the ways in which the genres might breach. We need a general sense as to the set of Boulding's "beautiful taxonomic boxes" and the poise with which to incorporate the unorthodox into the catalog of the accepted. We need the categories, but woe to them who are too strict in their categorization. It is in our flirting with the boundaries and our embroidery of the core message (both on the part of the sender and the receiver) that genre comes alive.

This is not to say that anything goes. It is naïve to think that forms of interaction arise and fall without leaving their impact on the moral landscape. Even though the boundaries are at best vague, they are nonetheless consequential. We must not blend genres in inappropriate ways. Were one, for example, to slip an out-of-place reference into eulogy (for example the time the deceased had a fling with another married woman), there would be confusion in the genres. A eulogy should praise the individual, place them into their times and help the family and friends to burnish their image of the individual. Within these boundaries, one can point to awards achieved, lighthearted stories that put the individual into a good light, etc. Both the person giving the eulogy and those who are hearing generally share these expectations. Off-color stories or the less fortunate chapters in one's life are often seen as being too far off-base to include in these situations.

This suggests that there are ethical rules associated with the production of communication. There is the good eulogy, e-mail, office memo or, for that matter, the good "dear John" letter (particularly from the perspective of the sender). Beyond individual evaluations there are more institutionalized forms of evaluation. There is a small industry associated with assisting us in the etiquette of writing letters, making after dinner speeches, proposing toasts and formulating thank you notes (Post 2002). The same is true of e-mail (Martin 2002) and indeed for SMS/MMS. There are committees (often sponsored by a local newspaper) that rate the best SMS joke during the summer vacation period and more recently the best MMS. All of these efforts point to the degree that interpersonal communications can be evaluated, that is the degree to which there is a common ethic associated with the various genres.

Table 1: The genres of SMS

Coded message types based on an analysis of 865 messages gathered from a random sample of Norwegians (all age groups) in 2002

Middle future coordination i.e. things that would happen in the next hours or next day	23%
Questions	11%
Grooming i.e. messages giving complements or engaging in "small talk"	10%
Near future coordination i.e. things that had already begun or would happen in the next minutes	8%
Short one word answers	8%
Emotional grooming	6%
Commands/requests	6%
Information	5%
Personal news	5%
Location information	3%
Sexually related jokes	2%
Distant future coordination	2%
Invitations	1%
Jokes	1%
Thank you notes	1%
Apologies	<1%
Safety issues	<1%
Creative messages	<1%

Genre – in the sense used here – is not a strict taxonomy nor is it large-scale groupings such as opera, fiction or rock music. Rather, it includes socially produced "reciprocal typifications" of communication events wherein the users (both senders and receivers) have a core sense of the typifications and some sense of the boundaries. These typifications need not be on a grand scale. Indeed the definition leads one to focus on the practices of the small group and their interpretation of the broader edicts of society. Further, the users need to have a sense of who constitutes the appropriate audience for a communication type and what makes up apt timing. In addition, they need to have a sense of the suitable content for a communication (Orlikowski and Yates 1998). Finally, there are various ethics that are applied to the communication. This is clear in the case of SMS, where the technology itself goes a long way in defining the formation of the messages (currently including text based messages that are 160 characters and which are usually entered via a so called 9-key system). It is also clear in the case of MMS and its grainy pictures and short captions.

Typifications of SMS

SMS messages have established nascent genre types, particularly among teens. An 18-year-old girl, Mona, provided a type of natural taxonomy of SMS messages when she said, "I send messages if I am planning something, if I am bored or if there is something important I need to say."[9] Her comments point to several typical uses of SMS wherein the sender and receiver share a common framework. She notes functional use of the messages as well as its more expressive use. While there are other types of messages. An analysis of over 865 messages established several types of messages. An overview of these is shown in Table 1, (ranked in order of use). These are categories that suggested themselves from the data. The codings were verified by separate analyses (Ling 2003).

Mona's general categories describe common – and commonly understood – examples of SMS genre. Informants note that this type of information exchange is a common use of the medium. This often takes the form of exchanging information that facilitates meeting.

> *Moderator: You write a text message "Where are you" for example. You do that a lot?*

> *Dorothy (15): Not a lot, but you do that often.*

> *Rune (18): I have about three of four that are like that [that are currently on my phone].*

> *Moderator: Agreeing to meet?*

---

[9] The citations in this section come from group interviews carried out by Telenor R&D. The names and identities of the informants have been change in all cases. The interviews were carried out in Norwegian and the comments have been translated for inclusion here.

Rune: Agreeing [to meet with messages like] 'Where are you now.'

Indeed analysis of SMS messages suggests that coordinating meetings is perhaps one of the most common themes in the messages (Ling 2003). As noted by Rune, messages such as "Where are you" are quite common. Other categories include greetings and "grooming" messages wherein one the goal of the interaction is the maintenance of contact.

Mona's second use of SMS was entertainment. In conversations with others, we have come across "chain" messages. These were generally impersonal messages, that is messages that were not necessarily authored by the sender and which were at least attempts at humor. They could take the form of either a type of pyramid letter, or that of a more traditional gag.

Nina (18): There are chain messages.

Moderator: Chain messages? For example . . .

Inger (17): Like dumb poems and things.

Oda (18): When we were having an exam I got one of those and you should send on to five others or you would have bad luck on the exam.

Here Oda describes a typical pyramid message where in order to have luck on her exam she needed to send the message on to five others. The other interesting thing in the sequence is the degree to which Nina's comment describing chain messages is taken and elaborated by both Inger and Oda. In this case, the two girls seem to have slightly different ideas as to the content and role of the message. Nonetheless there is a common sense that a chain message is that genre of SMS communication that attempts humor and is not necessarily authored by the sender. A little further into the session, Nina offers another example of what might be considered a "chain message":

Nina (18): I have a chain message here.

Moderator: Can you read it?

Nina: Yeah 'About 1 million people are having sex right now, and what are you doing?'

This seems to indicate that there is confusion as to the exact nature of what constitutes a chain letter; or that there are several variations within the grouping. On the one hand, it can be a type of pyramid message that one sends to a number of others. On the other hand, it is some type of joke that is not necessarily authored by the person sending it. These types of messages underscore the sense that SMS can be used as a form of entertainment or a way to kill time.

Andrew (17): A lot of times when you are sitting on the bus or the subway it is boring and then you can write messages. That is something to do when you are bored.

In this mode, SMS has the tone of being a rather impersonal form of interaction. The "chain" messages and the use of SMS to entertain oneself when bored describe a rather lax form of sociation. These comments give one the impression that there is no great investment of self in the messages either on the part of the sender or the receiver.

Bringing this back to the point of genre, the examples cited here show that these SMS users have a general sense of what constitutes a "chain" letter. That is, they have a rough sense, or typification of this type of communication. There is broad agreement between the sender and the receiver that these types of messages are intended to be amusing, though one can wonder as to the standards that are being applied. In contrast to the coordination messages described above, there is no real functional reason for the messages, except as a means to socialize and entertain. The social function of these messages is that they constitute a type of gift between the sender and receiver through which the friendship is maintained and developed (Johnsen 2000; Taylor and Harper 2001; Berg et al, chapter 13).

Coordination and entertainment are two emerging genres of SMS messages. A third example is the use of SMS for more personal forms of interaction (referred to as "grooming" in Table 1). In this case, the sender formulates the communications with the intention of communicating more or less exclusively with the receiver. The following is an example of this type of message:

> *"I PICKED EIGHT FLOWERS,WITH A CAREFUL HAND,TIED THEM*
> *WITH A BRIGHT RED RIBBON.INCLUDED EIGHT SMALL WORDS:I*
> *LOVE YOU MORE THAN YOU BELIEVE" (W 16).* [10]

There are clearly powerful interpersonal emotions at play. This short message lies somewhere between being a love letter and a card that one might include on a gift. It is intended to be a communication between two persons and it is likely intended to help cement a romantic relationship. In a similar vein, many teen and young adult couples send each other a final "good night" SMS. Indeed this can be seen as an obligatory reconfirmation of the relationship. Messages such as "goodnight" (W 15) "Good night and sleep well" (W18) and "good night I love you" (W 27) are a common theme. Other forms of these personal messages can include flirting messages, messages wherein one wants to avoid long drawn out conversations, "drunken" messages and even messages where one ends a romantic relationship (Ling 2004). In these cases, the communication often includes comments that are easier to deliver in mediated form than in a direct face-to-face interaction. Indeed the ability to be shielded in these situations is a characteristic of the genre.

While SMS messages are often intensely personal, the medium can also facilitate the collective evaluation of messages that otherwise might be seen as personal. In

---

[10] This example, as well as those in the following paragraph, come from a database of 882 SMS messages gathered from a random sample of Norwegians of all age categories in a nationwide survey carried out in the spring of 2002. The messages have been translated from Norwegian but the capitalization and punctuation is similar to that in the original messages.

this case, the message is actually authored by a known person (or at least it is attributed to a known person). Nonetheless, it is made available to the jury of the receiver's peers for evaluation, commentary and annotation.

Kristine (18): If you have gotten an SMS from the guy you are interested in then you can share it with others, perhaps even send it [via SMS]. You can even send it with comments.

This treatment underscores the relatively open nature of the messages. As with a letter, and unlike a conversation, the content of a communication can be shared. However, SMS can be shared and, indeed, broadcast with much greater ease. Assumptions as to the ultimate audience of one's communications is perhaps less precise than with other more traditional forms of interaction.

The messages can be authored by the sender, the sender in concert with others or even third parties. At the same time, the interpretation of the messages, and the way the messages are treated by the receiver can also vary. As noted above, Inger characterized chain messages as "dumb poems and things." Presumably Inger deleted these messages rather quickly. Another informant, Jenni took the opposite approach to some of her messages.

Jenni (18): Yeah I have [saved SMS messages].

Moderator: Why do that?

Jenni: Just like a letter, to take care of it. I print it out and I have a file folder. I am hopelessly romantic, but I have a box where I save cards and things like that that I have gotten from my husband and I have some SMS messages that I save in the same way that I save a nice card.

Boys also reported the same type of behavior.

Knut (15): You take care of only the ones you think are very personal or the ones that you want to save and then throw out the rest. You do that if you get a love letter and stuff like that. If you don't like it, you throw it out.

Kjell (17): If you have been let down by a girl, you know, you don't save that. That isn't too cool to read.

While the composition and reading of SMS plays on other forms of communication, there is a set of what one can see as native categories or mutual typifications. The classification into the categories has to do with the functional nature of the message, the authenticity of the authorship and the degree to which the communication is seen as being a personal or a public interaction.

The comments of the informants underscore the fact that there is a shared sense of the intention behind and interpretation of the messages. The coordination messages, the jokes or "chain" messages and the personal interactions are all familiar categories wherein the sender and the receiver have a mutual idea of the features that they one might expect in these forms of interaction. In this way, these illustrate budding genres of SMS messages in the sense that there is a shared typification. Clearly there are messages that resist this type of classification. The heavy use of abbreviation or the heavily expressive use of the medium might have meaning for the sender but not the receiver or, they may have meaning for the sender/receiver but not those who are outside the context shared by those two.

The context of SMS

Beyond the content of SMS, its genres can be seen in the particular context of use. This includes a sense of audience, a folk ethic that helps to define our sense of SMS's place and a sense of SMS vs. other forms of mediated interaction.

SMS is seen by teens as being a type of teen communication. Indeed, it was teens who first molded the use of SMS to their needs (Ling and Yttri 2002; Rautiainen and Kasesniemi 2000). Thus, teens do not necessarily expect that parents will understand the complexity of encoding messages.

> *Moderator: If you are going to contact someone in your family, your mother, father, sister or brother, what will you choose, SMS or calling?*
>
> *Lillian 18: Calling*
>
> *Berit 17: I call.*
>
> *Lillian: Not a text message to Mom. She can't answer one.*
>
> *Moderator: She can read a message though.*
>
> *Lillian: Yeah, but she cannot answer. She would use an hour.*

The teens' mastery of the communication form provides them with a seemingly greater ability to develop it. In addition, their recognition that parents are handicapped in their use of the technology means that it is seen as inappropriate to converse with them via SMS. Traditional voice telephony is a more appropriate form of communication. We come back here to the sense that the interlocutors need to have a mutual command of the genre before it can become a living communication form.

In addition to encompassing a rather clear demographic group, there is a type of folk ethic associated with the use of SMS. The content of some messages are good and some are bad. The use of SMS in some situations is seen as acceptable, and unacceptable in others.

An incomplete survey of these ethical considerations includes the sense, for example, that "drunken" messages are unfortunate, that sexually explicit messages (usually in the form of jokes or perhaps icons[11]) are a part of the game and that

---

[11] An icon is a picture formed on the screen of the mobile telephone. Some advanced icons include a primitive form of animation in that the icon is actually a sequence of several individual images.

messages, regardless of how personal they appear are not necessarily exclusive to the sender and receiver.

Moderator: Do you have to think through it before you send an SMS or call?

Thomas (18): If it is about flirting and things like that that seem very innocent, then I think that it has been completely discussed with friends and planned before it was sent you know.

So-called chain messages and routine coordination messages are of less value than those that are more personal. Mundane messages and poorly formed chain-messages are rarely worth saving. However, personal messages or particularly good joke messages might be archived (at least for the length of the relationship).

Another aspect of SMS's folk ethic is those situations where it should not be used.

Andrew (17): There are not too many people who don't even call and say happy birthday and send a message instead. That is going a little too far.

Here, the use of one medium as opposed to another is governed by a sense of that which is appropriate. While the boundary between what is appropriate and inappropriate changes with time, Andrew indicates that at this point in time, a type of boundary had been crossed if one only sends an SMS message on the occasion of a birthday. An SMS message is too impersonal or common in this situation. To use this medium would somehow mark one's communication as being inauthentic.

There is a convoluted value system here since as we have seen people are willing to send the most intimate greetings and remembrances via SMS. It is acceptable to send sexually loaded comments to one's partner, but not a simple birthday greeting. The former is probably an element in an ongoing rapport while the latter is a once-in-a-year occasion that, at least according to the sensibilities of Andrew, has stricter formalities. Nonetheless it is interesting that the informants were attuned to these issues and had an active sense of them.

The timing of SMS also sets it apart from other forms of interaction. There is the sense that SMS is more conversation-like than, for example, e-mail.

Per (24): For me it is like when I send an SMS that I expect to get an answer immediately. If you write e-mail then you think that it can go a whole day, not all the time, but you think that you will get an answer during the day. E-mail is often about things that you don't need an immediate answer to.

There is the sense in Per's comments that one has the right to expect the prompt attention of a communication partner in the case of SMS. This reflects the sense that SMS is often used to deal with immediate issues – such as coordination – where e-mail is used to deal with issues that are less time sensitive. Again, there is a paradox here. While there is a conversational tone to SMS, it is not necessarily a flowing conversation wherein turn taking is tightly intertwined. Rather, the conversation seems to be somewhat loose and there is room for other considerations.

Moderator: Why do you use text messages?

Anne (23): I don't always need to talk exactly then and sometimes it is better not to, you know and also [I can write a message] when I am doing something else and then send that and then after awhile I get a message back and then I hear the sound that I have gotten a message and I don't need to read it immediately. I can wait five minutes and then I can read it and answer back. I think that it is really easy.

The interaction is woven into other activities and allows one to carry out various tasks while communicating.

Thus, we assert that SMS communication is developing a set of everyday genres. That is, the users of SMS have a set of "reciprocal typifications" of communication events. Their comments indicate that they have a core sense of the typifications and some idea as to their boundaries. In addition to having a common sense of the content and form of the various genres – coordination, chain messages, personal interaction, etc. – there is a common sense of the context in which the communication takes place. They know whom the appropriate audience for the different types of SMS and they know apt timing and the appropriate stance to take when sending a message.

The MMS experience

Where SMS is, relatively speaking, an entrenched form of mediation, MMS is less so. The system is still in its early stages of diffusion and there is comparatively little agreement as to where, when and how to use the mediation technology. In spite of its immaturity, there were several genres or typifications that suggested themselves. These included humorous messages, "post cards," documentation of various types in addition to the genres discussed in the media, namely paparazzi and pornographic pictures.

Up to this point, one is not able to find, however, the more developed gradations that one sees in the SMS world. The categories here are generally those that have been promoted by the industry or broadly discussed in the media. Further, much of the focus in MMS has to do with the transmission of photos. In addition, the categories seem to focus more on the type of photograph in the message. The content of the text and/or audio portion of the message is not as central in the categorization of the messages. These findings, along with the others reported in this section come out of interviews from a pilot study of MMS use in work life. Telenor R&D carried out the study. It included approximately 25 users who received an MMS telephone during the spring and summer of 2003. The specific groups in the study were real estate salespeople, carpenters and sales people for a soft drink producer. These particular vocations were selected because their workers are nomadic, work in small groups and often have a need for information transfer while on-the-job.

At one level, MMS users reported seeing the service as a type of play.

Interviewer: What does [MMS] give as opposed to normal SMS?

Tor: . . . It is simply more fun.

The citation is interesting because it is less nuanced, or "shop worn" than the similar descriptions of SMS. Where the SMS chain letters were described as "dumb poems and things," the MMS system comes across as being fresh and promising. MMS was perceived of as simply being fun.

Figure 1

MMS as a post card

A second typification is the use of MMS "almost like a post card" to use the words of one informant. In this genre, MMS allows one to compose a photograph, write some text and send it to others as a type of greeting. In some cases, the exact intention of the sender is difficult to ascertain. Some users report receiving MMS messages of mundane objects such as salt shakers, escalators and the like. Here the receiver of the MMS may feel that it was perhaps nice to be remembered by the sender, but the exact intention of the message is obscure.

In other cases, the messages played on more familiar forms of interaction. These function as personalized post cards. MMS allows travelers to combine customized photographs of places visited. In one case an informant had received a photograph of a large dump truck from a colleague (see Figure 1). The odd juxtaposition of the large machine and the fellow in front of it made for an interesting motif. It allowed the sender to inform the receiver of his activities and also perhaps gave the two a common topic of conversation at their next meeting.

These often had texts describing their experiences in these locales.[12] Indeed, it was common for informants to discuss sending vacation pictures. One carpenter described this type of use:

Interviewer: You have sent some private pictures of things, are they entertainment pictures like the one you sent me or. . .

Alf: It is like fishing pictures and vacation pictures.

Interviewer: Why send pictures to each other?

Alf: It is fun, that is the way we are. .

Fredrik: I sent pictures from Torghatten and Syv Søstre (vacation locations) you know.

Tor: That picture I got from Rolf. I thought that was great, when he was on vacation he sent me a picture of, it was like a self lit logo [of a company that shared Tor's sir name].

Fredrik describes some more traditional "post card" messages. Tor's comments bring out the ability to personalize these greetings in a way that is not possible with traditional paper based post cards. In this case, the MMS sits on the boundary between being a post card and an internal joke. Since the motif in the photo plays on Tor's surname, Rolf could send a vacation greeting that also functioned as an inside joke. In this case, the intention and the interpretation of the MMS message were near at hand for both the receiver and the sender. Indeed, the photo was worth saving for Tor since he could use it in other contexts as a means of identity enhancement.

MMS in this sense sits at the nexus between the post card and the family album. It has the ability to capture travel experiences just as with traditional photography. However, it has the additional feature of allowing images to be sent to others like post cards. Thus, it helps us to integrate our sense of self with our social network.

Beyond simple photos, MMS allows for the recording and transmission of sound and a form of video. One informant combined these characteristics into a multi-media post card. He recorded portions of a rock concert by a well-known

---

[12] In SMS there is a limit of 160 characters to a message. With MMS there is no real limit on the length of a text message.

Norwegian singer in Copenhagen on his MMS telephone. This was combined with text and a photograph and sent to a friend. In this case, the photo, text and sound combined to provide the receiver a sense of the event. Given the quality of the recording technology, it was necessary for the sender to provide the receiver with audio, visual and most importantly supplemental textual information. Bringing the three elements together in a small production, however, was an enhanced souvenir when compared with a simple SMS. The meta-message of this activity was that the sender thought enough of the receiver to spend the time in making the multi-media message. On the one hand, this was a type of gift; on the other hand, it provided evidence of the sender's competence with respect to composing MMS messages. A key element here, however, is that the intention of the sender and the interpretation of the receiver are relatively harmonized.

MMS as documentation

Another emerging MMS genre is documentation. The soft-drink sales people discussed this. In this case, the framework did not derive from interpersonal relationships, but rather from formalized contractual considerations. In their work, they are extremely concerned with the placement of their products in the various stores. The competition between the different brands for optimal placement means that the territory within the store is carefully monitored. This is a relatively complex task in that there is not a standard floor plan for all grocery stores in Norway. Stores are often located in pre-existing locations making the floor plan unique from store to store. In spite of this diversity, there remains a keenly fought competition for optimal placement of products, as Terje explains:

> *Terje: So that the – in the stores – that the soft drink section looks the way it does is not by chance. It is all agreed on at the national level. That Coca-Cola is there and Pepsi-Max is there. It is all agreed on, yeah, actually through the whole store. They have worked out patterns for all the shelves in all the stores even including the cigarette displays by the cash registers. It is all agreed. It is not by chance in the stores, at least in theory. In practice it is a little different. It is not always so easy to carry it out in practice.*

The soft drink sales people found MMS useful in documenting, in real time, the placement of the product inside the store. The photos were taken, transmitted to their boss and interpreted vis-à-vis the agreements as to the contractual placement of the products. The intention and the interpretation were tightly connected and could be read in terms of the agreement for placement in that particular store. The MMS added timeliness to the photograph because it could be included in a communicative exchange when there was a question as to the boundary agreement for a particular situation.

Figure 2

MMS as quasi-technical documentation

Another form of such use of MMS is that of quasi-technical documentation as was seen in the photograph reproduced above (see Figure 2). One can see this in the attached photograph of the fire barrier being built by some of the carpenters. The text for the photograph noted the type of construction. In this situation it is also the case that the sender and the receiver had a common interpretation context. A carpenter described the following use of MMS:

Bjørn: Here a couple of days ago I sent a whole lot of pictures.

Interviewer: Who did you send them to?

Bjørn: To the architect. We were going to replace some things and the engineer had measured wrong. We were going to place a beam that was going to be over a door opening. Then we had to mark that and after that we had to screw in place an iron plate down in the joists and then I took a picture of the details and sent it to the consultant.

Interviewer: That was good.

Bjørn: It was also documentation; it is something that we will save. It wasn't a good picture, but it was good enough in case there is a question as to how it looks.

Both Terje, the salesman, and Bjørn, the carpenter, describe using the photos to document some type of regulated situation. In Terje's case, there are national agreements at stake, and in Bjørn's, questions about whether the work was done correctly might later arise.

These uses fit into a genre of documentation. Within this genre, both the sender and the receiver understand the intention and the interpretation of the photo and text in the MMS messages. Another carpenter described a situation wherein photos allowed for a more precise documentation of a situation. The interesting point here is that the intention in the production of the photograph is less precise than its interpretation by the receiver.

> *I am standing at a supplier and I needed to get some bearings for a sliding door and they didn't have what I needed and so [the next time I needed those bearings] I take a picture and send it and then he sits in his offices and gets that in his e-mail and that . . . that was very elegant. (Nr 4)*

A picture, at least in this case, is worth a thousand words: To describe these situations in text would demand time and a precision of description that is sometimes difficult to attain. In addition, the sender may not have the correct vocabulary or concepts with which to describe the particular situation, as was the case of the carpenter needing the bearings for the sliding door. He did not necessarily know the correct way to describe the specific items he needed perhaps in terms of size, model number, vintage etc. The supplier, however, could potentially read out of a photograph the cues that would allow him to apply specific knowledge of bearings.

From these examples, one can see the embryonic development of MMS genres. Humorous messages, "post card" messages, those intended for technical documentation and the transmission of emergent situations are some of the most often cited.[13]

Other MMS genres

Another MMS genre is the democratization of paparazzi and news reporting. The photograph of the celebrity caught in an awkward or compromising situation, that of the police acting unethically, that of the car pileup or the photograph of the natural disaster all become items of common interest. In addition they have a commercial potential. Many web sites advertise their interest in purchasing these types of photographs. The quick availability of a camera and the ability to immediately send and even broadcast these items makes for a powerful mixture. We are only now starting to arrange the moral furniture when it comes to MMS and camera telephones.[14]

Beyond these situations of more general interest, with the proliferation of MMS camera phones we are all potentially paparazzi, at least on a local scale. Teen informants noted this potential:

---

[13] Another theme that is often seen is that of pornographic images. While none of the respondents discussed this in the group interviews, they recognized its presence and, to some degree, had participated in the transmission of this type of image.

[14] In some situations such as in locker rooms, there are bans on camera telephones.

Jenni (18): You know, if I rush out the store in my pajamas without makeup and like that and the neighbor took a picture of me and sent it around and said, look here is how Jenni is.

Susanne (17): Uses it against you.

Jenni: Yeah, I don't think that it is so cool that everybody goes around with a camera and can snap pictures and send it to the Internet. That isn't so bad for me because I don't have anything to hide but there are a lot of people that are concerned about that.

Middle-aged women informants also quickly picked up on this theme.

Interviewer: We had a group interview with younger teens and they were all very concerned. They thought that somebody might take a picture of them and send it to the Internet.

Tonja: Yeah, you know that can be misused just like that. Girls at a party.

Lillian: Send that home to their mother

Tonja: Yeah

Lillian: That is super creepy . . .

Tonja: It is a little like "Big Brother is watching."

However, MMS lets one send the compromising photograph to the ends of the earth, or send it, in an enhanced form of direct mailing, to the segment of society that will be the most aghast.

One and all can potentially invade the privacy of others. This plays out in our sense of how we operate in the public sphere and even what we perceive of as the private sphere. As with SMS and mobile telephony in its time, we are only now starting to develop our sense of courtesy and propriety with regards to this new form of interaction (Choong 2003)

Textual and pictorial interaction

MMS is only now starting to be brought into our everyday experience. The material here, however, indicates that we have emergent notions of MMS genres. Should the technology be more widely adopted, photography and photographs will become more tightly woven into the daily fabric of life. Just as the transition from exclusively land-line based telephony to mobile telephony has made interpersonal communication more commonplace, increased access to photographs will make visual interaction more common. Rather than being the staged event that documents various phases in life, photography and the communication of these photographs along with their text and sound appendices will be closer at hand. The photograph may become more a mundane activity rather than the bracketed event to mark a special occasion (Ito 2003). Just as the e-mail and SMS have elbowed aside the traditional hand written letter, the ubiquity of photography can mean that the threshold of that which is photographed may be lowered.

As the mundane is elevated to a photographic object, the everyday is now the site of potential news and visual archiving. Sending camera-phone photos to major news outlets and moblogging[15] are one end of a broad spectrum of everyday and mass photojournalism using camera phones. What counts as newsworthy, noteworthy and photo-worthy spans a broad spectrum from personally noteworthy moments that are never shared (a scene from an escalator) to intimately newsworthy moments to be shared with a spouse or lover (a new haircut, a child riding a bike). It also includes neta [sic.] to be shared among family or peers (a friend captured in an embarrassing moment, a cute pet shot) and microcontent uploaded to blogs and online journals. The transformation of journalism through camera phones is as much about these everyday exchanges as it is about the latest headline (Ito 2003).

For this to happen, the creation process will have to become more grounded in our practice. Those who have had experience with the use of MMS telephones noted that the process of composing a message was not necessarily as intuitive as with other forms of interaction.

Kjell: We thought that the total experience with the telephone was negative. It was awkward and the pictures were bad and it was a frustration, the whole thing.

In any interaction, there are utterances that are more or less understood, interpreted and responded to. The mismatch between the intention of the utterance and its interpretation is a fixture of communication. In verbal communication, we often fish around for words with which to impart our intended meaning. The listener then does a better or worse job of interpreting the utterance and perhaps asks for a clarification or responds based on a more or less correct interpretation. As we move from textual to photographic communication, a different vocabulary arises and a new world of intention/interpretation is available.

The common MMS vocabulary of the sender and receiver, therefore, has to be in agreement. However, there is, it seems, a much broader potential for mismatch between intention and interpretation with MMS and photographic communications than with text. The photograph of the escalator or the saltshaker point to this degree of openness with which photographs and text can be interpreted. A photograph can be broken down into component elements, but it is not certain that two viewers will do this in the same way, or that a single viewer will do it consistently the same way from time to time. Text can be used to ground the photo and to give it "spin."

---

[15] Moblogging involves the posting of photos taken with an MMS telephone on a Web page along with text to illustrate and illuminate the photographs.

Nevertheless the breadth of color, juxtaposition, iconography and serendipity in the creation/interpretation of photos is much broader than for text, particularly when the text is limited to 160 characters or approximately six to twelve words with SMS (Hård af Segerstaad 2003; Ling 2004).

Interpretation is much less of a problem with text. There are well-engrained rules as to how one approaches reading words. A bounded set of letters are used to compose a relatively unbounded set of words that, in turn can be composed into a universe of SMS messages. With photos, one starts with the universe. With text, one starts one the upper left (or right as it may be) and proceeds linearly. Photographic interpretation is not nearly as linear or convention bound. There is a whole iconography that needs to be learned and that is often quite culturally specific. Abstract concepts are difficult to communicate pictorially and more open to misinterpretation. Interpretation of photographs can also be influenced by one's stereotypes and emotional state.

The nature of MMS means that both the sender and the receiver must rely on a different, perhaps more limited, ranges of interaction. Where the text of an SMS will, in all likelihood, be interpretable in 100 years, or by those outside the immediate interaction, an MMS message that bases itself on a photograph may only be understood in the immediate context. As one moves outside of the immediate social circle or as one moves into the future, it is more difficult to understand the importance of the event or the context being photographed. The photo of the young couple at a beach side restaurant with a text stating, for example "The view is beautiful, we have bought new things we feel good and we are soooo happy" sent to friends or family can be readily understood as young newlyweds on their honeymoon. A person who is outside their social circle can view the MMS and guess as to the situation, but the message is shorn of the deeply contextual information. The non-accredited viewer will not know that he has a sickness that requires frequent visits to warm climates; that they lost their luggage on the flight; etc. For those outside the circle the specific meaning of the pose, the artifact or the setting will be more difficult to interpret. For those who do not have the chance for such deep interpretations, that is those who are outside the circle – or only peripherally related – unintended or incomplete interpretations are easy to conceive of. In this case, rather than simplifying an interaction, at best it could cause the communication process to break down and at worst it could spin out of control into unintended misinterpretations.

When considered within the intimate sphere, the photograph can engender fond memories of times past. It is within this group that one finds the ability to interpret photographs. Thus the new father can send photos to new grandparents who will have the collective ability to interpret the meaning and magnitude of the situation. The child can send photos to parents while away at camp and the teen lovers can send each other silly photographs of the fellow next to them on the bus. The fact that MMS/camera phones allow for photography in more mundane situations means that the communications can potentially serve to strengthen ties at this level while excluding those who are outside the circle. MMS makes heavy assumptions on the knowledge of both the sender and the receiver. The sender has to know that the receiver will have associations with the items pictured. If one does not have knowledge of the persons involved, their preferences and characteristics etc., then the meaning of the photograph is lost.

SMS and MMS are developing as communications technologies that need to "hang together" in the eyes of the reader/receiver. As with the form and content of e-mail, their genres are in development (Baron 2000). To be successful, the communication has to lead the reader/viewer to anticipate and then, in turn, be gratified by the progression. Thus, the genre shapes our expectations as to what we will find in a communication. It also provides us with criteria as to whether the expectations have been met by the actual content of the communication. It may be that this is one of the key elements with MMS. That is, the communication form is only now establishing the reciprocally typified expectations that outline how communications should be approached.

Acknowledgements

This chapter was produced in the MEMO project, a project sponsored by Telenor R&D.

References

Baron, N. 2000. *Alphabet to Email: How written English evolved and where it's heading.* London: Routledge.

Berger, P. , and T. Luckmann. 1967. *The social construction of reality: a treatise in the sociology of knowledge.* New York: Anchor.

Boulding, K. 1980. *Beasts, Ballads and Bouldingisms: A collection of writings* by Kenneth E. Boulding. New Brunswik, NJ: Transaction.

Bryson, B. 2003. *A short history of nearly everything.* New York: Broadway Books.

Chandler, D. 1997. *An introduction to genre theory.*

Choong, A. 2003. "Camera-phone dos and don'ts." *Cnet* Asia.

Fischer, C. 1992. *America calling: a social history of the telephone to 1940.* Berkeley, CA.: University of California.

Gould, S.J. 1995. *Dinosaur in a haystack.* New York: Crown Trade Paperbacks.

Grinter, R., and M Eldridge. 2001. "y do tngrs luv 2 txt msg?" Pp. 219 – 238 in *Proceedings of the seventh European conference on computer supported cooperative work ECSCW '01,* edited by W. Prinz, Y. Jarke, K. Rogers, K. Schmidt, and V. Wulf. Dordech, Netherlands: Kluwer.

Haddon, L. 2001. "Domestication and mobile telephony." in *Machines that become us,* edited by J. E. Katz. Rutgers University.

Hård af Segerstaad, Y. 2003. "Language use in Swedish mobile text messaging." in *Front stage/Back stage: Mobile communication and the renegotiation of the social sphere,* edited by R. Ling and P. Pedersen. Grimstad, Norway.

Hashimoto, Y. 2002. "The spread of cellular phones and their influence on young people in Japan." Pp. 101–112 in *The social and cultural impact/meaning of mobile communication,* edited by S. D. Kim. Chunchon, Korea: School of Communication Hallym University.

Ito, M. 2001. "Mobile phones, Japanese youth and the re-placement of social contact." in *Society for the social studies of science.* Boston.

– . 2003. "Camera phones changing the definition of picture-worthy." *Japan Media Review*.

Johnsen, T. E. 2000. "Ring meg! En studie av ungdom og mobiltelefoni." in *Department of ethnology technical papers*. Oslo: University of Oslo.

Ling, R. 2003. "The socio-linguistics of SMS: An analysis of SMS use by a random sample of Norwegians." in *Front Stage/Back Stage: Mobile communication and the renegotiation of the social sphere*, edited by R. Ling and P. Pedersen. Grimstad, Norway.

– . 2004. *The Mobile Connection: The cell phone's impact on society*. San Francisco: Morgan Kaufmann.

Ling, R., and B. Yttri. 2002. "Hyper-coordination via mobile phones in Norway." Pp. 139 – 169 in *Perpetual contact: Mobile communication, private talk, public performance*, edited by J. E. Katz and M. Aakhus. Cambridge: Cambridge University Press.

Mante-Meijer, E. , and et al. 2001. *"Checking it out with the people – ICT markets and users in Europe."* Heidelberg: EURESCOM.

Martin, J. 2002. *Star-spangled manners in which Miss Maners defends American etiquette (for a change)*. New York: Norton.

Miller, C.R. 1984. "Genre as social action." *Quarterly journal of speech* 70:151 – 167.

Orlikowski, W., and J. Yates. 1998. *"Genre systems: Structuring interaction through communicative norms."* Cambridge, MA: MIT Sloan school of management.

Paragas, F. 2000. "A Case Study on the Continuum of Landline and Mobile Phone Services in the Philippines." in *The Social and Cultural Impact/Meaning of Mobile Communication conference*, edited by S. D. Kim. Korea.

Post, P. 2002. *"Peggy Post etiquette for today."*

PT. 2003. *"De norske marked."* Post and teletilsyn.

Rautiainen, P., and E-L. Kasesniemi. 2000. "Mobile communication of children and teenagers: case Finland 1997–2000." Pp. 15-18 in *Sosiale konsekvenser av mobile-telefoni: proceedings fra et seminar om samfunn, barn og mobile telefoni*, edited by R. Ling and K Thrane. Kjeller: Telenor FoU.

Sandvin, H.C., A. Dagfinrud, and J.P. Sæther. 2002. "Det norske telemarkedet – første halvår 2002." Oslo: Norwegian post and telecommunications authority.

Standage, T. 1998. *The Victorian Internet*. London: Weidenfeld and Nicolson.

Taylor, A., and R. Harper. 2001. "Talking 'Activity': Young people and mobile phones." in *CHI 2001 Workshop: Mobile communication: Understanding user, adoption and design*, edited by L. Palen. Seattle, WA.

Section Two: Texting and the Moral Order of Place

5   From Voice to Text: continuity and change in the use of mobile phones in France and Japan

Carole Anne Rivière and Christian Licoppe

Introduction

According to a questionnaire carried out by the sociologist Hashimoto Yoshiaki in December 2001 on a sample of 1878 people aged between 12 and 69 throughout Japan, the penetration rate of mobiles in Japanese homes has reached 75% (Hashimoto Yoshiaki, 2002). This indicates the considerable speed at which mobile phones have been adopted in Japan since their launch in 1987, especially when considering home ownership has risen by 25% since 1987 (an increase that took over 84 years to achieve for the fixed line phone). According to this same survey, 58% of Japanese with mobiles use email to contact on average 7.3 correspondents. Email is the written form of communication that was introduced to Japan to the detriment of SMS because of its lack of interoperability.

Although it is difficult to make direct comparisons, France can be said to have experienced a similar rate of mobile phone adoption, although with a slight delay: a sharp increase in 1998-1999 in the number of people having mobiles, and a situation today where the penetration rate leans towards saturation. But the adoption and use of SMS, starting from the summer of 2000, have exhibited different patterns in France and Japan. For example, in France, only a third (33%) of mobile owners were using SMS in December 2002[1], twice less than in Japan the previous year. Also, when examining the frequency of messages, French users limited their exchange of SMS largely to their closest correspondents. According to a statistical survey conducted in 2000, the number of SMS correspondents per week was 5, on the average[2]. This has not been the case in Japan where SMS messages have been exchanged with much larger networks of people. As we will see later,

---

[1] Figure produced by the operator Orange (do not take into account the usage of SMS with SFR and Bouygues subscribers

[2] Eurescom survey conducted in 2000

Richard Harper, Leysia Palen and Alex Taylor (Eds), The Inside Text: Social, Cultural and Design Perspectives on SMS, 103–126.
© 2005 *Springer. Printed in the Netherlands.*

differences between France and Japan are even sharper with respect to the balance and respective meanings of mobile voice and written forms of communication.

It has been argued that the success of mobile phone-based e-mail in Japan was partly serendipitous, and due to the lag in adoption rates of the internet in Japanese homes. Since this lag deprived many Japanese users of easy domestic access to PC-based e-mail facilities, users turned towards the more readily available mobile messaging services. Reporting on the low rates of micro-computer equipment in the home in comparison with the USA, Japanese analysts predicted that the use of PC-based e-mail would pick up, precipitating a slowdown in the uptake of mobile messaging services. This did not prove to be the case. PCs are now in 57% of Japanese homes (twice as much as the current rate for France) and there has been no slump in the growth rates of mobile messaging. The availability of high bandwidth access does not offer an explanation for the skewed demand for mobile messaging either, as Japan has a much higher penetration rate than France (at the time of study 25% of Japanese homes had ADSL access).

Japanese users place both mobile-based e-mail and PC-based e-mail at different points along the same spectrum, offering one possible explanation for the lack of any substitution effect between the two communication services. This is not the case in France, however, where e-mail and SMS are perceived as very distinct communication media. Such differences between the two countries suggests that a more detailed comparative investigation into the uses and understandings of the two services may go some way to providing an explanation for the differences in uptake.

We will start by comparing the use of text messaging in Japan and in France. We will show that in Japan, the use of mobile text messaging concerns a large number of correspondents for a given user, while in France the use of SMS is reserved to a core of close correspondents, and involves emotional bond management. In both configurations the discretion that goes with mobile text messaging is a strong motivation of use, but it is associated with different modes of management of social relationships in both countries. Japanese text messengers are very sensitive to the patterning of roles and obligations that a given relationship entails. They operate within a concentric model of social relationships in which different civility norms operate an inner and outer circle of social relationships. Text messaging is for instance a very useful resource for managing relationships within the inner circle, for text messages will often appear less intrusive and potentially embarrassing than phone calls. It also frees some exchanges from traditional etiquette, at least to some extent. French SMS users on the other hand are more sensitive to the proper patterns of behaviour in public and private spheres. The SMS technology provides opportunities to communicate with intimate correspondents from public spaces while keeping a proper distance and sense of privacy with respect to bystanders. Such a comparative study allows an exploration of the new forms of interactional norms that emerge from the diffusion of an array of interpersonal communication technologies, and of the way they are culturally shaped.

Our empirical data is based on two qualitative studies performed with 30 SMS users in France (2001 and 2002) and 40 mobile text messaging users in Japan (2002). These were in-depth interviews, two hours long on the average, exploring the conventions that govern the use of mobile text-messaging, the situations of use, the nature of correspondents, while trying to push systematically the comparison between the use of mobile text messages and voice-based phone calls.

Using Email and SMS in France and Japan

In Japan, communication via email is progressively replacing vocal communication to the point where it has become the dominant use of mobile phones. We have not observed any similar trend in France. where, on average, the use of SMS and mobile voice communication have grown together (except for the very particular case of students who do not have contract phones but prepaid ones). We will try here to provide evidence for these striking differences, and to emphasize the contrasts in the mobile communication practices in both countries.

Japan: switching from voice to mobile text

The qualitative interviews that were carried out in Japan on the daily usage of mobile telephones repeatedly highlighted the importance of written exchanges. When asked which mode of communication was used most frequently, all the interviewees with the exception of perhaps the elderly replied 'email'. E-mail was so pervasive that it was much easier for us to later characterise the usage situations and motivations linked to voice calls, as opposed to the raft of different uses and motivations associated with written communications.

The rationale for relying on mobile written exchanges has strong economic roots. It benefited greatly from the decision to include the relevant costs in the basic communication package. This made it highly comparable to vocal communication and highlighted its relative cheapness. When describing the advantages brought about by mail, the interviewed users often made the link between the banality and pointlessness of mobile written exchanges and the necessity for them to be as cheap as possible.

> "I use email when I don't want to use the phone because of the cost... for example yesterday there was a Japanese dance recital and so I received emails concerning my performance. Useless, unimportant information. E.g. I'm tired after work, or I want to eat together with someone or I would like to go to a good restaurant. Messages like that. A phone conversation always costs a lot, for emails it is not even 1 yen. So things that aren't really very important, I email. And if it's urgent I just call so and so."
> (Kanno, 28 yrs, female office worker)

So, for 90% of the people interviewed, vocal calls were reserved either for matters which were urgent enough to require immediate feedback or that necessitated complicated explanations and for which dialogue was more convenient than writing:

> *"When it is urgent, I telephone. For example, when I don't know where my lesson is taking place. There isn't much time so I telephone in order to get an answer straight away."*

> *"When I want a reply straight away, I telephone. When I am not in a hurry, I send an email." (Mika, 21 yrs)*

> *"When the subject of a discussion is important, the telephone is better. For example, when a friend has just changed job and she wants to talk about it with me, we use the telephone. Email would have been too short."*

> *"When it seems that writing an email would take too much time and that it seems easier to explain on the phone." (Igarassi, 20 yrs)*

A ubiquitous communication practice

Other reasons for relying on mobile written exchanges depended a lot on the type of relationships callers had with their correspondents. Though it is important to remark that mobile phone-based written sociability was not circumscribed to some privileged circle of intimate relationships (as we will show to be the case in France).

Mobile written communication within the first circle of close relationships

The first circle is made up of people that one meets everyday, with which one shares many common activities: it can be defined by the high frequency of occasions of physical contact and by the degree of geographical proximity. Emotional closeness is often involved, but some relationships in this first social circle may not elicit it. The first circle also includes one's colleagues which one sees everyday at the office (and with which one might go drinking and partying after office hours), 'student' friends belonging to the same campus, or mothers and housewives who meet up at their children's schools or get together for a drink during the day. The trivial and everyday dimension of the mails exchanged characterise these relationships where frequent and often daily face-to-face contacts are the norm, and where mobile e-mail therefore may assume a insignificant and informal character.

> *"When it was very hot, I asked for news. They said that you cannot leave your house because it is too hot or I tell them what I have done today or where I went today." (Tie Satou)*

> *"When I want to see someone after the lesson but this person is not in the same class, I ask via email when the other person finishes their lesson." (Aya, 20 yrs)*

"With some of my colleagues, three of them, we send each other emails about every two days. We rotate working in a book shop so I ask one of the three if they finish work at the same time as me. And if they say yeah, I ask them to meet me at Starbucks" (American coffee house chain), (Tiharu, 39yrs)

"With one of my friends, who comes from Tokyo, whilst travelling, we exchange emails. She tells me for example that it is too cold with the air conditioning in the train, that she has arrived at the station, etc." (Yosiko, 62 yrs)

An exception within the first circle: parents and or partners

On the other end of the first circle spectrum, we have these very close loved ones with a high level of emotional commitment such as parent/child, husband/wife, boyfriend/girlfriend relationships. These are the exception in the sense that the spoken word is more often relied on. For instance, voice phone calls are considered the most appealing and acceptable way to communicate between lovers.

"I know my girlfriend's timetable. So I know when I can telephone her. With others I prefer first to send an email." (Igarasi, 20 yr old student)

"I spend about 1 hour on the telephone a day, and this is only with my girlfriend. My girlfriend, 1 hour." (Yuki, 22 yr old student)

We will see that the situation in France is very different. There, a SMS is a sign of emotional attention that particularly befits amorous relationships, where the other person is considered a very special interlocutor (although this doesn't mean that you don't phone them too). In Japan, it is the opposite: first, to send an e-mail is very common and it is not a sign that you are paying particular attention to the recipient and second the perception that mobile phone calls are expensive explains why only certain privileged people receive voice calls.

In Japan, mobile messaging is not seen as acceptable in such contexts for another reason, namely the traditional relationship structure between partners. The latter is shaped from the original child/parent relationship that constitutes the intimacy circle par excellence. This 'inner circle' is the one where interpersonal etiquette is relaxed, and for which it is less necessary to anticipate the availability of the person and the embarrassment a call might cause. Such an empathy oriented towards the minimization of embarrassment in interpersonal exchange is indeed one of the main motivations for sending mobile e-mails, as we will see later, but intimate, e.g., husband/wife relationships, are relieved of some of these constraints:

"With the telephone, you have to think whether or not you are going to disturb the person you are calling. On the other hand, for my wife, I don't have to worry about her being available. She is the only person that I can phone whenever I want." (Tuyosi, 60 yrs)

Mobile written communication within the second circle of elective
friendships with regular (but not too frequent) encounters

A second social circle involving mobile e-mail exchanges would include for instance elective relationships for which face-to-face encounters occur less often than in the first circle. This covers many types of friends: friends from clubs, or hobby groups (which Japanese share frequently), former colleagues, former friends from school and university and which one sees from time to time, etc. Here mobile e-mail seems more oriented towards news updates and maintaining the bond between encounters.

> *"Myself and 5 or 6 of my friends exchange emails once every three weeks and I exchange emails regularly, perhaps, I don't know, a few times a year with former colleagues in order to hear their news." (Tie Satou)*

> *"With all my female and male friends, I send each one at least one email per week, to tell them what I have done during the week. These are the people that you don't see very often. So, I also want to hear their news." (Kanno, 28 yrs)*

> *"With the friends from where I grew up, we send each other emails every two or three days. For example, one of my friends tells me that his child has left for a school trip. We very rarely telephone each other, twice a year, when I go home to my mother, we see each other." (Tiharu, 39 yrs)*

Mobile written communication within the third circle of acquaintances with
no or almost no encounters

The third circle generally covers more diffuse relationships, acquaintances with which one may share a common activity (hobby club, a society, class) but towards which one does not feel compelled by a strong affinity. Encounters rarely occur outside the initial activity-oriented meeting place. It is necessary here to add that it is acceptable (if not customary) in Japan to exchange mobile phone numbers and addresses as soon as you have entered into a group. When returning to school or going into a new class, each person exchanges numbers, addresses with the rest of the group. Within this circle, mobile e-mail takes a more formal character and reasserts forms of social distance.

> *"To the other extreme, acquaintances whose emails do not give me any pleasure. To these people, I reply out of politeness if I can. These are people who I do not come across very much, that I know but who I do not wish to be friendly with and who send me emails. For example, in more concrete terms, members of a hobby club that I am part of who send me emails in order to send a message and on the other hand, bluntly, colleagues who I feel no sympathy towards, those I don't get on at all well with." (Youko, 30 yrs)*

Mobile email in Japan is therefore relevant to all types of interpersonal relationships but much less between husband and wife or boyfriend and girlfriend. This is in stark contrast to SMS usage patterns in Europe where messages are exchanged mostly within the first circle and, particularly, in amorous relationships. Given this difference and its apparent association with specific customs and forms of etiquette, it seems relevant to examine written communications against the backdrop of cultural systems and practices.

Mobile messaging and etiquette within inner/interior and outer/exterior social circles

Social distance in Japan is traditionally organized around the dual notion of interior/exterior in order to distinguish between different types of relationships and establish a kind of etiquette for governing these relationships. It is the presence or the lack of (or conversely, the need for) "enryo" ('reserve, restraint, discretion, hesitation') that is used to classify relationships in terms of the inner or outer circle of sociability (Doi Takeo, 1988). Relationships with parents, where no enryo is necessary, fall into the 'interior' circle. To the other extreme, tannins (firstly people who you are not related to, then people who you have no relationship with) constitute the exterior sphere and again a need for enryo is absent. Enryo is therefore unnecessary in either the closest social circle or at the periphery: in the first case because formal barriers are lowered between intimate family relationships and in the second case because social distance is so great that there is no need to exercise a proper formal etiquette and provide strong marks of respect.

The notion of "amae" helps to shed some light on this social distribution of enryo. Amae refers to that kind of indulgence or benevolence that one can/is entitled to expect from another in different daily situations. In the intimacy circle, this indulgence is considered implicit and unconditional and does not make the respect of a particular code of behaviour a precondition to be satisfied in order to get it. In social circles that concern mere acquaintances, the need for amae doesn't exist because nothing is expected from this 'circle of strangers.' But in the middle, there is a specific etiquette relevant to various situations of interaction. One has to play that coded game if one does not want to alienate "amae". [3]

Within the outer social circles, the need for enryo appears inversely proportional to the degree of intimacy and increases directly with social distance. Within that frame, phone calls are an occasion of great concern. One may breach etiquette and cause embarrassment to others if the call comes at a bad time or for an inappropriate reason. The sense of interactional empathy and attention to mutual embarrassment is so strong that there exists polite conventional sentences for the person who is called to apologize to the caller that he/she felt it was needed for him/her to call. We will see later how mobile e-mail is perceived as liberating

---

[3] Amae must be understood as a need to please in order to provoke a benevolent attitude from the other person. One example of this is in the devoted behaviour of employees in a company. When a mistake is made, amae will convey an indulgent behaviour towards the wrongdoer.

because it minimizes the risks involved in phone calls. The main motive given for using mobile messaging is usually "not having to worry about someone being available". Mobile messaging appears an effective and value-loaded medium for interaction in situations where enryo, as well as other social customs, are an issue, e.g., "giri" (obligation, duty) "ninjo" (human feelings, compassion) and "on" (debt).

SMS in France

SMS is perceived in France as completely different from any other form of electronic communication and is definitely not seen as another kind of email. The fact that the text is limited to 160 characters; the fact that one has to compose a phone number (and not an e-mail like address) to send an e-mail; the distinct places of the telephone and the personal computer within technological imaginaries; etc. have all served to sharpen the distinctions between SMS and email as communication media. Moreover, because of the pricing structure, SMS is considered to be an alternative to voice communications. When one sends an SMS in France, there is an additional cost that is not covered within the basic package, making it distinct from mobile-based voice calls. In summary, SMS in France appears to users as a rather singular form of communication.

> "I think the messages are nice. I don't know, I don't know how to explain. It changes, it changes the old methods of communication like the telephone. I don't know, it enables a change. It is another way of communicating." (Virginie, 19 yrs)

> "I don't know, the mini messages are really strange it is difficult to describe." (Marie-Hélène, 25 yrs)

While in Japan, mobile messaging was found to be one of the primary uses of mobile phones (making it easier for Japanese users to explain the particular situations in which they made voice calls), in France, voice phone calls remain the standard form of communication associated with mobile phones.

SMS writing games

Far from being standardized (as one might have expected from the 160 character limit), SMS messages offer a large variety of expressions and vocabulary; they refer to many styles and many genres, according to their contents, shape and the level of language used. The personalization of SMS messages is therefore strong. It is one of those forms of written texts that try to retain individuality and maintain integrity of meaning by drawing on spoken forms of expression[4].

---

[4] Patrick Williams found the same thing when he was studying Hungarian expressions in letters and texts. He shows that there is no difference between the written and spoken forms and he also shows how important it is to preserve individuality through writing like speaking, asserting an individual rather than collective identity through incorrect spelling and personal expressions. Fabre, Williams, 1997.

Some SMS users take a real pleasure in condensing their thoughts into a SMS message, in the way it gets them to condense their emotional thoughts, reduce ambiguity and synthesize ideas. In the words of one interviewee, it makes you "snappy": *"I am very very comfortable with these messages, where you have to sum up what you want to say in three phrases.... I think I must just have a precise mind. I get straight to the point and I think that I am a lot funnier..., that's how I see it."* (Stéphane, 28 yrs). Some get snappy indeed, but less through synthesis than through abbreviation and a telegraph-like way of writing. This is the case for Corinne: *"I write in a telegraphic style, I remove all the subjects but the words are whole. I write: broken down, the 4th road, outskirts, entry to St Ouen, don't know what to do."* *(Corinne, 37 yrs)*

For other users, it's just the opposite. They take pleasure in playing with words, shaping language, creating ambiguity, like Christian: *"Its often messages, its often messages with two possible meanings. You can say that there's a lot of play on words, lots of things like that. Because I find that the advantage of spelling is that it allows you to use to play with ambiguity, so it's good. It lets you use language to avoid messages that are a bit ambiguous, it's good."* *(Christian, 45 yrs)*. For Christopher, there is even some kind of poetry in this form of communication. He assumes a creative stance: *"When I write it is often in a playful way, to know that I have fun writing Alexandrian. So, also, it is funny because there is a reflecting side and a funny side. So, I often send poems. I am not a poet, it is more stuff, a bit like the style of Boby Lapointe with lots of plays on words, stupid things."* *(Christophe, 25 yrs)*.

These examples show the variety of exchange formats and writing practices that can be sustained in using the SMS medium. However, the playful dimension involved in composing SMS is very prominent in users' representations of this medium. The pleasure of inventing an original and creative language seems to overcome the more functional or utilitarian uses of communication in general and SMS in particular. The reduced size of SMS then becomes a positive constraint, that forces one to exert linguistic creativity, to the point that the form overwhelms the message. The form becomes the message, a point that Marion summarises well: *"It is a strange thing to write. In fact everything is in the shape: basically when you send a message for no particular reason, it is playful, punctuation games, little words that you use, it's fun."* *(Marion, 20 yrs)*.

With a close circle of friends

In France, SMS messages are mostly sent to close or intimate friends. Best friends and/or couples are the two relationships that are privileged with respect to the use of SMS, independent of age. Most people thus have, on average, 3 to 4 people who they send the majority of their messages to. This of course does not preclude occasional SMS exchanges with others falling into the extended social circles. Indeed, overtime we have observed that the uses of SMS have spread in 2001 (compared to the situation in 2000) towards other age groups[5], as well as the emergence of domestic SMS communications, for example between mothers and daughters. By and large, however, SMS communications with mere acquaintances or with professional contacts still remain the exception in France.

"Who do I send them to? Friends that are quite close. People that I mix with often, who I often spend time with. Either friends who I have known for a while, or friends in general from school." (Brice, 17 yrs)

"It is mainly my close friends and my girlfriend, and then acquaintances, but not that much." (Jaouen, 19 yrs)

"I have two people who I send them to: my girlfriend and my best friend." (Jouaen, 19 yrs)

"My best friend and I, who I see every two days, call each other as well as send messages. There is also a friend that I see everyday because we work together (Marie Hélène 25 yrs)

"My best friend" (Virginie, 19 yrs, Sandrine, 21 yrs)

"My boyfriend" (Pascale, 35 yrs, Florence 37 yrs)

The use of SMS to express emotion and maintain absent presence

The closeness of correspondents shapes the form, tone and content of the SMS messages exchanged. With close correspondents, the level of intimacy between the interlocutors will generally orient the message's content towards the expression of emotion. In some cases, 75% of mini messages can be of the "expressive" type.

Sending mobile mini-messages is both perceived as a step towards the ideal of ubiquitous communication or continuous presence "anywhere, any time", and as an impulsive practice.

"I do it when I want to." (Virginie)

"The mobile is in your hand. So if you really want to say something and to be able to say it straight away." (Marie-Hélène, 25 yrs)

The usage value of SMS is very often attached to their ability to materialise a "spontaneous" need for expression and emotional exchanges with close friends. Even where systematic SMS content analysis shows that a large share of SMS messages actually pertain to practical and utilitarian communications (mostly for coordination), emotion is inferred through little symbolic relevances; it appears to punctuate the functional SMS, making feelings pervasive. When sentimental messages are sent they are meant as a sign of the desire to share one's thoughts and

---

[5] Both because of the development of SMS exchange within older age groups and between different age groups, particularly intergenerational exchanges.

emotions, to remind the absent other of one's emotional presence, and to stress the continuity of the mediated relationship. They give way to and give form to almost any impulse to get in touch with the other, particularly when other modes of exchange are not deemed to be acceptable in a situation. In this sense, "emotional" SMS messages merge with other opportunities for "intimate" face-to-face and mediated encounters, without ever being expected to replace them.

"It's for telling someone you miss them and that you are thinking of them."
(Marie-Hélène, 25 yrs)

"It is for saying "I miss you and I'm thinking of you, things like that."
(Ghislaine, 20 yrs)

"I send nice messages. I mean a sort of replacement for love letters."
(Sébastien, 20 yrs)

"I send little messages to my girlfriend, something that tells her I am thinking about her, e.g. lots of love and kisses." (Jouaen, 19 yrs)

"In general, I send for example a friend messages saying how much I like them, or to my boyfriend that I am thinking about him. I send messages of love, I like it a lot." (Stephanie, 17 yrs)

"With my boyfriend all day I send only sentimental messages, emotional ones. I think that there are sentimental things that you say in life, you say them so that they are heard not just to get a response. So the mini message is excellent because even if you are far away from someone you can convey your voice through words, similar to letters and in a way that replaces them." (Florence 37 yrs)

Unlike the observations made in Japan, intimacy strongly shapes the development of the mini messages in France.

SMS still may develop within more widespread circles and/or along more practical uses. Informative messages often give you the opportunity to confirm an appointment, an address, a phone number or to tell someone you are going to be late. The arbitration between a phone call and the mini message then rests on how much time you are going to save with a mini message in relation to phoning, and the efficiency of a written message with respect to coordination purposes. Such messages may be a substitute for phone calls, as in Japan.

Motivations

Similarities and differences/continuity and change in mediated sociability

In this section we aim to shed some light on the dialectics of difference and similarity, continuity and change in France and Japan with respect to motivations for relying on mobile messaging for interpersonal exchanges, and interaction situations that are perceived to favour such exchanges between individuals. On the one hand, mobile messaging and its reliance on specific technological functions and features entrenches specific behaviours and motivations that are similar in both countries: the discretion of message exchange in public contexts; the possibility of an inventive and emotional writing game; the desire to escape some of the pitfalls of dialogic communication; etc. On the other hand, meanings associated with mobile messaging are not just determined by the material and functional features of the technology, they are also shaped by historical and cultural contexts. This shaping of the interaction medium can be argued to account for its different uses and meanings in different national contexts such as France and Japan. Taking a larger historical perspective, the behaviours associated with mobile messaging can be interpreted as part of general trends in interpersonal communication. We will question the growing rationalisation of sociability, the individualisation of communication practices, and the drift towards non-dialogic modes of interaction. The realisation of these overall trends in each country (through the way users have appropriated mobile SMS and e-mail) can be shown through such comparative case studies to be historically and culturally shaped.

An increased tendency to think in terms of the rationalization of interaction costs over different communication media

The avoidance of a phone conversation is one of the first reasons for using a written form of communication. It is justified by at least three basic arguments common in both France and Japan, that all pertain to the rational allocation of rare resources: economizing in money, economizing in time and economizing in personal investment into various projects (the rare resource here is the personal energy one has to commit).

The issue of comparative costs

Japanese users correctly insist on the fact that, overall, written messages are cheaper than voice conversations at the end of a month.

"Another advantage, it costs less than the phone." (Yuki, 22 yrs, student)

"And then there is the money worry. Emails are less expensive. If you are on the phone, straight away you have spent 20-30 yen, whilst email is a lot cheaper. And then with certain family reductions, for a short message it costs 1yen." (Seitti, 40 yrs, engineer)

French users indeed feel the same. Differences in the way mobile messages are billed in both countries are irrelevant here.

"Also when you have gone past the fixed price, it is cheaper than the phone." (Sébastien, 22 yrs)

"It is practical, it's quick and when you are outside the fixed price... the problem of being outside the fixed price is that a minute is 2,50F and the

mini message is 1F whatever happens. I am outside the fixed price at the end of the two weeks... (Laurent, 23 yrs)

"To call someone, it is long and will be expensive, so leaving a mini message will be a lot cheaper and won't last long." (Sebastien, 20 yrs)

The issue of time saving

Japanese users are sensitive to the fact that phone conversations takes time (even if attention to mutual embarrassment may lead participants to shorten their phone exchanges), and that mobile messages may save time and attention.

"Generally, when we start to discuss something on the phone, it will get longer and then will be expensive. As I am a housewife, I can phone from my fixed line. But recently I have realised that while I am on the phone, I can't do anything else, but with email. What was I saying? I can send a message when I have time and on the other hand, they can respond when they have time. And even if I sent them something late at night, they wouldn't be disturbed." (Atuko)

"With the telephone, for women, they tend to be long. Sometimes you can lose half a day speaking on the phone. Since my child has been at playschool, I have been busier. I make do with emails." (Kazuko, 36 yrs, Osaka)

This concern for time is even greater in France, where phone conversations are perceived to be allowed to run more freely than in Japan. French users regularly portray the phone calls between intimate correspondents as lasting for hours.

"Mini messages, when you send them, you don't need to talk for hours." (Arame, 15 yrs)

"Good, because in fact, talking on the phone can last a long time. I find that you can stay talking for hours and hours." (Virginie, 19 yrs)

Managing the energy investments required for different types of interaction and listening to your state of mind

Last, French users also develop a particular rhetoric of individualism through the idea of "being in the mood" for using a given communication medium – of being ready or not to invest in the necessary energy to handle a given type of communication.

"There are moments where I don't want to use the phone, so I send a mini message, with this I tell myself that it has all the information, and so there is no need to call. Sometimes that makes my head spin, it depends on the moment." (Jaouen, 19 yrs)

"It depends on my psychological state. If I am in a good or bad mood...if I'm in a good mood, I would tend to phone, I reckon." (Laurent, 23 yrs)

"It can also be when you have nothing to say, you want to hear news, but at the same time, when you don't really want to talk." (Virginie, 19 yrs)

Embarrassment and ordinary phone calls

In both countries, another very import set of reasons given for using mobile email and SMS services rely on their perceived properties as a medium that allows distant interaction in public environments, better management of potential embarrassment in interactions and puts less pressure on the immediate 'joinability' of correspondents.

Japan: interactional embarrassment management and liberation from formal codes

Since the Japanese culture is oriented towards a strict control over the public expression of emotions, the users of mobile messaging services immediately benefit from the discretion and diminished risk of embarrassment that characterizes written communication with respect to dialogic interaction. Mobile messaging has also contributed to the development of less formal exchanges, where users feel less compelled to worry about the usual social codes that can shape interpersonal relationships (writing a message, for example, is more direct and one can use any style without the need for the polite formalities necessary in phone conversations). This is reflected in the words of Japanese sociologists: "You know we have in Japan all these suffixes and verbal auxiliaries to mark respect. Now there is a tendency to omit all these markers in mobile written exchanges because of speed concerns, since one has to compose short messages. It is quite normal and tolerated to do so between comrades, but since they get used to that simplified way of writing they also tend to forget using the linguistic markers for respect in exchanges with older people, though these are mandatory in Japanese society. Students also speak more informally with their teachers (…) But these do not change deeply linguistic conventions for polite exchange. As soon as they are hired in a firm, they are re-educated very fast on that level."[6] (Hashimoto, 2002).

The most often quoted advantage of mobile email in Japan is that it does not rely on the immediate availability of the interlocutor. Because of this, Japanese users have hailed mobile messaging as a technology that has transformed interpersonal communication.

We can return to the notion of *"amae"*, developed by Doi Takeo, to account for the social behaviour in Japan and for the interpersonal relationship structures. Stemming from the primary relationship with the mother, all interpersonal relationships can be understood with respect to an ongoing need for *amae* in Japan.

---

[6] Interview, September 2002, Tokyo.

The *amae* relationship is therefore defined as a general attitude "that counts on the good will of others", and that is relevant to all kinds of social relationship. The child's need for *"amae"* leads him/her to engage in *"amaeru"*, i.e. the desire to be authorised by the other to benefit from his indulgence and to rely on the special bond that unites them. The Japanese therefore seem to internalize, at an early stage of their primary socialization, a high level of sensitivity to the emotional states of their interlocutors (especially with respect to feelings of embarrassment). Toi Dakeo highlights that *'enryo'* is a way of not being disliked by others. This behavior is made obvious in phone exchanges through the very explicit care Japanese users take to mobilize all the relevant politeness resources to smoothen the interactions, and to shorten conversations to minimize the disturbances it might cause others.

> *"Before I used to phone people but I was always worried about taking up the other persons time and now with email I am no longer worried about either sending or receiving messages." (Aya, student, 20 yrs)*

> *"With the telephone, there is always the worry that the person is not available or they are not there, and if I call their mobile it will show that I have called, and sometimes it is unnecessary for them to call me back because my call was not actually that important." (Eita, 25 yrs)*

Before the advent of mobile mail, signs of empathy and of the desire to be liked (displayed through the good will of correspondents) could be observed in phone conversations. For instance, the receiver of the call usually kept to the point and restricted his conversation initiatives so that the phone call would not cost the caller too much. Also, in certain circumstances, spontaneous use of the telephone would not match the social conventions used to guide normal interactions. Mobile email is felt to have a liberating effect at three levels. It relieves users from the psychological effort made to anticipate whether or the not the person is available. It frees them from many linguistic conventions and allows them to express themselves more directly and less guardedly. It relieves them of many concerns about costs, both for them and their correspondents.

> *"I tend to use email more because with the telephone you have to first think if the person you are calling is available. With email, I can send the message whenever, even if the other is at work." (Tie Satou)*

> *"People of my generation often have young children, so I don't want to ring and wake them up. With email I don't have to worry. I can send messages more frequently than telephoning. This allows me to maintain a friendship, something that would be more difficult with the telephone." (Tiharu, 39 yrs)*

> *"There is no particular slot in the timetable. It's just that I worry about disturbing the other person. With email I don't have to worry about whether the other person is available or not. Before phoning, you have to first think whether or not you are disturbing the other person. On the other hand, for*

my wife, I don't have to worry about her being available. She is the only
person I can phone when I want" (Tuyosi, 60 yrs)

The last extract nicely illustrates the implicit difference between interior and exterior relationships. Here, the relationship between partners is contrasted with exterior relationships. For the latter, discretion and reserve are deemed necessary but, between partners, the need for formalities is lessened because the presence of *amae* is not expected. It is important to understand that in Japan, it is the relationship structure and the individual's place in the different relationship circles that has a large part in determining social conduct. There is no real conceptual distinction of social behaviours using the two notions of *public* and *private*. These notions do not make sense because of the traditional way of understanding social relationships. That is, the distinction between interior and exterior relationships is unrelated to the division between public and private and in some sense transcends it: "We do not have a great commitment to the public good in Japan. The Japanese behave in a 'reasonable' way in an *enryo* context, but the context where *"enryo"* is required is felt as an inner world, in contrast to an outer world where no *"enryo"* is required, and which is therefore not a public space in the western sense. The distinction between 'inner' and 'outer' world, is relevant to a given individual. The principle of such a distinction is however approved and shared, which explains why a civic sense does not develop. It is generally accepted and explains why the sense of public spirit has not developed" (Takeo, 1988).

The main mobile phone-related behaviour in public situations (relating to the most extreme outer social circles) is very similar to Goffman's notion of civil inattention (Goffman, 1973). For example, in Tokyo's subways and trains, vocal announcements can be repeatedly heard reminding users to switch off their mobile phones, so that they will not risk causing interference with the pacemakers that some of their fellow travellers might be using. These calls are mostly ignored, and trains are commonly used as a place for sending e-mails. Travel time is seen to be convenient for composing and exchanging mobile e-mails. This behaviour is reminiscent of the capacity Japanese people have to negotiate indifference and establish a sense of privacy in public situations. Such 'ad-hoc' private spaces are produced on the spot, and range from unmediated embodied practices (e.g., easily falling asleep in public) to various forms of behaviour mediated through the use of material devices, such as the use of the walkman and now the use of mobile phones for interpersonal written exchanges. The fact remains that the decision to use e-mail is related, possibly negatively, to the ways in which the Japanese manage and arrange living amongst strangers.

France: individualization of communication and management of intimacy in public

Whenever discretion is evoked by French users as one of the main advantages of mobile messaging, it is usually referred to in discussions about individual freedom and the possibility of sending messages within the physical proximity of others and without breaching the etiquette of co-present interactions or co-existence in public spaces. Attitudes towards mobile e-mail communication are expressed with direct and explicit reference to the notion of public space and to the rules that govern the way a user might inhabit such an "open" space.

"In public places or in the office, it's very practical." (Stéphanie, 25 yrs)

"I always have to send messages when I am on public transport or in shops. I am a lot less comfortable speaking on the phone in public places, but on the other hand, mini messages, it is more comfortable because the people can not hear you." (Brice 17 yrs)

"You can use SMS even if there are loads of people around you and if you don't want people to hear what you are saying. Also when you are on public transport, it is noisy and so it is difficult to talk" (Sébastien, 22yrs)

"On public transport when there are lots of people around you, it is more discreet to send a message. I always get calls when I am on the RER, public places, which I don't like, it's better to get written messages." (Virginie, 19 yrs)

"When I am with other people and I need to say something to someone, I send a message and therefore do not disturb any of the others... for example when I am in the office at work. There are certain things that I don't want to say out loud." (M. Hélène, 25 yrs)

"Yes, I know it's annoying when you are in a group and the phone rings, even when it is my phone, I always keep it on vibrate. I prefer to send a mini message." (Ghislaine, 20 yrs)

"When I speak with my boyfriend, I know that my parents are listening." (Arame, 15 yrs)

"If I want to call someone and I know that it won't take long, I send them a message to check if they are not already on the phone or that they are not doing something else, that way I am certain ... If I know that I am not disturbing them, I call." (Virginie, 19 yrs)

"I have started communicating with my friends via SMS to see if I can phone them at that time, or just to say hello. When the person is not available, I call them back later." (Sandrine, 21 yrs)

What we see, then, is that the French use of mobile messaging for privacy is oriented towards a polite management of privacy in a public space, while the Japanese use is more sensitive to the nature of social relationships and the proper etiquette to maintain. In France, one is expected to behave neutrally in public places with respect to co-present bystanders (for example in a train): SMS then appears as a very useful resource to maintain silent behaviour and civil inattention among strangers while engaging in interpersonal communication. In Japan this is also a concern, but not the primary one. Japanese users are much more preoccupied with the potential embarrassment a phone call might cause to their interlocutors because of the traditions and the expected behaviour connected to each person's position in a relationship. As noted, mobile messages appear as a useful resource to achieve the obligations of *enryo*.

Mobile messaging and the display of emotions

The pleasure that one gets from the spontaneous expression of one's emotions, is a common theme in both countries with respect to mobile messages, but it leads to different kinds of practice. In Japan, the issue of expressive emotion through mobile messages is very much linked to the widespread use of pictograms, i.e. designs that represent different object categories, animals, weather, climate, facial expressions, and the use of which denotes a playful handling of the relationship. They cover different modes of engagement of the message writer, from the description of what he sees to the expression of the childish joy he feels in a given act of communication. In France, the sentimental value of SMS stems mostly from the way users will play with the standard conventions of writing to maximize the meaningfulness of a given message for his intended interlocutor. The written message is therefore often compared to a love letter that one keeps and reads over and over again.

Compared to a phone conversation that implies direct contact and a confrontation with the reactions of the other person, mobile message writing is perceived in both countries as a medium that can free the author from many inhibitions and modesties, as well as the fears usually associated to dialogic interactions or the formality of letter writing. Most forms of writing facilitate the expression of emotions because there is no direct trial of such expression as there is in dialogic interaction through the immediate response of the interlocutor. But emotional expression in writing can also work insidiously on the person it is addressed to. Though aggressive feelings (criticism, anger, excuses) will be less brutally imposed to the other and might not elicit an immediate outburst of violence in response, they can be read again and again, and thus cause deep forms of hurt.

France: A way to express emotion that remains anchored in standard writing practices

French users are very sensitive to the use of SMS to express feelings. Because of the asynchronous nature of text messaging and the lack of interactional cues, it is evident that the medium can free the author from many inhibitions and modesties in expressing his or her emotions. In this respect, SMS messaging is similar to conventional letter writing where the author is not subject to the immediate response of the interlocutor.

> *For example when talking with my boyfriend on the telephone, me personally, I don't like expressing my feelings on the phone. I don't know why, I block it out. But with writing there is no problem, I can express how I am feeling. You don't see the reactions. This makes communication easy.*

*Especially for a shy person, I don't know, I find that it makes it easier..."
(Virginie, 19 yrs)*

"And then in general, I find it easier when talking about love with your boyfriend or friends. It's easier to write to someone than to call them, and than to see them face-to-face. There are things that I dare to say with a mini message, but would not dare to say face-to-face." (Stephanie, 17 yrs)

"I find it easier to tell my girlfriend 'I love you' by writing it rather than saying it". (Sébastien, 20 yrs)

This controlled form of expression can also serve to emphasise the potential for the open shows of conflict that can ignite in verbal exchanges. Mobile messaging comes to be seen as a resource to avoid the potential conflict and minimize the vulnerability of face-to-face interactions or talk on the phone.

"I got home quite annoyed, so I sent a text. I think that it has an impact; I preferred to write it than to say it on the phone, because I think I would have been more unpleasant...It is not very straightforward but I didn't see any other solution." (Stéphanie, 25 yrs)

"I am very straightforward but I hate being unpleasant to my friends, that annoys me, so I prefer to send them a message. Perhaps I try to escape reality, oral confrontation. I am a very sensitive person and I would probably cry on the phone. With the mini message I can take a step back. Even when the person sends a really aggressive mini message, there is always the phone between us. It is less violent, I find you loose your temper less and you don't remember the aggressiveness of the voice." (Laurent, 23 yrs)

"The other day, I left slamming the door shut, I was angry and a quarter of hour late, I sent a message, but I didn't really want to phone the person and say 'I'm sorry' by actually saying sorry, I did the opposite and wrote it. For me, it is easier." (Pascale, 35 yrs)

Japan: Expression of emotion in mobile messaging and the use of pictograms

In Japan, emotional texts commonly make use of pictograms. These graphical forms of expression can be seen as an extension of established writing practices that rely on ideograms. But pictograms, alone, have contributed greatly to the increased usage of mobile email and are considered as a specific linguistic vehicle to convey serious feelings. Telephone operators provide about 200 pictograms in standard mobile phone menus, while standard PC interfaces allow only for conventional faces and smileys to be used. The size of a mobile phone's pictogram library is an important enough feature to induce a preference in using phone-based rather than pc-based e-mail. Pictograms can also provide an element of playfulness.

For example, users might compose a message made up of only the pictogram symbols, avoiding text altogether.

"How do you say it? I like to put a few pictograms into the text, not too many, so I can express my feelings." (Seiiti, 40 yrs)

"With the text alone you risk sometimes misunderstandings, so by adding a smile, a pictogram of a smile, I show that it is a friendly message. With such a large repertoire of pictograms, it seems to me that you can convey your feelings better." (Hiromi, 19 yrs, Osaka)

"Yes I really like them. I think that they convey feelings the text alone would not be able to communicate. For example, the sun pictogram shows that you are very happy and content. And when you are angry I use the fist. The rain, when I'm a bit sad. And then there are the faces that show psychological states. I often put them at the end of a phrase. If I only put a full stop or comma at the end, then the message isn't very friendly. It would seem like an administrative text." (Akiko, 42 yrs, housewife)

"I have a computer in my room, and from it you can integrate faces or pictograms so I am afraid that an email sent from the computer will be dry. Often I use the heart or the broken heart, the smile also." (Yuki Sinndou, student 22yrs)

For the Japanese, the meanings associated with conventional pictograms as a way to express emotions are particularly rich and deeply embedded in the context of their use. The use of pictograms in Japan is distinct in the sense that it represents more than a conventional sign language in which meanings are shared by all users. Their interpretation involves grasping a variety of nuances that are, at a semantic level, difficult to capture in words. Their power to evoke is greater and perceived as such by Japanese members. Such evocative power does not operate independently of the relationship between the message sender and its receiver. This explains the commitment of most of the users we interviewed to argue for the value of pictograms to express affects. Messages where a pictogram was used to express anger or an apologetic mode were deemed very particular and very important in comparison to ordinary messages.

"I always use pictograms. They represent my psychological state. When I am calm, I use animals that are more or less sweet: a dog, a cat, a rabbit. Because there are also tigers and other ferocious animals, there are even wolves. I use those when I am angry. When I am angry at someone and I want to send them a mail before I go to bed, I will send the tiger or even the wolf, or when I have a bad experience or even when I am unhappy with something at work, I put these animals in to make a final point to myself, to my feeling? I only use these pictograms with really close friends, so what I am trying to convey is understood. With acquaintances that I'm not close to, I don't make an effort by putting these pictures in." (Youko, 30 yrs)

As the above excerpt shows, pictograms may become a way to express strong negative feelings that one probably would not dare to express in direct interaction. While in France mobile messages could be seen as a resource to minimize vulnerability and the dangers of dialogues, in Japan mobile messaging and pictograms become a favoured resource for more direct expression of strong feelings (and particularly antagonistic feelings) than the ordinary conventions of dialogic interaction would normally allow.

Conclusion: the dynamics of direct and indirect exchanges in mediated communication

A functional representation of mobile messaging with respect to sociability therefore emerges, where it appears as a resource for avoiding phone conversations and the potential for dialogic 'violence' they entail. Two issues are compounded when Interpreting these new behaviours against the back drop of a general trend in interpersonal communication.

The first issue is that of rationalisation: becoming a *"homo communicio"*, the sociable individual is confronted by an increasingly complex and varied communication technoscape. An increasing amount of effort is needed to calculate which form of existing written or oral communication resource (e.g., email, fixed-line phone, mobile phone, face-to-face) is most efficient in a given context with respect to the costs involved in maintaining a proper interaction. What is at stake is the allocation of scarce resources such as money, time, effort and attention in order that one's mediated communication practices allow the management of one's social bonds in a way that fit with the (often) vague representations of propriety. Interpreted as a new communication strategy, you could almost say that this new social behaviour conveys a rationalisation[7] of sociable relationships (in the sense given by Weber) to the detriment of traditional and emotional uses (Weber, 1956). It is congruent with the consequences of modernisation described in terms of individualisation, of self-assertion and of autonomization. The diversity of interpersonal communication increases as a result of increased possibilities of personal choice across a variety of possible mediations: this entrenches notions of personal preferences operating over communication modes (written versus oral, direct versus indirect, etc.), and which seem to shape personal tastes rather than enforcing group-oriented norms.

Second is a drift towards increased reliance on indirect communication, particularly marked in the case of Japanese users' rather enthusiastic use of mobile messaging. This seems a current and general trend in the development of mediated communication. In recent statistics, we have observed that the use of indirect

---

[7] Max Weber distinguishes the rational activity against the traditional one and the emotional one. The first one is oriented by the final aims and by comparing, rationally, the means and the end, the end and the subsidiary consequences. He opposes rational action determination, seeing action instead to be oriented by the affects and/or the emotions, i.e., satisfying a feeling.

"messages" in the mass of contacts has been increasing at an equal if not faster rate than the overall growth in electronically mediated dialogue over the past ten years. Among the communication technologies that support indirect "messages" mobile phone-based written exchanges indeed figure more and more prominently[8].

The rationale for such an evolution appears very clearly in the case of "connected" relationships, in the context of the proliferation of communication devices and the fragmentation of activity (Licoppe, 2003). In "connected" relational practices, there is a seamless web of interactions, whether face-to-face, phone conversations or multiple forms of messaging (as opposed to dialogic communication) such as letters, voicemails, e-mail and most screen-based written exchanges, and now SMS. Because the attention of actors is a scarce resource, "connected" relationships are very limited, mostly to close friends that one sees often. This development of "connected" relationships brings some new constraints in managing social bonds. Since the attention and joinability of both parties is a rare resource, indirect "messages" are a particularly useful resource to evoke presence (when dialogue is impossible) and to produce the "connected" bond in the form of unceasing flow of reciprocal actions. This suggests a particular rationality involved in managing "connected" bonds in which both parties have to find a suitable balance between direct dialogic interactions (in which they are more vulnerable but which involve a high degree of commitment) and indirect "messages" (where they are less vulnerable to conflict and more generally to the difference in the Other, and also where commitment levels are less, even when taking into account the exacerbation of emotional expression).

These two observations, that of the increased rationalization of communication practices and that of a general drift towards an increased reliance on indirect messages may now be used to put our comparative data into a broader perspective. Such a perspective is not exempt from paradox, since mobile messaging could be seen as a "civilizing" technology leading to an "uncivil" social world.

The particular empathy of Japanese users and the attention they pay to potential embarrassment in interaction situations suggests that a key in understanding the drift toward indirect communication is to take into account the ways users assess the risks inherent in any form of embodied dialogue, whether face-to-face or on the phone. Displacing the balance between direct and indirect communication by relying heavily on mobile messaging can then be seen as using technology to domesticate that potential violence (whose perception depends on the meanings and positions of various technological mediations in a given state of the technoscape) and interiorising control of that violence through conventions regarding the proper use of communication resources. In that sense the development of indirect

---

[8] If we take all the various forms of communication, we know that the tendency of the French to communicate has increased 5 times between 1990 and 2000. We also estimate that it will double between now and 2010. When looking at all the factors that contribute to this evolution of interpersonal usages, the written forms of communication i.e. SMS, MMS and mail do and will constitute the main cause of this development.

communication and the success of mobile messaging could be read as a further step in the *"civilizing process"* (Elias, 1936) within the realm of mediated sociability.

Two tendencies seem to characterise the use of written messages. The first is that such communications emerge from the private sphere and increase the number of emotional contacts. Everybody is given the capacity to express their feelings at anytime and from anywhere. But the second shows a withdrawal from the public sphere evidenced by users isolating and absorbing themselves in their on screen writing (Rivière, 2002). Expressivity with respect to unseen correspondents and absorption with respect to bystanders fuse into new forms of articulation of the private and the public sphere.

From another point of view, it could be read as an indication of the growing incivility that goes with the "tyrannies of intimacy" (Sennett, 1979). Sennett has argued that the development of expressive and emotional communication in the name of the values associated to intimacy and personalization has led to the withering of the public sphere, as well as an increase in the difficulties of handling the risks that interactions with strangers are fraught with. He has suggested that the personalisation and emotionalisation of interaction has encouraged forms of socialization based on sameness of personalities and communion of souls rather than a commitment to joint action. Some uses of mobile messaging seem to reflect this. In France, mobile messaging has been predominant in sustaining very close, intimate bonds. In France and Japan, it is seen to provide expressive resources for communication, new ways to express affect and emotion as current activities unfold. Users in both countries also insist that mobile messaging allows them to engage into interpersonal communication in the public sphere without attracting any attention or breaching any code of behaviour. Intimate exchanges therefore gain ground in public contexts from which they were excluded. If we follow the political sociology of Sennett, mobile messaging contributes to the construction of an uncivil social world.

This ambivalent perspective is broad enough to encompass both the French and Japanese cases. However our study has also revealed distinct differences between these countries in the meanings and practices related to mobile messaging. The expectations and conventions regarding the mediated management of social relationships are culturally and technologically shaped. Because the use of the mobile phone is embedded in a wider cultural background that guides the acceptable ways of interacting with known and unknown persons, the proper balance between direct and indirect communications is negotiated very differently. The advent of new communication technologies redefines the resources available to users in finding the balance between dialogue and "messaging" to satisfy the need for social bonds. But such a balance will eventually remain shaped by the cultural context within which such expectations regarding sociability are constructed. Comparative studies in very different cultural contexts should prove an essential analytic resource to disentangle this interplay of culture, technology and sociability.

References

Hashimoto, Y. (2002) *The spread of cellular phones and their influence on young people in Japan.* In the proceedings of the conference on The Social and Cultural Impact/ Meaning of Mobile Communication, Chunchon, Korea: School of Communication Hallym University, 13-15 July.

Hashimoto, Yoshiaki, interview by Carole Rivière, Tokyo, September 2002.

Dagognet, F. (1985) *Rematérialiser*, Vrin.

Dagognet, F. (1989) *Eloge de l'objet*, Vrin, cité dans La technique, in *Notions de Philosophie* sous la dir de Denis Kambouchner, Folio Essais.

Takeo, D. (1988) *Le jeu de l'indulgence*, l'Asiathèque, Paris.

Goffman, I. (1973) *La mise en scène de la vie quotidienne*, (t.1 : La présentation de soi; t.2 : Les relations en public) Paris, Editions de Minuit.

La civilisation des mœurs (1936), coll Press Pocket, Calmann-Levy, Paris.

Licoppe, C. (2004) 'Connected' presence: the emergence of a new repertoire for managing social relationships in a changing communication technoscape. *Environment and Planning D: Society and Space*, 22, pp. 135-156.

Rivière, C. (2002) La pratique du mini-message. Une double stratégie d'extériorisation et de retrait de l'intimité dans les interactions quotidiennes, *Réseaux,* 112-113, pp. 141-168.

Riviere, C. (2002 – English translation) Mini-messaging in everyday interactions: a dual strategy for exteriorising and hiding privacy to maintain social contacts, *Revista de Estudius de Juventud*, 57, www.mtas.es/injuve/biblio/revistas/Pdfs/numero57ingles.pdf.

Sennett, R. (1979) *Les tyrannies de l'intimité*, Seuil, Paris.

Simmel, G. (1917), *Sociologie et épistémologie*, Puf, Paris.

Weber. M. (1956), *Economie et Société*, Agora, Paris.

L'écriture entre l'oral et l'écrit. Six scènes de la vie tsigane en France (1997), in Fabre D. (dir), *Par écrit, ethnologies des écritures quotidiennes*, Paris.

6   Intimate Connections: Contextualizing Japanese youth and mobile messaging

Mizuko Ito and Daisuke Okabe

Introduction

Ever since NTT Docomo launched its i-mode mobile Internet service in 1999, international attention has been trained on Japan as a hothouse for incubating the future of the wireless revolution. In particular, international technology communities have noted and often celebrated handset design by Japanese electronic manufacturers, third generation infrastructures, video and camera phones, and mobile entertainment. A focus on ever-new advanced technical functionality, however, can often lose sight of the social, historical, and cultural context through which contemporary Japanese mobile media is structured and has evolved. As Harper (2003, 187) has argued, "mobile society is not rendering our society into some new form, it is rather, enabling the same social patterns that have been in existence for some time to evolve in small but socially significant ways." In this chapter, we analyze messaging practices of Japanese youth as an outcome of existing historical, social, and cultural factors rather than as something driven forward by the inherent logic of new technology.

Based on the distinctiveness of young people's mobile media usage, we argue for the context specificity of meanings and usage of new technologies. Even as mobile phones have become common in all age groups,[1] young people use their phones more, spend more on them (IPSe, 2003), and have unique patterns of usage. Particularly distinctive is usage of mobile email.[2] 95.4% of students describe

---

[1] Since the late nineties, youth have had higher rates of mobile phone ownership than the general population, but the gap is closing. In contrast to a 2001 survey that documented how young people had higher adoption rates (Yoshii et al., 2002), a 2002 national survey of mobile phone communications conducted by Video Research (2002) found that the overall penetration of mobile phones in Japan was 73.7% with ownership by students age 12 and up at 75.7%.

[2] We use the term "mobile email" to describe messages (mostly text, but sometimes images) sent via short message services analogous to SMS, as well as mobile Internet services. Short messages can generally only be sent between subscribers to the same provider, and cannot be as lengthy as those sent

Richard Harper, Leysia Palen and Alex Taylor (Eds), The Inside Text: Social, Cultural and Design Perspectives on SMS, 127–145.

themselves as mobile email users, in contrast to 75.2% of the general population (VR, 2002) and they send a higher volume of messages.[3] They also tend to be more responsive to the email that they receive. Almost all students (92.3%) report that they view a message as soon as they receive it, whereas a slimmer majority of the general population (68.1%) is as responsive. May older users say that they view a message when convenient to them, or at the end of the day (VR, 2002). What is behind these distinctive patterns of usage by young people?

This chapter seeks to answer this question by analyzing ethnographic material on mobile phone usage in relation to three different contextual frames. One is ways in which mobile messaging has been structured by the power geometries of existing places of home, school, and public places. Next, the chapter presents the central social context in which youth peer messaging practice is situated, that of the intimate peer group. Finally, we analyze how this ethnographic material articulates with longstanding intergenerational dynamics in postwar Japan. Our focus is not on the uptake of a particular technology (ie. short text message services on the mobile phone), but on a historically continuous set of practices that have mobilized different technologies at different times. Because of the structural location they occupy in contemporary Japanese society, youth, particularly teenage girls, have spearheaded the development of what we call "personal, portable, and pedestrian" communication media practices (Ito, Okabe, & Matsuda, 2005).

Method and conceptual framework

Our research

This chapter draws from ongoing ethnographic research on mobile phone use centered at Keio Shonan Fujisawa Campus near Tokyo. We draw primarily from three different sets of data. One is a set of ethnographic interviews conducted by Ito in the winter of 2000 with twenty-four high school and college students about their use of media, including mobile phones. We have also conducted a series of observations on trains in the Kanto and Kansai regions of Japan, documenting instances of mobile phone use (Okabe & Ito, 2005). The central body of data behind this paper is a set of "communication diaries" and interviews we collected between July-December 2002 where we collect detailed information on where and when particular forms of mobile communication were used by a diverse set of people. We seek direct observational records in addition to interview data, as it is notoriously difficult to capture the fleeting particularities of mobile communication after the fact. Our diary was adapted from data collection methods piloted by Rebecca Grinter and Margery Eldridge (2001) where they asked ten teenagers

---

over the Internet. While users make case-by-case decisions about whether to send a message via short messaging or Internet, both types of messages are generally called *meiru* (mail).

[3] Teens send twice as many emails than twenty-somethings, sending approximately 70 a month in contrast to 30 for the slightly older set (Yoshii et al., 2002). In contrast to the general population (68.1%), almost all students (91.7%) report that they send over 5 messages a day.

No.	When	Who	Where	Sent or Received	Communication Type*	Reason for Choice	People in Vicinity	Problems if Any	Content
1	10:29	Friend S	Home	Received	KV		Boyfriend	Half-asleep	Canceling plan to go drinking together
2	12:19	Mother	Home	Sent	KV				
3	15:13	Friend K	Home	Received	KM		Boyfriend		Tell me your phone number
4	15:39	Friend K	Home	Sent	KM		Boyfriend	Couldn't respond right away	[phone number]
5	17:53	Friend M	Bus Stop	Sent	KM		Passer-bys		Confirming appointment to go drinking together
6	18:09	Friend M	Train	Received	KM	Cheap, in train	About 20 people	Train was crowded	Going to seminar and then out drinking
7	18:14	Friend M	Train Platform	Sent	KM	Cheap, in train	About 20 people		
8	18:20	Friend M	Train Platform	Received	KV				

Figure 1: Communication Diary Sample

*Communication types: KV=keitai (mobile) voice call, KM=keitai email to record the time, content, length, location, and recipient (or sender) of all text messages for seven days. As with interviews, this data collection method still relies on second-hand accounting, but has the advantage of providing much more detail on usage than can be recalled in a stand-alone interview.

We expanded the communication log to include voice calls and mobile Internet, and more details about the location and context of use. Participants were asked to keep records of every instance of mobile phone use, including voice, short text messages, email, and web use, for a period of two days. They noted the time of the usage, who they were in contact with, whether they received or initiated the contact, where they were, what kind of communication type was used, why they chose that form of communication, who was in the vicinity at the time, if there were any problems associated with the usage, and the content of the communication. After completion of the diaries, we conducted in-depth interviews that covered general attitudes and background information relevant to mobile phone use, and detailed explication of key instances of usage recorded in the diaries. Our study involved seven high school students (aged 16-18), six college students (aged 18-21), two housewives with teenage children (in their forties), and nine professionals (aged 21-51). The gender split was roughly equal, with 11 males and 13 females. 594 instances of communication were collected for the high school and college students and 229 for the adults. The majority of users were in the Tokyo Kanto region. Seven were recruited in the Osaka area in southern Japan to provide some geographic variation.

In addition to our own ethnographic work, we base our analysis on Japanese popular discourse and research literature on mobile phone adoption. In particular, we draw from research compiled by Tomoyuki Okada and Misa Matsuda (2002), collected more recently in English (Ito et al., 2005), which represents over a decade of work on youth mobile media. The final section of our paper brings this material to bear on our ethnographic work, analyzing current mobile messaging practices as an instantiation of longstanding intergenerational dynamics and a history of mobile media adoption. We turn now to the theoretical and conceptual framework for our analysis.

Conceptual framework

Countries with widespread adoption exhibit cross-cultural similarities in the intersection of youth and mobile phones. Richard Ling and Birgitte Yttri (2002) have coined the term "hyper-coordination" to describe the expressive and socially active uses of mobile phones by Norwegian teens. In contrast to the more instrumental uses that older subjects described, youths describe using phones for emotional and social communications, particularly for cementing peer relations. Ling and Yttri describe adolescence as a unique time in the lifecycle, how peers play a central role during this period, and how the mobile phone becomes a tool to "define a sense of group membership, particular vis-à-vis the older generation" (2002: 162). A growing body of work with teens in locations such as the UK (Green, 2003; Grinter & Eldridge, 2001; Taylor & Harper, 2003; Berg et al, chapter 13), Finland (Kasesniemi, 2003; Kasesniemi & Rautianinen, 2002), Norway (Skog, 2002), and Sweden (Weilenmann & Larsson, 2002), finds similar patterns in other countries. As documented by the chapters in this volume, text messaging, in particular, appears to be a uniquely teen-inflected form of mobile communication, and young people have driven adoption of SMS across the globe (Agar, 2003; Grinter & Eldridge, 2001; Kasesniemi, 2003; Kasesniemi & Rautianinen, 2002; Ling & Yttri, 2002; Rheingold, 2002). In the US, IM appears to occupy a similar structural role (Boneva, Quinn, Kraut, Kiesler, & Shklovski, Forthcoming).

Rather than locating the affinity between messaging and youth in the developmental imperatives of teens, we take a context-driven approach. In another essay, Ito (forthcoming) has argued that the practices and cultures of youth are not solely outcomes of a certain level of developmental maturity, or even of social relations, but are also conditioned by the regulative and normative force of places. In other words, rather than originating solely with the psychological, social and developmental needs of youth, text messaging practices are structured by institutional and cross-generational surrounds. We also argue that the historical development of certain mediated communication practices also construct a key structuring context that has made mobile messaging particularly amenable to young Japanese.

Behind our approach is the "new paradigm" in childhood studies that has argued that "youth" and "childhood" are categories constructed and consumed by people of all ages, and produced in particular power-geometries (James, Jenks, & Prout, 1998; James & Prout, 1997).[4] In other words, an understanding of youth practices needs to be located within an adult social structure that limits and regulates youth activity as well as cultural discourses that often construct youth as frivolous and socially immature. Most simply put, modern teens, despite their physical and psychological maturity, do not yet have access to a full repertoire of adult rights, responsibilities, and resources, such as their own homes where they can meet friends and lovers, or a workplace where they are considered productive members of society (as opposed to "consumers" and "learners"). Teens are also considered legitimate objects of external regulation, control, and redirection in a way that even young adults are not. Just as social theory has interrogated race, class, and gender, generational dynamics need to be analyzed with a similar social structural lens (Alanen, 2001). We cut our data along these lines as well. We apply the category of youth to those institutionalized as such – high school and college students who are financially dependent on adults.

In the section to follow, we posit that the institutionalized power-geometries of place (Massey 1991) are important factors structuring youth mobile phone usage. Youth communications are regulated by peers or adults depending on place and

---

[4] In her study of Japanese youth, Merry White (1994: 11) describes the differences between US and Japanese labels for young people. The category of "teenager" of "cheenayja" has been borrowed from English, but is not in widespread use. The native categories are *shonen* and *seinen* which are closer to the English term "youth" or "young person."

time of day, and access to mobile media takes a central role in managing and inflecting that control. Conceptually, our approach has much in common with Nicola Green's in her analysis of the role of mobile phones in surveillance and monitoring between adults and teens and among teens (Green, 2002: 201-218). Ling and Yttri (2002: 139-69) make similar observations of youth mobile phone usage and power relations in Norway. Cross-cultural similarities in mobile phone usage can be understood in relation to shared and different structural conditions in the lives of young people. While this paper does not present a comparative analysis, it does lay out conditions that contextualize Japanese youth's mobile phone use, and suggests that the cross-cultural similarities in mobile phone usage are partially an outcome of the similarities in the institutionalized status of youth. Specifically, mobile messaging helps compensate for the lack of social settings and places where youth can communicate privately among close friends and lovers.

Following our description of how mobile communications are keyed to existing power-geometries, we argue that youth mobile messaging has worked to construct alternative kinds of intimate "places" or settings where youth can be in touch with their close peer group or "full-time intimate community" (Nakajima, Keiichi, & Yoshii, 1999). In a different paper (Ito & Okabe, 2005), we have proposed a concept of "technosocial situation" to describe such settings for activity that span a range of physical locations but still retain a coherent sense of location, social expectation, and role definition exhibited in Goffman's (1963) analyses and other practice-based studies. Our general conclusion is that youth messaging can undermine certain adult-defined prior definitions of social situation and place, but also construct new technosocial situations and new boundaries of identity and place. To say that mobile phones univocally cross boundaries, heighten accessibility, and fragment social life is to see only one side of the dynamic social reconfigurations heralded by mobile communications. Mobile phones create new kinds of bounded places that merge the infrastructures of geography and technology, as well as technosocial practices that merge technical standards and social norms.

Our argument is that the social outcomes of technology use are a result of social struggle over appropriate usage rather than a "natural" outcome determined by a particular technological form; mobile media usage is a site of intergenerational struggle over what should be the structuring social institutions and relations for young people. The final section of our paper analyzes our ethnographic findings in terms of longstanding intergenerational tensions and cultural politics. Since the period of Japan's economic prosperity in the eighties, the older generation has struggled to regulate an increasingly vibrant and self-directed set of youth cultures. Current mobile media usage is simply the latest example of young people mobilizing new technologies and consumer cultures in their struggle to claim a space of autonomy outside of the purview of adult control.

Japanese youth and the politics of place

Doreen Massey has argued that "different social groups are placed in very distinct ways in relation to late modern flows of media, people, and capital" (1994, 61). While the mobile phone has often been touted as an "anyplace, anytime" medium, we have found that usage is keyed to the specific structuring dynamics of particular places, and an individual's relationship to the power geometries of that place. As in most postindustrial contexts, teenagers in Japan generally find themselves in places controlled by adults with certain degrees of power over their lives, particularly their parents and teachers. Most college and high school students move back and forth from the space of the home – where they may have some privacy and discretion over their activities, but lack physical access to friends – and the space of school – where they are physically co-present with their friends, but have severe constraints on forms of social contact. The result, not surprisingly, is that young people have very few places in which they can have private conversations with peers and lovers. Urban spaces such as the street and cafes become key sites for gathering on their own terms. Now, the mobile phone has also become a device for young people to construct a "place" for private communication that is not monitored by adults. The low-profile, unobtrusive nature of email on a small handset is particularly amenable to youth communication because it does not disrupt the norms of existing place and can escape adult surveillance. A more extended version of this argument can be found in a prior paper (Ito, forthcoming). Here we summarize the use of mobile email in relation to places that young people inhabit.

First, in the home context, youth report that they do not see it as a place where they can congregate with their peers and significant others. Through college, Japanese youths have less private space compared to their US and even European counterparts. The Japanese urban home is tiny by middle-class American standards, and teens and children generally share a room with a sibling or a parent. Most college students in Tokyo live with their parents, often even after they begin work, as the costs of renting an apartment in an urban area are prohibitively high.[5] Because of these factors, urban Japanese youth generally take to the street to socialize. For high school students, this usually means a stop at a local fast food restaurant on the way home from school. College kids have more time and mobility, gathering in cafes, stores, bars, and karaoke spots. Unlike the US, there is no practice for teens to get their own landline at a certain age, or to have a private phone in their room. The costs of running a landline to a Japanese home are very high, from $600 USD and up, about twice what it costs to get a mobile phone. It is thus extremely rare for a home to have more than one landline.

---

[5] Our sample of college students for the communication diary part of our study is a bit skewed in this respect, as our student pool at the Keio campus was largely comprised of youth living on their own. As a suburban campus of an elite urban university, the situation at our campus is unique in attracting students from around the country in an area with a relatively low urban density. Overall, our interviewee pool represented a range from mainstream middle class to elite.

Here is an excerpt from an interview with four high school girls who are close friends.

> *Interviewer: You all live close to each other. Do you visit each other's homes?*
>
> *Student1: We don't. It's not that we are uncomfortable, or our parents get on our case, but it's like they are too sweet and caring, and you worry about saying something rude, or talking too loud. You can't be too rowdy. So we don't meet in our homes.*
>
> *Student2: Occasionally. Maybe once a year. Actually, that's not even occasional.*
>
> *Student1: And if it happens, it is at a friend's house where they have their own room.*

This stance was consistent across the youths that we interviewed. Meetings among friends almost always occurred in a third-party space run by indifferent adults, such as a fast food restaurant, karaoke spot, or family restaurant. Even for college students living on their own, their space is generally so small and cramped that it is not appropriate for hanging out with groups of friends.

The phone has always provided a way of overcoming the spatial boundary of the home, for teens to talk with each other late at night, and shut out their parents and siblings. As noted in other studies (Green, 2002; Ling & Yttri, 2002; Skog, 2002), the mobile phone has further revolutionized the power-geometry of space-time compression for teens in the home, enabling teen to communicate without the surveillance of parents and siblings. This has freed youths to call each other without the embarrassment of revealing a possible romantic liaison, or at hours of the day when other family members are likely to be asleep. All that we interviewed were consistent in stating a preference for calling a friend on a mobile rather than home phone despite the higher cost. Youths now do not have the home phone numbers of any but their most intimate friends. Parents are generally tolerant of their children's mobile phone usage, and many mothers reported using text messages for family communication. At the same time, most homes had a rule against mobile communication during meals, and peer communication can be a site of parent-child conflict. All the parents we interviewed described a sense of unease and curiosity about their children's mobile communications. Conversely, all the children took measures to keep parents in the dark about the content of their email and calls. One parent voices what we take to be a typical parental stance.

> *Okabe: Do you have a problem with her using her mobile phone during meals, or after meals in the living room, when you are together?*
>
> *Mother: I don't have a problem with it when we are just lounging around. But during meals or when she is studying, I try to tell her to tell the other person on the line.*

Okabe: Are you curious or concerned about with who and what she is communicating?

Mother: I am concerned about all of it... though I can usually guess who it is.

Okabe: When you tell her to stop, does she stop?

Mother: She goes to her room ... if I am strict about it.

The constraints on gathering with friends in homes has driven youth to the personal medium of the mobile phone to cement peer communications. The places of school and public transportation have, more specifically, encouraged use of mobile messaging. While the home context supports communication by both voice and email, in the classroom and on public transportation, mobile email, rather than voice, is by far the preferred modality.

Schools vary with respect to how teachers deal with mobile phones, but without exception, voice calls during class are considered inappropriate. Almost all schools officially ban phones from the classrooms, but most students do use email during class at least occasionally. It is not uncommon for students to leave their mobile phones out on their desks during class, claiming that they use the clock function. All students, both in high school and college voiced the rule that they would not use voice communication in class, but almost all said that they would read and sometimes send messages. The mobile phone gets used most frequently during the lunch time hour and immediately after school, as students scurry to hook up with their friends.

We saw email being sent during class in only two of our communication diary cases, but almost all students reported in their interviews that they would receive and send messages in class, hiding their phones under their desks. Four students we interview specifically described conversations with students in the same classroom, making comments like "this sucks," "this is boring," or "check it out, the teacher buttoned his shirt wrong." More commonly, students reported that they conducted "necessary" communications during class, such as arranging a meeting or responding to an email from somebody with a specific query. The communications in class that we saw in the diaries involved coordinating meetings after school or receiving email from friends who were absent, asking for notes or other class information. In all these cases, mobile email is being used to circumvent the communicative limitations of the classroom situation, much as passing notes and glances across the classroom did in an earlier era. Perhaps more uniquely, the mobile phone in the classroom is a way to challenge the communication hierarchy of the traditional lecture format that insists that students passively listen to an active teacher. Mobile email enables students to resist their role in this one-way communication and to make more productive use of their attentional "dead time" between jotting notes and waiting for teachers to finish writing theirs.

In contrast to the home and school, which are under the surveillance of adults with a personal interest in individual youth, public spaces like the street and public transportation rely on a more distributed set of strategies for regulating communication. Most trains and buses display "no mobile phone signs," and announcements are made every few minutes specifying limitations on phone use. A typical announcement is: "Please do not make voice calls while on the train. Please turn off your mobile phone in the area surrounding 'preferred seating' [for the elderly and disabled]." The street and train platforms are open to voice calls, but are generally extremely noisy, and it is difficult to have a sustained conversation in these locations. In one of our studies, we have focused on uses of mobile phones on trains and subways (Okabe & Ito, 2005). While we commonly observed email use, voice calls are rare. For example, one 41-minute observation on a busy train line represented the highest volume of usage that we recorded. During the period of observation, there were 37 instances of observable mobile email usage (including both receiving and sending email), and 4 instances of voice calls. In a 30-minute observation with the lowest volume of usage, there was one voice call and 10 instances of email use. The overall average of voice calls in any given 30-minute span is 1-2 calls.

In our interviews, almost all responded that they would freely engage in email exchanges but were hesitant to make and receive voice calls. For example, interviewees described how they might decide not to answer a voice call if the train was crowded, or they might move to a less crowded location to take a call, or they might take the call but cut it right away. Most also responded that they were annoyed when somebody took a voice call on a train and talked in a loud voice. These responses were consistent across all age groups. Here is a typical response:

(High school student, male, 18 years, Kanagawa prefecture)

Interviewee: When I hear somebody's keitai go off on a train, it bothers me. I think, "I'll always keep mine in silent mode."

Interviewer: How about email in trains?

Interviewee: I do email a lot, to kill time. I think email is probably okay. If I get a call, I do usually answer it, but I keep my voice low. I do feel bad about it and don't talk loud.

Phone ringing is also considered a violation in public space. Interviewees who were heavy mobile users almost invariably reported that they put their phones in "manner mode" (silent mode) when they left the home. In the communication diaries, we saw only once instance of a voice call being initiated on public transportation, when the subject was the only passenger on a bus. The call lasted only a few minutes, and was cut as soon as another passenger entered the bus. Despite the virtual lack of voice mobile communication on trains in the Tokyo area, the announcements are relentless, attesting to a high level of social regulation work even in the absence of major transgressions.

In contrast to voice calls, mobile email is considered ideal for use in public spaces. Some trains announcements and signage specify no voice calls, thus implying that Internet and email use is permitted. While bus drivers will prohibit someone speaking on a mobile phone from entering a bus, we have not observed any instances of regulation of silent mobile phone uses. Just as the power-geometries of the home make email a privileged, private form of communication, regulatory efforts on public transportation have also contributed to the rise of email as a preferred form of mobile communication. Largely because of the risk that their interlocutor may be on public transit, a social norm has arisen among the younger generation that you should not initiate voice calls without first checking availability with a text message. Unless certain that their recipient is at home, most youths (there were two exceptions in our study) will send a message first asking if they can call.

Tele-cocooning in the full-time intimate community

The location-based contexts described thus far provide a picture of some of the factors that have driven Japanese youth's adoption of mobile email. Now we turn to the question of the kinds of social settings, or technosocial situations (Ito & Okabe, 2005), that youth are building through their mobile email exchanges. While there are a variety of different types of situations being built through mobile email, we focus here on ongoing contact in an intimate peer group.

Unlike voice calls, which are generally point-to-point and engrossing, messaging can be a way of maintaining ongoing background awareness of others, and of keeping multiple channels of communication open. This is like people who keep IM channels open in the background while they go about their work, but the difference is that the mobile phone gets carried around just about everywhere for heavy users. The rhythms of mobile messaging fluctuate between focused chat-like exchanges and a more lightweight awareness of connection with others through the online space. In our interviews with heavy users of mobile phones, all users reported that they were only in regular contact with approximately 2-5, at most 10, close friends, despite having large numbers of entries in their mobile address books. This is what Matsuda (2005b) following Ichiro Nakajima, Himeno Keiichi, and Hiroaki Yoshino (1999), describes as a "full-time intimate community." In a related move, Ichiyo Habuchi (2005) describes these online spaces, occupied by most Japanese youth as "tele-cocoons." She contrasts these intimate spaces with the more extroverted spaces of online dating and encounter sites frequented by a small but significant minority of Japanese youth.

While the scale of social relationships and content of communication appears to be similar to what other studies have found in other forms of mediated communication (eg., for IM and telephone, see Boneva et al., Forthcoming), the portable format of the mobile phone affords certain distinctive usage patterns. Heavy mobile email users generally expect those in the intimate circle to be available for communication unless they are sleeping or working. Text messages can be returned discreetly during class, on public transportation, or in restaurants, all contexts where voice communication would be inappropriate. Many of the messages that we saw exchanged between this close peer group or between couples included messages that informants described as "insignificant" or "not urgent." Some examples of messages in this category are communications such as "I'm walking up the hill now," I'm tired," "I guess I'll take a bath now," "just bought a pair of shoes!" "groan, I just woke up with a hangover," or "the episode today sucked today didn't it?"

These messages define a social setting that is substantially different from direct interpersonal interaction characteristic of a voice call, text chat, or face-to-face one-on-one interaction. These messages are predicated on the sense of ambient accessibility, a shared virtual space that is generally available between a few friends or with a loved one. They do not require a deliberate "opening" of a channel of communication, but are based on the expectation that someone is in "earshot." From a technology perspective, this differs from PC-based communication because the social expectation is to be almost always connected. This is also not a "persistent" space as with an online virtual world that exists independent of specific people logging in (Mynatt, Adler, Ito, & O'Day, 1997). As a technosocial system, however, people experience a sense of a persistent social space constituted through the periodic exchange of text messages. These messages define a space of peripheral background awareness that is midway between direct interaction and non-interaction. The analog is sharing a physical space with others that one is not in direct communication with but is peripherally aware of. Many of the emails exchanged present information about one's general status that is similar to the kind of awareness of another that one would have when physically co-located, a sigh or smile or glance that calls attention to the communicator, a way of entering somebody's virtual peripheral vision. This kind of virtual tap on the shoulder may result in a change of setting into a more direct form of interaction such as a chat-like sequence via texting or a voice call, but it might also be ignored if the recipient is not available for focused interaction.

Of particular interest are the logs of one teenage couple in our study, which is a somewhat more intense version of couple communications that we saw in other instances. Their typical pattern is to begin sending a steady stream of email messages to each other after parting at school. These messages will continue through homework, dinner, television shows, and bath, and would culminate in voice contact in the late evening, lasting for an hour or more. A trail of messages might follow the voice call, ending in a good night exchange and revived again upon waking. On days that they were primarily at home in the evening, they sent 34 and 56 messages to each other. On days that they were out and about the numbers dwindled to 6 and 9. The content of the messages ranged from in-depth chat about relational issues, to coordination of when to make voice contact, to lightweight notification of their current activities and thoughts. In this case, and to a smaller degree for other couples living apart, messaging became a means for experiencing a sense of private contact and co-presence with a loved one even in the face of parental regulatory efforts and their inability to share any private physical space.

While mobile phones have become a vehicle for youths to challenge the power-geometries of places such as the home, the classroom, and the street, they have also created new disciplines and power-geometries, the need to be continuously available to friends and lovers, and the need to always carry a functioning mobile device. These disciplines are accompanied by new sets of social expectations and manners. When unable to return a message right away, young people feel that a social expectation has been violated. When one girl did not notice a message sent in the evening until the next morning, she says that she felt terrible. Three of the students in our diary study reported that they did not feel similar pressure to reply right away. Yet even in these cases, they acknowledged that there was a social expectation that a message should be responded to within about thirty minutes unless one had a legitimate reason, such as being asleep. One describes how he knows he should respond right away, but doesn't really care. Another, who had an atypical pattern of responding with longer, more deliberate messages hours later, said that her friends often chided her for being so slow. In another instance, a student did not receive a reply for a few hours, and his interlocutor excused himself by saying he didn't notice the message. The recipient perceived this as a permissible white lie that got around an onerous social expectation. All students who were asked about responses delayed an hour or more said that they would generally make a quick apology or excuse upon sending the tardy response. These exceptions to the norm of immediate response trace the contours of the technosocial situation as much as do conforming practices.

With couples living apart, there is an even greater sense of importance attached to the ongoing availability via messaging. The underside to the unobtrusive and ubiquitous nature of mobile email is that there are few legitimate excuses for not responding, particularly in the evening hours when one is at home. Five of the ten student couples in our study were in ongoing contact during the times when they were not at school, and all these couples had established practices for indicating their absence from the shared online space. They invariably send a good night email to signal unavailability, and would often send status checks during the day such as "are you awake?" or "are you done with work?" We saw a few cases when they would announce their intention to take a bath, a kind of virtual locking of the door. Him: "Just got home. Think I'll take a bath." Her: "Ya. Me too." Just as mobile workers struggle to maintain boundaries to between their work and personal lives, youths struggle to limit their availability to peers and intimates. The need to construct and mark these boundaries attests to the status of this ambient virtual peer space as an increasingly structuring and pervasive type of technosocial setting.

Cultural politics of youth mobile media

We have described how youth mobile email use has grown out of the imperatives of existing places of home, school, and public space, and in turn, constructs a new set of technosocial places dominated by the logic of peer relations. In line with our overall context-driven approach to understanding youth messaging practices, in this section we analyze how these ethnographic findings articulate with longstanding cultural politics and intergenerational struggles.

Postwar Japanese urban culture has featured a succession of highly visible but transient youth subcultures, often led by young women. In their essay on Japanese women and consumption, Lisa Skov and Brian Moeran (1995) describe how young Japanese women's central positing in media imagery and cultures of consumption are an inversion of their weak position in the labor market. Consumption and style, particularly of youth street cultures, is one cultural arena where young Japanese women have taken the lead, in part because of this marginal social status. Feminine consumerism represents an escape from the dominant rhythms of salaried labor. The more recent history of mobile media adoption is in line with this characterization of postwar consumer culture as an arena where the disenfranchised have taken leadership and control. The micro-negotiations we have described though our ethnographic cases, where young people have appropriated existing places and new technologies to create spaces of self-determination, are tied to these broader historical and structural trends. Although corporate ventures are quick to capitalize on new consumer youth trends, these emergent cultures also invite a series of efforts to reinvigorate existing (and still hegemonic) social structures and norms. The case of youth mobile media, at both the micro and the macro level, is characterized by the struggle between youth at the social margins discovering new means of organizing and communicating (with the help of consumer capitalism), and adults in the social mainstream seeking to regulate and redirect these efforts.

Although we could trace the origins of current mobile media to diary exchanges and note-passing in class, most trace current mobile messaging back to the pager cultures of the early nineties, when teenage girls first hijacked the uses of mobile media for their social purposes (Matsuda, 2005b; Okada, 2005; Okada & Matsuda, 2002). Pagers were originally conceived of as business tools for companies to beep their workers in the field, but only became popular mobile media after teenage girls adopted them. Okada (2005) describes how 1992 was a pivotal year in the development of mobile messaging. Spurred by reductions in subscriptions rates and new pagers that displayed a callback number on the terminal (as opposed to simply beeping), young users began adopting this new medium. In contrast to prior years, where business uses were central, 1993 saw individual users, mostly in their teens and twenties, beginning to dominate, comprising 70% of new subscriptions. Taking their cue from these trends, providers released new pager designs that could receive text as well as numbers. At the peak of their use in 1996, 48.8% of Tokyo middle and high school students had a pager.

Mobile phone providers took note and began piloting inexpensive text messaging services for mobile phone handsets in 1996 through 1997. Young people soon jumped onto the short message services purveyed by the Personal Handyphone System (PHS) and then moved on to cellular phone-based messaging. By 2002 pager subscriptions were on the decline and young users had largely switched to texting via mobile phones. When mobile Internet services were rolled out in Japan in the late nineties, they integrated the messaging functions that had previously been restricted mostly to short messages sent between subscribers of a particular provider. Japanese mobile Internet adoption was driven forward by mobile messaging as young people, for the first time, were able to send messages of varying length across different terminal devices and mobile service providers. Within a space of a few years between 1995-98, mobile phones shifted from association with business uses to an association with teen street culture. Many of the young women we interviewed who are heavy texters had started with pagers in their middle school years, moved on to PHS in high school, and are currently mobile Internet users. They see the different technologies as upgrades supporting the same underlying set of social practices.

Kenichi Fujimoto (2005) has tied this shift from business to play uses of mobile media to the growing hegemony of young girls in public space. He calls this transformation "The Girls' Pager Revolution." Unlike the male *otaku* (techno-geeks) associated with video games and computers, media savvy girls have been associated with communications technologies such as pagers and mobile phones. Through the nineties, young women and girls gained more strength in defining street cultures, and in the mid nineties, the media attached a new label to street-savvy high school girls: *kogyaru*. In the late nineties, certain *kogyaru* in urban centers sported bleached and frosted hair, extreme tropical fashions, tanned faces, heavy make-up, and customized mobile phones, becoming the object of widespread imitation by youth across the country and moral panic among adults (Cohen, 1972; Matsuda, 2005a). We started our ethnographic research in the waning years of extreme *kogyaru* street cultures. Though the high school girls we interviewed would not self-identify with these subcultures, most adopted related cultural forms, such as bleached hair, brightly colored fashions, and conspicuous mobile media use. Even with pundits declaring the death of the *kogyaru* at the turn of the millennium, this youth subculture has a lasting legacy in mobile texting cultures and related public perception of mobile media.

In line with the moral panics over *kogyaru* street cultures, public discourse has associated pagers and mobile phones with bad manners, declining morals, and a low-achievement, pleasure-seeking mentality. Mobile phones continue to be iconic of a fast and footloose street culture beyond the surveillance of the institutions of home and school. For example, there is widely reported practice called *enjo kousai* that started in the nineties, where high school girls, particularly *kogyaru,* meet older men on the street and date them for money. Although anonymous dating and prostitution was supported with voice mail services using payphones and landlines, public reports have associated mobile phones with growth of these practices among minors (Tomita, 2005). In one example of public uptake, the popular weekly magazine, *Aera,* ran a series of articles about *kogyaru* and *enjo kousai,* depicting Lolita-complex middle aged men and "old man hunting" teenagers meeting on the street, keeping in touch with pagers and mobile phones (Hayami, 1996). Mobile phones have been linked as well to a more general decline in morals and manners. In the late nineties, a series of articles described the annoyance of having to listen to young people engaging in trivial chit chat via mobiles on trains and buses, and public transportation facilities started prohibiting voice calls (Okabe & Ito, 2005). A cover of a recent best seller, *Keitai wo Motta Saru: "Ningen Rashisa" no Houkai* (Monkeys with Mobile Phones: The Collapse of Humanity), features three *kogyaru* on a subway, clutching mobile phones, legs splayed, talking loudly (Masataka, 2002).

Social and cultural research paints a different picture of young people's mobile media adoption. The young people in our studies were highly conscious of mobile phone manners and used their phones to keep in touch almost exclusively with family and close friends from school. Others have argued that mobile phones have made youths' relationships selective rather than superficial (Matsuda, 2000), and only a small minority of youth engage in anonymous dating (Habuchi, 2005; Tomita, 2005). In an earlier study of American and Japanese youth, Merry White (1994) describes highly consumerist youth cultures that are likely familiar to North Americans, but she sees fewer conflicts between Japanese parents and youths. Dependency has less social stigma that it does among Euro-American youths, and this is institutionalized in the protective functions of family that extend through college and often beyond. White also describes how youth are defined by marital and employment status rather than by age, and "such institutional definitions have more weight than social and psychological identities" (1994: 11). Arguably, youth culture in Japan has been subject to more concern since the nineties, after White completed her work. Yet our ethnographic research supports her overall findings, in that the regulatory and protective functions of institutions such as family and school still dominate the lives of Japanese youth into their twenties.

Conclusions

The leaders of the girls' pager revolution and the anti-authoritarian subcultures of *kogyaru* were the early adopters or a new set of technosocial practices that have infiltrated the everyday lives of mainstream Japanese youth on the backs of new mobile media. Our ethnographic findings attest to less confrontational but more pervasive practices of micro-negotiations with the hegemonic structures of home, school and urban space that carve out new spaces of action for young people. Although the low-profile exchange of messages among full-time intimate communities is a far cry from the more extroverted practices of *kogyaru* extreme fashion and *enjo kousai,* both ends of the spectrum are indicative of young people's everyday struggles to push back at the adult-controlled structures that govern their everyday lives. Adults, too, push back through public demonization of deviant youth as well as more everyday efforts to regulate mobile phone usage in schools, homes, and public settings.

This chapter has described some of the social conditions that have contextualized the unprecedented adoption of the mobile Internet by Japanese youth. Rather than focusing on factors "inherent" in the personality and cultures of Japanese young people, we have suggested attention to a broad set of historical, social, and cultural factors. Among these are the unique history of mobile messaging in their intersection with youth street cultures, as well as the power geometries of place the regulate youths' everyday lives and social contact. We have described youth messaging as a unique response to these existing patterns of social life based on their sense of connection and accountability to their peer relations. The intersection between mobile email and the life situations of Japanese youth have created a new set of technosocial practices and situations in support of distributed intimacy and pervasive lightweight contact. These practices are both novel and situated within a broad set of historical, social, and cultural contexts.

Acknowledgements

Portions of this chapte were excerpted from two prior papers, "Japanese Youth, Mobile Phones and the Re-Placement of Social Contact," and "Technosocial Situations: Emergent Structurings of Mobile Email Use." Research described here was supported by NTT Docomo and "Docomo House" at Keio University Shonan Fujisawa Campus, as well as by the Annenberg Center for Communication at the University of Southern California. We would like to thank Kenji Kohiyama and Hiromi Odaguchi of Docomo House and our student research assistants, Kunikazu Amagasa, Hiroshi Chihara, and Joko Taniguchi. This work has also benefited from the comments of Alex Taylor, Richard Harper, Robert Kraut, and our colleagues at the "K-Times" workshop at Keio University (particularly Misa Matsuda), and reviewers and participants at the conference "Front Stage/Back Stage: Mobile Communications and the Re-Negotiation of the Public Sphere" in Grimstad, Norway.

References

Agar, J. (2003). *Constant Touch: A Global History of the Mobile Phone*. Cambridge: Icon Books.
Alanen, L. (2001). Explorations in Generational Analysis. In L. Alanen & B. Mayall (Eds.), *Conceptualizing Child-Adult Relations* (pp. 11-22). New York: RoutledgeFalmer.
Boneva, B. S., Quinn, A., Kraut, R. E., Kiesler, S., & Shklovski, I. (Forthcoming). Instant Message Connectivity: Securing Friendships for Adolescents. In R. Kraut, M. Brynin & S. Kiesler (Eds.), *New Information Technologies at Home: The Domestic Impact of Computing and Telecommunicatons*. Oxford: Oxford University Press.
Cohen, S. (1972). *Fok Devils and Moral Panics*. London: MacGibbon and Kee.
Fujimoto, K. (2005). The Anti-Ubiquitous "Territory Machine"--The Third Period Paradigm: From "Girls' Pager Revolution" to "Mobile Aesthetics". In M. Ito, D. Okabe & M. Matsuda (Eds.), *Personal, Portable, Pedestrian: Mobile Phones in Japanese Life*. Cambridge: MIT Press.
Goffman, E. (1963). *Behavior in Public Places: Notes on the Social Organization of Gatherings*. New York: Free Press.
Green, N. (2002). Who's Watching Whom? Monitoring and Accountability in Mobile Relations. In B. Brown, N. Green & R. Harper (Eds.), *Wireless World: Social and Interactional Aspects of the Mobile Age* (pp. 32-45). London: Springer-Verlag.
Green, N. (2003). Outwardly Mobile: Young People and Mobile Technologies. In J. E. Katz (Ed.), *Machines that Become Us* (pp. 201-218). New Brunswick: Transaction Publishers.
Grinter, R. E., & Eldridge, M. A. (2001). *y do tngrs luv 2 txt msg?* Paper presented at the Seventh European Conference on Computer-Supported Cooperative Work, Bonn, Germany.
Habuchi, I. (2005). Accelerating Reflexivity. In M. Ito, D. Okabe & M. Matsuda (Eds.), *Personal, Portable, Pedestrian: Mobile Phones in Japanese Life*. Cambridge: MIT Press.

Harper, R. (2003). Are Mobiles Good or Bad for Society. In Nyiri, Mobile Democracy, Passengen Verlag,Vienna, (pp. 185-214).

Hayami, Y. (1996). Toragyaru tachi no osorubeki enjo kousai (The dangerous prostitution of tiger-gals). *Aera, 62.*

IPSe. (2003). *Third Annual Consumer Report: Survey Results from Research on Mobile Phone Usage.* Tokyo: IPSe Communications.

Ito, M. (forthcoming). Mobile Phones, Japanese Youth, and the Re-Placement of Social Contact. In R. Ling & P. Pederson (Ed.), *Mobile Communication and the Re-negotiation of the Public Sphere.* New York: Springer Verlag.

Ito, M., & Okabe, D. (2005). Technosocial Situations: Emergent Structurings of Mobile Email Use. In M. Ito, D. Okabe & M. Matsuda (Eds.), *Personal, Portable, Pedestrian: Mobile Phones in Japanese Life.* Cambridge: MIT Press.

Ito, M., Okabe, D., & Matsuda, M. (Eds.). (2005). *Personal, Portable, Pedestrian: Mobile Phones in Japanese Life.* Cambridge: MIT Press.

James, A., Jenks, C., & Prout, A. (Eds.). (1998). *Theorizing Childhood.* New York: Teachers College Press.

James, A., & Prout, A. (Eds.). (1997). *Constructing and Reconstructing Childhood: Contemporary Issues in the Sociological Study of Childhood* (Second ed.). Philadelphia: RoutledgeFarmer.

Kasesniemi, E.-L. (2003). *Mobile Messages: Young People and a New Communication Culture.* Tampere: Tampere University Press.

Kasesniemi, E.-L., & Rautianinen, P. (2002). Mobile culture of children and teenagers in Finland. In J. E. Katz & M. Aakhus (Eds.), *Perpetual Contact: Mobile Communication, Private Talk, Public Performance* (pp. 170-192). Cambridge: Cambridge University Press.

Ling, R., & Yttri, B. (2002). Hyper-coordination via mobile phones in Norway. In J. E. Katz & M. Aakhus (Eds.), *Perpetual Contact: Mobile Communication, Private Talk, Public Performance* (pp. 139-169). Cambridge: Cambridge University Press.

Masataka, N. (2002). *Kehtai wo Motta Saru: "Ningen Rashisa" no Houkai (Monkeys with Mobile Phones: The Collapse of Humanity).* Tokyo: Chuko Shinsho.

Massey, D. (1994). *Space, Place, and Gender.* Minneapolis: University of Minnesota Press.

Matsuda, M. (2000). Friendship of Young People and Their Usage of Mobile Phones: From the view of 'superficial relation' to 'selective relation'. *Shakai Jouhougaku Kenkyuu, 4,* 111-122.

Matsuda, M. (2005a). Introduction: Discourses of Keitai in Japan. In M. Ito, D. Okabe & M. Matsuda (Eds.), *Personal, Portable, Pedestrian: Mobile Phones in Japanese Life.* Cambridge: MIT Press.

Matsuda, M. (2005b). Mobile Communications and Selective Sociality. In M. Ito, D. Okabe & M. Matsuda (Eds.), *Personal, Portable, Pedestrian: Mobile Phones in Japanese LIfe.* Cambridge: MIT Press.

Mynatt, E., Adler, A., Ito, M., & O'Day, V. (1997). Network Communities: Something Old, Something New, Something Borrowed... *Computer Supported Cooperative Work, 6,* 1-35.

Nakajima, I., Keiichi, H., & Yoshii, H. (1999). *Ido-denwa Riyou no Fukyuu to sono Shakaiteki Imi* (Diffusion of Cellular Phones and PHS and their Social Meaning). *Tsuushin Gakkai-shi (Journal of Information and Communication Research), 16*(3).

Okabe, D., & Ito, M. (2005). Keitai and Public Transportation. In M. Ito, D. Okabe & M. Matsuda (Eds.), *Personal, Portable, Pedestrian: Mobile Phones in Japanese Life.* Cambridge: MIT.

Okada, T. (2005). The Social Reception and Construction of Mobile Media In Japan. In M. Ito, D. Okabe & M. Matsuda (Eds.), *Personal, Portable, Pedestrian: Mobile Phones in Japanese life*. Cambridge: MIT Press.

Okada, T., & Matsuda, M. (2002). *Keitaigaku Nyuumon*.

Rheingold, H. (2002). *Smart Mobs: The Next Social Revolution*. Cambridge: Perseus.

Skog, B. (2002). Mobiles and the Norweigian teen: identity, gender and class. In J. E. Katz & M. Aakhus (Eds.), *Perpetual Contact: Mobile Communications, Private Talk, Public Performance* (pp. 255-273). Cambridge: Cambridge University Press.

Taylor, A., & Harper, R. (2003). The gift of the gab?: A design oriented sociology of young people's use of mobiles. *Computer Supported Cooperative Work, pp267-297*.

Tomita, H. (2005). Keitai and the Intimate Stranger. In M. Ito, D. Okabe & M. Matsuda (Eds.), *Personal, Portable, Pedestrian: Mobile Phones in Japanese Life*. Cambridge: MIT Press.

VR. (2002). *Mobile Phone Usage Situation*. Tokyo: Video Research.

Weilenmann, A., & Larsson, C. (2002). Local Use and Sharing of Mobile Phones. In B. Brown, N. Green & R. Harper (Eds.), *Wireless World: Social and Interactional Aspects of the Mobile Age* (pp. 92-107). London: Springer-Verlag.

White, M. (1994). *The Material Child: Coming of Age in Japan and America*. Berkeley: University of California Press.

Yoshii, H., Matsuda, M., Habuchi, C., Dobashi, S., Iwata, K., & Kin, N. (2002). *Keitai Denwa Riyou no Shinka to sono Eikyou*. Tokyo: Mobile Communications Kenkyuukai.

7 The Breakthrough of Text Messaging in Finland

Timo Kopomaa

Introduction

A visionary of the new uses of the computer, Nicholas Negroponte (1995), who has studied the typical characteristics of digital interactivity, has claimed that nobody is interested in just keying in numbers; what we want is to reach people by phone. However, the handling of easily portable nomadic devices must offer some satisfaction, since SMS messages, which require digital agility, became very popular, first among young people; the rest of us have now followed. Fiddling with some object – a string of beads, a bunch of keys, a cigarette, and now perhaps mobile phones – is probably a very fundamental part of human nature, a means of obtaining pleasure.

In principle, SMS is an entirely independent form of communication which has nothing to do with telephones. In the late 1980s in Finland, it was generally assumed that text messages would eventually replace pagers; the first text messages were only 20 characters in length (Helsingin Sanomat, November 1998; Iltalehti, October 1998.) The first SMS messages were transmitted by telephone in Autumn 1993. The following year, less than ten percent of mobile phone users were using their phone for sending text messages. Up to 1996, mobile phone text messages were mainly used within companies. The breakthrough of text messaging took place in Finland in early 1997, when competing teleoperators were offering the service free of charge. Informative messages were soon complemented by messages sent for fun. In January-August 1998, the number of text messages had increased sevenfold from the previous year. Operators reported that SMS traffic had increased by a factor of ten during a period when the number of GSM subscriptions had merely doubled. By 2000, around one billion short messages were sent on Finnish mobile networks (Suomen tekstiviestimarkkinat 1999 – 2002, 2001). SMS messages have become even more popular among young people than making mobile calls (Kasesniemi 2003). Messages are mostly sent using a mobile phone, although sometimes from the Internet as well.

Richard Harper, Leysia Palen and Alex Taylor (Eds), The Inside Text: Social, Cultural and Design Perspectives on SMS, 147–159.
© 2005 *Springer. Printed in the Netherlands.*

The following observations on the use of text messaging are based on group interviews and observations as well as on a pilot survey, in which school children were interviewed about the contents and significance of text messages (Kopomaa 2000, 133-135). Pilot study interviews were conducted with a total of 21 youths, of whom 18 were upper secondary school pupils of 15 to 18 years of age. Preparatory interviews had been conducted with three young adults, students of 19 to 22 years of age. The average age of the school pupils and students was 17. There were 10 males and 11 females among the interviewees. The interviews were conducted in Helsinki in October 1999. The school pupils were contacted at Malmi upper secondary school during a Finnish composition class. Interviewees were selected from among these youths who used text messaging and who said they were willing to take part in the interviews.

The interviewed school pupils sent an average of 3 to 7 text messages per day. The number of sent messages per day varied from one to twenty. Text messaging among the adolescents was interactive in the sense that they estimated that they received about as many messages as they sent. The eighteen school children interviewed sent messages more actively than the three students, who were a few years older. The average mobile phone bill among the interviewees was 44 € per month. The smallest reported bill was 10 €, the largest 150 € per month.

Continuous use

The typical things communicated by text messaging included the setting up of meetings, exchanging the latest gossip, giving information and reminders, or asking about shared activities from one's friends, for example: "Is there a training session today?", "Will you come to pick me up?", "What time does school start?". SMS transforms the mobile phone into a kind of electronic bulletin board, where you can post questions to await an answer. The sending of text messages also embodies the idea of living in synchrony. Everyday life and its activities are anchored to accessible people who operate in the same rhythm with oneself.

> *Some guy sends a message that he'll be coming on a certain train, that he'll be there at such and such a time. It's a bit like he was already there. (Topi, 26)*

SMS messages are the preferred form of communication when the message is concise and informative, with no need for discussion. Such messages include lists of things to buy at the store, and short, postcard-like greetings to brighten the day. Also, written messages can always be read again at a later time. The forms of contact-making clearly generated by the service itself include "idiot messages", specifically circular or chain messages whose purpose is to kill time and that are sent to several recipients at once, as well as jokes and funny images.

But why have text messages become so popular? What is the attraction? The threshold for making contact is lower with text messages than with voice calls. The reason for sending a text message may be just the desire to maintain contact, or to be polite. One of the interviewees made it clear that for him sending a text message felt often more troublesome than initiating a phone call. On the other hand, another summarised the advantages of text messages: "When the threshold of contacting someone is great, it becomes lower with the text message". SMS messages are a substitute for conversation and an alternative to being obligated to speak, which is why text messages are commonly used to ask someone out on a first date. With written text, it is sometimes easier to express your hopes and will in accurate ways.

One man in his twenties pointed out that the service is not used to send hostile or aggressive messages. A certain positive ambience and openness is characteristic of SMS messages. "Short" text messaging gives less possibilities for deep discussions compared to e-mail, for example, and in this way it is also probably a less confrontational medium.

Young people clearly appreciate the low cost of the service, especially when the alternative, even at its shortest, is a phone conversation demanding a modicum of small talk. As owners of mobile phones, young people keep a close eye on their phone bill, and they follow keenly which teleoperator has the lowest rates at any given time. The school children in the study estimated that just under half of their phone bills consisted of charges for text messages. Parents tended to pay part of their children's mobile phone bills. Most of the interviewees had also used commercial text message services. The services mentioned included directory assistance, account information, timetables, downloading images for the mobile phone screen, horoscopes or biorhythms, and the weather service. In addition, operators now offer charge limit services, which prevent phone bills from exceeding a set amount. In other words, this is a service to limit the use of the mobile phone, which suggests that indebtedness due to mobile phone use is a common problem.

Text messages are sent in much the same way as calls are made on the mobile phone: at home and at school, in the workplace and on public transportation. Messages can be read just like a pocket book, either on the move or while stationary. Girls used the service at home more than boys. Boys' use of text messages is more clearly associated with seeking contact with friends outside of the home, in the place of study or in transit, than is the case with girls. The fact that text messages are often sent while walking emphasises the "placeless" quality of mobile communication and its link with outward circumstances and needs ("I'm bored") rather than a particular place ("when you get a message"). When the interviewees were asked if there were any particular places they used for sending text messages, the answers included locations which represent the "living room" of the city: cafes and cafeterias, restaurants and pubs, or the bus. Messages are sent in various situations and states of mind, which include waiting, idleness, need for company and various pressing needs. One in four of the interviewees said that text messages are too cumbersome to send when you're busy walking down the street.

Adolescents also send text messages from places where other forms of communication are not possible, such as a cinema or a restaurant, where speaking is either difficult or impossible due to the situation or noise. Text messages can be composed not only in noisy environments, but also in areas where the phone connection is poor or with a phone whose battery is running low.

Text messages are a form of speech processing, a kind of visible speech. Opening and sending messages is used to fill otherwise empty moments; sending messages is a handy way of killing time. Composing text messages in all kinds of places is akin to the tendency, found in children's play, to move away from inactivity towards activity. The text message transports the sender's thoughts to the recipient, offering the sender freedom from the constraints of the immediate environment; the aim is escape. However, escape in this case is primarily based on the contact established with the recipient rather than a wish to get away from one's physical setting. SMS messages received at work offer a welcome opportunity to take a break, a moment for oneself. The senders and readers share a certain ritualistic relationship to the message: the message is a closed world, a joint arena for action for the senders and recipients alike.

Young people sending text messages to each other seem to derive only pleasure from the interruption caused by the arrival of a message. Messages fly back and forth in a merry dance, and the phone gives a beep to signal the arrival of yet another message. Of course, messages are also saved for perusal at a later time, for a more appropriate moment. Almost any situation can be suitable for sending a text message – even in the middle of the night, during a concert or in a cinema. The moment for sending and receiving text messages is less bound to time than making voice calls. In fact, there are no inappropriate times for this kind of communication. For example, users may send text messages to announce the score of a game in real-time, or the results of an examination or a medical test. Text messaging allows the maintenance of social contacts in an unobtrusive way. Interaction with others and the carrying of a phone and writing messages are the most natural things on earth.

> There's actually quite a lot text messages flying about. You can say you're moving to the next bar, or on the way to have a cup of coffee or something. It's like a kind of unnoticed continuous use. (Minna, 25)

Brevity and conciseness are key features of SMS messages. The writer must have mastered the art of abbreviation, otherwise writing would not be smooth. Like e-mail, text messages are a kind of conversational medium. In this respect, SMS messages differ from the postcard, although their brevity and content are akin to the telegraphic, condensed form of communication used in postcards. This postcard likeness is very clear especially now when people send photos using mobile multimedia, or MMS (Koskinen et al. 2002). In text messages, typically, many abbreviations and abbreviated words are used, as well as various catch phrases typically in English, such as *sorry, ok*.

The mobile phone seems to increase private communication – in spite of the fact that calls and messages are made from public places. Text messages are from the start, by their nature, private in the sense that letters are, but often messages are shared with others by reading them aloud. Indeed, the most serious mistake associated with text messaging is sending a private message to the wrong number, the wrong recipient.

Text messages are used to anticipate future meetings and to ensure that meetings are not missed. A message can include notice of an invitation or the necessary information such as time, sender, time of arrival, and place. Surprisingly, some youths had a critical attitude towards text messages as a medium for setting up dates, although half of the interviewees considered the service as a convenient way of doing so. Girls took a more positive view than boys towards using text messages for this purpose. A witty text message, one which the sender would not perhaps dare to say aloud, is interpreted as a friendly proposal or an attempt to create friendly contact.

> *What you can send [as a text message], it's something else, speech and written language are so different, so that when you write something, you can send as text verbal gimmicks which you'd never use in spoken language. (Iina, 21)*

> *That's right. (Marke, 24)*

> *Then there are lots of people, like, especially my friends send the kind of messages to, let's say some guys, that they'd never say aloud what they write. (Iina, 21)*

> *Then you have those animations, I've got my phone full of them right now (laughs). (Marke, 24)*

> Interviewer: *What kind of images are they?*

> *You know, sort of off-colour. (Tomi, 22)*

Those who prefer setting up dates by text message feel that it is socially less awkward than making a phone call. Sending an invitation by text message decreases tension and avoids embarrassment, and "getting turned down doesn't hurt as much". Reaction to the tone of the invitation and verbal interaction are temporarily avoided. SMS messaging allows the conditions of the meeting to be softened, so that perhaps only the time and the place are determined and the pressures concerning the success of the date are moved to a future time, to the actual time of the meeting.

Playful text messaging?

The focus of SMS messages is on entertainment and socialising but also in the exchange of information. Two-thirds of the school children interviewed said text messages are more for fun than for a serious purpose: on the average, 35% of the messages contained factual information, 65% were sent for fun. But for sure, both types were present. All of the girls interviewed emphasised the fun aspect of the messages rather than their informational content. With age, however, the proportion of informational messages is likely to increase. Messages can contain informational content among young people, for example, inquiries concerning what to buy something, asking a friend for an opinion about a CD or film, etc. Text messaging seems to be used often to seek support when the writer is feeling low or insecure (Kasesniemi 2003, 169). SMS does not appear to be purely a communication medium for light-hearted playfulness.

Only three of the interviewees had received hoax messages. These included messages like "Your phone has been disconnected", "Your phone bill has exceeded the limit", "Enter SIM code", "Give SIM card", "Keys locked", "Message centre informs", "Message received". Such hoax messages typically imitated notices from the teleoperator. According to information from a teleoperator in 1998, there were a number of hoax messages being sent around, although it would be more to the point to say that there were many active pranksters at work. Two of the young men had received advertisements telling them to call sex lines. Also "chain letters" are found among text messages. The usual reaction to such invitations to improve one's fortunes is humour, and if such messages are forwarded to others, it is usually done tongue-in-cheek. Instrumental, playful and perhaps even artistic aims become mixed in the domain of digital media. Most of the circulated SMS letters are local ones (see also Pertierra et al. 2002), but they might in some cases be global, written in English. Lately there have been stories in the media about cases of sexual harassment done via text messaging.

Text messages are often embellished with some kind of personal touch. Playful messages have a unifying social effect and leave no room for power games. In *Homo ludens*, a study of the play element in human culture published in 1949, Johan Huitzinga makes the observation that where the element of play increases, the importance of power correspondingly weakens. Inventing new combinations of signs to send others has a very strong playful element in it. A speedy reply is a sign of a warm and close relationship between the sender and the recipient. A clever or funny message also inspires the recipient to reply immediately, even when the sender clearly does not expect any reaction.

Mobile phones are "toy objects" (Morris 1977, 268), which affect a great shift with a small move: "press the button" and you are contacting people on the other side of the planet. As a tool for play – and games – the mobile phone has shown its social potential. With the simple action of pressing a button, users play games like shutting down the phone just when the call is being answered.

Users of text messages have used the signs available on the phone's keypad to make new combinations. Common elements in such messages are round brackets and other punctuation marks, which are used to create so-called *smileys* or *emoticons*. As their name implies, they imitate facial expressions, which represents an attempt to reclaim telephone communication or e-mail back into the realm of face-to-face communication (Kitchin 1998, 7). Also "animations", images that move at the press of a button, have been created.

Girls reported using special signs like smileys in their messages more than boys, indicating their greater commitment to the intimate, emotional register of communication. The images are usually used to express emotions, joy or sadness. The interviews contained a couple of mentions of a special Christmas icon, an elf. Other smileys used by girls included a smiling face, a rose, as well as the ready-made icons supplied with the phone, such as a heart, a handshake, or people. Downloadable icons are a popular mobile media feature.

:-)	Smile	:'-(	Tearful	<:-)	Christmas elf
;-)	Wink	%-)	Perplexed	:-X	Sealed lips or a kiss
:-(	Sad	:-D	Laughing	@-->-->--	A rose
:-I	Serious	^v	Speaking		
:-II	Angry	5:-)	Elvis		

Figure 1: Smileys used in text messages and e-mail

Some of the interviewed schoolgirls had drawn messages on paper to ensure the quality and correct outcome of the message. These messages contained both moving animations as well as static images. Such images – a cow, a teddy bear, a car – are intended as humorous, while an animated image is also an indication of the sender's creativity.

Often the adoption of a new technology takes place in discrete stages. Thus, we may say that the rapid spread of mobile phones was at first characterised by enthusiasm and novelty, then came a phase of sobering up and the transformation of novelty into invisibility. In contradiction to this stage of "sobering up", the playful attitude towards mobile phones is likely to survive into the future. There is also a huge trend to offer commercial media from popular culture, e.g. games, through mobile phones, in both visual and audio form. Besides young people and the business sector, women are perhaps the newest target group to request these latest applications.

Group messages

SMS messages are essentially private, but they can also be shared collectively. A message sent to a group of people reaches a limited circle of friends, who may perhaps read the message aloud or show it to others who happen to be present. Some Nordic studies on collective use of mobile phones, for example, reveal that teenagers share text material in concrete and symbolic ways. Text messages are circulated among friends, composed together, with fitting expressions or entire messages are borrowed from others. This collective behaviour contrasts with the emphasis placed on mobiles' private and personal nature by advertisers. As the message reaches a specified group of people, a kind of "instant community" is created in real-time. Thus mobile phones offer a forum for the circle of friends, allowing them to discuss shared interests or offer information about themselves.

Two-thirds of the school-aged subjects had sent messages to several people at once. The boys seemed to use this possibility slightly more often than the girls. The typical group message was one of a more general interest, or a funny story or joke. "Stupid" messages are often shown to friends: "Look what I got!" Messages that are difficult to decipher also generate shared readings, when the message requires interpretation by a friend.

Interview participants had not used the group text message service; instead, they had keyed in the recipients' numbers individually. This might provide the possibility to individualise the message for different recipients. The number of recipients of group messages varied from two to five. Thus the group of recipients comprised a small circle of close friends and acquaintances who have a mobile phone. The most common uses of group messages were for meeting arrangements, humorous texts, and other messages specially intended for circulation, e.g. chain messages, greeting texts. The aspect of synchronised time also emerged in that messages were sometimes composed when something peculiar appeared in the sender's surroundings, something that deviated from the ordinary course of events. The young people also used text messages the way they would greeting cards, to mark formal occasions. Such occasions included Christmas, New Year, First of May and Midsummer, as well as birthdays and name days.

Problems and luck in interpretation

Text messages form a complement to voice communication. Half of the interviewees used text messages as a substitute for a voice call; this applied especially to boys. One young man said that he kept in contact with a friend who lived in another city solely by SMS messages.

When asked whether they felt that text messages constitute a form of control, one-third of the interviewees gave an affirmative reply. One of the girls even felt that the messages represented "oppression". The controlling party was identified as a girlfriend, a buddy, parents, and even, in a way, the very existence of the phone. Although the mobile phone has increased parents' control of the whereabouts of their children, it also means that they are increasingly out of touch with their children's circle of friends (Coogan & Kangas 2001). Along with the new social forms of interaction, differences between the sexes in the use of telecommunication have attracted attention, with good reason (Moyal 1992). Although the use of SMS messages brings out the gendered power relations inherent in courting and dating practices, the messages are not only an indication of sexual control, but of attraction as well.

Areas which were the exclusive property of girls in the sphere of SMS messages included poems, horoscopes and biorhythms. Similar to the boys' messages on "things about women" which were shared with friends, the girls too had their own chain messages. Many girls said that boys tend to express things in their messages in a more direct way than girls, who have a greater tendency to beat around the bush.

Text messages are not always replied to with another text message. Often the reply took the form of a voice call, especially when there were lots of things to say, or the topic otherwise demanded it. The general tendency was to reply to a text message immediately after its reception. In this, the girls were perhaps a bit more conscientious than the boys. Sometimes the maximum message length was exceeded, in which case two separate messages were used, thus effectively multiplying the length limit of 160 characters. Such a message is no longer a "short message", as the name would imply.

According to some of the young people interviewed, text messages are not suitable for subjects that require extensive discussion. The problem is that the service encourages a concise, "telegraphic" style characterised by short lines and sometimes even a reckless disregard of the rules of written communication – "when you have to squeeze the message into a small space" – which can easily lead to misunderstandings. Sometimes, due to the formulation of the message, the gravity of the content or the intended mood of the message fails to come across. Some of the boys felt that the girls' written style was clearer than that of boys.

Unclear messages are interpreted with the help of friends. One half of the young people had asked a friend to help decipher a message. The person to whom the message is shown is usually a close friend, a buddy or a mate, or a relative. Some of these messages fail to be interpreted even with the help of another person, which makes them subject to special concern, although special attention is also paid to messages that are saved in the memory of the phone. Messages that are saved are usually text or images that are regarded as exceptionally rare, memorable or pleasurable.

One inherent quality of text messages, one that is perhaps even stronger than in the case of voice calls made on the mobile phone, is their capacity to surprise. The beep that signals the arrival of a message may bring welcome attention to the recipient when others are around to also hear it (e.g. in a quiet classroom). The downside was, according to the interviewees, that it may sometimes feel laborious to answer messages. Additionally, one young participant said that you may be looking forward so much to receiving a message that it is difficult to concentrate on other things.

One of the problems of SMS messages, and one that e-mail shares, is that the sender does not know if the message has been received, or when the recipient will read it. On the other hand, the recipient may be uncertain of the sender, specifically whether the message in fact originates from the owner of the phone.

The upper secondary school pupils who were interviewed did not generally use e-mail. This was also the reason why text messages are not a complement to their e-mail communication, which was not the case for the three older students who were interviewed. The fact that they do not use e-mail was one factor that intensified the popularity of text messages among the school children. Moreover, the personal nature and the here-and-now quality of SMS messages – with messages like "Hi, how R U doing?" – seems to serve the needs of the young very well. Some of the girls did report that text messages replaced their use of e-mail, which is probably connected to girls' tendency to send "chatty" messages. To some extent, text messages also serve as a substitute for letter writing.

The interviewees' comments regarding the speed or slowness of the SMS service may be explained by reference to time and schedules or their flexibility, as well as their pivotal status not only within the culture of mobile phones, but also in the "culture of textual messages".

Sharing the same rhythm – synchronous living

Mobile phone manufacturers have increased the typing speed of text messages by predictive text input and miniature keyboards. At the same time the writing skills of young people have developed significantly. The significance of SMS messages as a factor that dissolves the limitations of time and space is exceptionally clear in the everyday life of young people. Apart from the fact that they use text messages widely and flexibly in a variety of circumstances and situations, the exchange of text messages also represents a sphere of freedom, which lies outside the authoritative control of parents and teachers. It has been observed prior to the advent of mobile phones that new technologies, such as the portable transistor radio or the walkman, offer young people an instrument for spending time pleasurably. These portable companions have always been outside the control and influence of parents (Hall 1998, 586). The everyday life of young people is generally circumscribed by the rules and definitions of other persons telling them where and when and what they must or must not do.

The mobile phone does not eliminate situational or spatial existence and obligations, but it does introduce a new dimension to them, and the possibility to withdraw into another world mediated by text messages. Text messages are an instrument for avoiding or skirting the habitual boundaries and limitations of everyday life. When you have to be silent, you can still send a text message, and the same applies to noisy surroundings. It may be too late at night to make a phone call, but it's never too late to send a SMS message. And when you've forgotten to be in touch with your friend, a text message may still reach him or her "in time".

Descriptions of contemporary man as living in the "city of bytes" and in a networked society tend to emphasise the de-synchronization of life as a useful and important possibility that technology now affords (Negroponte 1995; Mitchell 1996; Castells 1996). However, in contrast to this observation, we see that modern everyday life is very often characterised by a tendency to live *in synchrony*. Text messaging, which allows constant interaction and near-instantaneous response, satisfies this desire, allowing the activities of everyday life to be tied to people who remain synchronized and accessible despite distance.

Conclusions

It is typical of people to find it is easier to send a text message than make a call to someone else at home, at work, at school or somewhere in between these everyday arenas. The threshold for making contact is lower with text messages than with voice calls. Users might find no reason to call, but surely they find one for sending a SMS. One common everyday exception of this is a situation, in which the caller finds it more burdensome to write down a text message and prefers to reach a person by making a call.

Text messaging is mostly used between friends or those one knows well – or might like to know. Sending messages is described as a communication media in between calling and sending email. Language seems to be less strictly regulated compared, e.g., to emails. People are skipping the conventional letter writing formalities in text messages.

By sending messages people act in a 'texting world', it is a communication sphere of its own. Writing and reading messages is a ritualistic process where the exchange of text messages is creating a closed world and a shared forum of participation between the friends. Sending SMS messages is not only a private form of communication but also a collective practice: texts are shared with others, shown to friends and sometimes circulated as group messages between (tele)partners. Digital communication has engendered shared, collective practices which are characterised by a new communality, nomadic tribes and digital neighbours.

People send text messages while waiting, when they are feeling idle, have need for company or other pressing needs for contact taking. Young people favour text messaging because they have found it to be cheap. The price of a SMS service is often compared to that of cellphone calls, not to the quantity or the value of the information of the sent message. In this context, such services as ring tones and icons have been surprisingly popular.

Free from the limits of time and space, the 'placeless' mobile communication, such as text messaging, is typically used in certain urban environments, on public transport, in cafés and in extreme environments of communication, such as noisy rock-concerts, silent libraries and dark cinemas full of people. SMS offers the sender freedom from the constraints of the immediate environment. People seek contact to the 'outside world' – and life always seems to be somewhere else!

The messages are used to reinforce the connection between people. Children primarily send text messages to their immediate family and close relatives, such as grandparents. Teenagers send messages to friends but also to family, parents and siblings to organise everyday life, such as agreeing on schedules or informing others about a change of plan. 'Family messages' are frequently practical. For elderly people text messaging involves a skill not yet available to everybody.

SMS is rarely used for deep discussions, though it is not an excluded alternative: good friends express their life experiences in real time or tell about serious things, they are not just about having fun. Some messages are valued with such a degree of pleasure, as being informative or memorable that they are saved in the phone's emory.

Having a mobile communication device allows people to live with acquaintances, in a situation in which time and space no longer restrict contact. SMS is a media for personal discussion and it requires an answer. With mobile phones the management of all kinds of affairs becomes a continuous project, while a 'culture of interruption' also develops as contacts wait to be consummated. Small wonder, then, that people find it difficult to distance themselves from this and to rationally select the information they want to receive. SMS provides an instant and mobile way to communicate *synchronously*. People reach out to act in synchrony, which also seems to be the case regarding video messaging. Early observations show that users will communicate about their feelings and events, in which movement is present. Moving pictures and digital still-photos about surrounding landscapes will surely strengthen the experience of the movement and give new meanings to the localities.

Acknowledgements

This chapter is an updated version of Chapter 4. SMS Messages – Visible Speech, from the book *The City in Your Pocket: Birth of the Mobile Information Society* (see Kopomaa 2000, pp. 60-77).

References

Castells, Manuel (1996). *The Rise of the Network Society*. Oxford: Blackwell Publishers.

Coogan, Kaisa & Kangas, Sonja (2000). *Nufix – Nuoret ja kommunikaatio-akrobatia. 16–18 – vuotiaiden kännykkä- ja internet-kulttuurit* [Young people and Communication Acrobatics. *The Mobile Phone and Internet Cultures of 16- to 18-year-olds*]. Elisa Research Centre, report no. 158. Elisa Communications and Finnish Youth Research Network.

Hall, Peter (1998). *Cities in Civilization. Culture, Innovation, and Urban Order*. London: Phoenix Giant.

Helsingin Sanomat, weekly supplement, 20.11-26.11.1998, 17, Digitaaliset muistilaput tulivat [Digital memos are here].

Huitzinga, Johan (1949). *Homo Ludens: A Study of the Play-Element in Culture*. London: Routledge and Kegan Paul; reprint, Temple Smith, London, 1970.

Iltalehti 24.10.1998, 13-17, *Täydellinen tekstiviesti* [The Ultimate Text Message].

Kasesniemi, Eija-Liisa (2003). *Mobile Messages. Young People and a New Communication Culture*. Tampere: Tampere University Press.

Kitchin, Rob (1998). *Cyberspace. The World in the Wires*. Chichester: John Wiley & Sons.

Kopomaa, Timo (2000). *The City in your pocket: Birth of the Mobile Information Society*. Helsinki: Gaudeamus.

Koskinen, Ilpo & Kurvinen, Esko & Lehtonen, Turo-Kimmo (2002*). Mobile Image*. Helsinki: Edita, IT-Press.

Mitchell, William J. (1996). *City of Bites*. Cambridge, Massachusetts: MIT Press.

Morris, Desmond (1977). *Manwatching: a field guide to human behavior*. London: Jonathan Cape.

Moyal, Ann (1992). The Gendered Use of the Telephone: an Australian Case Study'. *Media, Culture & Society,* 14(1), 51-72.

Negroponte, Nicholas (1995). *Being Digital.* New York: Knopf.

Pertierra, Raul et al. (2002). *Txt-ing Selves: Cellphones and Philippine Modernity.* Manila: De La Salle Press.

Suomen tekstiviestimarkkinat 1998-2002 [*The Short Messaging Service Market in Finland Between 1998 and 2002] (2001).* Publications of the Ministry of Transport and Communications 20/2001. Helsinki: Edita.

8   SMS Use Among Deaf Teens and Young Adults in Norway

Frøydis Bakken

Introduction

SMS is first and foremost a technology that gives the user an informal channel for communication across distance. Norway is among the countries in the world with the highest usage of SMS, with the penetration of mobile telephones among 13-20 year olds at 95% (Ling 2001a).

A feature in the adolescent culture is the need to coordinate interaction with friends and to be available in a social network. For many teens and young adults, it is important to be informed, to know the whereabouts of friends are and what they are doing. The mobile telephone and SMS was thus ideal for covering all these needs (Froenes and Brusdal 2000). The need to be available is a common one for all young people, regardless of their hearing status. Teens and young adults, both deaf and hearing, have the same social needs and seek devices that can help fulfil them.

Hearing status has inherent social implications, and many deaf people feel isolated because they lack a common form of communication. The deaf must participate in both the deaf and the hearing cultures, whether they like it or not. The official language of the country is Norwegian but the deaf use sign language, making them a linguistic minority. Within the deaf community, where all communication takes place in sign language, the interaction works adequately. It is only when society fails to meet the special needs of the deaf that deafness becomes and is perceived as a disability. Different forms of adaptation by the deaf themselves or by their surroundings may reduce the perception that hearing impairment is a disability. This chapter will explore the social implications of SMS use in relation to these issues of social networking and linguistic and social isolation.

SMS was brought into use by the hearing impaired through their own initiative. Adoption has literally taken place without the knowledge or intention of SMS developers and providers (Lindstroem 2001). First, the special needs of this group were not taken into consideration. Second, there is no obvious potential for the profitable production of specifically designed equipment. This means that the deaf

Richard Harper, Leysia Palen and Alex Taylor (Eds), The Inside Text: Social, Cultural and Design Perspectives on SMS, 161–174.
© 2005 *Springer. Printed in the Netherlands.*

represent a small group of consumers, and most of the other products developed for this group are financed by public sources.

The deaf and their technologies

The deaf in Norway

The deaf in Norway communicate in Norwegian Sign Language and, as noted, they are often considered a linguistic minority. Their first language is sign language, and their second language is written Norwegian. Statistically 0.1 % of the population is estimated to be deaf (about 4000–5000 people). In addition, many people who are hard of hearing are also users of Norwegian sign language. This latter group amounts to approximately 180 000 people (Oestberg 1998).

Hearing impairment can be divided into deafness and hard of hearing, although the research reported here focuses primarily on deafness. Deafness itself has been defined by several different professional disciplines. The three most central definitions are the cultural, the medical, and the social definitions of deafness.

Culturally, deafness is closely connected to sign language literacy. A person is defined as culturally deaf when he or she has a severely reduced hearing capacity and identifies himself or herself with the deaf community, i.e., he or she is part of a network in which communication is based on sign language (Breivik 2001).

A medical definition of deafness focuses more on the actual loss of hearing. This view is also known as the compensatory definition of deafness.[1] It considers loss of hearing as a defect and suggests measures to compensate for this. Cochlea Implants (CI), for example, are one solution that can improve hearing capacity, but will rarely be completely adequate. However, it provides the possibility to communicate using oral language. Another compensatory approach is the hearing aid, which can be useful if the person is not completely deaf.

Deafness can be seen in relation to both individual and group aspects, and as social and cultural phenomena. On an individual level, deafness can be compensated for by learning sign language or by using a CI to enhance hearing capability. Socially, access to information and communication within the deaf community as well as the broader community of the hearing is emphasised. The former reflects the medical perception of deafness, and the latter the cultural (Oestberg 1998).

Although the deaf are defined as disabled by hearing society, many hearing impaired people take deafness for granted and do not see themselves as different from the norm. The view often taken in the Norwegian society – that the greater the loss of hearing, the greater the deviation from what is normal – is a view held by hearing people, and is at odds with the view held among the deaf. Their identity is

---

[1] The assessment of a person's hearing ability is measured in decibels by audiographic equipment. Hearing capacity that is reduced by 30–90 decibels is defined as hard of hearing. Deafness is defined by loss that exceeds 90 decibels. According to the medical and compensatory definition, deaf people are considered disabled.

determined by their deafness, but that does not mean that they conceive this particular kind of condition as deviant. Rather their deafness has contributed to common experiences and has created a linguistic community with common values and interests. Measures aimed at restoring hearing ability, or alternatively compensating for hearing impairment, like the CI, are looked upon with reluctance by some deaf people, as it may imply that they are not accepted as they are (Ohna 2000).

The social, like the cultural, definition emphasises language, but it orientates towards the fact that so few in Norway understand sign language, and thus the deaf become isolated. The social definition stresses that deafness not only depends on the degree to which one has a loss of hearing, but also social interaction. It is not the degree of loss of hearing that is important; rather it is the loss of hearing's effect on the deaf person's possibilities for communication. According to this definition, a person is socially deaf when he or she has a reduced ability for communicative interaction with other people regardless of their degree of hearing loss. This definition sheds light on several aspects beyond the medical and cultural definitions, and will be the central definition in this chapter (Oestberg 1998).

Deafness also has social implications when the deaf are unable to communicate with hearing people who do not understand sign language. This problem is often perceived as a problem for the deaf person only, because the hearing person is considered to be normal, and the deaf deviant. The deaf participate in both the deaf and the hearing culture. When the deaf are together with other members of the deaf community, and all communication takes place in sign language, the interaction works well. It is only when society fails to accommodate the deaf that deafness becomes a disability. An example would be a television programme without subtitling. Thus, defining the deaf as disabled per se is not adequate, as it depends on the situation and to what extent society accommodates the group (Ohna 2000).

Technology for the deaf

SMS is considered a relatively new technology in Norway, with its breakthrough in the mid-1990s, when it soon after became integrated into the deaf community. Throughout history, however, several technologies have been presented as useful for the deaf and hard of hearing. Some of these were developed especially with the deaf in mind, while others were developed on a more general basis, though proved to be of great utility for deaf and hard of hearing. The domestic telephone with text function appeared in Norway for the first time in 1970's. This development was of great significance for the deaf, and was for a long time the only way they could communicate real-time across distance. Communication between two such telephones can be compared to today's chatting on the Internet. This analogy includes the implication that interlocutors both have such a special telephone. If a deaf person who possesses a telephone with text function, wants to call a hearing person who does not have access to a telephone with text function, it is possible to communicate through an interpretation service. In Norway, this service is accessed by dialing the telephone number, "149". The hearing impaired person using 149 types in a message that is then translated into oral Norwegian by the operator. The oral message of the hearing person is translated into text by the operator.[2]

The study

Methods

The findings presented in this chapter are based on data collected in 13 qualitative interviews with Norwegians teens and young adults who ranged in age from 15 – 27 years. The data collection took place in Spring 2002, from March through early June. Among these 13 interviewees, eight were deaf and five were hearing. Hearing status is an important dimension in this analysis and thus separate analytical categories of "deaf" and "hearing" have been used. The main reason for choosing to interview both deaf and hearing people was to see if and how hearing status might make a difference in the use of SMS technology.

The recruitment of the interviewees was based on two criteria. First, all had to be SMS users at the time of the study, although how long they had owned a mobile telephone was not taken into consideration. Secondly, they had to be either teens or young adults. The lower age limit was set to 15 years and the upper was loosely set at the mid-20s. Based on these criteria, the result was five subjects at the age of 15, one at 17, one at 18, two at 19, one at 20, one at 23, and two at 27. Only two of these were males, one deaf and one hearing. The hearing status of the others interviewees, all females, ranged from hard of hearing to deaf. For those hard of hearing, it was an important criterion that they used sign language so that they could be defined as culturally deaf. An interpreter was used in the interviews with the deaf.

Theoretical grounding

Network theory

In the article "The strength of weak ties" (Granovetter 1973), Mark Granovetter uses network analysis to explain processes of diffusion between individuals within social groups of different size. He argues that the processes that take place in interpersonal networks provide the most fruitful micro-macro bridge, where interaction on the individual level is translated into aggregated patterns which feed back into networks and small groups (Granovetter 1973: 1360).

Granovetter argues that to what degree networks of two individuals overlap varies with the strength of the tie to one another. The stronger the tie, the greater the

---

[2] Another technology that could be beneficial for the deaf is a telephone with the capability to transmit video signals. Those exist, but are not very widespread in Norway. It requires a very high transmission capacity, and has thus been considered too costly. However, the deaf have expressed that this is a missed opportunity. Along the same lines is the mobile multi MMS service. The use of MMS has recently exploded in Norway. This is technology that normally would fit the needs of the deaf, as many deaf tend to prefer visual communication over textual.

overlap in networks. Weak ties are relevant in relation to macro phenomena like diffusion and political organization. If one tells a rumour to all his close friends, and they do likewise, many will hear the rumour a second and third time since those linked by strong ties tend to share friends.

What is interesting in this process are weak ties because they tend to work as channels of communication and bring information to new networks. They also work as bridges in the process of diffusion and spread the information efficiently. A tie can be strong, weak or absent, and what decides "the strength of a tie is – a (probably linear) combination of the amount of time, the emotional intensity, the intimacy (mutual confiding), and the reciprocal services which characterize the tie" (Granovetter 1973: 1361). That means strong ties exist between individuals who are close to one another and see each other on a regular basis, while weak ties exist between individuals who see each other less frequently and with relationships based on a lesser degree of intimacy and emotional intensity.

By people moving from one network to another, links are established between networks. Examples of this kind of mobility are changes of jobs. Granovetter explains,

> *"Especially within professional and technical specialities which are well defined and limited in size, this mobility sets up elaborate structures of bridging weak ties between the more coherent clusters that constitute operative networks in particular locations. Information and ideas thus flow more easily through the speciality, giving it some "sense of community" activated at meetings and conventions. Maintenance of weak ties may well be the most important consequence of such meetings." (Granovetter 1973: 1373)*

Social networks and hearing status

One of the most interesting points with regard to the use of SMS by the deaf is that it is exactly the same service as that used by hearing people. This is important for the self-esteem of the deaf youth. In this phase of life, it is important to be like everyone else. The need for special treatment is an anathema in some respects. Using SMS like everyone else can impart feelings of independence and belonging. Other devices have been developed to help the deaf (for instance hearing aids, subtitling, and telephones with text function), yet SMS is unique because it is not a specially designed system. Rather, it is a commonly available technology that is also quite popular among hearing people.

According to Granovetter, within well-defined but limited technical or professional milieus, there exists a structure to connect weak ties. Information and ideas flow more easily through this special area or operational network, and may give the individuals a feeling of belonging to a society or a clearly defined group, which becomes underlined through meetings and gatherings. The most important effect from such interaction is probably the maintenance of weak ties (Granovetter 1973). Deaf people may be described as such a limited group both in terms of size and definition. Deafness in itself can be exclusive because of the lack of a common language to communicate with people outside this milieu.

Findings

Interview data reveal that the deaf community is perceived by those in it as fairly small, where seemingly everyone knows each other directly or indirectly. This is reasonable given that deaf people make up only around 4000-5000 individuals out of the Norwegian population of approximately 4.5 million (Oestberg 1998). The majority of the deaf are born into hearing families. Special boarding schools and associations for deaf children have been designed to accommodate their needs. These often become more central to their lives in terms of identity building than their real families. When a milieu is centered around a few different institutions and meeting places, there is a high possibility that the same people will meet regularly, though in different contexts. Those one meets may have strongly overlapping networks so that information or rumors diffuse efficiently.

The teens' and the young adults' perceptions of their network reveal that there are probably different structures in the networks of the deaf and the hearing. The networks of the deaf are more narrowly defined and the members are tied together through their common hearing status. The milieu for the deaf could be described as several groups attached together with ties of different strengths. Even though most deaf people have hearing contacts in their families, there exists a type of border around the members. For the young hearing, such borders do not exist in the same way. There are generally not any bigger cliques that together make up an exclusive environment. This is because these individuals do not have one particular trait that holds them together. Rather their ties go in several directions. There is thus no common denominator that clearly includes or excludes members. However, the research here shows that the border that has been drawn around groups of deaf people may be partially dissolved via the use of SMS.

SMS supports the development of ties both within the social networks of the deaf and hearing by making the networks easier to maintain. It is normal for teens and young adults to exchange mobile numbers upon meeting. In this way, a new contact point is established through SMS. This change, however, is a significant one for the deaf, as they establish bonds to entirely new networks. Previously this group can be said to have been isolated from others, but they can now develop and maintain the channels that connect them to others. Analysis shows that this change has had a greater impact on young adults than on teens perhaps because the young adults were older when the mobile telephone became a mainstream product. They were used to living without the possibilities of SMS, so the technological transition was more remarkable. The teens, regardless of hearing status, seem to take SMS more for granted.

SMS may serve both cultural and a compensatory/medical roles for the well-defined deaf community. Culturally, communication between members and maintenance of contacts are facilitated. According to the compensatory perspective,

SMS is a device or medium for communication, which can be used both internally in the group and externally to communicate with hearing people. SMS makes it easier to communicate with everybody, deaf as well as hearing, and thus makes it easier to communicate with an entire social network. SMS messages that are forwarded in this network can give people a sense of belonging to a group, and may have the same effect that Granovetter claims they have, namely to emphasise a sense of community.

A social implication of deafness is that one can easily feel isolated and become excluded from social settings that include hearing people because the deaf cannot easily follow a conversation. Many deaf can read lips, but once several people are involved in the conversation, this becomes more difficult (Haualand 2001). SMS has, to a large extent, replaced the text telephone as the central means of communication. This was confirmed through the interviews. Much of what was previously communicated through the text telephone is now going through the mobile telephone via SMS. The deaf stress in particular that it is convenient to be able to call without being home, a novelty for them since there are only a few text telephones publicly available on the streets.

Some of the deaf teens and young adults in the study have moved in order to attend special schools for deaf and were thus living on campus. Hanne, a deaf young adult, puts it this way:

> *"...What is positive with SMS is that I notice that I can communicate much more with my parents, without having to use the 149. I can also contact other family members, just sending short nice messages, that I have not done previously at all. Everybody in my family is hearing, and I feel I can talk with my mother more on a social basis when I am sending her messages...".* [3]

Since they do not have text telephones, hearing people have to go through the "149" telephonic interpretation service to communicate with deaf people. For deaf people this feels like a very impersonal way of communicating since a third person is involved all the time. They feel that things that could or should have been said are left out. The deaf are also aware that some hearing people are reluctant to use the text telephone. Because of this, there is less contact with these than they might otherwise desire. In addition, they note that there are frustrating errors of interpretation and misunderstanding. In this respect SMS is an improvement, and makes the maintenance of relationships easier.

With SMS, the deaf have an opportunity to keep in direct touch with their hearing family members and friends. This is important to them because they operate in both deaf and hearing cultures. This illustrates an effect that SMS has had when it comes to blurring borders that used to be easily drawn around networks consisting of only

---

[3] All quotes are translated from the original Norwegian.

deaf people. SMS has meant that deaf people have established lines of contact beyond the deaf community. Lisa, a deaf young adult, says:

"...But I notice that I am getting more in touch with hearing people. Among my friends for instance, are some hard of hearing. Hard of hearing are almost hearing so they have more friends with the ability to hear properly. And they want to meet me as well. [They say] 'Please give me Lisa's number and I will forward it to others as well.' That way I make more friends. I do not have to call. Sending a message is easier. It is easier for me, and previously. . . how could I get in touch with them? I had to call through 149, but I was normally too shy to make the call. The mobile telephone on the other hand is much better because it goes directly, and it is much more private."

The hard of hearing people, as mentioned here by Lisa, are sometimes perceived as social bridges. If two people have strong ties, then it is very likely that the others, to whom these two individuals have strong ties, will be introduced and that they themselves will develop strong ties to each other. This may have consequences for the integration between the deaf and the hearing. If some deaf people have strong ties to some hearing people, the others are likely to develop strong ties as well, and this can give deaf people better opportunities to increase their social base (Granovetter 1973).

There are also parallels when considering the adoption of SMS in the hearing and in the deaf communities. Deaf interviewees noted that the text telephone was used much less, though it was nice to have when making more formal calls, say to the bank or other public offices. This complementary use of the text and mobile telephone is also found among the hearing teens and young adults. Different mediums of communication are used for different purposes and different situations. SMS is perceived as being informal. Both the deaf and hearing still prefer the domestic telephone when making formal calls. SMS is preferred by the deaf when they are contacting hearing people for more informal interactions. They feel SMS has lowered the threshold for making contact. This is also partly because using the traditional landline text telephone is seen as a barrier for both the deaf and the hearing.

The possibility to make their own choices when it comes to choosing friends and acquaintances is made easier with usage of SMS. The interviewees in this study had both hearing and deaf friends, but emphasise that getting more hearing friends is not an end in itself, i.e., hearing status is not always an important criterion when getting acquainted with new people. Hearing status has, in a sense, become less important, because people can, to a greater degree, choose the friends they like and not be restricted to only those who have a similar hearing status. Some deaf wish for more hearing friends, while others prefer to stick to the members of the deaf community. These different wishes show that the deaf have individual opinions and needs in terms of their social lives. They have individual desires as to what they want, and whom they want to be with. Thus, the deaf are not a homogeneous group despite the seemingly strong cultural cohesion.

The mobile telephone may be of good use to the deaf, both for those who want contact with the hearing and for those who primarily want to communicate with other deaf people. For those who want contact with the hearing or new friends in expanded networks, the mobile telephone may reduce the threshold for achieving this, and make it easier to utilize the weak ties. For the hearing, SMS has allowed them to reach many people immediately.

Diffusion of information

The interviews reveal that, for all the interviewees, communicative speed and informal communication are important aspects in relation to the usage of SMS. The speed at which SMS messages are sent, together with the fact that content is seen as more important than perfection in language and spelling, is of significance to the deaf. The so-called SMS-language consists of abbreviations, acronyms and incomplete sentences, so the deaf who previously were ill-at-ease with writing Norwegian now face a lower threshold for sending written messages. (The deaf are often strongly attached to their first language, sign language, and are therefore less comfortable with written Norwegian.)

Speed is also of great significance when it comes to diffusion. Information can be spread rapidly, and how important SMS has become to deaf people in this respect is illustrated here by Lisa, who describes the period during which she was without a mobile telephone:

> "I was so isolated, very few bother to call on the text telephone. They used the mobile phone and sent messages about where we would meet, but I just stood there and no one told me what happened. I had to approach them, either call them or walk up to them directly, and ask where to meet. I was told it was difficult to reach me, and when I responded that they could use the domestic text telephone, they said they did not use it any more, as they had gotten used to SMS. When I got my mobile telephone back, it really changed my social life for the better."

When a person loses the opportunity to send and receive SMS, many of the channels for diffusion of information are lost. Information is important in order to know what is going on, and it is important with adequate channels for distributing information. If the costs of transporting the information becomes too high, the information will not reach its target, something that Lisa's comment underscores.

SMS may also have the ability to make use of weak ties within the deaf community easier. One of the deaf young adults, Ane, says that the deaf often send information to each other on special occasions. Hearing people can always get the news when they are on crowded buses or on the streets, but this is rarely an option for the deaf. The channels of diffusion that SMS provides are therefore more crucial for the deaf in this context. They are aware of the importance that they spread the news in their network, and make sure that if anyone receives important news, it is forwarded through SMS. Ane gives the example of what happened on September 11th 2001. On that day, she received several messages saying 'turn on the TV now!' 'It's war'. Because of these messages she, like many others, got to see the second of the two airplanes that crashed into the World Trade Center the moment it happened. She would sooner or later be informed anyway, but without the mobile telephone and the channels of diffusion of information it provides it would have taken more time. Having a mobile telephone means she could be easily reached, wherever and whenever, which thus makes the diffusion of information easier. SMS has in this sense led to a more efficient diffusion processes.

Personal independence and technological dependence

Independence is central to many SMS users. SMS gives one a feeling of independence in terms of both time and space. They can always reach others and be reached. Thus, they are more in control of their own situation since they do not have to sit at home and wait for a telephone call. They are free to do other things while waiting like, for instance, going out. One's location when the message is received becomes of secondary or no importance. This is also the case for the deaf, who are no longer dependent on being close to a text telephone, and that makes them more flexible when it comes to making appointments.

> *When asked whether she believes a mobile telephone will make her more independent, Lisa replies:*

> *"Maybe to a greater extent for the deaf than the hearing. The latter have always had access to telephones, and there are a lot of telephone booths around, although they are becoming more rare as most people have a mobile telephone. For hearing people then, calling to give a message has never been a problem. The deaf by comparison have not had this opportunity, until now with SMS. Previously I could not myself call my parents in order to have them come and pick me up, when I was out in the evenings. I had to write on a note and pass it on to somebody else with a request they make the call, for instance some staff in a kiosk or store. Today I just send my parents an SMS, that gives me a feeling of independence".*

Previously, Lisa was forced to ask for assistance in order to get in touch with her parents. The alternative would have been to agree in advance on an exact time and place for being picked up. SMS has changed all this and provided her with certain independence.

One of the main features of the mobile telephone and SMS are that they give the opportunity for a subtle, instrumental coordination, called micro-coordination. This term implies that it may not be necessary, or even so common any more, to make precise appointments. With a mobile telephone, one does not need to decide in advance where and when to meet. Rather vague appointments can be made and adjusted as the proposed time gets nearer, and those involved have a clearer idea of what will actually be most convenient. By doing it this way, one can more easily adjust to any surprises that may come along (Ling and Yttri 2002).

The traditional voice-based telephone covers more needs for the hearing than does the text telephone for the deaf. The hearing have always had access to telephone booths that provide some ability to micro-coordinate, although not to the same extent that mobile telephones allow. The ability to micro-coordinate that results from the mobile telephone can thus be seen as a more significant change for the deaf than for the hearing. With SMS, the deaf and the hearing are put on more even ground in terms of communication possibilities.

Sending SMS or making a call with a mobile telephone gives direct contact with a relatively small group, but there is always the possibility of sending the same message to several receivers, so that larger groups can be reached simultaneously. Granovetter claims that given the dichotomy between diffusion of information through formal mass communication on the one hand, and personal contacts on the other, the most efficient would be to go through personal contacts in order to achieve something, like for instance getting a job or asking people to come to gatherings. For the latter, be it hearing people or deaf people or both, the most efficient means might be to send an SMS with some personal content. Granovetter also says that in the cases where one wants to use information to achieve something, the information will be most efficient when sent for the first time, i.e., from the person the message originates. The interviews in this study reveal that it is easier to make people come to a gathering or party if the SMS is received from someone whom the receiver knows well, than if the information had gone through several others, including strangers.

Another aspect of independence is the problem related to unwanted contacts. This is relevant for the hearing as well as the deaf, though there seems to be a qualitative difference between the two groups. The hearing interviewees do not emphasise this to the same extent as the deaf, which may attributable to, as Lisa says in the above quote, the hearing always having had access to telephone booths in public places, as well as pagers. The hearing are in this sense more accustomed to being contacted by people they do not really like nor would like to be in contact with, but for the deaf, the channels of communication available with SMS exposes them to a new situation. The appointments the hearing made with those they did not really want to meet did not have to be as rigid or formal as appointments needed to be for the deaf, making it easier to avoid meeting altogether. In a case where one is not very fond of another person, but thinks it is wise to keep in touch, one can still send messages in order not to lose the relationship entirely. In Granovetter's terms, this is called "manipulation of the network," where one utilises the contacts that exist in order to achieve something (Granovetter 1973). An interview with one of the deaf teens revealed that some people are more central when it comes to arranging parties; it is considered important to be in this person's network if one wants to be invited. In the case that there is no tie to this person, the chances of getting invited are smaller than if a weak tie exists. Dina, a deaf teen, puts it this way:

"Some people are more popular than others, and they get invited to more parties. But for myself, I try keep in touch with some of the popular people because then I know it is easier to join them in weekends if I want to. With SMS it is easier to keep in touch with little effort. I just send nice messages now and then, like "how are you?", just so that they remember me, but I am not sure this strategy really works that well."

Dina's comment shows that SMS can open doors and make it easier to be included in social events. However it also underscores Granovetter's point that while a weak tie is not as a strong one, it is better than no tie at all.

Some of the interviewees also admit that they feel dependent on their mobile telephones. That is, they feel naked without them. They said that they physically feel that something is missing if it is not in their immediate proximity. It has at the same time been stressed, both by deaf and hearing users of SMS, as an important personal quality to be able to distance oneself from the mobile telephone and to be independent of the technology. One sees differences here when considering the situation of hearing and deaf teens.

The hearing teens and young adults emphasise that they try not to check the telephone for messages all the time. They say that they do not to take it with them unless they really need it. They try to manage without it in situations where it is possible. Dependence, however, is perceived somewhat differently among the deaf interviewees. They cannot hear when messages come in, so for them dependence means that they need to carry the telephone at most times, like the hearing, but also that they have to constantly check whether they have received any new messages. Vibration features for announcing incoming messages are perceived positively because it frees them from constantly visually checking their telephones for messages.

Dependence is also an issue for the deaf when traveling abroad. Opportunities to use text telephones are rare, and mobile telephony coverage is not guaranteed. This has posed problems and caused frustration for several of the interviewees. Many of them had also been in the USA, some up to a month's time. During this period they were totally without connection, both in terms of receiving and sending messages. They generally found it strange to be without their messages and missed their telephones. In some cases, however, they actually found it nice to be without them. They were on holiday and had more exciting experiences than in everyday life, therefore reducing their need for social contact through SMS. The consequences of being without a phone would have been greater at home, as they would have more distinctly missed their social benefits.

Many feel they get close to each other through sending messages, and that it is easier to write than to say the words face to face. The teens in particular, both deaf and hearing, find that SMS may be just as personal as a physical meeting. To keep in touch and exchange information, it is not even necessary to meet face-to-face; sending a SMS is in some cases sufficient. Sending each other some nice messages now and then becomes important for the preservation or development of a relation and the strength of the tie. One of Granovetter's requirements with regard to the definition of strong ties is the meeting frequency. For SMS users it is still important to meet, but SMS also makes it possible to have strong ties to people whom one does not often see.

Conclusion

This study of SMS use among deaf teens and young adults in Norway reveals several social implications the technology has had in maintaining and establishing networks. SMS has social, cultural and compensatory implications for the deaf teens and young adults. Culturally, SMS makes communication within the deaf community easier, particularly where the ties were weak initially. The compensatory implication is that the barrier between the deaf and hearing is reduced as a consequence of having a common means of communication that can be fully utilised by both groups. Because of SMS, the deaf have, if not closed the social gap between themselves and the hearing, have certainly made the gap smaller, by increasing communicative spontaneity and affording natural dialogue. Interviewees feel that this leads to a richer social life for those who are interested in becoming more integrated in hearing society.

The deaf interviewees now have an opportunity to exercise greater control over their own and other's activities by being readily available in their network through SMS. The interviews reveal that the most important aspect of SMS has been that it has made it possible to maintain strong ties in already existing networks in an efficient way, while at the same time making it easier to acquire more weak ties in one's network. While SMS technology has changed communication possibilities for all people who adopt it, the technology has been revolutionary to the deaf because it has decreased isolation by greatly increasing communications opportunities. Whereas the hearing have incrementally benefited by the evolutionary introduction of domestic telephones, public telephone booths, pagers, and mobile telephony, SMS represents a significant, emancipatory change in the lifestyles of the deaf.

Acknowledgements

This research was conducted while the author was a Masters of Sociology student at the University of Oslo.

References

Breivik, J.-K. (2001) Deaf identities in the making. Metaphors and narratives in translocal lives. In partial fulfilment of the Doctor Polit. Degree,Department of Social Anthroplogy, University of Oslo.

Frønes, I., and Brusdal, R. (2000). *På sporet av den nye tid. Kulturelle varsler for en nær fremtid.* Fagbokforlaget. Bergen.

Granovetter, M.S. 1973 *"The Strength of Weak Ties"*. American Journal of Sociology, Volume 78, Issue 6 (May, 1973), 1360-1380.

Haualand, H.M. (2000) *Døves tilgang til og bruk av informasjon: hva slags informasjon oppsøkes, og noen mulige årsaker til disse valgene.* Oslo: Norges Døveforbund.

Lindström, J.-I. (2001) *Universal Issues – what are the social impact from multimedia, broadband and universal mobile telephone systems?* Telia AB.

Ling, R. (2001) *Ownership and use of mobile telephones and mobile computing 1997-2001* Telenor R&D.

Ling, R., and Yttri, B. (2002) "Hyper-coordination via mobile phones in Norway." Pp. 139–169 in *Perpetual contact: Mobile communication, private talk, public performance,* edited by J. E. Katz and M. Aakhus. Cambridge: Cambridge University Press.

Ohna, S.E. (2001) *Å skape et selv. Døves fortellinger om interaksjon med hørende.* Det utdanningsvitenskapelige fakultet. Universitetet i Oslo.

Oestberg, T. (1998) *Døvhet og døve – belyst ved tre sosiologiske forståelsesmodeller.* Skådalen kompetansesenter, Oslo.

9 Mobile Communications vis-à-vis Teen Emancipation, Peer Group Integration and Deviance

Rich Ling

Introduction

The mobile telephone – often in the form of SMS – provides teens with a rich social life. It is used to coordinate activities and hold peer groups together. It is used as a symbolic umbilical cord to connect teens with their parents and it is a device through which teen's emancipation is mediated. Indeed, teens' adoption of the mobile telephone – and their intense use of SMS – is one of the surprises surrounding the technology. Reports from Japan (Hashimoto 2002), Finland (Kasesniemi and Rautiainen 2002), the general European scene (Mante-Meijer and al. 2001), the UK (Harper 2003) the Philippines (Ellwood-Clayton 2003) and of course Norway (Ling 2000; Ling 2001b; Ling and Helmersen 2000; Ling and Yttri 2003) all point in this direction. This point is also made in the chapters in this collection.

Emancipation, peer acceptance and the testing of various behaviors are a complex of activities that characterize adolescence. During adolescence, there is a strong motivation for teens to establish themselves as independent social actors who are outside the sphere of their parents. Indeed, emancipation from one's parents is one of the central issues for teens. The dynamic nature of modern society means that teens will emerge into a society that is at least somewhat different than that of their parents. Thus, the approach one takes to emancipation will be different from that of previous generations. This is simply because – unlike the situation in traditional societies – the situation changes from generation to generation. The skills needed, the technologies used and the educational background upon which one relies change and develop across generations. Because of this, the teen is an active agent in shaping his or her own socialization (Glaser and Strauss 1971, 57 – 88).

During this period, the peer group plays a central role in this transition. It provides the teen with a group in which he or she can help to decide on activities and where he or she can take part in establishing the fashion and mode of the group. The peer

Richard Harper, Leysia Palen and Alex Taylor (Eds), The Inside Text: Social, Cultural and Design Perspectives on SMS, 175–193.

group also helps one to work out a relationship to the various facets of adult life. This includes issues such as sexuality, forms of consumption, relationship to authority and degrees of social/normative deviance. Where the parents can provide the teen with an ordered sense of life, the peer group provides the teen with a sphere in which he or she can assert control and participate more fully in decision making (Giordano 1995; Harter 1990; see also Savin-Williams and Berndt 1990; Youniss 1980; Youniss and Smollar 1985).

The peer group provides teens with a sphere of life wherein they can experience reciprocal self-disclosure and emotional support outside family units. According to Fine, the peer group is protective of its members and it is active in the development of an ideoculture, that is, a whole system of nicknames, jokes, styles of clothing, songs, artifacts etc. (1987, 126).

While establishing a social profile often means simply interacting with others, it can also mean that one is increasingly drawn into a quasi-adult world. Indeed, there is a sense that teens need to test boundaries. They need to find the boundary between "appropriate and inappropriate" behaviors in conducting their lives. Parents can be a useful influence here, but their peers are also central in this negotiation. The peer group provides a context in which teens can try out various behaviors associated with the adult world. As noted above these can include decision making, compromise and conflict resolution. In addition, the peer group provides teens with a context wherein he or she can test various boundaries. It is often in the peer group that people first experience the use of alcohol and gain insight into sexuality. It is in the peer group that interaction with authorities – often in the form of teachers or school administrators – are either prepared for or are discussed after the fact. It is in the peer group that these interactions are set into a broader understanding of how teens treat and are treated by authority figures. Thus, there is a gray zone there between a rich social life and the engagement in illicit activities. The boundaries between acceptable socializing and mob actions are not always clearly defined.

The mobile telephone can play into the mixture. It lowers the threshold for social interaction and unlike the traditional house telephone, teens control their own communication channel. They can interact with others when and where it is convenient. There is no need to ask permission to use the phone nor is there the embarrassment of being overheard by others. This is a boon for teens since it allows direct and personally controlled access to their peer group. The negative side is that it is difficult for them to control the way that information is spread.

> *Geir, (15): I don't understand why people dare to have parties anymore because if the rumor gets out [via mobile telephones] you get a lot of people who steal and break stuff like that.*[1]

---

[1] The citations in this chapter come from group interviews that were conducted in Norwegian. The citations were translated into English by the author.

Gier's plight illustrates the dilemma for teens. On the one hand, there is a great premium placed on organizing social interactions that allow teens to come together and establish a social sphere. At the same time, the boundary testing of the peer group is executed with an uneven hand.

The social events organized by teens can range from innocent parties where friends simply want to be together to slightly more illicit interactions that include testing out their quasi-adult status through drinking and sexual interactions. They can also include blatantly illegal forms of behavior. Again, qualitative material points to the ways in which the mobile telephone – and its ability to quickly distribute information – means that a situation can spin out of control.

Interviewer: There are not only positive things about mobile telephony. I would like to ask you what are the problems?

Rita: (18): I have a good example. For example if there is trouble [i.e. fighting] and such it will be a bigger problem because of that. For example, if there is trouble you call to all your friends. That can be dangerous.

Erik: (14): That doesn't have to be dangerous.

Rita: Of course, because then they contact the others and it gets bigger you know. It is obvious that if there are 100 instead of two.

Erik: But it is good if there are 20 guys who want to beat you up.

Rita: But the problem is bigger you know.

This exchange points to the tension in teens' lives. Teens want to move out of their parents' shadows and develop their own social profile while, at the same time, it is not always easy to control the situation and to see the potential issues involved in their actions.

The decisions teens make and the council they receive from peers may help to provide them with the ballast they need later in life. However, there is also a chance that the situation will tip over to more serious types of deviance. The mobile telephone is becoming a part of this situation. Thus, it is important to see how its use covaries with other issues.

The analysis here looks into several dimensions in the greening of Norwegian teens. Specifically, it examines how mobile voice telephony and SMS play into the complex process of emancipation. This process can include a distancing from one's parents, tighter integration into the peer group, boundary testing issues such as drinking, sexuality and interaction with authorities, and in some cases, participation in clearly illicit activities such as stealing, fighting, and narcotic use. The emancipation process, peer acceptance and boundary testing is a well-rehearsed theme in the sociological (among many others Fine 1981; Fine 1987; Glaser and Strauss 1971; Lynne 2000) and the psychological literature (see for example Rubin 1985; Schneider and Stevenson 1999). The issue of teen criminality is also an area of intense investigation (Elliott, Huzsinga and Ageton 1985; Elliott and Ageton 1979; Hirschi 1969; Lemert 1967; Merton 1968). The role of mobile telephony among teens has also started to have a literature of its own (Ling and Yttri 2003; Rautiainen and Kasesniemi 2000; Skog and Jamtøy 2002). The goal of this paper is to go somewhat further in this analysis and to look at the role of mobile telephony and SMS in the broader social world of teens.

Method

The analysis described here is based on material gathered in the study *Ung i Norge* (*Young in Norway*) study carried out by Norwegian Social Research. This is a survey based on a questionnaire that was administered to 11 928 students from 47 randomly selected middle schools and 26 high schools. The data was collected in February of 2002. The material covers students from the 3 middle school years and the 3 high school years. There were approximately 2000 persons from each of these six grade levels. The age range was from 13 to 19 years of age.[2] There was a 49/51% split between males and females respectively. The material from the survey was compared to the general demographic for Norway. The gender balance, age, location, family sized and constitution and immigration status were compared. While some differences were noted, the general picture is correct (Rossow and Bø 2003)

The data material is the second in a series of studies done on youth in Norway by Norwegian Social Research. The previous questionnaire was carried out in 1992. That material has been used for various studies describing the situation of teens in Norway. In the intervening decade, one saw the rise of the Internet and mobile telephony. Thus, in addition to providing a second chance to see how Norwegian teens were faring, a new study also provided the chance to examine their use of these information and communication technologies, cultural items that were not as prominent in the lives of teen in the early 1990's.

The questionnaire covered a broad range of topics. In addition to the basic ownership and use of mobile telephony, respondents were asked to describe, among other things, their: 1) attitudes toward and participation in clubs and other social activity, 2) relationship to their parents, 3) sense of school and school achievement, 4) career choice and current work, 5) self-image, 6) general use of ICT, 7) romance and sexual activity, 8) participation in deviant activity, 9) use of controlled substances, 10) participation in physical training, political engagement and cultural activities and 11) spending of money on various activities. In addition, the sponsors of the questionnaire were generous in their willingness to include questions covering teens' use of Internet and mobile telephony.

The focus of the analysis was to look at different areas in which the mobile telephone and SMS might covary with important issues for teens. As noted above,

---

[2] The two older age groups and, in particular, the 19 year olds, were underrepresented since many of teens in these age groups had graduated.

there were four general areas of interest. These were that the mobile telephone is an element in teens' 1) emancipation from the home, 2) integration into the peer group, 3) boundary testing, including drinking, sexuality and interaction with authorities and finally 4) their eventual participation in openly criminal activities.

Based on these areas of focus, complex independent variables[3] were constructed from the material in the broader database. These complex variables were built up from the batteries of questions in the database. The relevant batteries of questions were first selected based on their usefulness for the analysis and then the complex variables were built with the use of factor analysis.[4] This resulted in a large number of complex variables. The next step in the process was to engage in a type of dynamic model testing wherein the different complex variables were assembled into that array that best explained the variance in the use of voice mobile and SMS.

Mobile communications access and use

The material shows that, overall, 94% of the teens in the study reported owning a mobile telephone. One can see from this that mobile telephony is securely institutionalized among Norwegian teens. When looking at the age-based ownership statistics, 88% of the 13 year-olds owned a mobile telephone while 97% of the 19 year-olds had one. More females (96%) than males (92%) reported owning a mobile telephone. There were significantly more girls than boys in the 13 to 18 year groups who had a mobile telephone (See figure 1). It is only among the 19 year olds that both genders are on par with each other. The finding that teen

---

[3] These independent variables are complex in the sense that the variables were constructed from various items in larger batteries of questions. Thus, each indicator contains the influences of several individual questions on the questionnaire.

[4] The material behind this analysis is a relatively large amount of data. It is, indeed, somewhat difficult to gain insight without simplifying the material in some ways. It is in this context that we drew on what is called factor analysis. This analysis technique searches through large batteries of data and seeks out those variables that co-vary. The point is to discover the underlying "factors" – that is the groupings of variables – that form together into identifiable complex-variables.

If, for example, one had a database that described preferences for various types of food, the individual variables might show that an individual liked hot dogs, ketchup, hot dog buns, potato chips and cola. The factor analysis would determine the underlying correlations between the individual's preferences for these items and it would suggest that these items could be placed onto the same "factor" that might be called something like hotdog preference. In addition, it would provide a weight for each of the individual items that would indicate their contribution to this particular factor. Presumably, the "weight" of potato chips would contribute less than that of hot dog buns, for example. Finally, based on this weighting, it can provide all the items cases in the database, that is, all the persons who provided their rankings, with a relative factor score. That is, the degree to which they felt that those items were preferable. Thus, one might expect that a "hot dog" factor would differ sharply from a "vegetarian casserole" factor in the analysis. That is, there would be little covariance between the meat eating hot dog lovers and the vegetarians.

After the factors are in place, one can then do further analyses on them to determine the demographic placement of the factors and the interaction between the factors and other items in the database. In addition, one can examine the factors in terms of other issues such as, for example, the proclivity to use mobile telephony.

girls are quicker to adopt mobile telephony has been found in other material (Ling 2004). Studies also often show that women are more skilled in using the telephone to organize social life and attend to the nurturing of others (Moyal 1992; Rakow 1992; Rosenthal 1985). The difference in ownership perhaps reflects the notion that women and girls have stronger social networking skills (Cochran 1993; Di Leonardo 1987; Moore 1990). There may also be a safety related issue associated with the gendered adoption of mobile telephones (Ling 2004; Rakow and Navarro 1993).

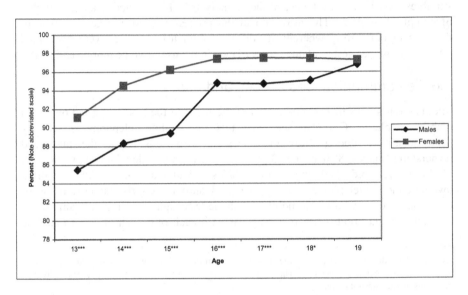

Figure 1: Ownership of mobile telephones by age and gender, Norway 2002 (n = 11,199). The symbol *** indicates a significance of less than 0.001. The symbol ** indicates a significance level between 0.001 and 0.01. The symbol * indicates a significance level between 0.01 and 0.05 and the symbol + indicates a significance level between 0.05 and 0.1.

The material shows that there were 5.7% of the teens who reported that they did not own a mobile telephone nor had they used one during the day previous to the administration of the questionnaire.

When considering use of the mobile telephone, all respondents, regardless of ownership status, were asked how many times they had talked on the phone and how many SMS messages they had sent and received the previous day. The median user had 1 – 2 conversations and sent 3 – 5 SMS messages. The teen girls and, in particular, the young teen girls are underrepresented among the non-users and over-represented among those making a moderate number of calls per day. When considering voice telephony, 29.6% of the informants with access to a mobile telephone had not made any calls the previous day; 35% reported making 1 to 2 calls; 21.2% reported making 3 to 5 calls; and the remaining 7.5% had made more than 5 calls. Broadly speaking, the same contours appear with SMS use. The girls, and in particular the younger girls are over-represented among those users who had sent a moderate number of SMSs the previous day (that is among those who had sent two to five messages the previous day), and the most intense use category is gender neutral.

The high use group – both when considering SMS but in particular when looking at voice telephony – is of special interest. It seems to be the extreme users who are driving some of the analysis. Its reported behavior and attitudes mark it as a special group. It is a relatively small group but its extended use of voice telephony – a less favored communication form among teens in comparison to SMS– has several interesting covariances that are discussed below.

The social context of teens

The "explanatory" variables[5] fit into the areas of parental control, peer acceptance, boundary testing and serious deviance. In addition, there were several variables describing other socio-demographic areas such as grade level and their spending levels.

The degree of teen emancipation from their home was seen in two complex variables. The first was the degree of parental control (reported parental insight into school assignments, marks in school, the teen's physical comings and goings, and the freedom with which teens told their parents about their free time activities). The second described the extent to which teens oriented themselves towards the home (the frequency which the teens were home with their parents and how often they helped with household chores). The data shows, for example that about 67% of the teens agreed with the statement that their parents usually know where they were. By contrast, 8% disagreed with this statement.

Social integration into the peer group was measured with complex variables describing the teens sense of their own popularity (number of friends, ease with which one can make friends, sense of popularity, feeling of peer acceptance), the time spent with friends, time spent at public locations outside the home ("hanging" on a street corner, a kiosk, a gas station or in a café or a snack bar) and their sense of loneliness. When looking at the latter variable, one of the component elements was "I feel that there are people around me but not with me." The data shows that 5% of the teens felt this often while 22% felt this on occasion. By contrast, 51% felt that they had a "many" friends.

There were several variables describing the degree to which the teens engaged in the minor deviance or the so-called status offenses. These included reported sexual activity (varying from "French" kissing to intercourse), drinking, truancy, being in trouble in school and on a slightly different tact, teens' sense of control over their school experience. If one examines sexual activity, 48% of the 8th graders[6] reported

---

[5] It needs to be noted here that I am not positing a causal direction, only a co-variance.

[6] Teens in the 8th grade were largely 13 years old with some 14 year olds among them.

that they had not had any direct sexual experience. This drops to 11% for those in the oldest group. The data shows that 44% of the teens had never drunken so much alcohol as to "feel drunk." This varies between 83% of the 13 year olds to 17% of the 19 year olds.

Finally, complex variables describing the teens' reported participation in openly illicit activities were developed. These variables described the teens' eventual engagement in rather severe activities. The items included a variable describing theft/fighting. [7] In turn this included the items "stealing more than 1000 kroner (approximately $145)," "theft of motor vehicles," "fighting with weapons (usually knives)" and "contact with the police." The variable describing narcotic use included both the use of marijuana as well as heroin. Thus, the activities described here are not simple "coming of age" transgressions, rather they are in many cases offenses for which one can be jailed. Just to give a sense of the incidence of these more serious offenses, the percent of teens who report having used marijuana or hash goes from 3% among the 13 year olds to 23% among the 19 year olds. When looking at hard drugs such as cocaine, LSD or heroin, the percentages go from slightly more than 1% to just over 8% for the oldest age group.

The teen's use of other information and communication technologies (ICTs) was also included in the analysis. These are not necessarily focused on the same issues as the emancipation/social integration/deviance variables described above. None-the-less they are a part of their everyday life. Because of this a complex variable describing the teens use of video and electronic gaming and another describing their use of the PC were included.

Results

Voice mobile telephony

The model with the greatest explanatory power was that describing the use of voice telephony. When looking at the entire sample, the model explained just over 28% of the variance.[8] There were many of the complex variables that showed high levels of covariance with voice mobile telephony.[9] These included a positive relationship between the use of voice mobile telephony and the teens' levels of sexual activity, reported monthly spending level, incidence of trouble in school, use of the PC, incidence of drinking or truancy in school, and time spent with friends (See figure 2; see also results in the appendix).[10]

---

[7] These two activities factored onto the same variable.

[8] The adjusted r^2 was 0.285.

[9] Again, I want to underscore the point that I explain covariance here, not causality.

[10] It is not surprising that this is the stronger of the two analyses. Voice telephony is not used as often among teens. It is more expensive and it is not as discrete as SMS. Finally, fewer persons used this form of communication. All of this means that it is easier to develop models describing the behavior.

To further examine the use of voice mobile telephony, I removed the most extreme voice mobile users as well as those who do not use voice mobile telephony from the sample in two respective analyses of the data. The point here is to determine differences between the extreme users and those who are closer to normal use.[11]

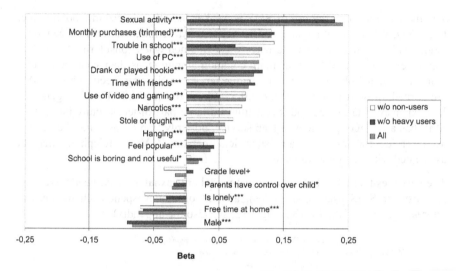

Figure 2: Regression results for voice mobile telephony

The analysis indicates that removal of the heavy user group causes greater changes than removal of the non-use group. Specifically, when the extreme-use group is removed, the variables describing narcotic use and stealing/fighting are no longer significant.[12] Other changes are that one is less likely to report being in trouble in school and is more likely to report being lonely. These latter variables are all significant in the model that excludes the heavy users, but their relative weight changes.

When the non-users are dropped from the analysis the only variable that is no longer significant is the variable describing school as being boring and useless.[13]

---

[11] The extreme use group was defined as those who make more than 6 calls a day. This group constitutes 7.5% of the total sample. Within this group 5.5% made 6 to 10 calls, 1.2% made between 11 and 20 calls and 1% reported making more than 20 calls a day. While six calls a day may not seem extreme, this is but the lower boundary for a category that includes extremely heavy users. One must also note that the cost of mobile voice telephony is often seen as a factor that limits use when compared to the relatively inexpensive landline telephony – particularly when it is one's parents who pay for landline telephony but not mobile telephony. The "non-ownership, non-use" group included all those persons who had no mobile telephone and who also reported not using one. This group is 5.8% of the population.

[12] The extreme users group made up 7.6% of the total sample.

[13] The non-voice mobile group made up 5.8% of the sample.

Thus, while there are only marginal changes when the non-users are dropped from the analysis, much broader shifts are apparent when the extreme users are no longer included in the equation.

SMS

The model describing the use of SMS is weaker than that describing mobile voice telephony. Where about a quarter of the variance was explained in the voice mobile model, only about 16% of the variance was explained when considering SMS.[14] By way of explanation, SMS is far more common among teens than voice telephony. Voice mobile telephony is the more unique service in Norway. Teens who use SMS are normal, those who use voice are different from the crowd. SMS is less generally less expensive than voice and it constitutes a large part of teens' daily interaction. SMS has a stronger profile as a teen service, possibly tipping over into being seen as a service for immature and superficial persons.[15] Voice telephony may be associated with mature, serious use.

The variables that contribute most to the model are sexual activity, gender (females are stronger SMS users than males), amount of money spent each month, and interestingly, use of the PC (See Figure 3; see also the appendix).

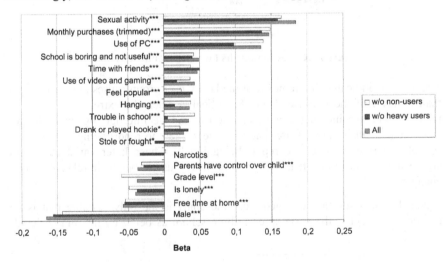

Figure 3: Regression results for SMS use

---

[14] The adjusted r^2 was 0.1608.

[15] From a methods perspective, since essentially all teens in Norway use SMS, it is more difficult to find independent characteristics with which to describe the use. Among 14–15 year olds, approximately 45% report using mobile voice telephony on a daily basis. More than 70% report daily use of SMS. The socio-demographic contours of use are less pronounced and this means that it is more difficult to tease out a model describing the use.

As with mobile voice telephony, extreme users were also of interest. In this case, the extreme high users are those who sent more than 20 messages a day.[16] Non-users were those who reported neither having a mobile telephone nor sending any messages.

There are significant differences in narcotic use, stealing and fighting, being in trouble in school and, interestingly, in PC use when comparing the whole sample to the sample minus the extreme users. In the case of narcotic use, the analysis shows that the variable goes from being inconsequential when examining the whole sample to being moderately (but significantly) negative when the extreme high users are dropped from the sample. Stealing and fighting goes from being positively related to SMS use – and significant at the 0.01 level – to being slightly negatively related and not being a significant contribution to the general model. The incidence of being in trouble in school also goes from having a positive relationship to SMS use to being inconsequential when the heavy users are dropped from the analysis.

A similar analysis was done by comparing the whole sample to the sample minus non-users. Grade level/age dropped out of the model as a significant variable in the analysis where the non-users were excluded.[17] Thus, the heavy users of both voice mobile telephony and SMS, to a lesser degree, mark themselves as being different from the masses on more dimensions than the non-users.

Discussion

Integration into the group

In addition to providing a mechanism for emancipation, the mobile telephone also assists in the integration of the teen peer group. Mobile telephony plays into the social life and the ability to organize one's own social activities. The analysis indicates that there is a covariation between use of the device and a reduction in one's sense of loneliness, one's sense of popularity, and in the reported time spent with friends. Specifically, the more one uses SMS and voice mobile telephony, the less one feels lonely.

Again, there are differences between the total sample and the extreme users. These are particularly strong when considering voice mobile telephony but also evident when examining SMS. There is a weak but significant relationship between SMS/voice and reports of feeling popular. There is a reasonably strong positive relationship between use of voice mobile and amount of time spent with friends. SMS shows a similar effect but not nearly as strongly as voice. One can observe a reasonably strong positive relationship between use of voice mobile and amount of time spent "hanging out."[18] The same is true of SMS but to a lesser degree. There

---

[16] The heavy SMS users made up 4.5% of the total sample.

[17] The non-SMS users made up 5.8% of the total sample.

[18] The indicators on this complex variable indicated the respondent spent time "hanging" for example on street corners, at local hamburger bars or gas stations (a popular location for teens in small isolated communities).

are some moderate differences when the extreme users are dropped from the analysis in that respondents reported less "hanging out." The voice/SMS differences may have functional as well as symbolic moments.

Boundary-testing

Another dimension of emancipation are various types of boundary-testing behaviors. These include the so-called status offenses wherein behaviors that are seen as deviant for teens are seen as being tolerated among adults (sexuality, drinking and missing mandated attendance at a social institution). In other cases, teens test boundaries through unguarded interaction with authority figures such as teachers and school administrators. These actions are not in themselves a transgression of law. However, a poorly calibrated interaction with a teacher can mean that a teen ends up in trouble.

Sex and sexuality are also boundary-testing behaviors, the contribution of sexuality to the model is the strongest variable in the analysis both in terms of SMS and the mobile voice telephony. In the case of voice telephony, it contributes almost twice as much as the next most important variable. Further, there are no clear differences in the covariance of sexual activity and mobile voice telephony when either the extreme users or the non-users are eliminated from the analysis. Thus, the use of mobile telephony – both voice mobile and SMS – has a relatively strong positive relationship to sexual activity among the teens in the study.

There is also a positive relationship between the complex truancy/drinking variable and mobile telephone use. This is particularly strong in the case of voice telephony. In addition, there is a positive relationship between reporting that one was in trouble in school and mobile telephone use. The removal of the heaviest users (both SMS and voice) results in a much weaker contribution of these variables to the model. Finally, there is a slight but significantly inverse relationship between SMS and mobile voice with regards to the sense that teens feel school is less relevant.

The material seems to indicate that mobile telephony has a role in teens' exploration of these boundary areas. As noted above, a part of the adolescent experience is the need to better define social boundaries and to better understand the consequences of transgression. The material here points to the notion that mobile telephony (including SMS) is a part of the boundary-testing complex.

Serious criminality

Finally, the analysis shows that there was a positive relationship between the respondents reporting the heavy use of voice/SMS and various types of serious criminality. There was a covariance between stealing/fighting and use of voice and SMS. The effect for voice is somewhat stronger than with SMS. The interesting thing here is that when one drops the extreme users, there is a dramatic shift in the contribution of this variable. For both voice and SMS, it goes from being a positive (and significant) relationship to being an inconsequential (and insignificant) relationship.

In the case of narcotics use, there is a positive relationship with voice telephony.[19] There is no real relationship when looking at SMS use. As with stealing/fighting dramatic differences arise when one drops the extreme users from the analysis. In the case of mobile voice, telephony the relationship becomes inconsequential and insignificant. In the case of SMS, the relationship actually goes from being inconsequential to being a significant inverse relationship.

The data shows that extended use of the mobile telephone for voice telephony covaries with the reported engagement in some serious forms of deviance. It also described the engagement in a variety of illicit activities such as breaking and entering, stealing, vandalizing and fighting with weapons.[20]

Mobile communication and teen deviance

When considering the extreme telephony users, one finds the incidence of the heavier types of deviance. However, it is important to remember that high use of mobile telephony is not necessarily causally related to deviance. This may well be the case of the tail wagging the dog. In other words, just because a person uses mobile telephony a lot does not mean that he or she will eventually become deviant. One who, for example, has responsibility for organizing choir practice may well use as much mobile telephony as a drug pusher. The point is that mobile telephony can facilitate activities and life directions that are chosen for completely different reasons. Thus, extreme use should be seen as a potential marker more than a slippery slope.

Three issues are at play here. The models indicate that voice mobile telephony and SMS use covary with the gender of the user (girls use more than boys); that there are a set of boundary testing behaviors that covary with use (in particular sexual activity); and, finally, for the extreme users, there is a covariance with illicit activities. The first finding, the gendered use of mobile telephony, confirms the results of other analyses (Ling 2001a; Ling 2003). It often seems to be the case that girls and women are stronger users of communications technology, particularly when it comes to remote care giving and social networking (Rakow and Navarro 1993). This is reflected here. It is also seen in the fact that voice mobile and SMS use covary with the social integration variables included in the analysis.

The second general finding shows that the mobile telephone has become an element in the boundary testing of teens. This is seen in the covariance with the variables describing the use of alcohol, truancy, the questioning of authority in school, but most directly in terms of the variable describing sexual activity. The fact that the device is a personal communication channel that is actually controlled by the individual means that communication is more precisely addressed; that is, one need not deal with the filtering effects of parents and other family members. This can

---

[19] The variable describing the use of narcotics included the use of relatively benign drugs such as marijuana but it also described the use of heavy drugs such as cocaine and heroin.

[20] In Norway, the usual weapon used in these situations is a knife.

have the effect of facilitating intimate interaction and other types of teen boundary testing. Although it is not possible to know from this data, other qualitative data leads one to the notion that teens arrange tête-à-têtes and other intimate interactions via SMS. This interaction has been suggested for the Norwegian situation (Pedersen and Samuelsen 2003), as well as in the anthropological analysis of courting behavior in the Philippines (Ellwood-Clayton, chapter 9; see also chapter 13).

Finally, there is the interaction between extreme mobile/SMS use and the heavier forms of criminality. There are many ideas as to why and how one becomes deviant and how this is translated into a culture of deviance. It has been suggested that criminality results if one experiences too great a gap between social expectations and their ability to fulfill these expectations (Merton 1968). It may also be such that criminality results when one is subjected to a public degradation. According to this approach, the subsequent labeling of someone as a deviant can then play into a self-fulfilling prophesy (Lemert 1951; Lemert 1967). Further, upon becoming a part of a deviant culture, one is held there by social forces such as attachment to others in the culture, commitment to one's position, active involvement in the culture that serves to refresh one's attachment and commitment, and finally one's belief in the centrality of the group to their life (Hirschi 1969).[21] It is this latter complex of a tightly bounded network that mobile communication can play into the picture. The low threshold for communication can facilitate the maintenance of a deviant culture in just the same way that it can facilitate the maintenance of the group of teen girls' mutual infatuation with a pop group. What is special here, however, is the relationship between these illicit activities and extreme use.

The material here suggests that the effects are stronger for those who use mobile voice telephony than for those who are extreme uses of SMS. There are several elements to consider here. First, voice mobile telephony is more synchronous than SMS. In a lifestyle wherein coordination is often of the essence, voice telephony would represent a preferred choice. Another logistical advantage to voice telephony is that it is ephemeral. There is no permanent record of the content of the interaction. For one who may have an interest in covering their tracks, this would be an advantage.

Second, there are symbolic issues at play. SMS can be seen as a service for immature superficial persons when voice mobile ties one into the world of powerful actors on an expansive stage. There is a "teeny bopper" image that can be associated with SMS where use of voice mobile has a more urgent and weighty image. The use of voice mobile marks one as having access to resources and being involved in breaking developments, be they legitimate or illicit. Indeed the culture of SMS is quite strong among teens and in particular teen girls (Ling 2003). Thus, teens that engage in the heavier forms of deviance may see the more extravagant

---

[21] Interestingly, these same elements can bind one to a "non-delinquent" life to the same degree that they can bind one to that which is seen as a delinquent life.

use of voice telephony as a way to further mark their distinctive lifestyle and to distance themselves from the immature image of SMS.

In sum, it seems that SMS and mobile voice telephony play into the adolescent experience in complex ways. These modes of communication facilitate emancipation; they assist in the bonding of the peer group and in some cases they play into more illicit activities. There is, however, a special role in terms of boundary testing behaviors that are, after all, a part of the emancipation process.

Appendix: Regression results

Regression results from the analysis of mobile voice telephony

	Unstandardized Coefficients		Standardized Coefficients	T	Sig.
	B	Std. Error	Beta		
(Constant)	0,783504	0,027015		29,00308	1,7E-178
Male***	-0,26058	0,021457	-0,11788	-12,1443	9,94E-34
Free time at home***	-0,09946	0,009675	-0,08696	-10,2799	1,11E-24
Is lonely***	-0,06253	0,010654	-0,05598	-5,86914	4,5E-09
Parents have control over child***	-0,02772	0,010009	-0,02436	-2,77001	0,005615
School is boring and not useful*	0,023902	0,00952	0,020746	2,510735	0,012062
Grade level***	0,031117	0,006668	0,046821	4,666837	3,09E-06
Feel popular***	0,061704	0,01121	0,052788	5,504444	3,78E-08
Stole or fought***	0,078138	0,009681	0,067804	8,070867	7,68E-16
Hanging out***	0,08006	0,009809	0,070002	8,16159	3,65E-16
Narcotics***	0,093074	0,009517	0,080765	9,779363	1,69E-22
Use of video and gaming***	0,111208	0,011044	0,09867	10,06974	9,45E-24
Time with friends***	0,127707	0,009616	0,111663	13,2808	5,93E-40
Use of PC***	0,130795	0,009336	0,116662	14,00974	3,16E-44
Trouble in school***	0,167186	0,009971	0,145074	16,76747	2,36E-62
Trimmed reported sum payments per month***	0,00014	8,17E-06	0,151057	17,17566	2,68E-65
Drank or played hookie***	0,224795	0,01179	0,195064	19,06653	8,33E-80
Dependent Variable: MOBTALK					

R	R Square	Adjusted R Square	Std. Error of the Estimate
0,504022	0,254039	0,252991	0,950171

Regression results from the analysis of SMS use

	Unstandardized Coefficients		Standardized Coefficients	t	Sig.
	B	*Std. Error*	*Beta*		
(Constant)	1,480885	0,040535		36,53349	2E-276
Male***	-0,59378	0,032197	-0,19186	-18,4423	7,36E-75
Free time at home***	-0,10987	0,014517	-0,06862	-7,56827	4,07E-14
Is lonely***	-0,06949	0,015986	-0,04444	-4,34705	1,39E-05
Parents have control over child***	-0,06167	0,015018	-0,0387	-4,10613	4,05E-05
Narcotics	0,015736	0,014281	0,009753	1,10188	0,270537
Grade level	0,01052	0,010005	0,011307	1,051522	0,293041
Stole or fought**	0,047114	0,014527	0,029202	3,243225	0,001185
Hanging out***	0,07287	0,014719	0,045511	4,950786	7,5E-07
Use of video and gaming***	0,077006	0,016571	0,048803	4,647014	3,41E-06
Feel popular***	0,080088	0,01682	0,04894	4,7614	1,95E-06
School is boring and not useful***	0,082034	0,014284	0,050859	5,742895	9,55E-09
Trouble in school***	0,0921	0,014961	0,057085	6,155923	7,72E-10
Time with friends***	0,09444	0,014429	0,058983	6,545362	6,19E-11
Drank or played hookie***	0,157787	0,017691	0,0978	8,919142	5,41E-19
Use of PC***	0,218396	0,014009	0,139142	15,59009	3,09E-54
Trimmed reported sum payments per month***	0,000212	1,23E-05	0,16278	17,26888	5,57E-66

Dependent Variable: SMS1A

R	R Square	Adjusted R Square	Std. Error of the Estimate
0,378271	0,143089	0,141885	1,425721

References

Cochran, M. et al. 1993. "The social networks of coupled mothers in four cultures." Pp. 86–104 in *Extending families: The social networks of parents and their children.*, edited by M. Cochran et al. Cambridge: Cambridge.

Di Leonardo, M. 1987. "The female world of cards and holidays: Women, families and the work of kinship." *Signs: Journal of women in culture and society* 12:440–453.

Elliott, D., D. Huzsinga, and S.S. Ageton. 1985. *Explaining delinquency and drug use.* NewYork: Sage.

Elliott, G., and S.S. Ageton. 1979. "An integrated theoretical perspective on delinquent behavior." *Journal of research in crime and delinquency* 16:3–27.

Ellwood-Clayton, Bella. 2003. "Virtual strangers: Young love and texting in the Filipino archipelago of cyberspace." Pp. 35–45 in *Mobile Democracy: Essays on Society, Self and Politics*, edited by K. Nyiri. Vienna: Passagen Verlag.

Fine, G.A. 1981. "Friends, impression management, and pre-adolescent behavior." in *The development of children's friendships*, edited by S.R. Asher and J.M. Gottman. Cambridge: Cambridge University Press.

——. 1987. *With the boys: Little league baseball and preadolescent culture.* Chicago: University of Chicago Press.

Giordano, P. C. 1995. "The Wider Circle of Friends in Adolescence." *American Journal of Sociology* 101:661–697.

Glaser, A., and B. Strauss. 1971. *Status passage.* London: Routledge and Kegen, Paul.

Harper, R. 2003. "Are mobiles good or bad for society?" Pp. 71–94 in *Mobile Democracy: Essays on Society, Self and Politics*, edited by K. Nyiri. Vienna: Passagen Verlag.

Harter, S. 1990. "Self and identity development." Pp. 352–387 in *At the threshold: The developing adolescent*, edited by S.S. Feldman and G.R. Elliott. Cambridge, Mass: Harvard.

Hashimoto, Y. 2002. "The spread of cellular phones and their influence on young people in Japan." Pp. 101–112 in *The social and cultural impact/meaning of mobile communication*, edited by S. D. Kim. Chunchon, Korea: School of Communication Hallym University.

Hirschi, T. 1969. *The causes of delinquency.* Berkeley: University of California.

Kasesniemi, E-L., and P. Rautiainen. 2002. "Mobile culture of children and teenagers in Finland." Pp. 170–192 in *Perpetual contact: Mobile communication, private talk, public performance*, edited by J. E. Katz and M. Aakhus. Cambridge: Cambridge University Press.

Lemert, E.M. 1951. *Social Pathology.* New York: McGraw-Hill.

Lemert, E.M. 1967. *Human deviance, social problems and social control.* Englewood Cliffs, N.J.: Prentice Hall.

Ling, R. 2000. ""We will be reached": The use of mobile telephony among Norwegian youth." *Information technology and people* 13:102 – 120.

——. 2001a. "Adolescent girls and young adult men: Two sub-cultures of the mobile telephone." Kjeller: Telenor R&D.

——. 2001b. ""It is 'in.' It doesn't matter if you need it or not, just that you have it."": Fashion and the domestication of the mobile telephone among teens in Norway." in *Il corpo umano tra tecnologie, comunicazione e moda" (The human body between technologies, communication and fashion)*, edited by L Fortunati. Triennale di Milano, Milano.

——. 2003. "The socio-linguistics of SMS: An analysis of SMS use by a random sample of Norwegians." in *Front Stage/Back Stage: Mobile communication and the renegotiation of the social sphere*, edited by R. Ling and P. Pedersen. Grimstad, Norway.

——. 2004. *The Mobile Connection: The cell phone's impact on society*. San Francisco: Morgan Kaufmann.

Ling, R., and P. Helmersen. 2000. ""It must be necessary, it has to cover a need": The adoption of mobile telephony among pre-adolescents and adolescents." in *The social consequences of mobile telephony*. Oslo.

Ling, R., and B. Yttri. 2003. "Kontroll, frigjøring og status: Mobiltelefon og maktforhold i familier og ungdomsgrupper." in *På terskelen: makt, mening og motstand blant unge*, edited by F. Engelstad and G. Ødegård. Oslo: Gyldendal Akademisk.

Lynne, A. 2000. "Nyansens makt – en studie av ungdom, identitet og klær." Lysaker: Statens institutt for forbruksforskning.

Mante-Meijer, E., et al. 2001. "Checking it out with the people – ICT markets and users in Europe." Heidelberg: EURESCOM.

Merton, R. 1968. *Social theory and social structure*. New York: Free Press.

Moore, G. 1990. "Structural determinants of men's and women's personal networks." *American sociological review* 55:726–735.

Moyal, A. 1992. "The gendered use of the telephone: an Australian case study." *Media culture and society* 14:51–72.

Pedersen, W., and S.O. Samuelsen. 2003. "Nye mønstre av seksualatferd blant ungdom." *Tidsskrift for Den norske lægeforeningen* 21:3006–3009.

Rakow, L.F. 1992. *Gender on the line*. Urbana: University of Illinois.

Rakow, L.F., and V. Navarro. 1993. "Remote mothering and the parallel shift: Women meet the cellular telephone." *Critical studies in mass communication* 10:144-157.

Rautiainen, P., and E-L. Kasesniemi. 2000. "Mobile communication of children and teenagers: case Finland 1997–2000." Pp. 15–18 in *Sosiale konsekvenser av mobiletelefoni: proceedings fra et seminar om samfunn, barn og mobile telefoni*, edited by R. Ling and K. Thrane. Kjeller: Telenor FoU.

Rosenthal, C. 1985. "Kinkeeping in the familial division of labor." *Journal of marriage and the family* 47:965 – 974.

Rossow, I., and A.K. Bø. 2003. "Metoderapport for datainnsamlingen til Ung i Norge 2002." Oslo: NOVA.

Rubin, L. 1985. *Just friends: The role of friendship in our lives*. New York: Harper.

Savin-Williams, R.C., and T.J. Berndt. 1990. "Friendship and peer relations." Pp. 277–307 in *At the threshold: The developing adolescent*, edited by S.S. Feldman and G.R. Elliott Cambridge, Mass.: Harvard.

Schneider, B., and D. Stevenson. 1999. *The ambitious generation: America's teenagers, motivated but directionless*. New Haven: Yale University Press.

Skog, B., and A.I. Jamtøy. 2002. "Ungdom og SMS." Trondheim: ISS NTNU.

Youniss, J. 1980. *Parents and peers in social development: a Piaget-Sullivan perspective*. Chicago: Univ. of Chicago.

Youniss, J., and J. Smollar. 1985. *Adolescent relations with mothers, fathers and friends*. Chicago: University of Chicago press.

10 Desire and Loathing in the Cyber Philippines

Bella Elwood-Clayton

Introduction

Ping-Ping & Albert part 1

Another text!

Ping-Ping is sure that it's a woman who recently has been texting Albert, her husband (asawa). More and more frequently, when Albert receives texts, his body language becomes awkward and his eyes avoid hers. And he's been receiving texts late into the evening!

The nagging feeling that something is just not right has made Ping-Ping wonder how she could, and whether she should, get her hands on his cell phone. If able to do this, Ping-Ping would be able to read Albert's inbox (the collection of messages he had received and chosen to save), scroll through the calls he most recently placed and received, and determine the existence or degree of cyber faithfulness that he had. If unable to discern traces of infidelity, Ping-Ping could also scroll through his address book with a keen eye for a female name Ping-Ping herself does not know – or perhaps a name she knows all too well.

All this is possible since besides a short password, which an intimate could easily observe and recall – no identification is needed to access one's cellular information. Manufacturing more sophisticated technology of this sort would certainly have a strong market, were rates of cyber (if not physical) adultery in the Philippines considered.

Paradoxically, an easy way to catch a cheating partner is to pay close attention to whom he/she is texting and to read his/her *inbox* when they are unaware. Yet, since texting is essentially silent (the sound of an incoming text can simply be deactivated) and often a solitary practice, texting also enables cheaters to transmit quick messages and confirm adulterous rendezvous.

Richard Harper, Leysia Palen and Alex Taylor (Eds), The Inside Text: Social, Cultural and Design Perspectives on SMS, 195–219.

The new type of communication that SMS provides its users is producing conditions whereby friends' expectations of each others' accessibility increases, and in which lovers attempt to monitor one another. Linked to this are themes related to *perpetual contact* (Katz 2002) and *absent presence* (Gergen 2002). This chapter pays special heed to the ways in which these fields of experiences – these increasing obligations to 'the other' – are conceptualised by texters in the Philippines. It highlights the ways in which texters respond to increased social pressures to be accessible to one another – whether through embracement or rejection of these new demands.

Copious numbers of text how-to books are sold in the bookstores of the Philippines – "Text to Text," "Ring Tones and Grafix," "The Lord is my Textmate." However, none provide tutorship about (the scholarly underrepresented yet highly active) group of texters engaged in text combat. "How To Deeply Wound Others By Text and Nasty Ring Tones," is not found in the commercial market. Let me speak to the adage, that *all's fair in love and war* – if this is not true, analysis of the texting phenomenon in the Philippines certainly highlights users fallible human preoccupations with both. I have discussed elsewhere[1] the ways in which texting is uprooting traditional courtship, and providing young Filipinas with a new site in which they can experiment with romantic agency and potentially subvert traditional gender ideologies in the domain of young love. Indeed, texting was found to be a particularly provocative way to seduce, develop intimacy, and fall in love. In contrast, in this work, besides highlighting the overall characteristics of texting in the Filipino setting, I treat the dark side of SMS: hostilities in cyberspace among intimates.

Specifically, in this chapter I examine texting as a medium that supports the identity exploration of social actors and acts to intensify and alter both virtual and lived relationships. By presenting empirical vignettes and the voiced experiences of Filipino texters, I illuminate intersecting dimensions of conflict in wireless cyberspace. I highlight themes relating to misinterpretation, anger, jealousy, gossip, issues concerning fidelity and deception, the termination of text and/or lived relationships by text, and text stalkers.

I will demonstrate the double-edged nature of texting in the Philippines. Locally appropriated by its users, texting is employed as a strategy to express the taboos of desire and loathing, and thus is utilized both as a romantic tool and a vindictive weapon. Unlike other researchers who posit that texting essentially acts to circumvent potential conflict (e.g. in the Philippines, see Pertierra 2002: 91; and in a comparative study of text exchange in France and Japan (see chapter 6; and in Japan chapter 7), my research indicates that although texting may indeed *sometimes* ward off conflict, it too has insidious, far-reaching effects which are played out among intimates in the social arena. Research findings indicate that texting in the

---

[1] See: Ellwood-Clayton, Bella, "Virtual Strangers: Young Love and Texting in the Filipino Archipelago of Cyberspace", in Kristof Nyiri (ed.) *Mobile Democracy: Essays on Society, Self and Politics*, Vienna: Passager Verlag, 2003. pp. 225-239.

Filipino context is often a form of artillery in personal combats and can, in fact, propel and increase peril among social actors, at times manifesting in different forms of trouble and/or (symbolic) violence.

In discussing the texting phenomena, readers will note my frequent reference to SMS communication as occurring in a site that is cyber. Cyberspace is derived from the Greek lexical item, *kyber*, which means 'to navigate,' and can be understood as a conceptual space within information communication technologies (ICTs) (Dodge and Kitchin 2001:1). Hayles (1999)[2] characterizes cyberspace as a distinctive realm of electronic connection that has resulted in the creation of new public arenas. She describes spaces such as these as essentially being a "continually evolving environment which provides an opportunity to meet and interact with others in that environment (p. x). Moreover, the new types of communication made possible through ICTs are "radically restructuring the materiality and spatiality of space and the relationship between people and place" (Dodge and Kitchin 2001: ix), and are thereby extending social action and interaction through new medias (ibid.).

Data in this article derives from ethnographic fieldwork conducted in Kalibo (from 2001-2003) on youth, sexual and reproductive health, and social change. Kalibo is situated in the central Philippines and has a population of 63,000 people, 90 % of whom are Catholic denomination.[3] Data-gathering techniques included standard anthropological methods: in-depth interviewing (with 60 respondents), survey, focus group discussions and participant observation, as well as analysis of popular culture. Through immersion in the everyday lives of my participants, I aimed to illicit contextualised and non-judgemental understandings of young women's lives in terms of their socio-cultural, economic, and historic surroundings and lived experiences.

Research respondents consisted mostly of young women (aged 15-29), although women from older age categories, (young) men, community players, and local health personal also contributed to the research endeavour. I was able to interview women from lower, middle and higher socio-economic brackets, and diverse educational standings.

Due to the ongoing nature of fieldwork, I also observed texters in Manila and in (holiday-destination) Boracay. In addition, by living in the local community, and by being in an age category that was similar to my participants, many of the "research subjects" became my close friends. The nature of our friendships allowed for easy sharing of mutual intimate narratives regarding (text) relationships.

Throughout this work, I employ fictional characters (e.g. Ping-Ping and Albert), based on the précis of accumulative research findings, in order to illustrate typical

---

[2] See Hayles, Katherine, "The Condition of Virtuality," in Lunefeld, Peter (ed.) *The Digital Dialectic: New Essays on New Media.* Cambridge, Massachusetts: The MIT Press, 1999.

[3] www.census.gov.ph.

text-scripts. I borrow the notion of *script* from Gagnon's and Simon's (1986) [4] work on sexual-scripts. Described as "a metaphor for conceptualising the production of behaviour within social life", scripts offer guidance to social actors, such as how operating syntax relates to language (ibid.).

Lexical moonshine

The ways in which language is "contaminated" in geographical space due to the popularity of text lexicon is being publicly criticized throughout the national forum. Analysis of popular Filipino culture (e.g. newspaper articles, talk shows, radio) and personal anecdotes revealed numerous stories about students handing in essay assignments in text format. (A cultural informant who worked as a high school teacher in Kalibo verified this as occurring in her classroom). Debates about whether texting, rife with incorrect grammar and misspelling, will result in the bastardization of language are a strong presence in the local media.

Texter's range of expression (unlike those engaged in Internet dialogue) is restricted by length, and debatably because of this, is considered limited in emotional substance. However, as I shall demonstrate, texting as a medium of communication is often far from superficial communiqué. The unique brand of shorthand often relied upon by texters can be conceptualised as a form of postmodern lexicon, which I would like to apply as something of a *lexical moonshine.* This term hints to that which is: (stylistically) mixed, illegal (illicit) activities, to moonlight (and thus clandestine meetings), the working of two jobs (or having perhaps a double identity) and potential drunkenness (lack of inhibitions); as does it suggest notions of substance-change or transformation through the distillation process. The concept of lexical moonshine demonstrates how information communication and technologies (ICTs) are providing new forms of communication that blend together written and oral styles to produce new linguistic registers and create new rules of language (see Reid 1994; Cherry 1995); and, in doing so, act to challenge modernist forms of communication (Dodge and Kitchin 2001: 21).

Like cell phones themselves (see Chapter 2), the linguistic typographies that texters choose to employ are highly individualized. This is especially apparent among youth (e.g. users' choice of full spelling or abbreviation, capitalization decisions, image-making, line spacing, and so on). By reinventing codes and concocting new vocabulary, young texters become co-producers of new styles of communication. Moreover, through the standardisation of their constructions, we can see how young users are agents in reconfiguring language. In many cases, they also exclude others (e.g. parents) who are unaware of these new styles and codes.

Whether a spontaneous or crafted endeavour, many SMS users enjoy the playful elements of text communication. During fieldwork I found that Filipinos send two

---

[4] W Simon and J.H Gagnon, "Sexual Scripts: Performance and Change", *Archives of Sexual Behaviour* 15 (1986) pp. 97-120.

types of messages to one another, what I have termed 'hallmark' (forwarded) and personal (self-composed) texts. Hallmark texts are often maudlin and corny, but there seems to be no stigma or irony involved in sending or receiving them. These syrupy clichés pertaining to love, God and friendship are sent like chain letters throughout the archipelago (Ellwood-Clayton 2003). Personalized text messages could include: invitations to parties, comments about a mutual friend, questions about a meeting time, or more intimate dialogue.

Riviere and Licoppe (this volume) note how texters in France "take pleasure in playing with words, shaping language, [and] creating ambiguity" (p. 111). I posit that the literary freedom which SMS communication provides its young users, and the inventive way that they, in turn, play with language, is somewhat akin to the work of e.e. cummings. Describing cumming's literary style, poet critic Randall Jarrell stated:

> *cummings is a very great expert in all these, so to speak, illegal syntactical*
> *devices: his misuse of parts of speech, his use of negative prefixes, his*
> *word-coining, his systematic relation of words that grammar and syntax*
> *don't permit us to relate – all this makes him a magical bootlegger or*
> *moonshiner of language, one who intoxicates us on a clear liquor no*
> *government has legalized with its stamp.*[5]

Texters too reject convention and propriety in their linguistic expression and thus create a bootlegged or moonshine form of language, which is sometimes used for good, and other times, as this article will testify, different degrees of "evil."

The Philippines – the text capital of the World

Before presenting empirical vignettes about hostility in cyberspace, let me first familiarize the reader with the general characteristics of the texting phenomena in the Philippines. I will briefly discuss economic rationale for such high rates of text exchange, explain who texters are, how users acquire cell phones and choose among payment options, and explore the sentiments of those who cannot afford a cell phone. I will then look at how cell phone discourse has become infiltrated into social life, and the locally perceived benefits of text exchange as likened to specific cultural values and social conditions.

The Philippines is heralded as the texting capital of the world, with one hundred million texts being sent around the archipelago daily (Pertierra 2002).[6] Although there are less cell-phone owners in the Philippines than in other countries, reports confirm that the number of text messages sent by SMS users is double the world

---

[5] As accessed on the Internet on October 19th, 2003, at site: http://www.empirezine.com/spotlight/cummings/cummings/com/html.

[6] As reported in Raul Pertierra, Eduardo F. Ugarte, Alicia Pingol, Joel Hermandez and Nikos Lexis Decanay, (2002) *Txting Selves: Cellphone and Philippine Modernity,* Manila: De La Salle University Press.

average (ibid.). Locally, many users are referred to as "generation texters". They are usually urban or semi-urban citizens, from lower-middle economic brackets and up, and are often students (fieldwork 2001-2003).

A main dominator in why texting has been so readily adopted by Filipinos is due to the inadequate infrastructure and notorious unreliability of traditional landlines (see Strom's 2002)[7]. The popularity of texting correlates directly to its low-cost. To send one text costs a mere Peso (approximately U.S $ 0.02) versus the relatively expensive rates of telephone calls made directly from cell phones. Despite the low-cost of texting, students (especially) use a large percentage of their spending money (given to them by their parents or relatives) on prepaid calling cards, resulting in many parents and/or elders/authority figures/community members, casting disapproving eyes.

Cell phone owners in the Philippines have the option to choose from competing networks (either SMART or GLOBE), and to decide which payment plan they prefer: either 'pay as you go' or a contract with monthly bills. Most Kalibonhons opt for the former as it grants them more flexibility over their spending. Prepaid calling cards can be bought ubiquitously (e.g. *sari sari* [corner] stores, supermarkets) and are offered in varying amounts (e.g. in 200 or 500 Peso quantities). Currently, 30 Peso "load" (credit) is now available in the Philippines; however, the credit expires within a three-day period.

Exploring the streets of Kalibo, an observer would notice an abundance of young teenagers and impoverished people texting on cell phones. How do the young, and how do the poor, acquire relatively costly cell phones? Questions such as these, concerning the process of obtaining a cell phone, and issues surrounding prioritising a cell phone over other purchases in "third world" or impoverished settings, deserves more academic attention. For example, as in the situation of my neighbours while in the field, would a family that ran a *sari-sari* (corner) store invest in one shared family cell phone, or put their small income towards their son's schooling? My neighbours opted for the highly visual, social status item: the cell phone. However, they would be able to utilize their cell phone as a business tool, for example, by being able to ensure supplies. In addition, by using a cell phone, my neighbours would have more direct control and awareness over their personal spending (versus relying on less regulated landline companies). Thus, their decision to purchase a cell phone can be viewed as a decision to actively embrace entrepreneurial agency.[8]

In terms of acquisition, it is common practice for young people to receive their cell phones as a gift from their parents or an elder sibling (as also reported as occurring

---

[7] George Strom, (2002) "The Telephone comes to a Filipino Village", in James E. Katz and Mark Aakhus (eds.), pp. 274-283.

[8] For related discussions regarding the relationship between mobile phone use and small enterprises in the Rwanda setting, see: Donner, Jonathan, (2003) "What Mobile Phones Mean to Rwandan Entrepreneurs" pp 393-411 in Kristof Nyiri (ed.) *Mobile Democracy: Essays on Society, Self and Politics*, Vienna: Passager Verlag.

among young people in Seoul, South Korea, see Yoon, this volume), or occasionally from a boyfriend, the latter being the ultimate romantic gift within the Filipino context due to the relationship between texting and romance. Besides the common practice of buying oneself a new cell phone from a retail outlet, or less commonly, the black market, other forms of acquisition included purchasing a second hand cell phone, or acquiring a phone through *pamilia* (family) networks (also reported by Yoon, this volume). In addition, it is common for people to purchase their cell phone through remittences from family members living overseas.

A strong example of how cell discourse has infiltrated social life as a powerful, far-reaching communication device is testified by its instrumental use in the overthrowing of Philippine president Joseph Estrada in January 2001 (for further discussion see Pertierra, 2002 and Paragas, 2003). Texting has become incorporated into local sensibilities, with many users dependent on this type of communication. Increasingly, many respondents – especially young users – consider their cell phone to be a necessity. Numerous humorous stories are told concerning *balik-bayans* (those who leave the country in seek of better employment opportunities – for example as a *yaya* [nanny] in Saudi Arabia) undergoing "text-sickness" as well as homesickness, when divorced from the text-friendly universe of the Philippines. In addition, popular culture analysis (of newspapers, magazines, talk shows, radio) found frequent reference to the onset of mild depression when one's cell phone is either lost or *snatched.* Cell phone snatching is an extremely common occurrence in the Philippines, particularly in highly urbanized areas. Cell phone owners are expected to have acute awareness at all times of the position of their phones and are highly aware of their vulnerability to theft.

Users cell phones are often highly individualized. Personalizing a cell phone is created by adopting new "casing" (the outer plastic which houses the cell phone) which can be bought in a plethora of colours and patterns (zebra, camouflage, cartoons); the use of waterproof protectors (sensible, considering the climate); different coloured screen lights (blue, orange) can be purchased; and phone jewellery may be incorporated (colourful straps, antenna caps, flashing and anti-radiation stickers). The cell phone as a fashion accessory has been reported in numerous cross-cultural settings (e.g. see in Italy, Fortunati 2002: 42-63). To further personalize one's cell phone, special interchangeable ring-tones and logos are commonly adopted. The symbolic values of cell phones vary among cell phone owners, with many young women particularly treating their cell phones with reverence. For example, it is not uncommon for young women to sleep with their cell phones on their pillow, and "dress" them in different looks, and thus attributing them with doll-like or pet qualities. It is interesting to compare this phenomenon to that of "virtual pets" in Japan.[9]

---

[9]Site http://www.virtualpet.com/vp/research/research.htm (as accessed on November 15th, 2003, has an excellent collection of virtual pet research, accompanied with an annotated bibliography.

Many Filipinos do not own a cell phone. In general, they are from the eldest and poorest sub-groups of the population. These cyber have-nots are severed from the excitement, enjoyment and convenience of the wireless world as well as the associated social status of being a cell owner. Almost all of my research respondents who did not own a cell phone expressed some degree of discontent about this. When asked how they felt about not having a cell phone, a common response was stating that they were upset "of course". One respondent commented: "it doesn't mean if you don't have any mobile, that you will be desperate and all that". Cyber have-nots often conceptualised texting as a "fad" or "trend". These concepts are most often used by those without mobile access as a strategy to counter the social importance of texting in the Filipino setting – for, important it is.

A small number of cell owners did not consider texting very important. Although they still noted the convenience of the cell phone (in communicating with friends or in terms of business interactions), for some, texting was not considered especially meaningful, e.g. "I just use it for work" said Karen (age 28, manicurist). Others considered the cost for a prepaid card disadvantageous. For example, Brenty (age 23, Mormon[10] high school student) commented that texting is "just important for communication, but not all the time, because I'm saving my load. I prefer to use my money in buying a dress than the cell card". Yet, in the majority of cases, texting has momentous importance in (young) people's social worlds and enhances users' quality of life.

Txt 2 txt

Q: Is having a cell phone important?

A: Yeah, that's my best friend (laughs). I can't live without my cell phone (name, age...).

What makes texting so enticing, and why has it become omnipresent in the Filipino setting? The following section explores the locally proclaimed benefits associated with SMS. Texting as a medium of communication is perceived to be: a superior form of communication due to mobility and practicality; an enjoyable form of recreation; a vehicle of "connection" which prevails over geographic space; a social support resource; means of gaining and nurturing friendships (and boyfriends) and; to "express what you cannot say" or, as enabling emotional bravery. Below, each of these chief attributes is discussed.

Texting: A superior form of communication: mobility and practicality

The use of the cell phone for young mobile youth whose daily life may often involve several venues ensures continuity of contact at all times. SMS users found texting to be a superior form of communication due to attributes associated with mobility and practicality. In particular, texting was viewed as a medium that offers

---

[10] Unless otherwise stated, all respondents should be presumed to be of Catholic denomination.

social assistance and cohesion to desired communicators. Not only was texting cited as "great for emergencies", it was especially favoured for its speed: "it's faster communication", explained one respondent, "through text you can say it right away". Another respondent commented on the convenience of SMS: "Unlike before, you have to call on the phone and you cannot reach them if they're not at home or [at the] office; at least now you can reach them anywhere". Thus, a chief benefit of SMS was cited as being able to track/have access to (or leave a message for) the person one desires to communicate with. "Of course", said one respondent, "it makes life easier for you because you can get in touch with people wherever they are".

In addition, text communication was found to be "easy" at an operational level and inexpensive. For those in the formal labour industry, SMS was commonly cited as improving business relationships and making work-related interactions swifter. Thus, youth are concerned with removing spatial boundaries and cell phones allow for control over other people's movements, which is particularly important for business partnership. These combined benefits further SMS into local status as a superior communication device.

Texting: An enjoyable form of recreation

A pastime occupies one's thoughts and time and oftentimes acts as a pleasurable diversion away from the concerns of everyday life; it relaxes and amuses. Respondents perceived texting as a pastime that was "fun" and entertaining. It was also conceptualised as an activity that acts to alleviate boredom (as also reported by respondents in Yoon's 2003 study, this volume). Describing this, Arwen, a twenty-three year old college student, explains:

> It's just a pastime when you're bored. You text so you can have communications [sic]. Like when I'm alone, my uncle goes out, I don't have anything to do, [so] I text.

In addition, fieldwork supports that in Kalibo, despite sometimes working long hours, office and government workers, as well as many young professionals and those in the service industry, are positioned in relaxed atmospheres and allotted with generous 'free time.' This situation allows for dense amounts of discreet text exchange during working hours. For example, one of my research respondents working as a lawyer receives up to 6-10 texts from her boss *before* her lunchtime break, on a daily basis.

Here we can see the enjoyment associated with the repetitive nature of SMS-ing versus other forms of enjoyment, which require different degrees of imagination and skill (e.g. reading) or interpersonal skills (face-to-face communication).

Texting: SMS connection prevailing over geographical space

Keeping in touch with a loved one (family member or friend) and being able to "communicate even if you're far apart" was expressed as a major advantage of text communication. In a national economic situation of high relocation and migration overseas,[11] participants found texting to be an affordable, fast and endearing way to keep in touch, "so I feel like they're here with me". As other respondents expressed: "keeping in touch with someone far away, you text *ok na yon* [that would be ok], even if you can't hear his voice"; and, even if a loved one is far away, it "feels like he is just nearby". The extent to which people use SMS for work or study commitments, which act to prevent them from visiting family members, is also high. Texting supports the maintenance of social relationships despite crossing regional boundaries. Thus, SMS provides a financially solvent and particularly rewarding form of adhesion in maintaining familial and social relationships – a domain almost rhetorically important (Tan 2002) in the Filipino setting.

Texting: A social support resource

> *Sometimes the messages my friends send me are inspirational and they make me feel better when I'm down. Sometimes it's coincidental they send me messages that I need to hear. (Melinda, age 29, married mother, housewife).*

Many respondents also articulated the emotional support associated with text exchange. If, for example, a person is feeling sad or lonesome, she can find solace in receiving an unexpected kind text message, or, she can communicate her predicament to a *textpal* (a close platonic text friend). As one respondent explained, "it uplift[s] you when you are sad. Then you can talk to someone, so it helps". Or another: "Picture messages and some messages are quite significant in your daily life. It's good to have someone reminding you how wonderful life is!" Certainly, texting can operate as a celebrator of life, friendship and love. For example, receiving a text such as the following in the morning could instil pleasurable feelings: *"SACRED HEART of JESUS CHRIST shower d person readn dis wid ur blesngs 2day & always."*[12] (Here we can see how the symbolic value of text messages whereby they do not need to be individualized – as the meaning is attached to the shared values incorporated into messages.)

Even if the said person is not feeling particularly "blue," text messages are found to provide inspiration to those who send and receive them. Texting can often be perceived as social 'pick-you-ups.' The exchanges act as reminders of faith, love and friendship, and reinforce cultural values of enjoying the good that life has to offer despite numerous external hardships. A joke received during a "brown-out" (loss of electricity), or a poem about friendship, charge texters with a sense of being cared for and remembered. Texting, in a sense, acts as a form social or

---

[11] For example see, "Government debate rages over foreign workers", *The Post,* Jan 16 – Feb 12, 2003, p. 6.

[12] Due to space limitations, I will not further discuss dissemination of religious ideas through the vehicle of SMS. However, I am currently working on an article that responds to these themes.

emotional hospitality – hospitality being a highly honoured Filipino (e.g. Agoncillo and Guerrero, 1977[13]) – and certainly Kalibonhon (Reyes-Tinagan, 2001[14]) trait. Thus, inspirational text messages can be understood as goodwill enacted on a micro level through cyber means, and enacting goodwill, vis-à-vis text communication, only takes minutes – or even seconds.

This notion of goodwill can be likened to Mauss's (1924) conceptions of gift giving and reciprocity (as also briefly linked to texting by Taylor and Harper, 2002; Kasesniemi and Rautianen, 2002; Pertierra; and Yoon 2003). In *The Gift*, Mauss argues that reciprocity is not only situated through economic exchange, but is found to operate in social systems. Mauss argues that parties are obligated to exchange goods *appropriately* and this is dependent on the specific cultural context. Thus, texting can be viewed as a somewhat balanced form of reciprocity, where like is exchanged for like (text for text). In addition, although there is no time set for "text repayment," differing assumptions regarding *appropriate* SMS communication is cause for strife among social actors, as the later sections of this article testify.

Texting: Gaining and nurturing friendships (and boyfriends)

Texting has a strong presence in the enriching of social relationships. As reported as occurring in other settings (e.g. see Ling and Yttri, 2002: 160; Yoon, this volume), in the Philippines the mobile phone operates to assist the development of newly acquired friendships. Young people, in particular, spoke of SMS as a means to gain new friends: "you get to know different people and you get new acquaintances", and: "well, you get to have more friends". Texting is also said to support friendship, by way of "thoughtfulness", and was perceived as a tool to nurture close relationships. Texting was also reported to be a key method in finding, experimenting and nurturing amorous relationships (see Ellwood-Clayton 2003).

People form various types of text-relationships in numerous ways, resulting in diverse outcomes. Two areas are central to understanding the configurations of text relationships – the degree of prior knowledge of the texter and textee, and the overall type of exchange in terms of emotional intention. Thus, the chief formulae in understanding text relationships is whether the parties stem from existing or new acquaintanceship, whether their central relationship is cyber or embodied, and whether the exchange is platonic, possibly amorous (in many cases, this is quite difficult to determine) – or clearly amorous.

In terms of existing acquaintanceship, people text acquaintances, friends, family members, and/or work colleagues. Through exchange of texts, these relationships are often fostered and in some cases, altered. In addition, people text existing

---

[13] Agoncillo, Teodoro and Guerrero, Milagros,(1977) *History of the Filipino People*. R.P Garcia: Quezon City.

[14] See for example, Reyes-Tinagan, Marcella. (2001) *Viva! Kay Senor Santo Nino. Viva!* National Commission for Culture and the Arts: Manila.

amorous relations, i.e. possible suitors, suitors, boyfriends and husbands, thereby also (often fostering) and changing relationships. People also text as a method to make *new* acquaintances, friends and romantic relations.

The process of turning a stranger into an acquaintance, an acquaintance into a friend, and to convert friends and acquaintances into romantic partners, is heightened through text communication. Anonymous texters act as the wild card in the formation of text relationships. Appearing mysteriously from the abyss of the cyber universe, high rates of "anonymous texters" are found across the Filipino archipelago. In most cases, mutual friends aid anonymous texters by giving them the cell phone numbers that are so desired. Another common means to locate a person desiring a "textmate" (close text friend) is through personal adds in the back of comic and music magazines, as well as in text how-to books. The following example comes from "Text Friends (Text me Forever 5): The Texter's Latest Guide on Friendship, Dating, Romance and Real Love."[15]

Hey watz up? Txt me if ur doin' nothing...c")	*I luv sweet msgs. But I love most... sweet people!*
Kid/ 20/ f	*Rose/ 23/ f*
09182489784	*O9195680530*

After initial preliminary questions (e.g. usually finding out the gender, age and availability of a textee) or almost immediately, the anonymous texter will ask: *"can I b ur txtm8?"* (can I be your textmate?). It is not unusual for virtual strangers (anonymous texters and receiving textees) to later form (varying degrees of intimate) relationships.

Texting: As enabling emotional bravery

Well, you know sometimes you cannot express [yourself] personally, so you can resolve it through texting (Inday, age 33, young professional).

Finally, texting was frequently conceptualised as a medium where respondents felt comfortable communicating otherwise difficult information. As one respondent said, "important matters could be discussed even in texting alone". Users' acknowledgment of SMS as a medium to express what they would not feel comfortable communicating in person, manifests itself richly when analysing the expression of desire and loathing. Texting was found to instil personal bravery among its users (as findings from studies conducted by Kasesniemi and Yttri, 2002, and Pertierra, 2002, concur). Key in terms of romance and conflict, texting can be conceptualised as enabling emotional bravery, sometimes offering its users a

---

[15] King, David. 2001. Wordlink Books: Manila.

medium of personal liberation from perceived restraints of traditional communication.

In summary, we can see how the use and appreciated advantages of SMS relate to specific social conditions (e.g. poor telecommunications infrastructure, notions of alienation in the modern world due to urbanization, relocation) which ultimately lead to fragmented communication, of which SMS is one way of combating that isolation. The conflicting nature of texting, which is itself, fragmented, but also serves to overcome fragmentation of an individual, is also linked to cultural values (e.g. the importance of maintaining familial relations).

Moreover, texting provides a vehicle in which to communicate privately in a setting of general governmental and religious conservatism (CPA 1999: 42, Law 2000). Interestingly, this conservative climate is juxtaposed to strong operating romantic discourses (Tan 2001: 82). During fieldwork, respondents described the "Filipino" disposition as being "emotional", "loving", and "romantic": in sum, a "sentimental" people. Indeed, ideas of romantic love are pervasive and central in the social scripts involving dating, courtship and marriage in the Filipino setting (Tan 2001: 82).

Thus, the relationship between technologies, and the ways in which different groups use these technologies, benefit from anthropological analysis. As Penley and Ross (1991) have so aptly stated:

> *Technologies are not repressively foisted onto passive populations... they are developed at any one time and place in accord with a complex set of existing rules or rational procedures, and... popular desires.*

Technologies are incorporated in relation to users desires. The ways in which texting is appropriated is culturally and historically specific (as addressed by Riviere and Licoppe, this volume) – although, as the authors (Riviere and Licoppe) state, within a wider historical framework, localized findings can also generate overall insights about the direction of interpersonal communications.

Part II: Albert & Raquel

> *Three months ago, Albert texted Raquel for the first time and, in doing so, turned Raquel's life upside down.*

> *She'd been hanging out at a new fast-food restaurant that had opened in Kalibo, enjoying a* halo-halo *(cool dessert) and the air-conditioned relief from the outside heat when she received a text from an unknown number. It read: "helo Raquel, havn a gud day?"*

> *She typed in the immediate response: "who s dis?"*

> *"a special frend... I hope???"*

> *"who gave u my name n numbr?"*

"I hav d best connectns n town ☺!"

Raquel let the cell phone sit in her lap, took a spoonful of ice cream, mused about her response for a moment and then sent: "wel, atleast uv got gud taste, huh?"

At that moment, Ping-Ping started back towards the car. Seeing her, Albert quickly slid his cell phone into his pocket and turned to help his wife with her shopping bags.

Equipped with a cell phone and linked to disembodied cyberspace, texters experience a release from geographical constraints, as well as freedom from context-based interpersonal communication. Other researchers such as Pertierra (2002: 91), maintain that texting generally aids in *avoiding* possible confrontations and conflict in the Philippine setting, Riviere and Licoppe (this volume) assert that SMS acts in a similar way in France, i.e. "Mobile messaging comes to be seen as a resource to avoid the potential conflict and minimize the vulnerability of face-to-face interactions ..." (p. 121). I argue, however, that particularly for young people who have less experience in expressing "embarrassing feelings" and in a culture that seeks to avoid interpersonal conflict (see e.g. Tan 2002), feelings of both affection *and* odium are expressed with less restraint through mobile communication.

Indeed, users rely on texting to coordinate meeting times and for other trivial social detailing, yet, it is also used to voice, to give life, to passions. This section of the chapter examines symbolic violence as experienced through texting. As Rapport & Overing (2000: 382-384) state, violence can only be understood anthropologically as a meaningfully experienced within the context of socio-cultural interactions. Moreover, the socio-cultural context of violence may be expected always to encompass both the done and the said, such that no ontological disjunction is positable between 'real' violence and 'symbolic' violence' (ibid). It may be an exaggeration to frame symbolic violence as equivalent to physical violence, one might say, they are almost the same.

Fighting among friends and lovers: 2 txt or nt 2 txt?

Fighting by text among friends and/or boyfriends was reported to be a common occurrence. Many of the respondents spoke freely of how easily they found it to "tell someone off" by way of text. This idea can be linked to Internet "flaming:" characterised by foul language and the abusive/disruptive posting of personal attacks and/or insulting, argumentative, or chastising messages. The palpable expression of anger through this medium was first brought to my attention during a focus group discussion with 15-year-old high school students (as the following excerpt demonstrates):

Hershy: *There are many people who deceive through text. There are those* bastos *[rude people]. If you're angry at a person, you just text him and he won't even know it's you texting him. You can text* gago *[crazy/stupid* *things], and whatever bad terms you want to say, that you can't say in person, you just text.*

Bella: *So you do that? You quarrel with someone through text?*

Group: *"Yeah". "Sometimes". "Grabe" (so bad)!*

When Hershey states that "he won't even know that it's you", she is referring to deceiving a textee by either contacting him whilst using a different SIM card (owning multiple SIM cards is becoming increasingly common) and thus becoming unidentifiable by cellular number, or using someone else's phone who the receiving textee would not have filed in their address book. Here too, the overt expressing of anger/dislike provides a solid example of how cyberspace 'permits' identity exploration (see Turkle 1995), especially with what is associated with the taboo. Following this theme, Gloria (age 27, young professional) explains:

> *...because in texting, you can say anything you want to. Example, if you don't have the courage to say it face-to-face, then you can text him, say, I don't know, you don't like him, or you don't like the way he acts or she acts, whatever (name, age...).*

Texting boosts users to communicate in ways they would not in person, e.g. "For instance, I'm really mad at this person and I can't tell it [sic] to his face... I really swear at him! I say to myself, okay, I swore at him, so what?!" Respondents articulated a changeover of character, made possible through the technology of SMS: "I'm not a sarcastic person, but when it comes to texting, it's easy for me to be harsh with someone", said one respondent. By assuming a different identity, texters embody the role of actors.

Specifically, perceived *bastos* (rude) text messages/"jokes" (some accompanied with "lewd" graphic images) served as a catalyst for the onslaught of text-conflict. During fieldwork, for example, one of my *bakla* (homosexual) friends forwarded to me the following message, of which many of a similar calibre are passed around the archipelago:

> *d polic hav found a badly decomposd body o a womn w no recognizble featrs xcpt a rily BIG VAGINA. So, m jst chekn- r u alryt? Pls reply.[16]*

A large number of interview respondents reported being upset by *bastos* "jokes" such as these – "usually, the green jokes which I really hate. Sometimes it's below the belt, right"? In turn, many retaliated with text combat. For example, Cherry recalls: "There was a boy who texted me some rude words, so I text him back. I told him if he wanted to text anybody just show some respect". Examples such as this demonstrate how social norms when communicating face-to-face are not

---

[16] This translates as: The police have found a badly decomposed body of a woman with no recognizable features except a really big vagina. So, I'm just checking—are you all right? Please reply.

adhered to in texting. Social boundaries are crossed in terms of age, gender and social class, as well as in terms of the content of communication.

Rivierer and Licoppe (this volume) highlight Japanese texters' use of pictograms to relay "serious, non-anecdotal feelings." Specifically, angry respondents spoke of using images such as a fist or tiger to convey their antagonism. Thus the authors conclude, that in Japan SMS and pictograms are becoming the favoured ways to express strong feelings, versus their findings in France, whereby SMS is often used to downplay conflict. We have been speaking about symbolic violence, however, in terms of physical violence, texting too acts as a medium to intimidate. For example, according to the Edinburgh News, SMS accounts for more than half of the threats of violence and/or intimidation in The Lothians area in Scotland.[17]

Albert & Raquel

After determining that Raquel's acquaintance had been the one to give Albert her cell number, the two settled into regular correspondence. Over the months of June, July and August, Raquel received texts from Albert on almost a daily basis. He would text her in the morning to wish her a good day, again, in the evening to make sure she had eaten. He filled her hours with small text surprises: jokes, sweet quotes, compliments and flirty banter, which she grew to treasure more than any exchanges she had with people in her physical life. At night she dreamt of Albert and in the morning she woke thinking of him.

By September she knew what she was feeling for Albert was love. Unable to suppress it any longer, she texted: "I thnk we shud meet".

Albert didn't reply for two whole days, and when he finally did, Raquel was at a loss to understand his message:

"o o (yes), lets meet... pero (but) it cn nvr wrk btwn us, I have a secreto (secret). Dnt b disapntd n m, sige (okay?)."[18]

Generally the domain of flirting too is a site of cyber contention. Text communication is often ambiguous (for example, is his *"gud nyt, sweet dreams"* text platonic or amorous?) and thus rife for misunderstandings and possible offence. That texting provides a space whereby communication is perceived to be less significant than a telephone call in terms of dating scripts, or face-to-face encounters, allows users to send messages which could be interpreted in many ways, to transmit double entendres and thus feel out the response of a given textee.

---

[17] See Mitchell, Simone, (2003) "RU IN2 SMS, THE GR8 NU WAY 4WARD," in City Careers, November 27th, p 9, Melbourne, Australia.

[18] This translates as: Yes, let's meet, but it can never work out between us, I have a secret. Don't be disappointed in me, okay?

An example of this may be a man sending his girlfriend's female friend the following SMS:[19]

HELLO	GooD Morning AND DAY	S W E ET E	t A K E	C A R E AND	G O D	B L E S S	U U UU U U	e --,) e	((--,) ((

How would the young woman respond to this text? What if more kept being sent, of an increasing romantic nature? For example: "Everyone wants 2 b the sun dat lights up your life. But id rather b ur moon, so I can shine on u during your darkest hour when your sun isn't around." What if the man's girlfriend found out about these texts exchanges? Although flirting by text can create discord, issues related to notions of perpetual contact were heralded as one of the most significant causes of strife among mobile users.

Shunning notions of perpetual contact

On a tram in late spring of 2003, in Melbourne where I was writing up my thesis, I overheard the beginnings of an argument between a young couple two seats behind me.

"Well, why didn't you answer it?" the man accused.

"My hands were wet," she tried to explain, speaking quickly. "The phone was in my bag."

In Katz's 2002 work, *Perpetual Contact*, he writes about ownership of a mobile phone as creating "the internal psychological feeling of being accessible or having access". As a consequence, social relationships are changing due to new pressures and obligations (p. xxi). Gergen (2002) specifically discusses this in terms of the notion of "absent presence" whereby "one is physically present but absorbed by a technologically mediated world of elsewhere" (p. 227).

Interview respondents reported quarrelling among their same-sex friends due to perceived obligations related to connectivity, e.g. "We usually end up fighting when I don't reply as soon as they [my friends] want me to". Certainly, evaluating the time lag between sending and receiving a text message serves a common *cyber* bone of contention when messages are not immediate returned. The time of text response provides a tidy way to judge the nature of one's relationship. Moreover, *not* responding to a text sends a larger message than any written form of

---

[19]This text was found in King's (2001: 58-61) text how-to book.

communication could. A non-response creates not only the feeling of absent presence, but more so, the sentiment of *present* absence presence: the recognition that one's gesture has been regarded as insignificant.[20] Texters, aware of their obligation to respond, have adopted routine comebacks to justify their unaccountability – *"low bat"*, *"no signal"*, or *"no load"*, all work – whether true or not. We can see how strife originates directly from this new sense of accountability. This plays out in terms of romance too, whereby perpetual contact and accountability uproot individual's privacy within romantic couplings. Amplifying the agony of the "waiting by the phone" scenario, mobile communication intensifies psychological levels of anxiety among romantic intimates. Rather than leaving a message on some ones' answering machine and resigning oneself to wait until the desired party is home (which is impossible to determine), texters have the ability for *constant* access, and are thus "waiting by the phone" in all locations throughout all days and nights.

Data accumulated during fieldwork indicates that many couples (boyfriends and girlfriends, husbands and wives) frequently fight by way of text. Below Lorna speaks to this:

> *Yes, I guess one example is my boyfriend before [previous boyfriend], 'coz I can't always keep track of him, he always turns off the cell phone – especially when he goes out with his* barkadas *(group of male friends) – maybe [there are] other girls around (age 24, service industry).*

Lorna's comment highlights some key issues regarding the ways in which mobile communication operates in a couple's life. Lorna states clearly that she relied on cell phone discourse to "keep track of her boyfriend" (not dissimilar to the desire of parents to monitor children though cellular communication). Here, we could argue that the cell phone was being used in attempts to monitor, and therefore potentially control a lover's actions. Lorna's boyfriend, aware of this, was able to counter her attempt to control his behaviour by simply turning off his cyber gate: denying her access and thereby disavowing her perpetual contact. Lorna further speculates that her boyfriend may have shut his phone off because "other girls" were "around".

The story of another young couple I knew in Kalibo can be juxtaposed neatly to Lorna's account. Maria, a young middle class high school student, and her older *noybo* (boyfriend) Joni, were so in love and so willing to demonstrate their unimpeachably to one another, that they created a cyber pact. The couple decided to switch cell phones with each other for "an entire week". By allowing each other privy to their personal cyber universes, they were thus able to prove that nothing romantically untoward was occurring, and possibly alleviate fears and solidify trust in their relationship.

While conducting fieldwork, I had a young friend (age 25) named Honey. Her boyfriend was so jealous that she would be castigated if she did not answer *his*

---

[20] I would like to thank Mark Poster for pointing this out to me during a shared happenstance flight across continental Europe in spring, 2003.

telephone call when out in the evenings. His jealousy became extreme. For example, after asking her at which establishment she would be patronizing, he would later text, asking: *wat color dres r u wern?*[21] Discerning that Honey's dress was pink, he would call the establishment and ask a staff member if a woman wearing a pink dress with Honey's height and hair length was indeed there, and then further question the employee about her companions. Sometimes, if, disliking the sound of her companions, he would call Honey's best friend – who was usually by her side – and interrogate her about Honey's activities. Then, when Honey found herself next with her boyfriend face-to-face, he would often reveal the different ways he monitored her behaviour and question her about the omissions she made by text about her activities.

Although the narrative of Honey's boyfriend reveals an instance of an excessively jealous man (rather than an instance of general behaviour, although certainly jealousy plays a strong role in both men's and women's sexualities in the local context), this brief anecdote points to the far reaching effects advanced technologies have in terms of surveillance of the romantic other. Particularly, it sheds light on issues associated with controlling behaviour, and highlights how new forms act to restrict women and men in their social activities. It takes little imagination to envisage how picture and video messaging services too will contribute – or reek havoc – upon couples in romantic unions, in terms of monitoring each other. (As would it not be difficult to imagine how these same services could promote sexual exploration and heighten long-distance love affairs.)

Perpetual contact, or rather, perpetual access to the other, is made possible merely by having the cell phone number of another party. Even if one desires to discontinue communication, advanced technology situates it so one does not necessarily choose whom they receive messages from.

The text *stalker*

Frequently, amorous feelings are not felt both parties, and young romances often turn sour. In the wireless Philippines, cases such as these commonly result in text stalking (there are no names given to this widespread text-type within the local vernacular). This term denotes the receiving of drunken and/or angry and/or love-filled texts or phone calls from admirers, ex-boyfriends, or anonymous texters. Occasionally these exchanges turn hostile and result in women desiring a new SIM card – the only way to ensure discontinued communication.

This also relates to the dangers of the spontaneous text – watch out for drinking, tantrums and text declarations. Here we see users initiating crimes, or rather, texts of passion. "Missed calls" and "oops texts" (pretending one didn't mean to text or call the person) are also strategies to track unavailable heart throbs, all different methods in the game of love and war (by text). There is no legal precedent to establish text-stalking as harassment in the Philippines.

---

[21] This translates as: what colour dress are you wearing?

Another serious, far-reaching effect of SMS is increased access to the commercial sex industry. For example, through texting, clients can easily arrange underground meetings with female or male commercial sex workers, at sites that may them as vulnerable. Or, as found in the classifieds of the Australian Herald Sun[22], women advertising commercial sexual relations through SMS again can increase their risks.

Symbolic violence: Gossiping by text

Gossip is an extremely popular activity in the Kalibonhon, and arguably Filipino landscape (e.g. see Rodell 2002: 196-199); in fact, it is so widespread, that many refer to it as the national pastime (with SMS texting running a close second). Texting offers a way to increase the speed of disseminating gossip, rumour and/or slander and thus acts as escalating symbolic violence. In Kalibo, public presentations of the self are highly gendered, and the potential cost of damaging one's reputation acts to both restrict and define women's public actions and the expression of their personal desires. (At this juncture I am only addressing women's relationship to gossip due to the limits of my data, which focused only on women in this regard.) Women are aware that their public actions, if at all inadmissible, will likely surface vis-à-vis word of mouth. Thus, in order to counter potential damage to one's reputation, young women's desires are often met through surreptitious means (with texting undoubtedly aiding the process, e.g. the arrangement of clandestine meetings). However, research findings indicated that the chief threat in the management of young women's social reputations was *tsismis* (gossip). Moreover, gossiping by way of text was reported to occur frequently among both men and women. It is not difficult to imagine how widespread access to an instantaneous communication device within enhanced social networks will heighten the ability to spread rumour and have insidious affects for people attempting to pursue private pleasures and or activities. Discussing the relationship between gossip and power, Manderson and Allotey (2003: 16) have written:

> *Embedded within gossip is the ability to control. Conventionally, gossip controls individual behaviour and mortality, including sexuality, because the stories of which it consists operate as moral tales for both the tellers and the listeners: either might be the next subject of rumour.*

Thus, *tsismis* in Kalibo can be conceived as sometimes operating as symbolic violence, with a high cost ratio (as affecting women's reputation and thus future prospects). Texting provides a neat avenue to destroy another's reputation speedily – an instantaneous way to disseminate fact *or fiction*.

Fidelity, adultery and something in between

> *On a ferry from one island in the Visayas, the central Philippines, to another island, I began speaking to a young Catholic priest in his mid thirties. Although he provided service in Manila, he was here to visit his*

---

[22] Herald Sun, Saturday, January 3rd, 2004, p. 74.

sick nanay *(mother)*. *Settling comfortably in our seats, by a wide window that housed cerulean waves, we talked about our lives, our different studies, and ideas. After learning that my project centred on sexuality, and that I was becoming increasingly interested in how texting was affecting romantic relationships, the Priest shook his head.*

"So many times in confession," he told me, "men speak about cheating on their wives. That they found new girlfriends by texting."

Raquel's dilemma

Raquel was in love. So in love. Albert was funny, and sweet, and when she had a problem, he's the one she turned to. They met last month, in person for the first time. Met, during a festival in the poblacion *(town centre), so that it was crowed and no one would report to her family that they saw her with an unknown man. He looked as she had imagined he would, not really* gwapo *(handsome), but strong-looking and kind. And she could tell from his eyes that he felt the same way about her.*

Sometimes he called on the landline now too. Their talks had become more serious. He had eventually confided in her about his secreto *(secret) – he had a child, a little girl who was six already. But he hadn't explained where the mother of the baby was, and whether they had married or not...*

Since in virtual relationships there are no non-verbal cues to go by, dishonesty and miscommunication abound. Texters can own different SIM cards and thus numbers, and potentially, identities. Locally, people are aware of the probability of deception, e.g.: "You know that a single person can own so many numbers because of the SIM, *di ba* [right]? You have to be very careful" (Novie, age 24, service industry).

When texting the opposite sex (as in Internet communication), traditional lines of faithful/or not so are blurry. To physically flirt with someone standing beside you is something – there is some form of commitment in the act, as it is seen, dually experienced, tangible. But, when the entirety of the crime is the typing of generally unimpeachable prose: who can contend? The fact of the matter is, this subtle, safe boy-girl texting is as perilous as can be, for the movement from friend *lang* (only) into something 'in between' is as swift as the transmitting of the message itself.

Texting is a handy tool for the cheater and cheatee. During fieldwork, numerous people informed me that married men often pretend they are single and woo women by text. (No such cases of married women were thus reported; however married women do flirt with single men, although their intentions are rarely to consummate this in an embodied way.)

By the time the texting parties have met, usually the duped woman is already 'in love' with the married man, making future physical transgressions more probable.

Breaking up in cyberspace: rituals to forget

Raquel turned to me, "I erased his number".

'You didn't'! I cried. Poor Raquel, this was serious.

Albert had come clean. He was in a loveless marriage, and only married the woman since she had become pregnant. It was Raquel who he desired, to cherish, to be close with. His feelings were real. Raquel knew this to be true. Knew he was a good man, who she had grown to love, but a man who was someone else's husband. When Ping-Ping had texted her three nights before, avenging her to never text her husband again, Raquel knew she must stop, and trusted in God that someone more suitable would come along to love her.

As the research indicated, many modern relationships in the Philippines either originate or are nurtured through text discourse, and so too, texting plays a vital role in 'breaking up.' Both virtual and embodied couples were found to use texting as a stratagem to terminate romantic relations. For example, as found especially within the younger cohort, once a woman finds herself unhappy in a virtual or lived relationship, it would be common for her to simply text the (young) man "don't text me anymore", signifying her desire to terminate future communication. Sometimes this wish was expressed in person, or through the telephone, as Gloria described below:

Last April I had a textmate. He asked me if we can see each other in person. Then, I kept on replying to him. He was so annoying. So, I got mad at him. I called him up and told him not to text me anymore (age 17, high school student).

At this juncture, it would be common for the woman to *erase* her former partner's number from her cell directory – symbolizing the act of forgetting, a significant ritual of lovers breaking up or not being textmates any longer. (Friends too use this ritual of erasing a contact's name from their cyber address book if they have been hurt and aim to discontinue the friendship.) In both platonic and romantic relationships then, if the former friend or lover does text again, since their names have been removed from the said cell directory, the textee would most likely reply, *"who s dis?"*[23] an insult and overt cultural indicator that the former person has already been "erased" them from the other party's cell phone, and thus vanished from their ordered world of importance. Here we can se the concept of *virtual exclusion* at play, whereby mobile communication acts to severe rather than enhance communication among social actors.

---

[23] Only a few respondents had older cell phone models that were not capable of storing names as well as telephone numbers. In such cases, respondents often memorized the numbers (particularly the last few digits) of more intimate contacts.

Although the act itself takes only a few seconds, when the techno-savy youth of the Philippines neatly "erase" a person's cyber identification from their cell directory, the emotions involved range in intensity and can cause great suffering. If the relationship had solely been a cyber exchange, often both texters would mourn the end of their cyber time together but perhaps contain some hope, as they knew there were numerous other texters to find in the unknown world of cyber exchange. If the relationship was, however, an embodied affair (although some couples end their relationships amicably), most avoid their ex like the plague.

Conclusion

In summary, we can see how the use and appreciated advantages of SMS relates to specific social conditions (e.g. poor telecommunications infrastructure, notions of alienation in the modern world due to urbanization, relocation) and are linked to cultural values (e.g. the importance of maintaining familial relations, as enabling emotional bravery, within the context of strong discourses of romantic love and of general governmental and religious conservatism). Texting provides a vehicle to express desire and loathing, and is done so in abundance in the Filipino setting. Misinterpretation, fighting, jealousy, the monitoring of romantic couples (leading to interpersonal surveillance), texting as a device to ascertain whether a lover is up to no good, gossiping and slander, repetitive inappropriate text communication (leading to possible harassment), increased access to the commercial sex industry, and adultery are all increased through widespread mobile use. The relationship between advanced technology and intimate relationships, for example, Princess Dianna using number recall to determine Charles's last call was placed to Camilla, a wife's discovery of gay porn on her husband's PC, or a girlfriend's reading a love-text he sent someone else, all illuminate the ways in which technology is and will alter intimate relationships. Mobile communication raises questions about this, as well as issues associated with appropriate contact, privacy invasion, and issues relating to social control.

I will conclude this paper by rescripting my views about contemporary urban legends in the Philippines. I had argued that:

> *texting in the Philippines is transforming conventional fairytales. Not unlike a Cinderella-themed narrative: the ballroom can be conceived as cyberspace, where instead of dancing, Cinderella and the Prince text one another. The fit of the glass slipper can be compared to text skill. The fairy godmother can be envisioned as technology; the evil stepsisters: a stolen phone, a faulty SIM card, and no signal (Ellwood-Clayton 2003: 235).*

However, taking into account ethnographic findings presented in this article, we could see how easy it would be for one sister to sabotage Cinderella's chance with the Prince, (by perhaps stealing his cell phone and telling the prince she no longer loved him and to not text again). Or perhaps the Prince, after winning his sweet Cinderella, would get bored and begin initiating anonymous text relationships with other women.

Acknowledgments

I would like to thank the Australian government for granting me an Australian Postgraduate Research Award, and the University of Melbourne for awarding me the Asian Travelling Fieldwork Scholarship. Special gratitude to my supervisors, Professor Lenore Manderson and Dr. Milica Markovic, for their sound editing and insights, as do I appreciate Dr. Linda Bennet's comments on this work. I am indebted to the people of Kalibo, and particularly those who acted as cultural informants, research respondents, and, in many cases, friends. Thank you for sharing your stories and experiences with me.

References

Agoncillo, Teodoro and Guerrero, Milagros. (1977) *History of the Filipino People,* R.P Garcia: Quezon City.

Berg, S Taylor, A. & Harper,R. (2004 *The Gift of the Gab*, Chapter 15, this volume.

Dodge, Martin and Kitchin, Rob. (2001) *Mapping Cyberspace,* London: Routledge.

Donner, Jonathan, (2003) "What Mobile Phones Mean to Rwandan Entrepreneurs" pp 393-411 in *Mobile Democracy: Essays on Society, Self and Politics*, edited by Kristof Nyiri. Vienna: Passager Verlag.

Ellwood-Clayton, Bella, (2003) "Virtual Strangers: Young Love and Texting in the Filipino Archipelago of Cyberspace", pp 225-239 in *Mobile Democracy: Essays on Society, Self and Politics*, edited by Kristof Nyiri. Vienna: Passager Verlag.

Fortunati, Leopoldina, (2002) "Italy: Stereotypes, true and false", pp 42-63 in *Perpetual Contact: Mobile Communication, Private Talk, Public Performance*, edited by J. E. Katz and M. Aakhus. Cambridge: Cambridge University Press.

Gergon, Kenneth (2002) "The challenge of absent presence" pp. 27-242 in *Perpetual Contact: Mobile Communication, Private Talk, Public Performance*, edited by J. E. Katz and M. Aakhus. Cambridge: Cambridge University Press.

Hayes Hayles, Katherine, (1999) "The Condition of Virtuality," in *The Digital Dialectic: New Essays on New Media*, edited by Lunefeld, Peter. Cambridge, Massachusetts: The MIT Press.

Kasesniemi, Eija-Lissa and Rauntianen, Pirjo. (2002). "Mobile culture of children and teenagers in Finland" pp 170-192 in *Perpetual Contact: Mobile Communication, Private Talk, Public Performance,* edited by J. E. Katz and M. Aakhus. Cambridge: Cambridge University Press.

Katz, James and Aakhus, Mark (ed) 2002. *Perpetual Contact: Mobile Communication, Private Talk, Public Performance.* Cambridge: Cambridge University Press.

King, David. (2001) Text Friends (Text Me Forever 5): *The Texters Latest Guide on Friendship, Dating, Romance and Real Love.* Wordlink Books: Manila.

Kristof Nyiri (ed.) 2003 *Mobile Democracy: Essays on Society, Self and Politics*, Vienna: Passager Verlag.

Ling, Richard and Yttri, Birgitte. (2002) "Hyper-coordiantion via mobile phones in Norway." Pp. 139-169 in *Perpetual Contact: Mobile Communication, Private Talk, Public Performance,* edited by J. E. Katz and M. Aakhus. Cambridge: Cambridge University Press.

Manderson L, Allotey, P. (2003) *Story telling, marginality and community in Australia: How immigrants position their difference in health care settings.* Medical Anthropology 22(1): 1-21

Mauss, M. (1969). *The Gift* (I. Cunnison, Trans.). London: Cohen & West.

Paragas, Fernando Paragas (2003) "Dramatextism: Mobile Telephony and People Power in the Philippines. pp 259- 285 in *Mobile Democracy: Essays on Society, Self and Politics,* edited by Kristof Nyiri. Vienna: Passager Verlag.

Ross, Andrew and Penley, Constance. (1991) *"Technoculture."* Minneapolis: University of Minnesota Press.

Raul Pertierra, Eduardo F. Ugarte, Alicia Pingol, Joel Hermandez and Nikos Lexis Decanay, (2002) *Txting Selves: Cellphone and Philippine Modernity,* Manila: De La Salle University Press.

Rapport, Nigel and Joanna Overing. (2000) *Social and Cultural Anthropology: The Key Concepts.* New York: Routledge.

E. Reid. (1994) *Cultural Formations in Text-Based Virtual Realities.* PhD thesis, University of Melbourne, Available at ftp://ftp.lambda.moo.mud.org/pub/MOO/papers.

Reyes-Tinagan, Marcella. (2001) *Viva! Kay Senor Santo Nino. Viva!* National Commission for Culture and the Arts: Manila.

Riviere and Licoppe (2004), *From voice to text*, chapter 5, thius volume.

Rodell, Paul. (2002) *Culture and Customs of the Philippines,* Westport, CT: Greenwood Press.

Simon, W. and Gagnon, J.H. (1986) "Sexual Scripts: Performance and Change", *Archives of Sexual Behaviour* 15 pp. 97-120.

Strom, George. (2002) *"The Telephone comes to a Filipino Village"*, pp. 274-283 in *Perpetual Contact: Mobile Communication, Private Talk, Public Performance,* edited by J. E. Katz and M. Aakhus. Cambridge: Cambridge University Press.

Turkle, Sherry. (1995) *Life on the Screen,* New York: Touchstone.

Internet

As accessed on the Internet on December 16th, 2003, at site: www.census.gov.ph

As accessed on the Internet on October 19th, 2003, at site: http://www.empirezine.com/spotlight/cummings/cummings/com/html.

As accessed on November 15th, 2003, at site: http://www.virtualpet.com/vp/research/research.htm

Newspapers

Herald Sun, Saturday, January 3rd, 2004, p. 74. (no author listed)

Mitchell, Simone, "RU IN2 SMS, THE GR8 NU WAY 4WARD," in City Careers, November 27th, 2003, p 9, Melbourne, Australia.

"Government debate rages over foreign workers", *The Post,* Jan 16 – Feb 12, 2003, p. 6. (no author listed).

Section Three: Designers' Text

11   Usability Issues of Sending Text Messages

Matthias Schneider-Hufschmidt

An introduction to text input technique

Have you ever looked at teenagers writing a short message on a mobile phone? Using the standard 12-keypad of their mobile phones they seem to be able to write text faster than most of us can write text on a computer keyboard. For most mobile phone users, however, typing a short message is a difficult and tedious task. Typing text with a keyboard that has less keys than there are characters in your alphabet is inherently difficult and hard to learn. The easiest solution for this dilemma would certainly be to provide enough keys for each character to be entered by hitting just one key, but the size of today's devices and the size of our fingers makes this option invalid. You need a much larger device to implement this option (see Figure 1).

**Figure 1: My son's idea of the ideal mobile phone user interface
when he was six years old**

Sending text messages is three-step activity. After typing the text of an SMS, users need to select the phone number or the name of the recipient of their message. Finally, the SMS is sent from the mobile phone to the user's service provider.

If we look at these activities with the eyes of a human factors expert only the first activity is truly interesting. Selecting a phone number is fairly easy for most users

Richard Harper, Leysia Palen and Alex Taylor (Eds), The Inside Text: Social, Cultural and Design Perspectives on SMS, 223–236.
© 2005 *Springer. Printed in the Netherlands.*

as they know this task already from setting up a standard phone-call. And sending a message requires usually only a very small number of button presses. If a message cannot be successfully sent or the user has dialed a wrong phone number the device may display information which is confusing to the user, but the steps to get out of these error situations are usually quite well supported by the implementations of the various devices.

How to write text messages

Entering the text of a short message on a small device is the hard part of text messaging. Many ingenious people have thought of clever ways to make this task easier for users. Some of these methods use the standard 12 keypad that we know from our mobile phones. Others require specific hardware integrated on the mobile device. Out of these many possibilities, so far only those which do not require additional hardware have been a commercial success.

Let us first look at various hardware and software solutions for text input:

• The standard solution for writing text is to use the keypad that is already available on a mobile phone. The difficulty with this solution is that normal western languages have far more characters that need to be typed than the phone has keys. So either the user has to make the mapping from the character to be inserted to a key sequence or the device needs some clever algorithm to disambiguate the user's input. There are a variety of software solutions trying to solve this mapping problem, some requiring additional hard or soft keys, and we will look at the usability issues related to these solutions later.

• A second group of possible input technologies is based on the use of a touch screen. The most comfortable technology, but also the one with the most usability issues is handwriting recognition. This input technique is only viable if the recognition rate is very high and the system is able to disambiguate the user input based on knowledge about the grammar and vocabulary of the user's input language.

• Based on a touch screen another option is the use of short hand writing and gesture recognition. To use this from of input the user has to first learn the gestures that will be recognized by the device for each characters. The system with the widest usage based on such a gesture-based writing style is the Graffiti system used in Palm-based personal digital assistants. The advantage of these systems is that the recognition rate of the device software can be raised considerably, but the related cost is the effort that the user has to invest in order to learn the characters (see Figures 2, 3, 4 and 5) for an example of such a shorthand alphabet). Additional problems can come up when special characters or numbers need to be inserted which very often results in mode changes hard to understand for the average user.

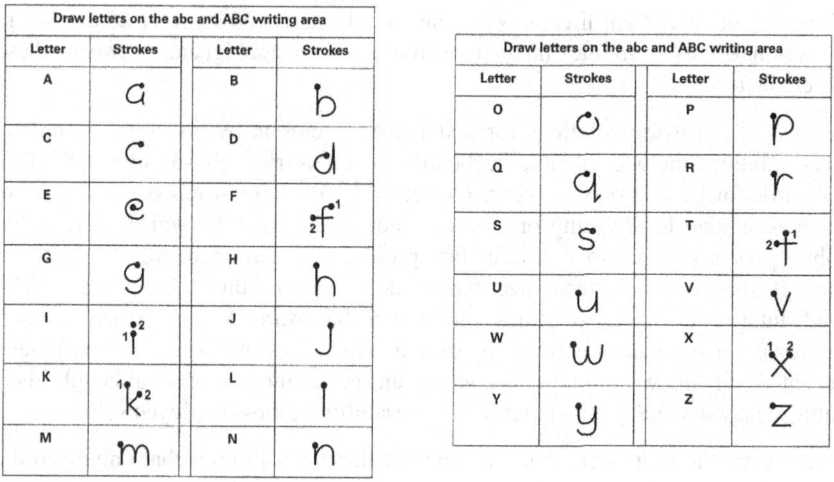

Draw letters on the abc and ABC writing area			
Letter	Strokes	Letter	Strokes
A	*a*	B	*b*
C	*c*	D	*d*
E	*e*	F	*f*
G	*g*	H	*h*
I	*i*	J	*j*
K	*k*	L	*l*
M	*m*	N	*n*

Draw letters on the abc and ABC writing area			
Letter	Strokes	Letter	Strokes
O	*o*	P	*p*
Q	*q*	R	*r*
S	*s*	T	*t*
U	*u*	V	*v*
W	*w*	X	*x*
Y	*y*	Z	*z*

Figures 2 and 3: Graffiti short-hand alphabet

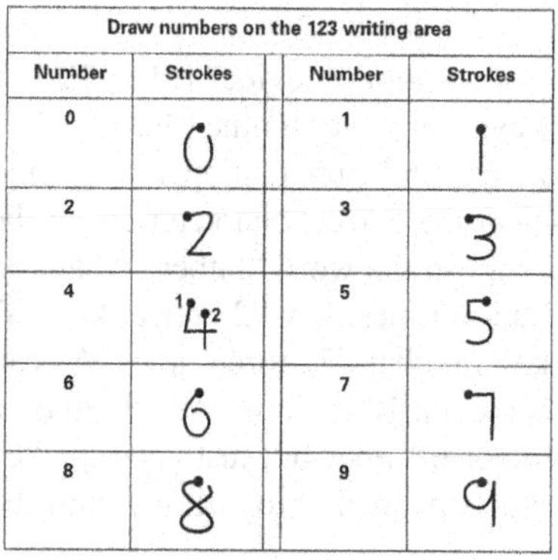

Draw numbers on the 123 writing area			
Number	Strokes	Number	Strokes
0	*0*	1	*1*
2	*2*	3	*3*
4	*4*	5	*5*
6	*6*	7	*7*
8	*8*	9	*9*

Figure 4: Numbers in Graffiti

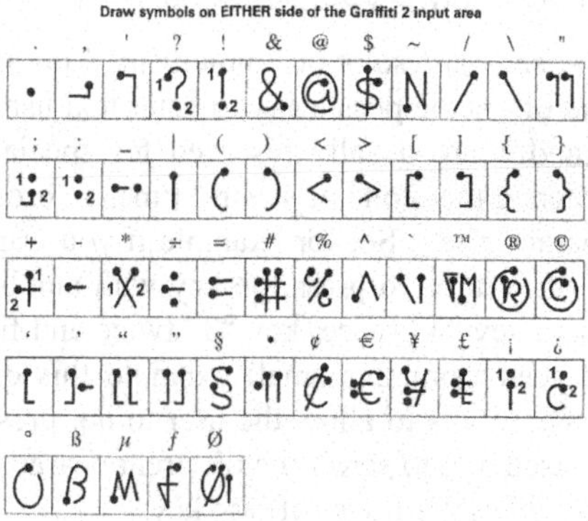

Draw symbols on EITHER side of the Graffiti 2 input area

Figure 5: Symbols

- On the basis of a touch screen one can finally use what is called a virtual keypad, a software program able to display a miniaturized keypad on the device. With the use of a pen, or possibly also with the finger, the user types text as on a standard keyboard, one character at a time. In addition to the usually very small size, which makes it hard to touch the right key, there is also the problem of mode switches for the input of special characters or numbers which needs to be understood by the user. Given that the screen of most of today's devices is fairly small, the display of a keypad may obscure most of the text which the user is just then trying to compose. We will discuss some usability issues of virtual keyboards later.

- Through a navigation key or a joy stick which is normally used for moving inside a menu or for navigation with the cursor on a 2-dimensional plane it is possible to input simple gestures which can then again be interpreted as characters of an alphabet. Simple mathematics shows that if we have a key that can distinguish four directions (up, down, left right) and we have 26 characters we need to combine three movements to disambiguate between these characters.[1]

This list of hardware solutions for text input systems is by no means complete. Other solutions include foldable keyboards as accessories, clip-on mini QWERT-keyboards for mobile phones, pens, connected by cable or wireless to the device, which recognize handwriting or gestures and transmit the recognized text to the mobile phone, or accessory devices that project a virtual keyboard on a table in front of the user and recognize typing activities on this table surface. The disadvantages of these solutions (additional hardware to be carried around, additional energy consumptions as well as the cost for these solutions) have prevented all these solutions becoming an economic success, although their usability may well be much higher than the usability of most-deployed solutions.

So let us now look in more detail at some of these possibilities that only need the standard key pad of a mobile phone.

Multiple key presses for text entry

The standard solution implemented on almost every mobile device with a 12 key pad offers the possibility to enter text using the keys from two to nine (the keys 0, 1 # and * are usually reserved for special characters and punctuation marks) and pressing them one or several times in order to select the correct character out of the character set[2]. So, for example if you want to compose the word "father" what you need to do is to press the key with number "3" three times, key "2" once, key "8" once, key "4" twice, key "3" twice and finally key number "7" three times. As can be seen from this small example this can become fairly tedious. An alternative possibility is to allow the user to not press a number of times but just keep the key pressed and to scroll the different characters that are mapped onto one key until the user takes the finger off the key.

The number of key presses necessary to write text using that method is fairly large. Somewhere between one and four key presses are necessary just for twenty-six characters of the standard English alphabet. If you look at European languages with

---

[1] As a matter of fact, we can disambiguate 64 characters with three key movements which gives us the possibility to enter upper and lower case, numbers, and a few special characters. Alternatively we could shorten sequences for the most common characters but each sequence of two movements takes away four unique sequences of three movements.

[2] The mapping between the English alphabet an the keys of the telephone keypad was standardized only at the end of the last decade. Before this standardization took place different countries used different keypads. In particular, the United States and France used a different key mapping which was not easier to learn and remember than the on now in use worldwide. Needless to say that this did not make the task of text input easier. The staendard now has the following mapping: "ABC" on 2, "DEF" on 3, "GHI" on 4, "JKL" on 5, "MNO" on 6, "PQRS" on 7, "TUV" on 8, "WXYZ" on 9. For other European languages ETSI (the European Telecommunication Standardisation Institute) has defined an additional European standard mapping additional characters to the same 8 keys.

the multitude of different characters one can easily imagine that it might take up to seven or eight key presses just to write one specific character. Since the characters are ordered alphabetically on the keys with 3 characters per key with the exception of the "7"- and "9"-key which have 4 characters assigned to them, there is no optimization possible to reduce the number of key presses. So we can expect that it will be necessary to press close to two keys per character inserted. For non-English alphabets with accents and special characters which are also assigned to these 8 keys the average number of required key presses may well get higher than two.

A number of mobile phone manufacturers have tried to make the process of text input easier for standard situations by providing standard text templates ("I will be xx minutes late.") which can easily be modified by users without being forced to type lengthy character sequences. The standard text is usually not modifiable, only the place holders, as the "xx" in the above example, can be replaced by digits or letters. At the end of such a pre-defined message the user can add arbitrary personal text.

Predictive text input

The term "predictive text input" is now used to describe a number of text input technologies which allow to reduce the number of necessary key presses considerably[3]. The first possibility to lower the number of necessary key presses is based on the insight that if we press every key just once instead of a number of times we might end up with a set of words that could be written using one specific sequence of keys, however in most languages only very few alternatives make sense. In the English language the maximum number of words that can be written with one specific sequence consisting of 4 keys is seventeen. So, in the worst case, a user has to select one out of seventeen possibilities after typing 4 characters[4]. In most cases, however, there are only one or two possibilities left after the user has hit those four keys. In these cases it is not a major problem to select the correct one of these alternatives if the system cannot disambiguate simply by the key sequence that has been pressed. If we use such an assistant the number of keys that need to be pressed per character goes down from somewhere between one and a half to two

---

[3] Most of the systems in use these days are not really predictive. Their algorithm is based on an analysis of the vocabulary in the user's input language. True prediction, i.e. the selection of an entire word based on the beginning which the user has already typed (with additional interesting usability issues popping up) is not used by many systems. The term "predictive" has, however, become common for the entire group of vocabulary-based text-input support systems. "Predictive text input requires one key-press per letter. After each key-press predictive text input returns matching words or stems of words ordered by frequency of use" [Pim van Meurs, Tegic; private communication].

[4] A colleague of mine told me that he and his wife would not disambiguate between options when typing text messages but instead they would send their messages with the first option offered by the database and leaving the interpretation of what has been meant to the reader. While this may be a hilarious experience for expert SMS interpreters it is probably beyond the abilities of most SMS users [Mark Dunlop; private communication].

and a half very close to 1.1 or even below. So, using this technology it is much faster to input text into a mobile device[5].

Prediction

Another step forward is the possibility to combine vocabulary based input assistance with true prediction. If we know the vocabulary which can be entered then in many cases it is possible to recognize the word – or at least part of the word – that the user wanted to insert after just a few keystrokes of the user. In this case we can offer the user to complete the missing characters and thereby reduce again the number of necessary key presses. In many cases it will be possible to even get below one key press per character on the average.

It should be obvious that the integration of such support systems raises a large number of additional usability issues. While the solution with multiple key-presses is fairly straightforward and creates only limited usability problems, predictive text input systems make it much easier to input standard text while at the same time creating new usability problems in case of user errors, when something unexpected happens, or unknown words need to be inserted in the text. In the next section we will discuss how to measure the ease of use of these different systems and will analyze major obstacles for the average user of these systems.

Usability measurements for text input

The most obvious value that can be measured when we look at inputting text is time per character. We observe users while they type in messages and measure how long they take to write the entire text. However, time is not the only important factor. Another relevant measurement is the number of errors that a user is likely to make when inputting text. And, finally, it is also important to evaluate how long it takes to correct an error in case the user has made a typing error.

For the user the quality of a text input system is directly linked to the time and effort necessary to type the intended text message. Underlying this subjective measure are these objectively measurable values of typing speed, error probability and ease of error identification and error correction.

Usability issues for text input systems

Typing errors

Multiple key presses are obvious reasons for typing errors. People are not good at counting key presses, they are also not good at keeping the time in-between key

---

[5] An alternative way to reduce the number of keystrokes necessary to type text is the use of a shorthand form ("T42" being interpreted as "tea for two") to write text. This option was and is actually chosen by many teenagers making their messages easy to type and hard to understand for the non-knowledgeable recipient of their messages (see Grinter and Eldridge 2001). It does not, however, work together with predictive text input technologies.

presses so that a sequence is recognized as one character instead of two characters. So if the user is too slow at doing multiple key presses instead of getting a B by pressing the "2"-key twice he or she may get two As in the word instead. The problem may also come up the other way around. If a user wants to get twice the same character and doesn't leave enough time between the input of the first and of the second character of the key sequence, the input may not be interpreted correctly by the device. One might consider how to adapt the timing behavior of a system to the behavior of an individual user, but even with such solutions the problem cannot be solved because users' behavior might change over time.

This problem of wrong interpretation of multiple key presses obviously does not show up if we use either vocabulary based input assistance or predictive text input, because in these systems the user usually only types each key once and every key press is interpreted as one character by the system.

Correcting mistakes that arise from misinterpretation of multiple key presses is fairly straight forward. The user can immediately see that he has done something wrong, rubout the character in question and retype.

Even for experienced users of multi-key-press-input it is usually not possible to type text without looking at the screen. For acceptably fast input it is therefore important that the user is able to find the correct keys without looking at the keypad. If users are not able to type text blindly their input speed will again be reduced dramatically.

The entire picture changes with vocabulary-based input assistance. Obviously the number of key strokes and thereby the time necessary to type a sequence of words is reduced dramatically as well as the probability of a typing error. But there is a flip-side to the coin.

When using predictive text input technologies it is much harder to see that an error has occurred in the first place. During the typing of a word there may always be ambiguous interpretations of the entered key sequence. So, while typing the users may or may not see the beginning of the word that they intended to type. They might look at a word that looks totally different and changes with each additional key press. The interpretation might change during typing because the system knows which words are used most often in the specific language that the user tries to write and utilizes this information to always present the most probable word.

For this reason it is advantageous for most users not to look at the display while typing their text. If at the end of the key sequence leading to a word the system doesn't display the correct word users may experience serious difficulties trying to identify the reason for the unexpected result and the necessary steps to reach their intended goal.

If the system does not display the word that was intended there are a number of possibilities of what might have gone wrong. The first possibility is that the user has typed a wrong key sequence. Another possibility would be that the vocabulary is incomplete or that the word to be entered is not part of the vocabulary of the device. Let us look at these issues and the problems that users have to solve if they occur.

Typing errors

Let's assume the user has typed a wrong key sequence while trying to enter the word "object" using a predictive text input system. The correct key sequence would be "625328". The sequenced used was, however, "62538", the second-last character is missing. What the user now sees on the display is the word "makeu". Scrolling through the list one might see other word stems like "malfu", "maket", or "malev". After circling through these options the phone will ask the user to define an unknown word. At that point the user might come to the conclusion that the input sequence was incorrect. But where was the mistake? To identify the exact position of the wrong or missing character it is necessary to undo the mapping which was performed by the device earlier. If the user succeeds he/she will find out that the mistake was made at the second-last character and can correct the mistake.

The entire process is in reality at least as complex as the description in the last paragraph. Most users are not able to correct typing errors using predictive text input systems. It is often much easier to erase the entire word and start over. Both solutions have, however, a fatal effect on the typing speed which we identified as an important usability measure.

Incomplete vocabulary or missing word

If the intended word is not part of the systems' vocabulary, the user needs an option to insert the word, either only into the text or additionally also into the vocabulary of the system. In order to achieve this goal it is usually necessary for the user to fall back to multiple key presses as the only available means for character disambiguation. Most systems will not allow the user to choose if the word should only be entered into the database, with the disturbing side-effect that misspelled words will find their way into the vocabulary of the device and show up later as potential sources for new mistakes.

Current predictive text input systems lead automatically into the learning mode of the program if the user encounters a situation with a missing or unknown word. After entering the unknown word using multiple key press disambiguation the database of the predictive text input system is updated accordingly. In addition, the word will appear in the user's SMS since this was the original intention of the user.

Most predictive systems have the ability to adapt their database to the specific word selection of an individual users. If a word that appears only rarely in standard English texts is used often in messages of an individual, the word is moved to the front of the list of ambiguous words. This reduces the number of necessary keystrokes for this individual user, for other users typing on the same device this may lead to some puzzlement since this device behaves differently from any other device.

Usability issues of touch screen solutions

Devices with a touch screens (as e.g. PDAs (Personal Digital Assistants) or so-called smartphones) offer a wide variety of different technologies to input text. Besides Graffiti-like solutions and handwriting recognition which were already mentioned, the most effective solution for text input is the use of a virtual keyboard. A keyboard is presented to the user and characters are inserted in text by selecting the respective virtual key with a pen. Since the ordering and relative position of these keys is not fixed as in hard keyboards, the designer of such a device has the option of optimizing the layout of a keypad.

When evaluating a virtual keyboard a number of new usability measures can be applied:

- The *accuracy*, with which a user is able to hit a specific key, is a measure for the number to typing errors and is usually directly related to the size of the individual key.

- The *distance* between two keys that need to be pressed sequentially is a parameter for the typing speed. The size of the target is a second factor for predicting the time needed to hit a specific key.[6]

It is obvious that the task of text input with a touch screen can be optimized by finding the optimal key size and the optimal layout of keys on the display. There are, however, a number of other aspects to be considered when designing touch screen input systems.

First, on a portable mobile device screen estate is usually rare. This implies that either the number of keys that can be displayed becomes small, thereby forcing the user into mode switches when typing text, or alternatively the key size becomes too small for accurate and fast typing. Both solutions will lead to sub-optimal typing behaviour. In many cases the disadvantages of both solutions are apparent as exemplified in Figure 7, which shows the different virtual keypads of a Palm handheld.

Another possibility to enhance the typing speed on virtual keyboards is to optimize the ordering of keys on the screen. Many devices use either a standard QWERTY layout or an alphabetical ordering on a matrix of keys starting with "A" in the upper left corner. While it is well known that these orderings are sub-optimal in terms of input speed and accuracy, they are certainly easy to learn and to remember. For these reasons they are the most commonly used realizations. Optimization of the key-layout, for example by circular or hexagonal ordering of keys as in a beehive may lead to much better typing results for experienced users. For the average user who is no expert in text input the disadvantages of having to learn a new keypad

---

[6] According to Fitts' law the average time needed to move a pen from one key to another with a given distance D and a key size S is $t=a+b(\log (D/S +1)$ where a and b are empirically determined values characterizing the device and the ability of the individual user [Fitts 1954].

layout will often outweigh the advantages of shorter pen movement or greater accuracy.

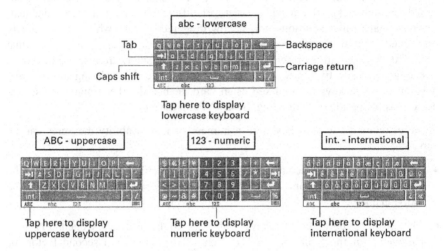

Figure 7: The different virtual keyboard of a Palm handheld device

Chord keyboards

Chord keyboards are actually quite well known to most users, the best-known example is probably the piano. As a piano player creates music by hitting a number of keys (and the right keys!) at the same time to create a chord, chord keyboards can be used to select single characters by hitting a selected number on keys of a keyboard at the same time. Unfortunately, the analogy carries even further. It is as important for the piano player to learn the technique and "vocabulary" of the piano as it is necessary for the user of a chord keyboard to learn which combination is necessary to result in a specific character.

The most widely used chord keyboards can be found on so-called Braille-input devices for blind users. The Braille language presents each character as a combination of at most 6 dots on paper. Obviously it is fairly easy for blind people who know Braille to use a keyboard with 6 keys for text input[7].

Users with wearable computers with head-mounted displays have been using chord keyboards for a long time. Text input with chord keyboards is difficult to learn as the user needs to memorize the mapping from a character to a combination of keys. Also, many users have difficulties pressing several keys at the same time, or at least within a very short time interval. After mastering the technique, text input with chord keyboards can, however, be extremely fast and efficient. For experienced

---

[7] For computer systems a Braille alphabet with 8 dots is in use, resulting in 256 characters (including a space character) to be distinguished.

users the number of errors done during text input becomes negligible using chord keyboards.

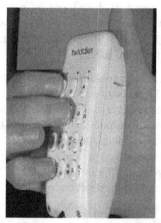

Figure 8: One-handed chord-keyboard for text input

Text input for users with special needs

Text input can become a very hard or impossible task for people who have special requirements due to cognitive, motor, or sensory impairments. For these groups of users it is necessary to develop specific devices or software solutions which help them to overcome these problems.

Users with motor impairments may have problems targeting specific keys or pressing these keys hard enough to create input. Also, regular repetitions of key presses as in the multiple key press solution can become major obstacles for motor-impaired people. Similar problems arise if users cannot recognize fast enough that a specific character has been typed and press the correct key too often due to the cognitive problem of mapping their sensory input to the appropriate (non)-movement. In these cases there are both hardware and software solutions available. Most prominent are clip-on keyboards which provide larger keys or keys with more or less pressure needed for typing. Alternatively, software solutions similar to those available on a computer can help to radically reduce the need for motor coordination. Solutions which require explicit switching to the subsequent letter may often take away the stress of having to hit one specific key long and often enough at the appropriate speed to achieve the input of a specific character.

Users with limited eyesight often have no serious problem with typing, besides the fact that they may have trouble finding the correct keys on a telephone keyboard. To solve this issue a marking on the "5"-key which is central on the keypad has become a required feature on mobile device keypads. This marker should be located preferably on the key and prominent enough that it can easily be experienced. Alternatively, many manufacturers mark the area above, below or around this key with markers on the housing of the device.

Unfortunately, knowing how to type does not solve another problem with which users with limited eyesight are confronted. Most input technologies only work for users who can control the result of their input by reading. Multiple key presses require constant attention to detect wrong key presses while predictive text input need eyesight during the process of disambiguation and error correction. These problems can be very hard for blind users.

One option to solve the feedback problem is the use of synthesized voice output to reflect the users input. These voice output systems must be able to spell unrecognized words in order to achieve their task. Alternative solutions are the use of Braille keyboards and Braille output devices, the first to speed up user input and allow the use of a familiar device, the latter device for control of input for subsequent correction. Figure 9 shows an assistive device for blind users which can be connected to a mobile phone. This device integrates a Braille chord keyboard, the functionality of a PDA and synthesized voice output.

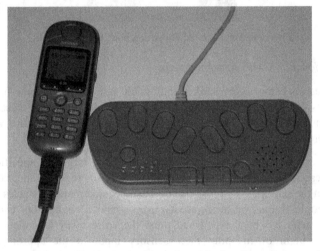

Figure 9: The paddy, an assistive device for users with visual impairments allowing fast and efficient text input.

The future of message input

Which technologies will be in the focus of the users of tomorrow's devices when it comes to text input on mobiles? For a variety of reasons, one of the most important being the desire and requirement for privacy, text input using keyboards or touch screens will probably remain the predominant style of text input for the foreseeable future.

An obvious alternative to typing is the interpretation of spoken input. This approach which could also solve most of the problems of users with limited eyesight, can replace the activities of typing and looking at the result with speaking and listening to the output of the voice recognition system. We may expect the first devices capable of recognizing spoken English language with sufficient reliability within the next decade. Until then, alternative solutions could be implemented in the mobile network with remote speech recognition systems able to interpret pre-processed speech input from mobile devices.

The main challenge for user interface designers in the foreseeable future will be the integration of other types of messages (sound, video, pictures) in multi-media messages. With the advent of MMS the complexity of message input will increase by dimensions (with text input still being the most tedious part). To master the full complexity of this task is probably beyond the possibilities of most users, even with elaborate support systems for content creation and synchronization.

Many of the technologies and tricks developed for text input will not work for pictures and sounds in the same way. Text input is a tedious task but users were and are willing to spend time and effort to create valuable contents which they want to send to the recipients of their messages. Using a camera or a microphone it is much easier to create contents. If this perceived ease of creating messages will eventually lead to a de-valuation of messages in the recipient's estimation can probably only be answered after MMS has become the standard messaging system.

Another question that remains unanswered for the moment is, if a message created using a microphone has any advantages over standard voice-mail functionality found in today's mobile communication systems. If you use an answering device much of the freedom of being able to compose a message asynchronously is being lost. We have, however, today no easy solution to compose voice messages and combine them with pictures and/or written text and comments.

While the selection of predefined text, as described above, is employed by many users because they want to pass on valuable information, the same technique, selection of predefined message parts, becomes much more difficult if pictures and/or sounds can be selected from predefined lists. Although in theory the process is identical, I would assume that people are more reluctant to choose from predefined pictures or sounds when composing a personal message. Personal messages to a friend or spouse should not contain segments which can be easily identified as pre-defined.[8]

Not only for the composers of multimedia-messages, but also for human factors engineers, this change from text to the combination of text, sound and pictures will bring new challenges. While text-input technologies could easily be evaluated and compared in laboratory settings and the results of these evaluations could well be transferred to real-world settings this will no longer be true for the composition of multimedia messages. When people start using cameras and microphones to create the contents of messages it will be necessary to take the environment into account in which users will create their messages. The challenge for the human-factors community will be to find the right combination of lab-based evaluation and

---

[8] Would you want to embellish a personal letter with graphical elements that could easily be identified as being publicly available? Using well-known clip-art is likely to diminish the personal value of a message.

context-aware evaluation technologies in the users' actual environment. Only with hybrid evaluation techniques it will be possible to correctly identify the advantages and disadvantages of different input techniques for multimedia messages.

To develop these evaluation techniques and associated tools and to bring the results of these evaluations into the user interface design process will remain a most fascinating task for human factors engineers.

References

Berg, S., A.S. Taylor and R. Harper (2003) *Mobile Phones for the Next Generation: Device Designs for Teenagers* CHI 2003, April 5-10 2003, Ft. Lauderdale, Florida, USA, Vol. 5, Issue 1, pp 433-440.

Butts, L., and A. Cockburn (2002) *An Evaluation of Mobile Phone Text Input Methods.* AUIC2002, Melbourne, Australia, Conferences in Research and Practice in Information Technology, Vol. 7, pp 55-59.

Fitts, P.M. (1954) *The information capacity of the human motor system in controlling the amplitude of movement.* Journal of Experimental Psychology 47, pp. 381-391.

Grinter, R.E., and M. Eldridge (2001) y *do tngrs luv 2 txt msg?* in Prinz, W., Jarke, M., et al. eds. ECSCW 2001: Proceedings of the seventh European conference on computer supported cooperative work, Kluwer Academic Press, Dodrecht, 2001, 219-238.

James. C.L. and K.M. Reischel (2001) *Text Input for Mobile Devices: Comparing Model Prediction to Actual Performance.* SIGCHI 01, March 31 – April 4, 2001 Seattle WA, USA pp 365-371.

MacKenzie, I.S., H. Kober, D. Smith, T. Jones and E. Skepner (2001) *LetterWise: Prefix-based Disambiguation for Mobile Text Input.* UIST 01 Orlando FLA, 3 (2) pp 111-120.

MacKenzie, S. (2002): *Mobile Text Entry Using Three Keys* NordiCHI 10/02 Arhus Denmark, pp 27-34.

MacKenzie I.S. and R.W. Soukoreff (2002) *Text Entry for Mobile Computing: Models and Methods, Theory and Practice.* Human-Computer Interaction, 17, pp 147-198

MacKenzie, I.S. and R.W. Soukoreff (2002) *A character-level Error Analysis Technique for Evaluating Text Entry Methods.* Proceedings of the Second Nordic Conference on Human-Computer Interaction – NordiCHI 2002, pp 241-244.

Silfverberg, M., I.S. MacKenzie, and P. Korhonen (2002) *Predicting Text Entry Speed on Mobile Phones.* CHI 2000 The Hague, Amsterdam, Vol. 2, issue 1, pp 9-16.

Soukoreff, R.W. (2002) *Text Entry for Mobile Systems: Models, Measures, and Analyses for Text Entry Research.* A Thesis presented to the Faculty of Graduate Studies of York University in partial fulfillment of requirements for the degree of Master of Science, June 2002.

Zhai, S., M. Hunter, and B.A. Smith (2002) *Performance Optimization of Virtual Keyboards.* Human-Computer Interaction, Volume 17, pp 89-129. Lawrence Erlbaum Associates.

12 Design for Richer Reachability: Mobile inspection in building maintenance

Sarah Olofsson and Mårten Pettersson

Introduction

Mobile technology makes it possible for people or technical systems to be accessible when out of the office or the control room. It opens up possibilities for an individual to be accessible everywhere, anytime. Today's mobile phones contain traditional functions such as speech as well as non-traditional ones, such as data transfer. When we start to study such matters in the context of design and actual appliances we find that one single function or a narrowly defined set of functioning devices can lead the way towards realising exciting possibilities for combining new artefacts with the phone – which still remains a core communications tool (Brown, 2001; Norman, 1998; Sharpe, 2001).

Today buildings are being equipped with automatic heating and ventilation systems which make it easier to, for example, control the temperature and monitor other details in order to establish whether they correspond to the desired settings. In the boiler rooms of these buildings we nowadays find highly sophisticated control systems, which support communications within the buildings, as well as to more remote locations. In these rooms there are sensors and remote-controlled radiators. As older systems are being replaced, the number of buildings that are connected to local or wide area networks is on the increase. The control room is not the only place where heating and ventilation information is accessible, but in many cases it is the place where the co-ordination of work is done; the setting, in its entirety, is accessible from the control room.

This chapter is based on an ethnographic field study of building maintenance work. The aim of the field study was to investigate everyday mobility among maintenance workers by combining findings from studies of work practice with the actual design of mobile services and products. We wanted to understand how mobile services are used within the community today and to identify services based on current technology. The building maintenance worker works in a control-room setting

Richard Harper, Leysia Palen and Alex Taylor (Eds), The Inside Text: Social, Cultural and Design Perspectives on SMS, 237–252.
© 2005 *Springer. Printed in the Netherlands.*

(called the control and surveillance centre, CS-centre), and can also be found out in the 'field' inspecting different building automation systems. In this work we observed him using an SMS-alarm triggering system. The system forwards automatic alarms, which are sent from the CS-centre in the form of an SMS. The alarms are an integrated part of his workday, allowing him to be reached by automatic alarms when out in the field and to access information in buildings he is supervising.

This chapter focuses on a design issue that is based on a picture that has emerged in studying these SMS alarms. From this perspective, we ask how might technology be designed so that it utilises data – from sensors, cameras and positioning systems – to support both the work in control rooms as well as out in the field? Our central aim here is to consider how maintenance workers might be better supported when they are away from the control room and, in particular, how they might gain a better overview of a building's condition when mobile. Based on the experiences we have gained in studying how SMS alarms are used, we will discuss design issues concerning what we have chosen to call *richer reachability*. In exploring the concept of richer reachability we address the question of how we might design systems that take into account the increasing amount of data from different systems. We suggest that one way to access information is to allow the worker to '*interview the field*' – making it possible for the building maintenance worker or other operators to ask questions of, interrogate or inspect the different systems.

Related research and background

Within the research fields of Computer Supported Cooperative Work (CSCW) and Human Computer Interaction (HCI) there are numerous accounts of ethnographic studies of work in control rooms (e.g., Bowers & Martin, 1999; Goodwin & Goodwin, 1993; Harper & Hughes, 1993; Juhlin & Weilenmann, 2001; Martin, Bowers, & Wastell, 1997; Pettersson, Randall, & Helgeson, 2002; Suchman, 1993). The studies often focus on what people actually do in their work, e.g. how they use different technological artefacts. Suchman (1993) refers to control rooms as "centres of coordination"; that is, they are "centres for the coordination of human activity... constituting *spatial* centres within an extended system of distributed activity" (ibid, p. 113). In this sense, she focuses on the physical space where people are co-located and the distributed activities that constitute the work of operators. Along these lines, she suggests that to coordinate a system of widely distributed activities, personnel within the site must have access to others who might be dispersed in space and time (ibid, p. 115).

During a study at the Swedish emergency service centre we have observed how operators handle different kinds of emergencies based on interviews with callers and triggered by automatic alarms, e.g. fire alarms (Pettersson et al., 2002; Pettersson & Rouchy, 2002). We have noticed that often those alarms are opaque in their design. That is, there is no other way for the operators to determine whether there is a fire or if it is a false alarm. The alarm systems that we have seen thus far cannot be interacted with to get more detailed information. In this respect, these systems are similar to the SMS alarms that we will focus on in this paper.

There are several studies that aim to move the focus beyond the control room and rather focus on what people do in the field. Heath and Luff (1998) report on the mobility of the staff working for the London Underground. They point out that as soon as the staff leave the control room they loose the access to updates about the state of their station even though real-time updates can be crucial, for example, during peak hours or during situations of evacuation. The authors point out that thought should be directed at determining what devices might support this mobile monitoring. For example, they suggest that the small screens on handheld devices might not be suitable to display the images from surveillance cameras.

Similarly, several ethnographic studies have been carried out at wastewater plants focusing on the design of information technology within as well as outside the control room (Nielsen & Søndergaard, 2000; Nilsson, et al., 2000; Bertelsen & Bødker, 2001). The studies highlight the importance of the mobile aspects of the work. For instance, they reveal that when out of the control room, wastewater plant workers use their sense of smell and hearing to gauge the state of the processes they monitor. Drawing on these findings, Nilsson et al. (2000) present a prototype called the Pucketizer. The Pucketizer is designed to support "a more dynamic and flexible configuration of process monitoring than provided in a traditional control room context" (ibid, p. 44). For example, the Pucketizer allows the wastewater plant operators to retrieve data from different components, such as motors, sensors and valves, when out at the field. The values from the components are displayed in the Pucketizer and may also be shown on different screens throughout the wastewater plant.

Nielsen and Søndergaard (2000) design a personal digital assistant solution to complement the work in the control room. They introduce a mobile device in order to make information from the system and an overview of the process available when on the move. They conclude that it should be possible to access some information when on the move and other information in the control room; it is not a matter of supporting information anywhere, anytime. They stress that an important question to ask is what information should be available where. This should determine how the mobile device functions.

Bertelsen and Bødker (2001) report on the cooperation in a wastewater plant. They point out that many mobile technical solutions take as a starting assumption that it should be possible to access everything, everywhere and that the information should be presented in the same form, independent of media and device. Drawing on their own work Bertelsen and Bødker reveal that needs vary and that different forms of information are needed in different places and times. In their field study of a plant they describe how although there are two control rooms where the workers may access data and obtain an overview of the plant, the workers tend not spend a lot of time in these rooms. Rather, they walk around in the plant, taking samples and repairing equipment. In doing so, their specific information needs depend on their particular physical location and a general overview of the plant or process is obtained through the individual tests and sampling procedures.

Findings from the field

The Control and Surveillance Centre

This study has been carried out in the municipality of Karlskrona, in the south east of Sweden. Karlskrona is a large city in Swedish terms with approximately 75,000 inhabitants (Figure 1). The city is located on the coastline and several of the sites are located in the archipelago. This means that the area is expansive. The control and surveillance (CS) centre, located within the technical department, is responsible for maintaining a range of facilities within the municipality including schools, plants and ferry terminals. The CS-centre provides a remote overview of what is going on, although it is often necessary for either the building maintenance workers or caretaker to go to their respective buildings and resolve problems on site. In the CS-centre there are a total of six personal computers with control systems. There are several different control and surveillance systems in use. The systems include control systems for heating and ventilation, elevators, burglary and surveillance alarm systems, etc.

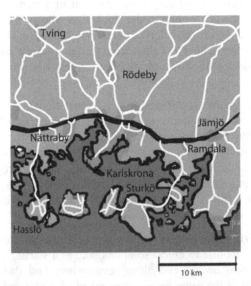

Figure 1: The municipality of Karlskrona covers a large area. From the CS-centre it takes about 30 to 40 minutes to reach Tving in the north or Sturko in the south. This corresponds to approximately 30 kilometres.

A large part of the building control systems are connected to a Local Area Network (LAN) or available via modems. Each system that is monitored in the CS-centre also has a local node, often placed in the maintenance centre in a building – the boiler room. With some of the newer systems it is possible, for example, to see the current temperature in a specific room from the CS-centre. If there are anomalies in the system an alarm triggers. The alarms from some systems are automatically forwarded to an SMS server and then sent to the building maintenance worker's mobile phone (Figure 2).

Building maintenance in the municipality

An array of different mobile technologies are currently used within the CS-centre, of which we will report on the use of a few. Mobile phones, PDAs, global positioning devices, paper and pagers with text capabilities are all routinely used. The building maintenance worker has a mobile phone, a Sony Ericsson T68i and uses a Bluetooth headset when driving. He uses the mobile phone in order to make phone calls to service technicians, janitors and suppliers.

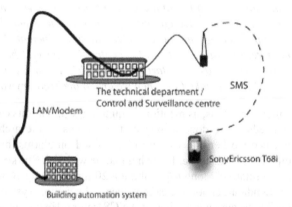

The technical department /
Control and Surveillance centre

SMS

LAN/Modem

SonyEricsson T68i

Building automation system

Figure 2: The sketch shows a schematic view of how the SMS alarm works. In the buildings there are automation systems. The systems are connected to the CS-centre via either a LAN or a modem. The systems are accessible at the CS-centre. Alarms in priority 1 and 2 are automatically forwarded to a SMS-server that transmits over the phone.

The building maintenance worker starts his workday in the CS-centre. He checks through the systems to see if everything is all right regarding e.g. heating and ventilation. Sometimes he adjusts the systems via the control system. Other times he has to go to the boiler room or the location where the problem has occurred. His role, in cases where something has happened, is to inspect and if possible fix the problem temporarily and then investigate what further action has to be taken. He coordinates this with the service technicians at the service contractors or suppliers. The municipality has service contracts with developers, but must sometimes announce jobs on the open market. The costs and benefits of repair work are assessed against the replacement of broken or damaged systems.

Examples from the field

Below we present three different examples from the building maintenance worker's workday. Each example shows what he does, how he plans where to go and what artefacts to bring. The first example describes how he plans to visit other buildings within a certain area when he is there for a single errand. This example opens up the possibility for design recommendations based on "when-you-are-there-anyway" alarms. The second example shows how he uses the mobile phone, alongside thermometers and printouts, when diagnosing the state of radiators in a room that are too hot. The third example shows how the SMS alarm is used as both a trigger to draw attention to a new problem and as feedback to relay that the problem has been corrected.

Example 1: Problems with remote access

The building maintenance worker looks at the overview map of the Sturkö School. He made an adjustment to the floor heating in one room some weeks ago, and now it is too hot in there. He prints an overview map to the ink jet printer next to PC1. He continues to look at the Ramdala School, where he has a problem getting access to the local equipment. This means that he cannot receive alarms at the CS-centre, but instead has to check them on location. He needs to restart the system locally in order to regain access. He says, "We can take that when we are in the area anyway".

The area of the municipality is, as mentioned, quite large and in this case there is an adjustment that needs to be done at one of the schools in the archipelago. The building maintenance worker plans where to go based on alarms, but also on the state of the equipment and distance. Knowing that he will visit Sturkö, and that it is, according to him, a relatively long trip – about a 20 minute drive away – he checks the status of the Ramdala School. He cannot access the control system in Ramdala, making it impossible to get an overview at the CS-centre. He will probably have to go and look into the problem at some point, and so decides that while in the area he will test whether resetting the system will fix the problem. Thus, he takes the opportunity to visit the nearby school and deal with the problem when he is in the vicinity, as he says in the example.

Example 2: Searching for errors at location

When arriving to the Nättraby School he walks around in the room. In order to sense whether the heat is on or not, he places his hand on the radiators. The radiators are controlled remotely via the heating systemand each radiator has a control device. He sits down on the floor next to one of the radiators. He sees that the control device seems loose; it does not close properly. He returns to the car to pick up the thermometer. He brings two thermometers, one that allows him to measure the temperature at specific points in the room, and a larger one that gives him the general temperature in the room.

The sensor that reports the value to the control system sits next to the door in the room and he compares the reported value that he has on the printed screen with the one he gets via the smaller thermometer. He then calls the supplier using the phone and discusses the problem in detail with them. They agree that the supplier should take over since there are several radiators not working.

This example shows how the maintenance worker decides what is wrong, looking for errors with the heating in a room. He takes the opportunity to contact the supplier and to discuss the problem and possible solutions when in the field. He makes the call from the room where the problem is and this makes it possible to describe the problem with the supplier and also answer questions.

The overview that the building maintenance worker mentions is interesting. He has a laptop computer, but it is old and too large to bring and he is currently waiting for a new smaller one. The printouts from the system are easier to bring and although they do not represent real-time values, he uses them to compare the values he gets in the room by using the thermometers. The printout may be placed almost anywhere, while the laptop is heavy and needs to be connected to a modem or local network. It is important to emphasise the role the printout plays when diagnosing what is wrong. The building maintenance worker diagnoses the room at the Nättraby School by juxtaposing the values on the printouts with the thermometers whilst he is on the phone. He says that the figures that the system provides him with are an overview of the state that he cannot get locally in the boiler room. This overview is provided by the control and monitoring systems at the CS-centre, but he cannot access it locally.

Example 3: SMS alarm and reset

During the coffee break he receives an SMS from the school in Tving. When he returns to the CS-centre he goes through all alarms that have been triggered while he was gone. The alarm from Tving was about warm water having too low a temperature. He drives to Tving in his car, it takes about 30 minutes.

(...)

After about 25 minutes of error detection near the boiler he picks up a notepad. He says that he thinks the pipes are placed wrongly. He makes a drawing of the construction – he wants to discuss it with an expert, since he thinks it does not look right. He turns around and walks away to the pipes at the other end of the room. He then notices that the warm water circulation is closed. Someone has closed it. He turns it open and then returns to the boiler. The temperature increases another five degrees in a shorter time than before. He consults the display at the local node of the building automation system (see Figure 3). He says that he thinks he's fixed the problem. Just before leaving the boiler room he receives an SMS with a reset notice of the alarm.

**Figure 3: The temperature increases. The building maintenance worker says:
"It looks good"**

The example shows how the SMS triggered by an alarm is used both as a notice about the alarm and as feedback when it is fixed. The SMS alarm is an extension of the systems at the CS-centre; they are based on the information stored in the systems. The SMS alarms give the building maintenance worker a hint that something has happened that should at least needs to be considered. The SMS alarms consist of extracted alarms, where only the system alarms with high priority are delivered via SMS. Notably, although he goes alone, the maintenance worker keeps in touch with other colleagues using various techniques. Above, for instance, he wants to discuss the construction of the boiler room with an expert and thus makes a sketch in preparation.

In the above example, we also see how the SMS alarms operate "one way only". The system triggers an alarm and reset alarm, both of which trigger the sending of an SMS message. However, there is no mechanism to interact with the system. Although there is no direct interaction, the feedback received from the reset alarms via SMS serves as an important resource when planning the work and when determining whether a problem has been dealt with. If an alarm is received and then followed by a reset, there is probably no need to go to where the problem occurred – getting an overview of what is going on is sufficient.

Designing for richer reachability in building maintenance work

What do we know?

The SMS alarms are useful for the building maintenance worker in that they inform him of high priority system alarms wherever he is. He always checks his phone for the alarms, unless he is in front of the PC when the alarms appear. The application that he uses to investigate what has caused the alarm gives him an overview of e.g. what valve is open and which part of the system is not operating at the right temperature. As noted, when out in the field he does not have access to real-time overviews of the system. In the boiler room, for instance, it is difficult to get an overview – the same data is available for inspection, but the presentation is different from that displayed on the PC monitor. He manages this constraint by bringing printouts of the system and comparing these with the readings and conditions he is able to work out in the field.

Not all system faults and triggered alarms require him to go to the source of the problem in person. Sometimes he is able to coordinate with others who are able to fix the problem or give him a report of what has happened. Other times he must personally inspect and diagnose the problem. This is important, not least because one single problem may have several causes. He keeps in contact with people in the field: caretakers, janitors and service technicians through his mobile phone. Some of those people are experts on specific parts of the systems or buildings. He plans his workday according to the priority of alarms, the distances he must travel and kind of problems that are to be dealt with. For instance, in the first example we see how he takes the opportunity to visit another school that is near to a site that has a reported problem. This means that he does not have to revisit the area on two separate occasions, saving him time and miles.

The priority of the alarm is programmed when the alarm system is installed and is dependent upon the sensors that are triggered. A priority 1 or 2 alarm, that needs to be dealt with promptly, is forwarded via SMS, while lower priority alarms are only made available on the PCs in the centre or locally in each boiler room. For example, in some buildings that need to be air-conditioned because they contain sensitive equipment, the alarm for malfunction may be set to priority 1. In other cases the mal-functioning of the air-conditioning may not be that important, making the problem a lower priority. Notably, the incorporation of location-based services could provide additional methods for augmenting this existing priority-based solution. Since distance is important to the maintenance worker, a positioning service that allows alarms in a specific area to be triggered could be useful. This would allow the building maintenance worker to receive alarms of lower priority when in a nearby area. Expanding the features of the positioning system, notes and memos might also be made available at locations and at times that suited the maintenance worker's movements.

At each site, information from sensors that detect other sources of information and that combine different recordings might also improve the alarm system. The operators we have talked to mention the possibility of combining data from smoke detectors with heat sensors in the walls. This would help in the location of fires and possibly also pass on information of the exact location to fire fighters. The existing sensor/alarm systems might also be combined with video or still camera footage, for example. Adding new kinds of sensors to the automatic alarms, the aim would be to provide the operators with a richer, more detailed, account of a location.

Similarly, camera phones could provide an opportunity to get more information related to a system's physical condition and setup.

Figure 4: The mock-up phone with an SMS alarm in priority 1.

In future services it would be interesting if the phone could be used in order to ask questions to the building control system. The building automation system could answer either via the phone display, e-mail, SMS or fax. It could also be possible to determine other reasons for the alarm by investigating possible causes. When interacting with the technical system in this way we use *interviewing the field* as a metaphor. That is, the operators have the possibility of interrogating the technical systems and thereby get retrieve answers about the their current states, allowing for richer possibilities for interaction with the systems. This is one way to achieve richer reachability.

Below we present a short scenario that aims to illustrate richer reachability through interviewing the field. We use mock-ups (i.e. simple paper based prototypes) as tools to think with and to reason around design issues. The building maintenance workers also get an idea, a feeling, of what it would be like to work with artefacts similar to the mock-ups in the future. The mock-ups encourage active user involvement (Ehn & Kyng, 1991), which makes it easier for the user to reason and talk about their ideas.

Figure 5: The PDA device and the phone. The SMS alarms are shown on the device and is received by bluetooth.

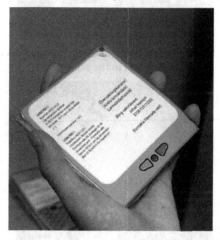

Figure 6: The menu shows different options for gathering more information.

Scenario

An SMS alarm with priority 1 reaches the on-call building maintenance worker, at 05.53 in the morning. The mobile phone displays a short description about the alarm; low temperature in a computer room in the Ruterfors School. Some additional information is also available, such as the current temperature indoors, the divergence from the preset temperature and the current temperature outdoors. There is also added value information about an associated alarm that has been sent to the guarding company United Guard (Förenade vakt), and the time when the message was sent (see Figures 5 and 6).

The building maintenance worker deals with the priority 1 alarm. He walks to his car where he has his PDA-device, which, as soon as he is nearby (within approx. 10 meters), connects via Bluetooth and receives information about the Ruterfors

School alarm (see Figure 7). The device shows additional information concerning the alarm, e.g. that it is a burglar alarm that went off because of a broken window. There is also additional information about the associated alarm: the security company went to inspect the premises.

Figure 7: For example, further information could include pictures from the surveillance cameras in the area.

Figure 8: A diagram of how the temperature in the room has changed is shown, as well as a nearby alarm-a reminder for low priority alarm nearby.

A touch screen menu presents different options for interviewing the field (see Figure 7):

- Surveillance cameras
- Other alarm transmitters
- History of alarm transmitters
- Call janitor: Johan Ivarsson, 0708-55511233
- Contact the security company

The building maintenance worker first chooses to take a look at the surveillance cameras. He retrieves a picture over the broken window in real-time, and also an overview the row of windows in which the broken one is located (see Figure 7).

After he has taken a look through the surveillance system he chooses to view the history of the alarm, e.g. actions that have been taken. He gets an overview of the temperature presented in a diagram (see Figure 8). There is also additional information such as probable cause of the broken window, a tree that has fallen down. The security company has temporarily fixed the window.

The history shows that the temperature has started to increase. A "reset alarm" is expected around 8 o'clock.

An alarm with priority 3 is displayed on the screen. It is a low priority alarm, but it is displayed because the maintenance worker is near to the location of the problem; it is a reminder triggered when within a set distance to a problem.

How to get there

We envisage the possibility of designing for richer reachability in at least three different steps. The first step is based on the capacity the user has to ask questions to the system by replying to SMS alarms or sending predefined SMSs. There are examples of these kinds of systems controlled by SMS available on the market already, for example burglar alarms. The second step relies on being able to get hold of increased information from the system via, for example, a WAP-interface. The building maintenance worker may retrieve the same data from either the remote centre or directly via Bluetooth access points in the different on-site rooms. The third step is to enable an infrastructure in which several different systems can connect with each other, opening up for a possibility for the different sensors to know what other sources are available and to make it possible to access information from those sources.

Undoubtedly, there are certain constraints that the mobile phone places on this vision of richer reachability. The mobile phone's display is designed for SMS, a short text message, or possibly MMS. 'Interviewing the field' opens up the possibility for new sources of information and consequently puts new interactional demands on the phone. However, wireless connectivity designed for device-to-device communication (such as Bluetooth) makes it possible to design artefacts that communicate with the phone. Thus, rather than placing all new functionality onto the phone a system might be designed so that functionality could be distributed across numerous inter-connected artefacts, e.g. more traditional PDAs, alongside the phone. Further research is needed to determine the balance to be found between placing demands on phones and other wireless, multi-functioning devices.

We have briefly shown the mock-ups to the employees at the CS-centre, the building maintenance worker and the system administrator, in order to get feedback on the ideas about richer reachability. They liked the concept, but pointed out that some of our thoughts about connecting cameras and getting pictures from the field might be problematic because privacy issues.

Conclusions

Since the building maintenance worker finds it easier to get an overview in the centre, it is a challenge to support this when out in the field. Being in the field means having to be at several different locations outside the control room e.g. the car or the boiler room at a school. Today, the SMS alarms provide a limited snapshot of the state of the systems in the buildings. The possibility of getting a rich picture is missing when out in the field. In the centre, the alarms are presented as a list on a PC-monitor. This list provides an overview of all alarms on a moment by moment basis. The building maintenance worker may also access the system and look at the current state of e.g. the ventilation system that triggered an alarm. In contrast, the SMS alarms are separate from the system and only allow information to be sent in one direction – from the system to the phone user. That is, there is no direct way to access the system via the phone. Moreover, the phone is only able to display one alarm at a time. Thus, in order to access the real-time representation of system in the field, the building maintenance worker must either consult the display at a local node or connect to the CS-centre via a laptop using a modem.

The two handheld devices presented in this chapter are not considered to be the perfect alternative. The mock-ups were made in order to think through cases where richer reachability could be a matter of importance. We would like to stress that we consider the design sketches to be tools to consider designing for richer reachability. By this, we mean that it is the possibility to connect different systems with each other, and how to access them at different places that are important, not the sketches *per se*. However, we have found the sketches useful when thinking through the design ideas and the scenarios. We have also shown the sketches to the building maintenance worker and his colleague in the CS-centre, and described the general ideas about artefacts communicating with each other by using the same scenario presented in this paper. Our experience, from this project, was that the mock-up helped the discussion about different technology. Although, e.g. video is not available today, the sketch gave an idea about how *it could* function. This opened up a discussion about new sensors that are available, that the workers were aware about.

The SMS alarm, which we have described in this chapter, is a first step in making information from the building automation systems available when on the move. There is a great deal of interest from the workers in the CS-centre to develop new artefacts supporting the work practice. For example they are looking into the possibilities of using PDAs to store information about buildings, manuals for correcting malfunctioning systems, etc. Possibilities to access other systems and knowing what is going on, not just in the building-control system, but also in other systems such as burglar alarms etc. may be of use for the building maintenance worker. There are several different kinds of sensors in the market that may be integrated into the alarm systems, e.g. microphones that may be used to be able to hear if the ventilation fan sounds are operating correctly and humidity sensors detecting water on the floor. Currently the system's designers have not begun using surveillance cameras, but they are very interested to look into the use of them. How to combine these different systems and make them available outside the CS-centre is also of great interest to them. Our interest in this domain is guided by the aim to develop new ways to interact with the systems. We will continue to investigate how to design technology in order to support the overview of the current state of the system, and how to combine different artefacts in order to interrogate the automation systems, to access real-time data that is not available locally.

The question that continues to motivate this research is how to design artefacts that allow the information to be accessible when requested by the building maintenance worker. In this chapter, we have referred to this as interviewing the field. We see this as taking three primary forms:

- ask for data e.g. from temperature sensors in the room in order to compare values from other thermometers

- access data from other systems in the building, such as burglar alarms, surveillance cameras etc

- receive low priority alarms, or locally available alarms

There are several examples of research about mobility issues in work places such as wastewater plants pointing out the need for specific information at specific times. It is important to retrieve information from the control system when out in the field and on the move. However, the building maintenance work is somewhat different from wastewater plants. One difference is that the field is distributed in location. A second difference is that the building maintenance worker is not always the expert in solving the problem. He has told us that he tries to fix the problem temporally and then attempts to coordinate subsequent actions that have to be taken that may well be beyond his remit. Often it is important to carry out an inspection of a reported problem with a janitor or some other staff member. Richer reachability in the distributed field demands a design that allows access to data at several different locations outside the CS-centre. Information can be needed when on the way to problem sites or in specific circumstances at the sites.

In these terms, *Richer Reachability* sets out a design challenge for requesting and accessing specific data at specific times.

Acknowledgements

We would like to thank the building maintenance workers working at the CS-centre in Karlskrona municipality for their co-operation and helpful explanations during our ethnographic work. Also our sincerest thanks to professor Jeanette Blomberg, professor Bo Helgeson, Marine Karlsson, Björn Stille and our colleagues at the Work Practice Laboratory at the Blekinge Institute of Technology for their helpful comments.

References

Bertelsen, O. W., & Bødker, S. (2001). Cooperation in massively distributed information spaces. In W. Prinz, M. Jarke, Y. Rogers, K. Schmidt & V. Wulf (Eds.), Proceedings of the Seventh European Conference on Computer Supported Cooperative Work (pp. 1-17): Kluwer.

Bowers, J. M., & Martin, D. (1999). Informing Collaborative Information Visualisation Through an Ethnography of Ambulance Control. In S. Bødker, M. Kyng & K. Schmidt (Eds.), ECSW '99 Proceedings of the Sixth Conference on Computer Supported Cooperative Work (pp. 309-330).

Brown, B. (2001). Studying the Use of Mobile Technology. In B. Brown & R. Harper (Eds.), Wireless World.

Ehn, P., & Kyng, M. (1991). Cardboard Computers: Mocking-it-up or Hands-on the Future. In F. Kensing & K. Halskov Madsen (Eds.), Design at Work: cooperative design of computer systems (pp. pp. 169-195). Hillsdale: Lawrence Earlbaum.

Goodwin, C., & Goodwin, M. (1993). Formulating planes: Seeing as a situated activity. In Y. Engeström & D. Middleton (Eds.), Communication and cognition at work (pp. 61-95). Cambridge University Press.

Harper, R. H. R., & Hughes, J. A. (1993). What a f – ing system! Send 'em all to the same place and then expect us to stop 'em hitting. Managing technology work in air traffic control. In G. Button (Ed.), Technology in Working Order. Studies of work, interaction, and technology (pp. 127-144). London and New York: Routledge.

Juhlin, O., & Weilenmann, A. (2001, 16-20 September 2001). Decentralizing the Control Room: Mobile Work and Institutional Order. Paper presented at the Proceedings of the Seventh European Conference on Computer Supported Cooperative Work, Bonn, Germany.

Luff, P., & Heath, C. (1998). Mobility in Collaboration. Paper presented at the Proceedings of the CSCW '98, Seattle, ACM.

Martin, D., Bowers, J., & Wastell, D. (1997). The interactional affordances of technology: An ethnography of human-computer interaction in an ambulance control center. Paper presented at the People and computers XII, Proceedings of HCI'97, London.

Norman, D. A. (1998). The Invisible Computer: Why Good Products Can Fail, the Personal Computer is So Complex and Information Appliances are the Solution. Cambridge, Mass.: MIT Press.

Pettersson, M., Randall, D., & Helgeson, B. (2002). Ambiguities, Awareness and Economy: A Study of Emergency Service Work. In C. M. Neuwirth & T. Rodden (Eds.), CSCW 2002 (pp. pp. 286-295). New Orleans: ACM Press.

Pettersson, M., & Rouchy, P. (2002). 'We don't need the Ambulance then' – Technological Handling of the Unexpected. Paper presented at the Presented at the XV World Congress of Sociology, 7-13 July 2002, RC.25 Language, Technology and Work, Brisbane, Australia.

Sharpe, B. (2001). Information Appliances An Introduction. Unpublished manuscript, Bristol, UK.

Suchman, L. (1993). Technologies of accountability: of lizards and aeroplanes. In G. Button (Ed.), Technology in Working Order. Studies of work, interaction, and technology (pp. 113-126). London: Routledge.

13   Working Text: Texting Work

Keith Cheverst, Dan Fitton and Mark Rouncefield

Introduction

In 'Smart Mobs' Howard Rheingold (2002) makes some dramatic claims about the social and political impact of texting – with interesting and insightful comments on 'thumb tribes' and 'generation txt' and claims about the impact of texting on practices as diverse as teenage mating rituals and demonstrations. This chapter considers the impact of texting in a far more mundane, though no less important domain – the everyday world of work. Here our interest is in people texting into their workplace – 'texting work' – and how texting is used in work to perform or support various communicative functions – 'working text'. Like Rheingold we are equally interested in one of the most surprising phenomena to have occurred within the field of mobile computing within recent years – the uptake of text messaging. According to the Mobile Data Association (MDA), the total number of chargeable person-to-person SMS text messages sent across the main four UK GSM network operators between 31st December 2003 and 1st January 2004, was 111 million, an 8% increase compared to figures over the same period the previous year (http://www.text.it/mediacentre) – and new uses of SMS messaging are emerging, for example in conjunction with interactive TV services.

One use of SMS texting that has received little investigation to date is its use as a means of enabling a (potentially mobile) user to message a situated display at work rather than another mobile device owned by a particular individual. Such a facility has clear potential in co-operative work settings when, for example, the context of interaction means that messaging to a particular place – a workplace – is more appropriate than messaging directly to a particular individual. The utility of such situated displays is considered by O'Hara et al (2002) when they write:

> In recent years, more and more information is being presented on dedicated digital displays situated at particular locations within our environment. At their most basic, digital display technologies allow information to be more easily updated dynamically and remotely. However, these new kinds of interaction technologies also allow people to use these situated displays in novel ways both as for the individual's purposes and in the support of group work (O'Hara et al 2002).

Richard Harper, Leysia Palen and Alex Taylor (Eds), The Inside Text: Social, Cultural and Design Perspectives on SMS, 253–269.

They particularly refer to the potential for texting to and updating situated displays remotely, and it is this functionality that forms the focus of this chapter. We describe and provide an analysis of two application case studies – Hermes and SPAM – both of which enable users to text to and update situated displays remotely. In the first case study we describe our experiences with the Hermes system which enables users to interact remotely with office door displays via their mobile phone using SMS. The SPAM messaging system evolved from our experiences with Hermes and provides the focus of the second case study. This system also enables users to remotely update situated displays (using SMS) in order to facilitate coordination and cooperation with remote work colleagues.

Technologies for texting: Hermes and SPAM

This section provides some technical details of the Hermes and SPAM systems. These descriptions of the technologies may be of little interest to social scientists (who historically have displayed little interest in any of the actual details of the technologies they comment upon (Button 1993)). But in describing the technical features of the systems deployed, two features of the designs, two important and related aspects of the assembly of what were essentially 'off-the-shelf' components, may be of some relevance. That is, they may be of some value in thinking both about how the technologies were designed and assembled and how they got used and thereby incorporated into everyday work. These related notions are what Erickson and Kellogg (2000) call 'social translucence' and Anderson and Sharrock (1993), following Gibson's original formulation refer to as 'affordances'. As Erickson and Kellogg comment, when designing systems to support communication and collaboration 'socially translucent systems' enable people to draw upon their social experience and structure their interactions with each other (using text in our case). This contrasts with digital systems in general which are 'socially blind' because they make no use of our social abilities, our ability to respond and improvise using our knowledge of or awareness of other people and their interactions. The qualities that make systems socially translucent are those of visibility, awareness and accountability and our interest was in assembling systems that might draw on these qualities in order to ensure greater usability. Social translucence emphasizes making socially significant information visible. Awareness involves awareness of others and their actions, rights and obligations and accountability concerns being held accountable for actions drawing on a range of norms, rules, and customs about reasonable workplace behaviour. In texting to situated displays users of the Hermes and SPAM systems make available to others their location, plans and activities and thereby draw upon and reflect aspects of everyday social life that are a fundamental requirement for supporting communication and collaboration. Accountability in these circumstances encompasses the everyday activities whereby members produce and manage their organised everyday affairs. Texting enters into this as one instance of a range of practices. As Garfinkel (1967) suggests such practices consist of an endless, ongoing, contingent accomplishment:

"In exactly the ways that a setting is organised, it consists of members' methods for making evident that settings' ways as clear, coherent, planful, consistent, chosen, knowable, uniform, reproducible connections, – i.e., rational connections. In exactly the way that persons are members to organised affairs, they are engaged in serious and practical work of detecting, demonstrating, persuading through displays in the ordinary occasions of their interactions the appearances of consistent, clear, chosen, planful arrangements. In exactly the ways in which a setting is organised, it consists of methods whereby its members are provided with accounts of the setting as countable, storyable, proverbial, comparable, picturable, representable – i.e. accountable events" (Garfinkel, 1967: 34)

Another way of thinking about the Hermes and SPAM technology is in terms of 'affordances' (Anderson and Sharrock (1993)) and the notion that; ". we can treat ... phenomena .. as affording knowledge and as having been designed with this possibility in mind". Here our interest is how the different features of the assembled systems are constructed so as to 'afford knowledge' as to, for example, the working division of labour by which the various tasks associated with a residential hostel or a university department are performed. The notion of affordance used here treats perception as resolutely embedded in particular cultural practices. Just being fully enculturated members of the university or the staff of the hostel means being able to use the texts presented by the systems to see certain things – that somebody is 'running late', 'in trouble', 'under pressure' etc. – unproblematically. Simply by becoming a member of staff and becoming familiar with the organisation, 'learning one's way around' involves learning how to 'pick-up' such organisational information from the environment.

In this way, and given that the division of labour in organisations is often a division of responsibility and accountability it is evident how the technology of Hermes and SPAM can also be viewed as 'technologies of accountability' (Suchman 1994; Bowers, Button and Sharrock 1995) – in making work tasks available to others, thereby playing an important role in the 'real world real time' social organisation of work. The texts, to both Hermes and SPAM, are both the focus for work and a visible record of work that has been done or remains to be done. What these representations do, as we document later (and as we have already suggested with the idea of 'social translucence'), among other things, is make everyday work 'visible' so that it can be 'taken note of', 'reviewed', 'queried', and so on, by others involved, putting the work on display so that others may be aware of it.

Hermes overview and requirements

The original idea for Hermes (Cheverst 2003c) was (at least in part) motivated by a desire to explore whether the traditional way of leaving messages on post-it notes in 'semi-private' places could be enhanced with a digital equivalent, e.g. one that supports remote interaction. In order to explore this area, we have designed and deployed a digital asynchronous messaging system (called Hermes after the messenger to the gods in Greek mythology) within the main computing building at

Lancaster University. The Hermes system supports remote interaction by allowing messages to be created and read via the web or a mobile phone. We hoped that by supporting remote interaction and observing how the new system was used over a significant period of time we would gain some useful insights into the relative importance and interaction of 'place' 'space' and 'text' within this application domain. For example, what kinds of messages would members of university staff post on their door when texting remotely?

Work on developing the Hermes system started in October 2001 and the first unit was installed outside one of the offices in the computing department in March 2002. The system comprises a central server and a number of wall or door mountable units (referred to as Hermes displays). Figure 1 illustrates the first Hermes display to be deployed in the department.

Figure 1: Example of an early Hermes display

The physical deployment of the Hermes displays within the university department was subject to four main requirements, namely: units should comply with university safety regulations, units should comply with disabilities legislation, units should be straightforward causing minimal disruption to offices and units should be relatively secure. At present we have 10 units deployed on one floor of the Computing Department at Lancaster. Owners of Hermes displays currently include departmental secretaries, lectures and research students.

Hermes functionality

One of the challenges with a system such as Hermes is to avoid trying to implement every feature technologically possible. Our intention was for Hermes displays to have the ease of use and dependability associated with an information appliance, i.e. to perform a small number of tasks simply and well. The functionality supported by the system can be considered from two main perspectives, namely: the perspective of the *owner* of the Hermes display and the perspective of a *visitor* (see Cheverst et al 2003c). The system provides the owner of the Hermes display with two key functions:

1.   the ability to create a message to appear on the display, and,

2.   the ability to read messages left by visitors.

Typically, the owner will create a message to appear on their Hermes display by entering some appropriate text using the web interface (Figure 2.) The web interface can also be used to upload a graphical image for display, such as an animated GIF.

Figure 2: The Hermes web interface (Cheverst 2003b)

One of the issues that we wished to explore was the implication of supporting remote interaction with Hermes displays. Consequently, we designed the system such that (in addition to using the web interface to create a message) the owner could also use SMS via his or her mobile phone in order to text a message to appear outside an office door on a Hermes display. In part, this facility was motivated by the concern of one of the designers that he might become delayed during his daily commute to work and not be able to notify a student that would he would be late for a given appointment. Interestingly this particular Hermes owner rarely makes use of the remote messaging facility but the type of usage for which the facility was developed (i.e. notifying students of lateness) is used extensively by another Hermes owner who was not a member of the design team.

The overall system architecture of the Hermes system is illustrated in Figure 3. In this figure, the oval represents the typical entities associated with a given user. At the heart of the system is a single central server application written in Java that runs on the Linux platform and provides the following key functions:

1.   centralized storage for messages and user profile information,

2.   communication with the SMS Gateway,

3.   hosting of the web portal.

The system utilizes both wireless (802.11b) and wired Ethernet network infrastructures. In order to support the reception of SMS messages, the central server communicates with a Wavecom DB02 GSM terminal.. The web portal is implemented using Java servlets and this enables the dynamical generation and publication of html web pages. The Hermes displays themselves run the CrEme Java virtual machine running over the PocketPC operating system.

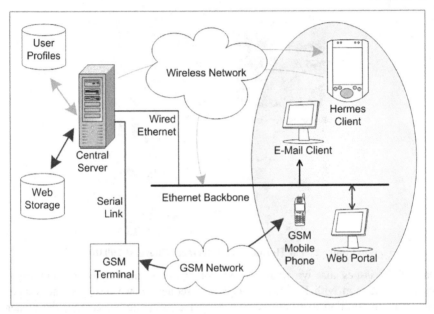

Figure 3: The system architecture of Hermes (Cheverst 2003b).

SPAM overview and requirements

The SPAM system has been developed to support cooperation between staff working at two associated sites located in Carlisle, a small city in the North of England. Both sites are managed by a charitable trust and provide varying levels of residential care support for former psychiatric patients. The hostel is the first step for patients leaving the psychiatric wards of local hospitals, which are currently being closed down. The overall aim of these facilities is to gradually introduce patients back into the community and allow them to support themselves. This general objective means that any technology introduced into the setting should enable staff and residents to arrive at this outcome, rather than foster dependence, and raises the very real problem of identifying requirements in complex and unconventional domains (Crabtree et al. 2003).

At present staff activity is coordinated through the use of a diary, notice-board, a telephone answering system and an on-call pager system. However, observations revealed a number of instances where communications proved less than satisfactory: where the manager would lose track of workers' whereabouts or staff would be unable to contact their colleagues in order to alert them to relevant circumstances.

The requirements for SPAM were obtained through ethnographic study, cultural probes (Gaver et al 1999) and design workshops with the staff (see Figure 4 below).

Figure 4: Design workshop

The workshop gave staff the opportunity to cooperatively analyse our early design concepts for a messaging system and to articulate changes and amendments. During the workshop, a number of possible scenarios were outlined involving situations in which residents or staff members needed to inform the site of their circumstances. The first scenario involved a situation where staff might need to send a message to the office – in this case a visit to the hospital with a resident where the visit is taking longer than anticipated. The second scenario concerned residents needing to send messages to the hostel. Here the scenario was of a resident returning by train to the semi-independent living accommodation, their train is delayed and they have forgotten their keys, so they need to have a message relayed to the other site to ensure they can get into their accommodation. In each case the staff at the workshop were asked to:

Consider scenarios – how would you cope with them now? Would a text messaging system be useful? What problems might there be?

Think of other scenarios – where do you think current systems have problems? – where text messaging may be useful...

Think of 'designing the interface' – how should messages be displayed, transferred etc- would you want separate spaces for staff and resident messages? would you want some way of indicating urgency? Would you want some way of ensuring privacy? The transfer of personal messages? etc

The implausibility of our first scenario was rapidly revealed – since mobile phones cannot be used in hospitals – but alternative, similar and plausible scenarios, based on staff experience, were rapidly suggested. The workshop also revealed a number of other circumstances where some form of messaging system might prove a useful addition to current facilities. So, for example, members of staff reported that they often found it problematic to communicate effectively using only the phone. *"The phone is constantly engaged at the hostel, its just luck that you get through"* was a common complaint among staff. Following the discussion of these scenarios, possible problems and solutions in terms of some form of visible display in the staff rooms were discussed. This discussion was based around the current 'Hermes' system being deployed at Lancaster University and was illustrated via the following slide (Figure 5).

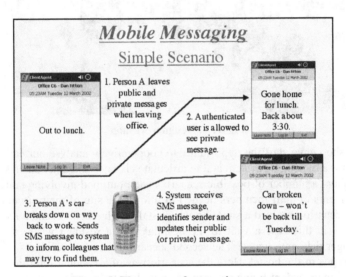

Figure 5: The proposed messaging system

The overall response to the idea of a messaging system was extremely positive. In particular, such a system was viewed as another, alternative, tool for communication capable of supporting staff in their everyday work and interaction with residents. This, then, became the rationale for the construction, testing and deployment of the SPAM system.

SPAM functionality

Based on the requirements obtained from the workshop, we embarked on developing an SMS public display system. The SPAM system has been designed to run an SMS messaging application, allowing staff from the hostel office to communicate easily with staff from the semi-independent living accommodation office (and vice-versa) by composing messages using an on screen keyboard displayed on a touch sensitive screen (see figure 6). When messages are received by a SPAM unit they are displayed on the screen until deleted by a member of staff.

Staff can also use their own mobile phones in order to send text messages to the SPAM displays when they are out of the office and to receive messages originating from a SPAM display. In addition, the system also provides residents located off-site with an additional means (i.e. in addition to the phone system currently installed) to communicate their situation to staff, e.g. I've just missed the last train back to Carlisle and don't have my key!

The overall design of the system architecture is shown in Figure 7. This highlights the way in which SMS messages sent via mobile phones and by the SPAM units themselves are handled by the system.

Figure 6: One of the SPAM displays showing messages received

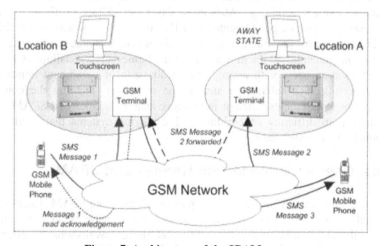

Figure 7. Architecture of the SPAM system

The typical scenario is illustrated by SMS Message 1, i.e., the message originating from a mobile phone is successfully delivered to the permanently staffed hostel (Location B) and the transmission of a 'message read' acknowledgement is triggered by a member of staff reading the message. Message forwarding is performed by the system if a message is sent to the semi-independent living accommodation (Location A) at a time when no member of staff is providing cover (denoted by AWAY STATE). In this case, the message (Message 2) is automatically forwarded to the display of the hostel with 24-hour cover. The two SPAM displays were deployed in the two offices in October 2002. Since that time the units have been used on a daily basis.

One of the key issues with both texting systems is the need for users to have a strong trust in the reliability of the system, i.e. a strong belief that any SMS text message that they send to a situated display will (indeed) appear on the situated display and remain there for an appropriate period of time. In the case of Hermes this means staying there until removed or replaced by another message while in the case of SPAM it means staying visible until deleted by a member of staff. Of course, in order to encourage users to trust the system, they need to see the system functioning correctly over a protracted period of time, i.e. months rather than minutes. We have found achieving this kind of dependability difficult, especially for the Hermes system. The ideal situation would be to develop a system in which all components work faultlessly or at least have an extremely long mean time to failure (MTF). However, such a situation is indeed ideal. For example, SMS messages are not always delivered in a timely way by a given GSM service provider (especially where a message requires routing between different service providers). It has been interesting to observe how some users have developed coping strategies to deal with early reliability problems. For example, on one occasion, a user's Hermes display did not update properly so that for a week while he was away his door displayed "I am in! Alan". Now he always includes with such messages an explicit date, e.g. "Alan in all day today, Thurs 13th". In this case because Alan possesses a good 'mental model' of the Hermes system he was able to adapt his behaviour, i.e. through a subtle change in message composition, to overcome the potential problem caused by a Hermes update failure (Cheverst 2003a). Providing users with appropriate feedback is of paramount importance when supporting such interaction and is one means for tackling the complex dependability requirements inherent in systems such as Hermes and SPAM – the quantum leap in difficulty of building and deploying systems that need to be operational on a constant basis.

Issues: User experience with Hermes and SPAM

This section presents some reflections on how the Hermes and SPAM systems have been used in practice. This emphasis on studying technology in use – using ethnographic observation, cultural probes and design workshops – reflects a longstanding tradition, even, perhaps, orthodoxy in CSCW (computer supported cooperative work) research (Hughes 1994; Randall et al 1995). Our interest is in texting as 'phenomena of everyday life' as 'everyday' occurrences. We assume that any setting (a university department or hostel) and its associated activities make sense to the participants and the interest is in careful descriptions and account of those activities. New technology is, as Harvey Sacks (1992) would say, 'made at home' in this world – a world 'that has whatever organization it already has' (Sacks 1992: 549). Our concern is then with how this technology finds a place within the 'working sensibility' of those under study. This interest is, perhaps, remote from the kinds of general reflections that someone in an occupation (university lecturer, care worker) can produce, and much more engaged with their consciousness and attention when they are 'at work'. What kinds of things do they take for granted or presuppose in going about their work, what kinds of things do they routinely notice, what kinds of things are they 'on the lookout' for, how do they 'tune themselves in' to the state of being 'at work', how do they react to events? In particular we are interested in the use of texting in developing this working sensibility and in how and in what circumstances do they react to or decide to initiate text messaging? The development, deployment and evaluation (to date) involved in the Hermes and SPAM case studies have revealed a number of interesting issues in this regard.

'Working Text': Usage and sharing context

The SMS messaging capabilities of Hermes and SPAM have both been used effectively. Examples of messages sent remotely to door displays in Hermes include:

> *"am running 20 mins late",*
> *"On bus – in shortly",*
> *"Gone to the gym",*
> *"Johm – in ww burger joint.".*
> *"Maomao going to be late –will catch up later. A."*
> *" In big q at post office.. Will be a bit late"*

Similarly, SMS messages sent to SPAM include:

> *"SORRY IM GOING 2B LATE DARRIN"*
> *"blocked in snow will be late"*
> *"Snow problem please ring Barbara"*
> *"I keep ringing and noaody answers? Can ynu ring me please i cbn nmt get out yet bd"*
> *"Penny am with mr gate closed bvt not locked"*
> *"Hold up with s m money will be delayed back a s a p Barbara"*

A large proportion of the messages shown above illustrate an explicit sharing of context in order to support (or potentially support) cooperation with colleagues.

In both the Hermes and SPAM studies, the user has significant control over the information that is shared but may be prepared to forgo some control in terms of who is able to view the information. For example, if you've arranged to meet John in your office but realize that you won't be able to make it on time then you might

SMS the following message to appear on your door display: "John, I'm in the Café with Jim". This message clearly indicates the desired recipient and you (simply) accept the fact that anyone walking past your office will be able to view the message. Of course this kind of message posting was possible with post-it notes. For example, your secretary could leave a message for John on your behalf or if you thought it likely that you were going to be delayed in the café then you might have left a note on your door 'just in case'. Again the system simply provides an additional (but very useful) facility for letting John know that you have been delayed in the Café that is more immediate because it does not require you to pre-empt the fact that you might be delayed or require you to try phoning a secretary.

There is, perhaps unsurprisingly, some similarity between our studies of workplace SMS texting and other studies on workplace instant messaging (IM). Like Nardi et al (2000) and Isaacs et al (2002) we were interested in the communicative functions of texting, for example, for quick questions and clarifications – *"do you know if Helen has any medicine.."* *" wot time is paul calling to c hh"*

Similarly there was some evidence from the logs that texting was useful for various kinds of coordination and scheduling, particularly when either immediate responses were required or when other forms of communication such as the phone were engaged or being kept free.

"D... XXX has to have blood test at cc at 10 30 i will take him can you tell him to be ready – let me know if you have got message"

"Got message have cancelled his taxi"

"Barbara will you bring a spare medication strip (empty day one) On the front desk office"

Texting is then used as part of a process of negotiating availability and determining or switching media – changing to phone, email or face to face – if, for example, the conversation was complicated or too much typing is involved – or, especially in this workplace, if the other technologies – phone, fax and email are already in use or being kept clear in the anticipation of urgent use.

" please phone house when you are able"

Or to alert each other to technology failures.

"put the phone on to answerphone"

"please switch the mobile phone on"

"u r blocking the phone line after someone telephoned here it sounded like mike. Please sort out as we can not use the mobile if needed"

What becomes obvious in reading the message logs is the flexibility of text messaging in terms of the everyday work (of the hostel or the department) that it supports. So, for example messaging is used for clarification *"what have you done to 136", "complaints form 136 updated"*; to delegate and coordinate tasks *"alison can you ask terri to ring me when she comes in about the swop.."* *"can you tell margaret that the decorators plan to start on her flat tomorrow"*; track schedules *"what shift is steve doing tomorrow and where", "alison on visits and has mobile. Brian out with hh and has own mobile"*; and ask favours *"can I possibly get a lift into town"*.

Another noteworthy feature of the text messaging was its 'expressive' character – even without the addition of emoticons that has only gradually developed – allowing for affective communication about work, work crises, jokes and general social banter.

> *"... I can hear a kind of jingley sound and there are animals on the roof what does this mean?" "It means that Santa is passing over the house and making his way down to see me"*

> *"Help please its all too much on my first day back"*

> *"hello ian i was wondering if everything was alright?"*

> *"A man went to the doctors with a lettuce up his bum and the doctor said 'its just the tip of the iceberg im afraid'..."*

As Nardi et al (2000) argue:

> *"It is interesting that a lightweight technology consisting of no more than typing text into a window succeeds in providing enough context to make a variety of social exchanges vivid, pleasurable, capable of conveying humour and emotional nuance." (Nardi et al 2000: 4)*

Of particular interest is what Nardi et al (2000) call 'outeraction' – where messaging does more than support rapid informal communication but "facilitates some of the processes that make communication possible". This includes negotiating the availability of others for conversation – *"plys phone the house when you are able"*. Such negotiation requires some sensitivity towards the work and pace of work of others; recognition about appropriate and inappropriate times and modes of interruption and so on. Texting addresses these issues in that it is less obviously 'in your face' than some other forms of communication, permitting delayed response or easy acknowledgement (pressing the acknowledgement button) and facilitating multi-tasking – allowing workers to monitor texts whilst engaged in other jobs. Texting in the hostel allows workers to negotiate their availability and maintain their connection with the rest of the staff – knowing who is around, what people are doing for example at weekends or during sleepovers at the main hostel – that is, setting up the basis for a range of possible interactions.

Concluding remarks

*"HOW DO U TURN A DUCK IN2 A SOUL SINGER? – PUT IT IN THE
MICROWAVE UNTIL ITS BILL WITHERS"*

In this chapter, we have explored the design, deployment and evaluation of two groupware systems both of which support remote text messaging to situated displays. Having installed the text messaging equipment, ensured it functioned adequately and demonstrated it, the systems have now been in constant use for some time. General reactions, for example to the SPAM system, have been excellent: *"... we're delighted with it ... we've all started to use it very quickly ... and we're using it a lot ..."... "... I think people at first thought it was going to be really complicated but it couldn't be easier ... we find it extraordinarily useful."*. Examination of the logs suggests that current usage seems focused on confirmation *("Has Fax, email got through? Has x left yet?")*; coordination between sites *("Pizza & and chips are ready come on in :-)")*, simple queries *("which keys should we hand over?")* to signify delays *("please ring car wont start")* and so on. The logs also reveal a growing familiarity with SMS or 'textspeak' *("what does 18tr mean?" .. "later in sms speak, get with it babe")* and its use to tell jokes *("how do u turn a duck in2 a soul singer – put it in the microwave until its bill withers")* suggests the technology is slowly becoming organizationally embedded.

When designing and deploying the systems we have been careful to strive for what Pullin (2003) calls 'lightness of touch', an attempt to find resonance between the diverse needs of different people and a diversity of appropriate tools. The Hermes system has been designed to loosely support cooperation and coordination within a university department and the remote messaging functionality supported by the system has been used ostensibly by one or two lecturers in order to perform the electronic equivalent of sticking a post-it note on their display to state (and perhaps explain why) they are not in their office. The SPAM system was developed following an extensive period of ethnographic study and design workshops in order to support communication between staff working in remote but associated offices. This system uses SMS messaging as a network transport between each of the SPAM units situated at the two offices but also enables members of staff to use a mobile phone in order to text messages to one or other of the SPAM units. It is important to emphasise that the systems described are intended to supplement and certainly not replace existing person to person communication and this has indeed been very much borne out in practice.

In both systems, the situated location of the displays raises interesting issues relating to the public and private character of text messaging in the workplace. There are, of course, issues of confidentiality and privacy to be considered and these concerns have already been anticipated. Initially, in the hostel setting, for example, we wondered if the issue of confidentiality might arise because residents are generally assigned to a single staff member who visits them and coordinates many of their activities such as visits by their psychiatric social worker etc. Displaying text messages on-screen and viewable by other staff members might be regarded as a possible breach of confidentiality. We had some concerns that messages sent by residents to an individual team member should only be readable by that member – suggesting a design solution in terms of the transfer of messages to individual staff mobiles. However, the staff argued forcefully that they worked as a team and the team overrode any such issues of confidentiality.

> *"I don't think having the message relayed to an individual's mobile is (a good idea) ... we work as part of a team ... ".*

> *(Researcher explains ... maybe that particular resident won't want to talk to anyone else?)*

> *" ... it can happen but ... we don't encourage it ... we actively discourage it ... when you're working with personality disorders ... (we don't want) for them to create a dependency on a single person which can happen ... "*

> *"... we also make it fairly plain that anything told to (an individual team member) is shared ... is told to the team ... you've got to work as a team and share as much information ... "*

In a similar fashion the staff argued that concern about security and the requirement for some system of authentication was not necessary because any screen was never going to be accessible by residents since the staff were always in the staff rooms or the doors were locked. At the same time the messaging system was perceived as having some advantages over the current answer phone when it came to issues of privacy:

> *"... people talk at different volumes ... there's always the chance of people overhearing ... and the messages you receive ... "*

Nevertheless a number of further requirements and suggestions concerned with connectivity, interface and usage have been articulated and incorporated into the design. Emerging requirements have included a facility to block numbers (to prevent abuse from residents); facilities for multiple messaging; emoticon buttons (to 'soften' the perceived harshness of textspeak); a menu of regular messages for saving time and a 'hide' facility (to ensure privacy).

However, these issues have not been the focus of this chapter. Instead, this chapter has focused on the everyday use and issues that arise through supporting remote messaging to situated displays. Crucially, we believe that it is important to deploy such systems in the long term. This is necessary in order for users to have sufficient time to make the systems 'at home', to 'domesticate them by adapting them to particular features of the domain or to develop new forms of use – innofusion (Fleck 1998) – with the technology. Our interest is in what has been characterised as 'co-realisation' (Hartswood 2003). Here the key issue is not only 'design', but also 'use', ensuring that user requirements for messaging systems, that we suggest can only be identified in the context of, and through, use, are indeed adequately captured and understood. Our interest is in making these particular text messaging systems work for these particular users, in this particular workplace and at this particular time.

Acknowledgements

This work described in this chapter has been conducted under the auspices of the CASCO project (grant number GR/R54200/01), the Equator IRC (www.equator.ac.uk) and Dependability IRC (www.dirc.org.uk) funded by the UK Engineering and Physical Sciences Research Council. We would also like to acknowledge the members of Lancaster University's Computing department and the Croftlands Trust for their continued tolerance and support.

References

Anderson, R.J., and Sharrock W.W (1993) 'Can organisations Afford Knowledge/' *Journal of Computer Supported Cooperative Work* (JCSCW) Vol 1, No. 3, 143-161.

Bowers, J., Button, G. and Sharrock, W. (1995) 'Workflow from within and without', in *Proceedings of ECSCW '95*. Stockholm, Sweden, Kluwer Academic Publishers

Cheverst, K., Dix, A., Fitton, D., Friday, A. and Rouncefield, M. (2003a) "Exploring the Utility of Remote Messaging and Situated Office Door Displays", *in Proc. of the fifth ACM International Symposium on Human Computer Interaction with Mobile Devices and Services (MobileHCI '03)*, Udine, Italy, Lecture Notes in Computer Science, Springer-Verlag, pp. 336-341, September 2003

Cheverst, K., Dix, A., Fitton, D. and Rouncefield, M. (2003b) "'Out To Lunch': Exploring the Sharing of Personal Context through Office Door Displays", in *Proc. of International Conference of the Australian Computer-Human Interaction Special Interest Group (OzCHI'03)*, pp. 74-83, ISBN 1-8649-9738-9. November 2003.

Cheverst, K., D. Fitton, and A. Dix. (2003c) "Exploring the Evolution of Office Door Displays", in: *Public and Situated Displays: Social and Interactional aspects of shared display technologies*. K. O'Hara, M. Perry, *et al* (Eds). Chapter 6, pp. 141-169, Kluwer. ISBN 1-4020-1677-8. 2003.

Crabtree, A., Hemmings, T., Rodden, T., Cheverst, K., Clarke, K., Dewsbury, G. Hughes, J. and Rouncefield, M., (2003) "Designing with care: adapting cultural probes to inform design in sensitive settings", in *Proc. of International Conference of the Australian Computer-Human Interaction Special Interest Group (OzCHI'03)*, pp. 4-13, ISBN 1-8649-9738-9. November 2003.

Erickson, T., and Kellogg, E. (2000) "Social translucence – an approach to designing systems that support social processes," *ACM Transactions in Computer-Human Interaction*, vol. 7 pp. 59-83.

Fleck, J. (1988) Innofusion or diffusation? The nature of technological development in robotics, Edinburgh PICT Working Paper No 4.

Garfinkel, H. (1967) *Studies in Ethnomethodology*, Englewood Cliffs: Prentice-Hall.

Gaver, W.H., Dunne, A. and Pacenti, E. (1999) "Cultural probes", *Interactions*, vol. 6 (1), pp. 21-29.

Hartswood M, Procter, R, Slack R, Voss, A, Büscher, M, Rouncefield, M. and Rouchy, P. (2003) "Co-realisation: towards a principled synthesis of ethnomethodology and participatory design", to appear in the *Scandinavian Journal of Information Systems*.

Hughes, J. A., King, V., Rodden, T., and Andersen, H. (1994), "Moving out from the control room: Ethnography in system design," in *Proceedings of CSCW '94*, Chapel Hill, North Carolina: ACM Press

Isaacs, E., Walendowski, A., Whittaker, S., Schiano, D., and Kamm, C. (2002). The Character, Functions, and Styles of Instant Messaging in the Workplace. *Proceedings of Conference on Computer Supported Cooperative Work.* New York: ACM Press.

Mobile Data Association, (2004) http://www.mda-mobiledata.org/resource/hottopics/sms.asp

Nardi, B., Whittaker, S., Bradner, E. (2000). Interaction and Outeraction: Instant Messaging in Action. In *Proceedings of Conference on Computer Supported Cooperative Work,* 79-88. New York: ACM Press.

O'Hara, K. E. Churchill, M. Perry, D. Russell, N. A. Streitz, (2002) Public, Community and Situated Displays: Design, use and interaction around shared information displays, Call for papers, available at: http://www.appliancestudio.com/cscw/cscwdisplayworkshop call.htm

Pullin, G. (2003) 'Inclusion, inspiration and lightness of touch' in Clarkson, J., Coleman, R., Keates, S., & Lebbon, C. (eds) (2003) *Inclusive design: Design for the whole population.* London: Springer-Verlag, pp.558-564.

Randall, D. Rouncefield, M. and Hughes, J. (1995), "Chalk and Cheese: BPR and Ethnomethodologically Informed Ethnography on CSCW", *Proceedings E-CSCW 1995,* Stockholm ACM Press, pp.325-340.*l*

Sacks, H. (1992). *Lectures on conversation.* 2 vols. Edited by Gail Jefferson with introductions by Emanuel A. Schegloff. Oxford: Basil Blackwell

Suchman, L. (1994), 'Working relations of technology production and use', *CSCW,* 2: 21-39.

14 Gift of the Gab

Sara Berg, Alex S. Taylor and Richard Harper

Introduction

With the immanent arrival of 3G wireless communication systems in Europe and the US (and their recent deployment in regions of South East Asia), mobile phone manufacturers and network operators are in search of features and services that will make use of the promised technological advances (e.g., increases in bandwidth, 'always-on' connectivity, etc.). They are also seeking to identify those solutions that will revive consumer interest and boost waning sales of both mobile phone handsets and service contracts. Various possibilities have been suggested to meet these demands. MMS, for example, has been designed to extend the SMS facility, available on existing digital networks, by enabling users to exchange still images, sound and video content. Also, through the much used 'anytime, anyplace, anywhere' slogan, location-based services are said to offer a means to provide context-sensitive, commercial services to consumers when they need it (i.e., 'push advertising').

Despite these offerings, however, serious concerns have been raised about the financial commitment made towards the 3G venture. There is no certainty that the pay-outs made by the manufacturers and operators will result in the much needed increases in revenue. It seems confidence has dwindled because of the lower than expected demand for advanced services, based on WAP (wireless application protocol) for example, and the overall slump in the mobile telephony market. Nobody seems to be sure about how to make the most of 3G and, perhaps more importantly, what services will be popular amongst mobile phone users.

In an interesting strategic twist, manufactures and operators seem to be turning to so-called 2.5G as a means to test out features such as camera enabled phones and MMS services. 2.5G has offered an interim test bed through which the manufactures and operators can explore markets and consumer needs before making yet further commitment to the costly 3G infrastructure (Gibson, 2002; Hoffman, 2002). Unexpectedly, technological progress appears to be outpacing economic and marketing developments, providing space to assess the feasibility of particular services and features.

Richard Harper, Leysia Palen and Alex Taylor (Eds), The Inside Text: Social, Cultural and Design Perspectives on SMS, 271–285.

In this chapter, we demonstrate that as well as investing in this 'build-and-see' approach, there is still much to be learnt from detailed investigations into current phone use. Specifically, we aim to reveal that ethnographically oriented field studies of phone users can be used to inform the design of particular interactive features and the form phones might take with the advent of 3G systems. The research presented here draws on an ethnographic study of teenage mobile phone users and presents an early design concept of a mobile device based on the field investigations. Using this research as an example, our aim is to illustrate how ethnographically informed studies offer a viable approach to determine how the 3G infrastructure might be used more fruitfully and what services might be well-received by consumers.

In the next section we outline the fieldwork study of teenage mobile phone users and briefly describe the findings. Following this, we report on the design of a concept for a mobile device. We reveal how the design was influenced by the fieldwork findings, briefly describe the design process itself and present an overview of the device's interactive features and its form. We also offer some insights gained from preliminary reactions by potential users of the device. We conclude the chapter with some general comments on the use of an ethnographic approach to inform design.

Field study

The fieldwork study of teenage mobile phone users took place at a sixth-form college located in an English suburban town. A familiar part of the English education system, sixthform colleges are institutions in which students between the ages of 16 to 19 are taught for two years in preparation for their advanced level examinations. These examinations qualify them for entry into university – determining whether they can attend university, what university they attend and what subject they might study.

Run over a five-month period, the study employed various qualitative procedures, including observational and interview techniques. The observations took place in and around the college premises, including in the college cafeteria, in the classrooms and hallways, and in playgrounds and parks near to the college. The interviews were held over ten weeks with six of the college's students – five girls and one boy. Held weekly, the interviews were used to clarify points of interest raised in the observations and to learn more about those activities that could not be observed, such as phone use at home or in private. During the interview period, the students were given still cameras, audiocassette recorders and diaries to record their phone-related activities.

The field study resulted in a substantial collection of both observational field notes and group interview transcripts. Some of the results of the field study have been reported in detail elsewhere (Taylor & Harper, 2002; 2003). In this section, we briefly describe the key findings from this work and, specifically, those that relate to the design exercise we describe later.

Social exchange

One of the overriding themes to be uncovered through theethnographic field study was that the teenagers who were observed and who took part in the interviews appeared to use their mobile phones to participate in the social practices of exchange. Specifically, their phone-mediated activities sometimes resembled the patterns of *gift-giving* described in the anthropology and sociology literature (Berking, 1999; Mauss, 1999; Sahlins, 1972; Scwhartz, 1967). This literature has its routes in the early ethnographic studies of tribes in Polynesia and Melanesia (Malinowski, 1926; Berking, 1999), but has also received attention in more recent research (Appadurai, 1986; Cheal, 1986). Generally, gift-giving is described as the exchange of material objects that embody particular meanings. It is also viewed as subject to the obligations to give, receive and reciprocate, and available as a means to demonstrate social ties and allegiances.

Embodied meaning

Amongst the teenagers, the phones were regularly used as a way to *embody* particular thoughts, feelings and meaningful events. For example, the text messages that were exchanged were sometimes described as objects that evoked particular memories. The messages were the embodiment of something personal that could be stored, retrieved, re-read and shared, becoming tangible mementos for individuals and groups. Thus, the phone appeared to provide a means to participate in social exchange in so far as it enabled particular objects to take on symbolic meaning and for the objects to be seen as meaningful between people.

From this perspective, the mobile phone might be seen as a tangible memory store or 'box' of sorts; as one of the interviewees contemplated, the phone is "like a box of stuff that reminds me of certain people... It's like a diary isn't it?" Phones and, in particular, text messages are thus seen as sentimental objects with emotional and social value. As with the gift exchanged, the value is not merely determined by the object's material features but also through its presence in and contribution to social exchange.

Obligations of exchange

In the fieldwork, it was evident that phones enabled teenagers to meet what are termed the *social obligations of exchange*: to give, receive and reciprocate. This was achieved in clear and observable ways through the exchange of text messages. The mechanisms for sending, receiving and replying to text messages allowed the exchange with relative ease. Text messaging, or 'texting' as it is colloquially known, provided the teenagers with a means to make the offer of something special or personal, to receive that offer in a mutual show of solidarity, and to reciprocate, completing the unspoken contract that establishes the bond between giver and receiver.

As well as text messages, the phones and the credit used to pay for call charges also served to meet the obligations to give, receive and reciprocate. Both were used as offerings in larger systems of exchange. For example, call credit might have been given in return for say a drink and the phones were swapped so that the charges imposed to call phones on different networks were avoided.

Some of these forms of exchange were made poignant through their role in ritual ceremony. The 'goodnight' messages sent between boyfriend and girlfriend demonstrate this. The messages of well wishing are sent nightly and performed in an orderly sequence of turns so that each party can meet their obligations of exchange and, in doing so, occasion a mutually constituted ritual that has its own unspoken rules and formalities.

Demonstration of social networks

The phone-mediated forms of exchange that took place between the teenagers in the fieldwork also had much to do with the building of allegiances and the cementing of social networks. The phone, and its content, seemed to offer a means to demonstrate the ties between social groupings and, occasionally, the status of friendships or possible rivalries.

Ties would be made observable through the use of the phone. The teenagers would frequently write or read their text messages together, passing the phone from person to person or leaning over each other to view the displayed messages. The mere sharing of a phone and the coordinated participationin texting would serve to bring individuals together and demonstrate their intimacy with one another. Test messaging was shown to be a collaborative endeavour through which teenagers found a way to reinforce their social networks and demonstrate their friendships with their peers.

The status of relationships would be played out through the obligation of *reciprocity* in exchange. By not replying to received messages or reciprocating with offerings of lesser value, teenagers could display the tensions between sender and recipient. The use of free messaging services provided on the Internet was seen, for instance, to be cheap and an affront to the mutual and fair exchange of text messages.

The mobile phone's roles in the embodiment of meaning, the obligations of exchange and the demonstration of social networks point to the ways in which the practices of exchange are present in teenagers everyday lives. Importantly, they reveal how the use of the phone has offered new ways forteenagers to participate in these practices and, in doing so, organize and manage their social relationships. In the following section, we describe how we worked with these findings to consider what features a phone with 3G services might have to accommodate the points raised above. Crucially, this investigation has been guided by our belief that practices such as social exchange are commonplace in everyday life and that digital technologies provide ways for them to be practically accomplished.

From the field to design

The main points to be taken from the field study for the purposes of design can be summarised as follows:

- Phones and their content are used to participate in the social practices of exchange.

- Phones and particularly text messages embody meaning for teenagers, meaning derived from their form and the syntactic and grammatical style messages take.

- Through their phones, teenagers are able to participate in the obligations of exchange: to give, accept and reciprocate.

- The participation in the ritual ceremony can make the exchange special because it evokes a mutual and shared understanding.

- Social ties and rivalries can be demonstrated through the participation in phone-mediated exchange.

Informing design

With this understanding of teenagers' mobile phone use we set about considering how a device might operate and what it might look like if it were to take advantage of 3rd generation technologies. Given that much of our research confirmed what has been recognised as the popularity of text messaging amongst teenagers (Grinter & Eldridge, 2001; Kopomaa, 2000; Ling, 2001), we chose to focus on developing a MMS facility for teenagers and a method for displaying contacts designed to support this. Importantly, the design ideas that we considered were not necessarily chosen because of their novelty, but rather to develop a set of features that tied into our findings on social exchange.

In the following, we describe how a number of the early design suggestions were born out from the forms of phone mediated exchange that were seen to take place between teenagers.

Information capture and communication

In considering a MMS system, particular attention was paid to the capture and communication of information. These concerns were seen to be closely tied to the issues related to exchange. The ways in which information was reportedly entered and communicated using the mobile phone, for example, was closely related to the embodiment of meaning in exchange. The success of text messages in this respect appeared to rely on the manner in which text messages could be crafted and personalised for specific recipients using particular abbreviations or language styles.

Thus, in sharing multimedia messages, we felt it to be important to capture the significance of a particular exchange of messages and to allow possibly meaningful information to be associated with the messages so as to personalise them. As with text, then, the mechanisms for capturing and inputting content, would have to be designed so that information could be combined in unique ways – ways that would allow meaning to be crafted into the message. For example, one possibility might be to allow video to be combined with talk, or to incorporate text or hand drawn sketches with still pictures.

So as to make the delivery and receipt of messages meaningful, a solution might also allow communications to be made in playful ways that may not, for example, rely on the explicit or obvious methods for exchanging information, but rather allow contact to be made using more subtle means. Particular information crafted by a sender could be displayed on a recipient's screen, for instance, so that it might be discovered through a passing glance. This would allow surprise 'gifts' or possibly 'gifts' intended to be understood only by the recipient.

Sorting and organising information

The sorting and organising of content on the mobile phone was seen to be another way in which teenagers managed their participation in social exchange. With texting, messages that were important and those that had personal significance were stored so that they could be reread and sometimes shared. The teenagers in the field study came up with inventive ways to get around the limitations of memory capacity by, for instance, moving their messages to their phones' outboxes (from the inboxes). Some of the study's participants also reported writing out their messages by hand so as to preserve their content, if not their form. Notably, the name, time and date stamps attached to messages were seen as important to teenagers because they provided yet another means to place significance upon a message.

In considering multimedia messaging, these features could be augmented so as to provide new methods for teenagers to store and organise their messages. A system might be designed so that messages could be marked and personalised by the recipient. Information about when a message was sent, or when it should be sent in the future, could also be added, thus allowing the obligations of giving, receiving and reciprocity to be tracked and organised. This would offer users with the ability to withhold messages, to be sent when they saw fit, or to give messages on special occasions.

Recipients might also be given a greater capacity to arrange their messages into meaningful groups and do so in a way that adds to the idea of messages having embodied form. For example, messages might be stored in virtual containers or boxes that could be labelled. These boxes could also be shared, thereby solidifying the ties between groups or possibly sustaining rivalries; 'boxed' messages might be shared amongst friends or kept from rival groups.

Displaying social networks

Also of interest with respect to design was the problem of displaying social networks on the mobile phone's small display. As we have noted, teenagers appear to have established several ways to demonstrate their social ties based on physical proximity; the phone offers a legitimate reason to bring people into close proximity and also to exclude others. Teenagers have also found that their use of particular features and services have value that can be used to display their allegiances to one another – conforming to common abbreviation methods, for example, reveals a teenager's alliances to particular social groupings.

Thought was given to how the design of features on the phone might contribute to these demonstrable practices. The address book on phones was seen as one possible facility to augment. Address books on existing phones are relatively restricted, showing basic details of contacts and, occasionally, offering an ability to display photographs. Using animated graphics, an address book might be designed to incorporate the sense of networks and people's social proximity. For instance, the navigation between contacts could simulate 3D space, where contacts move closer or further away based on their social allegiances. Contacts might also be able to display expressions through their pictorial icons to demonstrate their feelings towards the phone user.

Design concept

To help develop our ideas and to support the design activity itself, our attempts to draw on the field study's findings were combined with lo-fidelity prototyping using paper models and Macromedia Flash animations.

Feedback from people who were thought to be potential users of the concept device was also used throughout the design cycle. The feedback was obtained through individual interviews with twenty-two young people, aged between 15 and 25. The interviewees were asked to respond to various questions and materials including questions on their current Internet use (including instant messaging), their opinions of existing PDA and camera devices, and to provide their responses to the early mock-ups.

In the later stages of the design exercise participants were also asked for their responses to the device using three scenarios. One of the scenarios had the participants imagine they were exchanging "goodnight" messages with their partners. A significant problem raised from this scenario was the lack of expressiveness provided using existing text messaging services. A second scenario was based on the collaborative use of a phone and the sharing of the phone in small groups. Here, one common problem was that of display size and the problems encountered with sharing the phone with several people. One other issue was that of negotiating access privileges to content (i.e., how phone users manage who can view the display). The final scenario offered an example of a chance meeting in a public space (i.e., a hallway) through the phone. The points raised here had to do with displaying one's identity and social status.

Overall, the iterative and cooperative prototyping process helped to uncover a number of usability issues, as well as obtain some reactions to the device's capacity to support social exchange. The usability issues and people's responses to the mock-ups gradually evolved into a broadly encompassing set of criteria that guided the ongoing design. Some of the criteria that related to social exchange were:

- Admit usage/viewing of content in small groups (2 to 4 people).

- Admit combination of photos, sounds, type and drawing in same message.

- Provide individual memory sticks for saving messages/ other content.

- Admit communication of identity, feelings, mood and other status of users.

- Express and add to the user identity.

- Express the preciousness of a private object.

- Express playfulness.

Although, individually, these criteria seem fairly modest, we believe their strength lies in viewing them together and considering how they might guide the design of a device so that it can contribute to the practices of exchange. In the following, we present an overview of one concept that came out of this process and describe a few of its features that relate to the field study's findings.

Concept overview

A mock-up of the user interface for the phone, offering basic functionality, was designed using Macromedia Flash. Figure 1 presents an overview of the user interface and general form of the device.

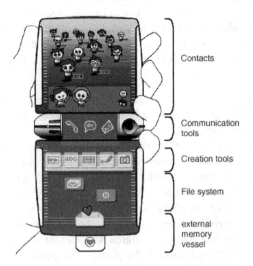

Figure 1: Overview of design concept

A physical model of the device was also produced using foam material (i.e., Ureol and Sibatol) to allow a sense to be had of the size, shape and feel (e.g., Fig. 2). The device has a 'flip-open' or 'clamshell' form. It has been designed to look and feel like a personal, private object: a container of personal information, similar to a box or diary. A camera and microphone are built into the phone and can be used when the device is closed.

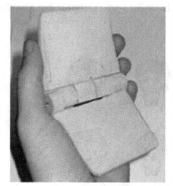

Figure 2: Physical model of device

Open, the device provides two, 55x70 mm, touch-sensitive displays that can be controlled either by hand or with an input device such as a pen. On the left and right sides of both displays there are narrow, touch sensitive areas to scroll through the respective screens. These areas are operated by sliding the finger along their surface. The microphone and camera, which can point towards or away from the user, are placed in-between the two displays. At the bottom of the device is an input so that additional memory modules can be attached.

Contacts

The view at the top of the device displays the user's contacts (equivalent to an address book) in a 'virtual world' (Fig. 3) that can be navigated using the scrolling areas on the sides of the display.

Figure 3: Contacts view

In the Contacts view customised icons represent every contact added to the device. These icons are designed individually by each contact. This way an icon can express the 'identity' of the person it represents. The icon can also express a particular mood or emotion. Thus, a contact may choose to present himself as angry or happy. The icons are composed on the phone by combining hairstyles and faces and setting simple animations (Fig. 4). The icons belonging to the contacts are arranged according to the frequency of communication, so an icon representing a person the user often communicates with will, for example, be shown in the foreground.

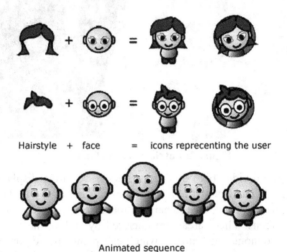

Figure 4: Composing icons for contacts

At the bottom of the Contacts view is the 'Myself' area where the phone user's own icon is displayed. The icon shows the 'default identity' the user has chosen to display to her social network and the specific mood she has chosen for a selected contact. To set or change her icon or alter the mood expressed, the user selects the face icon on the right-hand side of the Myself area and chooses from a variety of displayed options.

The Contacts view is designed to reflect the social ties of the user. People, such as friends and family, who are frequently communicated with are presented as closer in proximity. Contacts are also able to express their form of friendship – their allegiances or possible rivalries – using customized 'gift' icons that can be picked from the menu displayed when the present/gift icon to the right of the Myself area is pressed. These customised 'gift' icons could be used to offer a gift of sorts. In the form of a flower, a heart or a short text message, such icons could serve as simple expressions of emotion displayed at a poignant moment. An expression of love might, for instance, be displayed at night along with the regular goodnight ritual.

In addition, it could be envisioned that contacts might be grouped into certain areas in the virtual world, reflecting the frequency of communication between several people. This would display not only the relationship between individual contacts and the user, but also social groupings.

Communication and creation tools

The three tools for communication are placed in a "communication area" that connects the two screens. The tools allow three different forms of contact to be made:

- Two-way, real-time visual and audio communication.

- Synchronous chat, featuring photo, type, drawing and sound input and transfer facilities.

- Asynchronous messaging, featuring photo, type, drawing and sound input and transfer facilities.

To start communicating with a person/group the user drags the person(s) to the Myself area and pushes one of the communication tools (Fig. 5). The device then switches to the chosen mode of communication.

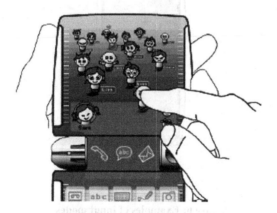

Figure 5: Dragging contact to begin communication

The creation tools are used to select the type of input. There are four different input modes: audio, type, drawing and picture taking (e.g., Fig. 6). The user can combine all four tools any way she wants to and when she is satisfied with the created content she pushes "submit" and the content is submitted into the ongoing communication.

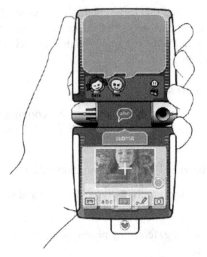

Video input mode

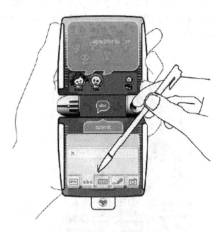

Type input mode

Figure 6: Examples of input modes

The communication and creation tools are designed to enable users to combine information in creative ways. As with the object of exchange (e.g., the gift), communications made with the phone can be crafted and made special for particular people – through the creative combination of tools, the communication is transformed from the exchange of words or talk to the sharing of personalised and meaningful objects.

File system and external memory vessel

The file system and external memory vessel are located in the bottom half of the device. Both offer 'space' to save communications and created objects. The file system operates in a similar way to the desktop on a personal computer. Collections of, for example, communications from particular people or specific types of content can be stored, organised and managed. The external memory vessel is a storage facility that allows collections to be saved on an external medium. The vessel can be removed and replaced, or exchanged between phones.

Both the file system and memory vessel provide a mechanism for communications, such as audio conversations or text messages, to be further embodied. The file system allows communications to take on a form that can be grouped, stored, labelled and arranged in meaningful ways by the user. The external memory vessel takes this a step further, allowing collections of messages and objects to take on a tangible form so that they can be physically kept, swapped or, possibly, disposed of. It is envisaged that memory vessels might take on several forms so that they can be, for example, worn as rings on attached to a necklace.

The preliminary tests of mock-ups of both the user interface and form of the prototype indicated that the device had a high level of acceptability. The size and form of the device were much appreciated amongst the young people. The methods for input also appeared to work well: the touch sensitive areas on the sides of the device were intuitively used for scrolling, selection was intuitively done by pointing with a finger at the object of interest on screen, and the drag and drop functionality was adopted with ease. The overall structure of the graphical user interface was also easily understood, even without instructions. Functions were found quickly by trial and error and the user interface was found to have similar features and parallels with chat and instant messaging services used on the Internet.

The presented design concept offers an indication of how a mobile communications device might be designed using the field study analysis alongside various established prototyping techniques. By paying particular attention to the ways in which teenagers use the current generation of mobile phones and their views of other communications systems, we have designed the features of the concept device to support the participation in social exchange. In a specific attempt to consider MMS, a 3G service, we have attended to the ways in which media can be used and combined in message exchange. We have chosen not to detail the low-level interactions with the device in this chapter. Although these are important, we see them as peripheral to the primary purpose of the chapter: to illustrate how field studies can be used to inform the design of next generation mobile technologies.

Conclusions

Broadly speaking, various criticisms have been levelled at the use of ethnographic field studies that aim to inform design. The approaches have been described as focused on the wrong level of detail for design, producing design requirements that are too vague or modest, and concerned with commenting on existing practices rather than prescribing new forms of computer-mediated activity (Grudin & Grinter, 1995; Hughes, et al, 1992; Rogers 1997).

In the work presented, we have attempted to tackle this problem of using field studies to inform design. We provide a practical example of how fieldwork and qualitative analysis can produce specific and concrete design suggestions for future 3G mobile devices. We describe the concept for a mobile phone that offers just one possible set of features that might be derived from ethnographic field data. As a whole, the user interface and form factor of the phone aim to support teenagers' social practices and specifically, their participation in gift-giving.

By tackling the problem of using ethnographic field study data to inform the design of mobile devices, we have come to see the possibility of an approach that may be generally applicable. This approach is based on the premise that some social practices are relatively persistent within social groups. It follows that if these practices can be uncovered, the potential exists to propose and consider future technological solutions that are likely to be compatible with and useful in people's everyday social lives.

This approach could be targeted at discovering those social practices that are common amongst people and, importantly, *how* such practices are routinely accomplished. It could then be used to consider the ways in which new technologies might impact upon and either contribute to or detract from commonplace, social activity. To explore this possibility further more studies that aim to reveal persistent social practices need to be undertaken. Time could also be given to investigating a more systematic method for uncovering and using such practices to inform design.

Acknowledgements

A version of this chapter was first printed at CHI 2004, Ft. Lauderdale, Florida, ACM Press, pp. 433-440 (by permission ACM Press).

References

Appadurai, A. *The Social life of things: commodities in cultural perspective.* Cambridge University Press, Cambridge Cambridgeshire ; New York (1986).

Berking, H. *Sociology of Giving.* Sage, London (1999).

Cheal, D. The social dimensions of gift behaviour. *Journal of Social and Personal Relationships 3*, (1986), 423-439.

Gibson, O. *Vodafone Looks for Life After Text.* Guardian Unlimited, http://media.guardian. co.uk/city/story/0,7497,723669,00.html (May 28, 2002).

Grinter, R.E. & Eldridge, M.A. y do tngrs luv 2 txt msg?, in Proceedings of Seventh European Conference on Computer Supported Cooperative Work, ECSCW 2001. (2001), 219-238.

Grudin, J. & Grinter, R.E. Ethnography and design. *Computer Supported Cooperative Work 3*, (1995), 55- 59.

Hoffman, M. *3G: Why European Operators are Backing Off.* Mobile Commerce World, http://www.MobileCommerceWorld.com/Tmpl/article.asp?CID=1&AD=16002&SCID= 1&TCode=FT&T1=10/9/2002 (2002).

Hughes, J.A., Randall, D., & Shapiro, D. Faltering from ethnography to design, in *Proceedings of Conference on Computer Supported Cooperative Work, CSCW '92*. (1992), 115-122.

Kopomaa, T. The City in Your Pocket: Birth of the Mobile Information Society. Gaudeamus Kirja, Helsinki, Finland (2000).

Ling, R. *Norwegian teens, mobile telephony and text messages* (Report No. 2-2000). Oslo: Technical Newsletter from Telenor Research and Development, (2000).

Malinowski, B. *Crime and Custom in Savage Society*. Routledge, London (1926).

Mauss, M. The Gift: The Form and Reason for Exchange in Archaic Societies. Routledge, London (1997).

Rogers, Y., Reconfiguring the social scientist: Shifting from telling designers what to do to get more involved, in *Social Science, Technical Systems, and Cooperative Work: Beyond the Great Divide*, Bowker, G.C., et al. (eds.). Lawrence Erlbaum Associates, London (1997), 57-77.

Sahlins, M.D. *Stone Age Economics*. Aldine-Atherton, Chicago (1972).

Schwartz, B. The social psychology of the gift. *American Journal of Sociology 73*, 1 (1967), 1-11.

Taylor, A.S. & Harper, R. Age-old practices in the 'New World': A study of gift-giving between teenage mobile phone users, in *Proceedings of Conference on Human Factors and Computing systems, CHI 2002*. (2002), 439-446.

Taylor, A.S. & Harper, R. The gift of the gab: a design oriented sociology of young people's use of mobiles. *Journal of Computer Supported Cooperative Work (CSCW)*, (in press).

15   Swarm: Text messaging designed to enhance social coordination

Pedram Keyani and Shelly Farnham

Introduction

Martin Cooper's invention, the cell phone, has gone from a large, expensive gadget of the business elite to a small, stylish device that people from all walks of life can afford. Cell phones, also known as mobile phones, allow people to communicate with others while being just that, mobile. This newfound ease of mobile communication is creating new opportunities for meaningful social interaction, such as keeping in touch with and coordinating activities with friends and family.

Cell phones have become an integral part of the feeling of connectedness that people share with one another. However, cell phones also have negative social implications because just as they allow people to reach out to the world, the world can reach back at any time, posing problems of interruptability, split-attention, and politeness in public settings (Pale, 2002). While voice communication is very natural and expressive, it also requires immediate attention, occasional privacy, quiet surroundings, and does not scale well for coordinating within large groups of people (Grinter & Eldridge, 2001; 2003).

The goal of this work is to employ group-based broadcast text messaging to overcome the limitations of voice communication while creating an increased sense of social connectedness. We have created a social communication system, called Swarm, with both the broadcast powers of email distribution lists and the lightweight peripheral information provided in IM (Instant Messenger). The combination of these properties creates a medium through which social groups can communicate, coordinate and feel connected in an unobtrusive and natural way. We chose text messaging because it is mobile, does not require immediate attention and can be used in a number of settings where a phone conversation would be socially unacceptable.

Swarm is designed around a simple command language which works without any installation on all SMS-enabled phones. In order to use Swarm, a user sends text messages to the Swarm server access number. The messages then get rebroadcast to

Richard Harper, Leysia Palen and Alex Taylor (Eds), The Inside Text: Social, Cultural and Design Perspectives on SMS, 287–304.
© 2005 *Springer. Printed in the Netherlands.*

the user's group. Swarm recognizes a set of commands for creating, managing and communicating with social groups.

In this chapter we (a) provide a background discussion of digital communication and Smart Mobs, (b) describe the objectives of our work and provide an overview of the Swarm command syntax and architecture, (c) discuss the findings of two user studies that explore Swarm's impact on group awareness, coordination, and convergence, and (d) outline the redesigns that resulted from user observation and feedback.

Background

Different forms of communication have varying levels of media richness, broadcast ability, peripheral information, asynchrony, message persistence and mobility. These factors have important implications for social communication software. Designing social communication software also requires an understanding of the social context within which it will be used; group size, attention limitations, ambient noise in public settings, and many other variables must be considered.

Important characteristics of digital communication

In the following section we discuss several types of communication mediums to better understand the role a group-based text messaging system may play in people's social lives.

Voice communication

Voice via phone is an extremely rich form of communication. It is a natural way to communicate, since it feels like a face-to-face conversation, and can express paraverbal information not found in text communication (Forlizzi et al, 2003; Short & Christy, 1976). *Media richness* describes a media's ability to transmit explicit and implicit cues and provide timely feedback in a natural and intuitive manner (Rice, 1992; Short et al., 1976). Face-to-face communication is often used as a baseline in evaluating media's richness as information is conveyed explicitly through voice and implicitly through body language; feedback is immediate since the participants are in close proximity. However, the intuitive and expressive nature of voice communication can inadvertently lead to untimely, lengthy conversations which can deter people from calling one another at times (Nardi et al, 2000; Woodruff & Aoki, 2003). Voice communication requires full attention, making it a central, not peripheral means of acquiring information which prohibits multitasking. This makes mobile phone conversations very difficult, if not rude, in many social settings (Palen, 2002).

Coordinating with one person via phone is efficient but becomes time consuming for larger groups because the same information must be repeated to each individual. At the desktop a viable solution is to email a group of people but when away from the computer people must contact each person individually or use some form of group-coordinated phone tree.

Text

All forms of text communication share the ability to capture, store and easily retrieve the content of the communication both synchronously and asynchronously. This proves to be crucial in many social settings where the point of the communication is to convey a phone number to call or an address at which to meet. While this is also possible with voice messages, reviewing is much more difficult due to the ephemeral nature of sound. Background noise during sending and receiving can also drastically affect the quality of the message.

Email

Email enables asynchronous communication. *Asynchronous* communication is time independent, such that the people communicating are not required to respond immediately to each other. This translates to a high amount of acceptable lag between turn-taking in a conversation. With increased acceptable lag between turn-taking, participants are able to fit the conversation into other aspects of their current activities and triage more effectively.

Email distribution lists also provide a good model of group-based message broadcasting because they are easy to create and manage, and they provide a topic-specific (work, sports, friends, family, etc.) virtual social space for group communication. *Broadcasting* is the ability to send one message to many recipients with roughly the same effort as sending to just one recipient. It becomes a crucial capability for communication within large groups where information needs to be repeated for each member.

Due to the disinhibiting effect of email (Walther, 1996) and the decentralized nature of email distribution lists, email tends to have more equal participation across group members than face-to-face communication. No one person is in control of the group's communication, resulting in more efficient and democratic decision making than in face-to-face meetings (Erickson & Kellogg, 2000).

Instant Messaging

As the cost of interrupting someone goes up, more consideration must be given to the interruptability of the recipient. The fear of interruption can result in situations where both individuals want to talk but hesitate to call each other. A powerful feature of IM clients is the personal status message which presents information peripherally. Users can either explicitly set their status along with a message, such as "I am taking a nap", or their IM client can set it automatically based on user activity. This information changes the user's appearance on their friend's "buddy list", giving them a simple visual cue of presence status. *Peripheral information* refers to the low level of interruption and attention required by the recipient to process information.

Text Messaging

SMS is a lightweight text communication medium for cell phones. As the name implies, messages are very short, limited to 160 characters for most encoding schemes. SMS allows one person with an SMS-enabled phone to send a text message to another person with an SMS-enabled phone. While SMS lacks many of the features and capabilities of email and IM, very few mobile devices have the computing power and form factor necessary to support these advanced communication applications. SMS-enabled phones are in widespread use in Europe and Japan and gaining acceptance in the United States. As mentioned earlier, voice communication is very expressive but not necessarily the most efficient or appropriate way to coordinate social activities. It requires contacting each person explicitly, interrupting that person's current activity, and the receiving party having a means of capturing the conversational details. Our goal is to overcome these limitations through lightweight group-based text message communication and coordination.

Smart Mobs and text messaging in social groups

The term Smart Mobs – coined by Howard Rheingold – refers to the enhanced ability of groups of people to coordinate and cooperate based on digital communication (Rheingold, 2002). The defining characteristic of these 'smart mobs' is their ability to mobilize very quickly. An extreme example of the power of smart mobs is the ousting of President Joseph Estrada of the Philippines by way of peaceful demonstrations organized by text messaging. Within hours of the first message "Go 2EDSA, Wear blck" thousands of protesters converged, to be accompanied by over a million more within a few days (Rheingold, 2002).

Despite the short message length of SMS and impoverished text input mechanisms of most cell phones, text messaging is the dominant form of mobile communication for young adults in much of Europe and Asia (Grinter & Eldrigde, 2001). Part of the reason behind its widespread use is that it fits well into the social behaviors of young adults. Mobile phones and SMS foster a sense of intimacy of being always on and always connected to each other outside parental control (Ito, 2001; see also chapter 6). Teenagers find it very important to always be available to their social networks whether or not they are co-located (chapter 6). They use cell phone address books and text messaging as ways to show allegiance, rivalry and to strengthen ties with one another (Chapter 13; Grinter & Eldridge, 2001; 2003; Taylor & Harper, 2002). As Howard Rheingold notes, text messaging became an integral part of social coordination for teenagers.

> *Linturi, the father of teenage daughters, was one of the first observers of the way young people use text messaging to coordinate their actions: 'there were endless calls "no, no, it's changed – we're not going to this place, we're going over here. Hurry!" It's like a school of fish'. By the time Linturi and I met in May 2001, the term 'swarming' was frequently used by the people I met in Helsinki to describe the cybernegotiated public flocking behavior of texting adolescents (p. 13, Rheingold)."*

With all its important social uses, text messaging in its basic form lacks features to support social activities such as coordinating plans with a group of friends.

However, the simplicity of text-based messaging systems offers flexibility in creating new services on top of it. Companies like blah.com and upoc.com have developed similar group-based text messaging services (http://www.upoc.com; http://www.blah.com). These services are generally used for larger, less connected groups. Our goal with Swarm was to design a lightweight coordination tool for smaller groups of friends intent on spending time together. Given the importance of social groups to people who actively use text messaging, how would combining the broadcasting ability of email with text messaging enable group level awareness and coordination?

SWARM

Swarm is a group-based text messaging systems that enable time- and location-independent "always on" group awareness and communication capabilities, which we refer to as hyper awareness and hyper coordination (Ling & Yttri, 1999). The design of Swarm centers on the important role that social groups play in our lives. In Swarm, groups are the primary mechanism for supporting social communication and coordination. Swarm groups are similar to email distribution lists to which each member of the group can send messages. Swarm takes into account the multi-faceted and dynamic nature of social groups by allowing people to easily create and alter multiple Swarm groups to match the social groups in their lives.

Hyper awareness

We use the term hyper awareness to refer to the sense of social awareness that individuals share with one another by constantly staying in touch across different locations. Text messaging enables hyper awareness because it allows people to communicate their current status to each other in noisy environments, with minimal interruption to their current activities, and without breaking norms that prohibit voice calls. This creates a multitude of new opportunities for social exchange.

Hyper coordination and smart convergence

Hyper coordination is the process by which people plan and re-plan the time, place and details of an event up until the moment that it occurs (Ling & Yttri, 1999). This fluid form of negotiation is becoming a common trend among the mobile masses and allows groups of friends to coordinate more spontaneously and converge more often (Nardi et al, 2000). Smart convergence is the improved capability to meet at optimal locations resulting from continuous lightweight communication and decision making.

The Swarm command language

Interacting with Swarm is done by sending text message commands to the Swarm server's access number. The goal was to make the command language simple, short and easy to remember. Table 1 describes all the commands in the Swarm language.

Managing groups

Creating a group in Swarm is done by issuing the command "create <group>". At this point the user can add people to this group by issuing the command "add <name> <number> to <group>". People are removed through the command "remove <name> from <group>". Users can also remove a group by issuing the command "remove <group>".

Broadcasting

Broadcasting a message is done by sending "(<group>) <message>" to Swarm. The first word is the name of a particular group that the sender belongs to followed by the content of the message. If no group is specified, the message is sent to the default group of the person. The first group people create or join becomes their default group and they can change their default group at any time through the Swarm website which we describe in a later section.

Polling

In order to set his or her status, a user issues the command "status <personal status message>". Polling is done through the command "poll <group>", the result is a list of names and status pairs for those in the group that have set their status within the last 24 hours. Given the limited size of SMS messages, no additional status timestamp information is included.

Command	Description
Add <name> (<number>) (**to** <group>)	Adds a current or new friend to a specified group or to the default group
Create group <group>	Creates a new group
Edit name <name>	Changes username in Swarm
Give <name> <group>	Makes <name> co-owner of <group>
<group> **on** or **off**	Turns a group on or off for message reception
Help (<command>)	Returns general help on using swarm or detailed help for a specified command
Poll (<group>)	Returns the status of friends in a group or the default group
Remove <person> (**from** <group>) **R**emove <group>	Will remove a particular person, group or person from a specific group
Status <personal status message>	Sets a status message
Who <group> **W**ho <name>	Returns the list of people in a group or the name, number and status of a specific friend
(<group>) <broadcast message>	Broadcasts a message to a particular group or the default group
xyz: x is a shortcut for the command xyz (x) : x is an optional part of the command <x> : x is a user defined field	

Table 1: Swarm command language

Architecture

Getting started using Swarm simply requires knowing the phone number of the Swarm server and a subset of the command language which can be learned by sending Swarm the message "help."

On the user side is a basic SMS-enabled cell phone that interfaces with the cellular infrastructure. Swarm interfaces with this infrastructure through a standard SMS-enabled phone that is connected to the Swarm server via a serial port. The entirety of the Swarm hardware, drivers, application log and data persistence reside on the server. A key advantage to this design is that users can start using it without installing any programs on their phones. This loose coupling allows us to constantly add functionality and improve Swarm with no adverse effects to the end users. One of the most useful advantages of this architecture is that we are able to log user activities automatically, which served very useful for our user studies.

Swarm notifications

As users interact with Swarm, they receive notifications of changes in status in the Swarm system. For example, if added to a group, a user receives a message indicating that they have been added to a group, and what to do if they want to be removed from the group. When sending messages to a Swarm group, the messages are automatically prefixed with the author and name of the group (e.g., "shelly to party: let's meet at joe's!"). People receive copies of their own messages so that they can see their messages were successfully broadcast by the Swarm system.

Swarm website

The Swarm website allows users to create, manage, and communicate with their Swarm groups from the Internet. Once users logs in, they are taken to the Swarm Group list page (Figure 1) which lists the groups they belong to and allows them to remove themselves from the group, ignore or un-ignore the group, and set a group as the default group. Users can also click the name of each group to be taken to the group detail page (Figure 1), where they can see the people who are in the group and messages sent to the group. As well as seeing group details they can send messages through the web, if they are the owner of a group, they can add and remove people from the group as well as giving other members of the group owner privileges.

User studies

We conducted a group scavenger hunt study to compare how people coordinate and cooperate using SMS broadcasting versus mobile voice communication. We then had a real social group use Swarm over six months to explore how it might be used in every day social settings.

Scavenger Hunt Card Game study

We explored how people would use cell phones to coordinate group activities through a distributed scavenger hunt card game. We recruited groups of 3 to 10 people to complete the game twice, once using mobile voice communication and once using text messaging. The point structure of the game was such that the team as a whole would get higher points if people converged on the same hands. We expected that people would converge on common hands more easily through text messaging because they could broadcast their messages to the whole group.

Participants

32 men and 18 women participated in the game in seven teams of three to ten people. Participants completed the study in exchange for a t-shirt, latte, or piece of software. People were recruited if they were SMS-enabled, and were instructed to bring their cell phones to the study session. The average participant age was 35.5 years, 90% had at least two years of college, and 52% had at least intermediate experience with text messaging. However 48% had no experience with text messaging or classified themselves as beginners.

Procedures

Participants first completed a questionnaire that asked about their demographic background, and then asked how they used technology in their social lives. As they were completing the questionnaire we created a Swarm group for the team. We then introduced them to the Swarm system and had them practice sending messages to the group. We explained the game to them, and then had each team play the game twice, once using voice communication through their cell phone, and once using the Swarm system. The order of type of game was counterbalanced. Before each version of the game, we gave the teams a few minutes to talk about an effective strategy for the game.

The game was designed to model a social convergence situation (such as meeting at a bar on a Saturday night), where each person has individual preferences, and as a group they had many potential convergence points. If people are communicating effectively, they should converge on one or two places. For the game, participants were instructed to make the best hand possible out of five cards. The team that earned the most points per person would win an additional prize. They were each given two cards, and sets of three cards were pinned to ten trees around a park. Team members were given maps that indicated the placement of the trees, and were each assigned a different tree to start with. Although they could use any tree's cards in their hand, they could each only visit two trees, so were required as a team to communicate with each other to earn the most points possible.

Results

Preliminary questionnaire

We asked participants to indicate how they were using different communication methods to interact with their friends socially. We found that people spent as much time interacting with friends overall through the use of technology as they did face-to-face (Figure 2). Chat or IM was the most commonly used form of interaction, with cell phones and emails following close behind. Text messaging was the least used form of technology, with 62% of our participants indicating they never used text messaging to interact with their friends. If the use of a technology facilitates face-to-face interactions, they should be positively correlated. We found that time spent using text messaging was the only form of communication significantly correlated with time spent in face-to-face interactions ($r=.31$, $p<.03$). Communicating through technology such as broadcast emails ($r=.35$, $p<.02$) and IM ($r=.31$, $p<.04$) were positively correlated with feeling like a part of a community.

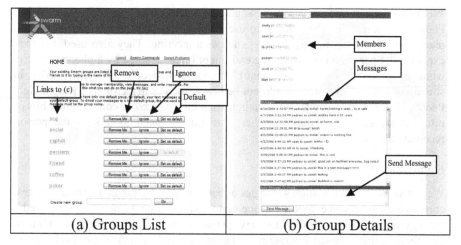

| (a) Groups List | (b) Group Details |

Figure 1. Swarm website.

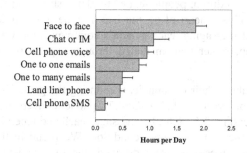

Figure 2. People spend a lot of time socializing through computer-mediated communication.

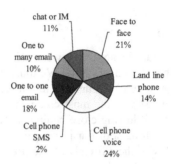

Figure 3. People actively use cell phones and broadcast messages to coordinate social activities.

We asked people to indicate what percentage of their social activities was planned by different types of technology. We found that voice over mobile phone was most commonly used, and then broadcast emails (Figure 3).

We asked people who used text messaging to discuss why and when they used it. People mentioned that they tended to use it when they were in a situation where a phone call would not be appropriate, such as a meeting. They also used it if they expected the person on the receiving end might be interrupted by a phone call (e.g. while in a meeting or while sleeping). A couple of people said they used it in situations where their voices would not be heard, such as in a crowd or a night club. People also tended to use text messaging when they needed to convey small bits of information, such as a flight number, but did not need to talk to the person receiving the information.

Game results

We noted the communication strategies adopted in playing the game across the two conditions. In the voice condition, one team had no strategy, two teams adopted a strategy of each person calling the next person in their list with their information, and three teams adopted a strategy of having a point person whom each person called, and then that person called each player in turn with the full information. In the text messaging condition, people tended to plan a shorthand for communicating card info (e.g., "h6" is a heart of 6), but had no other communication plan. Thus with broadcast text messaging, each person's communication was always directed to the entire group, rather than mediated through a point person as with voice communication.

We asked people about their communication during the game itself, and we found that people had on average 6.7 (SD=4.7) phone conversations in the voice condition, while sending 3.5 (SD=.95) messages each and receiving 11.4 (SD=4.8) messages each in the text messaging condition. We found in the text messaging condition that many messages were dropped due to technical problems. Some participants reported sending up to 4 messages that were lost in the system. People reported using their phone conversations and text messages to communicate the tree hands to each other, and which tree would be the best to visit next. People learned on average 6.2 hands from their teammates in the phone condition, and 5.2 hands in the text messaging condition. See below for an example SMS game conversation.

Bob: Al has 2 of diamonds and the 8 and 3 of clubs going to hal next

Jane: Ed then jenny 5c 8d tend

Jane: jenny has 5s ahearts 2h

Mark: Carl jd 7c 4d fred 9h 8d qs

Bob: I can pick ed or hal

Jane: What does hal have

Bob: HAL has 3 of hearts and, 10 and ace of clubs

Jane: ed works best for me

Bob: ED it is

In terms of performance we found that while people were significantly slower to complete the game in the text messaging condition (27 minutes vs. 22 minutes, $F(1,5) = p<.05$), there were no differences in average scores (25 and 27 points respectively, $F(1,5) = 1.0$, ns). As mentioned earlier, the game was designed so that team members should converge on one or two hands if they were communicating effectively (depending on the size of the group). We found in both the phone condition and the SMS condition that on average 46% of the team players were converging on the same 1.8 trees.

After participants completed each game, we had them rate their enjoyment, satisfaction and confusion during the game experience. We also had them complete measures of presence, social presence and feelings of group conflict or togetherness.

Response	Phone	SMS	*diff p* <
enjoyment	4.4	3.7	*ns*
confusion	3.2	3.4	*ns*
satisfaction	**5.3**	**4.0**	.07
conflict	2.2	2.4	*ns*
presence	3.1	2.7	*ns*
social presence	**4.8**	**3.3**	.05
togetherness	**4.5**	**3.1**	.03

Table 2: Self-report responses to game experiences

We found that people were significantly more satisfied in the phone condition, and reported a greater sense of social presence and togetherness (Table 2).

In sum, we found that people were able to converge in the game as expected using text messaging, however there was no improvement in level of convergence or points earned over mobile voice, and they took more time. We did find that people communicated more hierarchically in the voice conditions, with half the groups using a point person to convey information to others in the group. Furthermore the average number of communication exchanges was smaller with voice than with text, because of the reliance on pair-wise interactions. Even so, participants reported feeling more social presence and togetherness in the voice condition.

Post games Swarm feedback

After participants completed both games, we asked for general feedback about the Swarm system. Participants reported finding Swarm somewhat easy to use (4.5 on a scale of 1 = not at all and 7 = extremely so). People were fairly neutral in their liking toward Swarm, with 42% indicated they did not like Swarm, and 50% indicated they liked it. 45% said they were not likely to interact with people in their day-to-day life with Swarm, and 42% said they were, with 61% giving us their emails to sign up for subsequent studies using Swarm.

We asked people to explain what they liked and disliked about Swarm in a series of open-ended questions. The majority of responses in favour of Swarm indicated they liked the group communication feature. When asked what they disliked, most focused on the messages that were lost or delayed, and a few people could not figure out how to send text messages or found the use of text messaging itself cumbersome.

When asked how to improve Swarm, most indicated improved speed and reliability was very important. A few suggested features for easily adding and removing the self from groups. Finally we asked participants under what circumstances they might actually use Swarm in their day-to-day lives. People mentioned they would use Swarm to coordinate games or hobby groups, arrange meetings, or arrange a party or gathering at a night club. Three people said they would use Swarm to broadcast information such as a new phone number.

Some participants expressed frustration at how slow text messaging was due to using numeric keypads. We feel that this frustration may have more to do with their lack of practice with text messaging. Studies of European mobile phone users shows that one of the reasons they prefer text messaging over calling is the increased speed of messaging (Grinter & Eldridge, 2001). Many of our users had done very little text messaging. It appeared their experience with the numeric keyboard was limited to adding entries to their address book.

A number of users expressed frustration about using Swarm due to their lack of text messaging experience, the clunky input device, and the extreme message latency of certain service providers. At the same time, while talking to users we found that a sizable portion of them liked the idea of Swarm and wanted to use it with their friends. A few of our participants had a great deal of text messaging experience, they said that their use of text messaging was quickly adopted by many of their friends. This viral spread of text messaging suggests that once it reaches critical mass it will quickly become widely spread in use. The adoption of new technology requires people to change their current behaviour, which is often not instantaneous (Flores, et al, 1988).

Lessons learned from Scavenger Hunt study

Although we did not find that group text messaging improved people's coordination during the scavenger hunt game, we did learn some important lessons from the study. First, we found that people were as capable of playing the game through text messaging as through voice, and did so with less hierarchical communication structures. In the real world, we would expect that people would use a combination of text messaging and voice in coordinating their social activities. Second, we found that although most people were SMS-enabled, they were surprisingly not knowledgeable in how to use text messaging to communicate with each other. We found that we spent considerably more time providing people with lessons on how to use text messaging than we anticipated. This suggests that in the United States, difficulty using text messaging is still a barrier to entry for everyday use. Third, we learned that it took a great deal of time to set up a Swarm group through the SMS command system. Sending one message for each person added to the system was quite cumbersome and a real barrier to use. Finally, we found that people were very frustrated when their messages were dropped. The inability to communicate their status to their team mates, and their uncertainty about whether their messages got through, highlighted the importance to us of a) re-architecting our system to ensure a high degree of reliability, where messages may be received and sent simultaneously, and b) providing users with notifications from the system confirming when their messages were successfully received.

Focus group and design evolution of Swarm groups

We had a focus group create a Swarm group and send messages to it to assess people's abilities to create and use a Swarm group in their real social settings. The social awareness and coordination features of Swarm are designed around the concept of social groups. Our original design of groups allowed each person to create their own private contact lists for posting and polling. This design allowed the owner to broadcast messages to their group but recipients could not broadcast responses back to the entire group. Our intent was for message broadcasting to serve as a catalyst for convergence (e.g., automatically going to the sender's favorite bar). We envisioned scenarios where messages of the form "Beer?" or "party at John's" from a sender to their close friends would carry enough tacit information to elicit action.

Feedback from users during the focus session showed that private, individualized broadcast groups did not offer enough flexibility for the types of interaction they were interested in. They found Swarm to be a natural "place" for discussing plans and voting on activities. To support this type of activity, we extended the design of Swarm to include community-owned contact lists where each member can send messages to the group. While this raises issues of permissions, we felt the added complexity was outweighed by the sociability gained.

Informal observation of Swarm in a real social setting

In order to explore how Swarm might be used in a real social setting we recruited a set of our friends to try out Swarm, and then observed their use of the system over six months. We were concerned with a) whether people would use Swarm in a real friendship group, b) what problems might arise in trying to implement and maintain a Swarm group over time, and c) would use of Swarm have a meaningful impact on the group's sense of connectedness and social coordination. These friends were recruited for the informal study because they were very socially active and already used mobile phones to coordinate their social activities.

We created a group called "party", and told people it was for sending reports on social events. The group originally had eight people in the list, and grew over the months to over twenty-five people. Users were trained in the use of SMS as needed. As a member of the friendship group, the experimenter was able to directly observe the use of the system in social settings and ask users for feedback. The usage of the system was also logged, and at the end of three weeks and fourteen weeks we had group participants complete a small questionnaire asking what they liked and disliked about Swarm, and how they might improve it.

In the first weekend of Swarm's use, people successfully used the system to converge on the best social event. Three people went to three separate parties. The first person reported through Swarm that his party was "slow" and left, but thought it might "pick up later". Later, the second person went to the same party with her friends, and reported that it had indeed improved and was quite fun. By the end of the evening, all were at the same party. The following excerpt from our logs for the following weekend illustrates the reporting nature of the system.

John to party: anybody at Jims or Nancys? Report?

Kat to party: I am going to Nancy

John to party: Nancy report?

Mary to party: So uh, oh yeah, where is Nancys?

Sally to party: Nancy at goldies. we at chac

Larry to party: dont know anything about Nancys ... Jims is pretty mellow

Over the course of the six months, the size of "party" increased to over twenty-five people. The level of use was consistent over that time, averaging five to ten messages a week, most highly concentrated on Thursday, Friday, and Saturday nights between 8pm and 2am (Keyani & Farnham, 2004). The majority of the messages were party reports (50%), some of which included addresses (9%). People also sent invitations to converge (18%), and questions (16%). Only 15% of the messages were general chat. A total of 56% of message gave recipients enough information to converge on a location. Because this was a group of friends, messages like "good jazz at chac", provide enough location context for people to meet up at their local coffee shop.

In the questionnaire responses, people reported liking Swarm (M = 3.7, where 1 = strongly disagree and 4 = strongly agree), that it made them feel more connected (M = 3.5), and that it helped them figure out where to go at times (M = 3.8).

In the open-ended responses to Swarm, a few people reported having negative initial reactions, they were concerned that they would get too many messages, or that the text messaging was too difficult to use. However they tended to change their minds with use.

> *I first thought that it would be useless and not fun. Spamming people with party messages didn't seem like a good idea. Then once I actually heard about a party going on that I didn't know about, Swarm became cool – I had a great time at the party and would have missed otherwise. One such time is enough to get you addicted.*

Only one person out of all twenty-five that were added ever asked to be removed from the system.

People liked the peripheral awareness of the group's activities, and the sense of connection that it provided.

> *I liked hearing from people I knew, getting little updates. It was like little windows into my friends' lives.*

About eight people actively posted to the group, however all users reported reading their Swarm messages. At one point a couple of lurkers who never sent messages or participated in the group's social activities were removed from the group. They became upset and insisted they be added back, saying they liked that feeling of knowing what people were up to even though they were not that actively involved with the group. Similarly, a couple of people could not receive messages for a week because of technical reasons, and reported feeling very disconnected from their friends. One participant, upon having his technical problem fixed, sent an email thanking us for adding him back to the group, and that "you saved my social life." One group participant expressed concern about the Swarm group discontinuing: "If this is a research project, what are we going to do when the study is over?"

People were also explicitly aware of the role Swarm had in planning their social activities, and reported appreciating the in-time, in-place coordination.

> *it helped me get together with them at a cool place, which I definitely like...*
> *I also loved it when I was at a party and wanted people to come, I could just fire off a message and a few minutes later, people were on there way from multiple locations.*

> *i really liked being at a party, standing in a group of people talking – my phone would signal a new swarm message and rather than having to leave the circle to answer the phone and give the caller my undivided attention, i was able to maintain interaction with those around me while i checked the message, got their feedback and replied.*

Over time other people in the party group's social circles became aware of Swarm, and the experimenter received frequent requests for announcements to be made to the Swarm group, or requests to be added to the Swarm group.

In naming the project Swarm, we tried to capture the essence of what we were trying to accomplish; namely, to make it fast and easy for social groups to communicate, coordinate and converge together. We found that the name had a significant impact on how people perceived the project. While Swarm is both a noun and a verb, participants quickly adopted it into their language as an active verb; "I'll Swarm you later!", "Swarm me when you find a cool party!", and "Let's Swarm later" were commonly spoken by users of the system.

Although most of the group's users were initially new to text messaging, they quickly developed conventions within the system. For example, people would send "up?" for "what's up?" Because of the initial concern about being spammed, messages without party reports were generally discouraged, unless the message referred to some important or unusual occasion. For example, people would say hello when out of town "Hi from san fran!", or announce an upcoming wedding "N & L are getting married!"

When asked for suggestions for improving the system people reported finding it difficult to create groups or to remember the less used commands. Initially we envisioned people creating groups and adding and removing people while on the go. From observation of Swarm usage, it became clear that only a small subset of swarm commands were ever used. The majority of people only interacted with Swarm to broadcast messages to their groups. We found that generally the only commands used in the social, mobile context was the 'add' command and the 'who' command. When being added to a group, people often asked to see who was already in the group. Users were not generally creating their own groups. Only highly motivated, social leaders in their own friendship circles asked how to create their own Swarm groups.

People also wanted to be able to opt in or out of "monitoring" the group. They might know that they have no intention of interacting with any of the group on a particular night, so would not want to receive messages.

> *My phone kept ringing all the time, once after I was in bed and it woke me up. It would be great to have a super simple I'm swarming/I'm not swarming toggle.*

Design lessons learned from informal observations

From observation of Swarm usage in a real friendship group, it became clear that only a small subset of Swarm commands were ever used. Part of the problem, we believe, is that most people are unwilling to commit a large set of text commands to memory. While this is a reasonable assumption, it made it difficult for us to understand how people would use Swarm if they belonged to multiple groups. Our response was to create a Swarm website where users create, manage, and communicate with their Swarm groups.

Even those who did not send messages to the group or go to many events still found the messages they received important parts of their social lives. They liked knowing what their friends where doing, even if they could not join them. However, user feedback also suggests that it is important to be able to turn off message receiving so we added a command to allow users to turn off and on their Swarm groups.

The initial design of Swarm did not include default groups. It seemed reasonable to assume that users would remember to prefix their messages with the group name. This turned out to be a problem because few people remembered to prefix the group names. We solved this problem by adding the ability to set a default group.

Conclusion and future work

Swarm is a group-based text messaging system that enables hyper awareness, hyper coordination, and smart convergence. Controlled user testing showed that users were able to converge in a distributed scavenger hunt game using Swarm as well as with voice-based mobile phone communication, though they took more time. Using Swarm also resulted in more decentralized communication and decision making. Some users initially found text messaging to be confusing and difficult to use but this was largely due to their lack of experience or technical difficulties with their service providers. They generally reported that Swarm would prove useful in a social setting.

We found that in a real world setting, people actively used Swarm to coordinate their social lives. People liked being aware of what their friends were up to, and actively used the information to intelligently converge on optimal social occasions. The group's usage patterns of mainly sending party reports on the weekends stems from their goal of finding fun social events. While they reported spending more time with one another and feeling more connected, they rarely used Swarm to chat.

Future work will deploy Swarm to user groups in a more controlled user study. We expect that the impact and use of Swarm will depend on a number of variables, including people's life stage. The desire for hyper awareness and hyper coordination is probably much greater in younger populations, for whom friends are at the center of their social lives.

Acknowledgments

We would like to thank the Social Computing Group at Microsoft Research who helped guide the design of Swarm. We also want to thank all participants in our user studies whose valuable feedback was invaluable. Special thank goes to Jens

Riegelsberger for diligently reading and rereading many early versions of this chapter.

References

Erickson, T. Kellogg, W.A. Social Translucence: An Approach to Designing Systems that Support Social Processing. *ACM Transactions on Computer-Human Interaction*, 2000, 59-83.

Flores, F., Graves, M., Hartfield, B. Winograd, T. *Computer Systems and the Design of Organizational Interaction*. ACM 1988.

Forlizzi, J., Lee, J., Hudson, S.E. The Kinedit System: Affective messages using dynamic texts, to appear in *CHI'2003 Conference Proceedings*.

Grinter, R.E., Eldridge, M. y do tngrs luv 2 txt msg? In *Proc. Seventh European Conference on Computer-Supported Cooperative Work ECSCW 2001*, 219-238

Grinter, R.E., Eldridge, M. Wan2tlk?: Everyday Text Messaging. In *Proc. ACM SIGCHI 2003*, 441-448.

Ito, M. Mobile Phones, Japanese Youth, and the Re-placement of Social Contact. *Proc. Ann. Mtg. Society for Social Studies of Science*, 2001.

Keyani, P., Farnham, S. *Group-Based Mobile Text Messaging Towards Hyper Awareness, Hyper Coordination and Smart Convergence*, In submission, 2004.

Ling, R., Yttri, B. *Nobody Sits at Home and Waits for the Telephone to Ring: Micro and Hyper-Coordination Through the Use of the Mobile Phone*, 1999.

Nardi, B.A., Whittaker, S., & Bradner, E. Interaction and Outeraction: Instant Messaging in Action. In Proc. *ACM CSCW 2000* 79-88.

Palen, L. Mobile Telephony In A Connected Life. *Communications of the ACM*. Vol 45, No.3, March 2002.

Rheingold, H. *Smart Mobs: The Next Revolution*. Perseus Publishing, Cambridge, MA, 2002.

Rice, R.E. Task analyzability, use of new medium and effectiveness: A multi-site exploration of media richness. *Organization Science*, 1992, 3(4), 475-500.

Short, J., Williams, E., Christy, B. *The social psychology of telecommunications*. Chichester: Wiley. 1976.

Taylor, S.A., Harper, R. Age-old Practices in the "New World": A Study of Gift-Giving Between Mobile Phone Users. In *Proc. ACM SIGCHI 2002*, 439-446.

Walther, J.B. Computer-mediated communication: Impersonal, interpersonal, and hyper-personal interaction. *Communication Research*, 23, 1996.

Woodruff, A., Aoki, P.M. Media Affordances of a Mobile Push-To-Talk Communication Service. *Computing Research Repository* (CoRR) Technical Report http://arxiv.org/abs/cs.HC/0309001, 2003.

16   Default Thinking: Why consumer products fail

Scott Jenson

Introduction

SMS, more commonly known as texting, is a typical killer application. It is not only popular but also profitable, bringing in significant revenue to network operators. There is even a strong after market selling RingTones, info alerts and crude interactive games. A great technological irony is that such a successful product is so under appreciated. For all of the frenzied SMS marketing discussion, the product has hardly changed over the last few years. Given its success, you would think the industry would put more effort into understanding the value SMS offers to consumers and then produce new services that extend this value.

Instead, the next services trotted out by the industry were WAP, Instant Messaging on the phone, and SyncML. These services, for all of their hype, are but a pale shadow of their original expectations. None of these services are building on the success of SMS. It's as if the industry turned its back on text messaging.

You may think I've forgotten about Multi Media Messaging or MMS. This is perceived as a substantial upgrade to SMS, allowing the sending of rich text, photos and even sound clips within the same message. However, MMS under appreciates SMS as well. It does this in two ways. The first is that its new application interaction is far more complex; it effectively ignores the powerful simplicity that made SMS so popular. The second is that MMS doesn't add any substantial value for consumers. I will explain both of these points in more detail later in the chapter.

However, MMS is just an example of a broader trend. The true culprit here is the approach to product design that sets up these products and considers them valuable. It seems all too easy to create products that misinterpret the true needs of the consumer, creating products that engender little enthusiasm. The marketing failures of both WAP and Instant Messaging should be an enourmous cautionary tale to us all.

I call this shallow approach to product design "Default Thinking". I have seen this throughout my career in product discussions within many companies. By

Richard Harper, Leysia Palen and Alex Taylor (Eds), The Inside Text: Social, Cultural and Design Perspectives on SMS, 305–324.
© 2005 *Springer. Printed in the Netherlands.*

identifying the components of Default Thinking and showing how it affects product design, I'm attempting to create a better vocabulary: a starting point in how to discuss product design issues in more detail. I'll use MMS as an example, showing how it contains many instances of Default Thinking. This is not to prove that MMS is doomed but rather to show how this new vocabulary can be used as a communications tool. The goal is to encourage a more insightful discussion of mobile service issues.

The analysis of MMS will show many weak points of the product but it will also encourage a broader discussion of mobile services in general. A basic tenet of design is that it is very easy to criticize and much harder to create. In order to show how this process can be used creatively, I'll build on this analysis and finish the chapter by brainstorming a series of new mobile services.

Default Thinking

I wouldn't be surprised that many readers may not share my concerns over MMS. My goal isn't to imply MMS is fatally flawed, only to say that there isn't a very mature way for us to discuss its pros and cons. Take for example the fairly innocent phrase, "MMS is an extension of SMS and therefore a natural progression for the industry". This is an exact quote I lifted from a well-known industry speaker. I would claim there is an entire world of assumptions and potential misunderstandings in that phrase. How can we pull it apart and discuss it further?

That phrase is infused with 'Default Thinking' which is the underlying way people manage the complex process of product conceptualization. Product design is a rather soft discipline. There are no equations for insight or no guarantees of success. In order to cope, most people use a personal set of beliefs to base their work. The problem is that such intuitive rules are rarely exposed. In most cases, few people really have a strong understanding of how they internalize the design process. They have a weak collection of axioms of design, broad market visions, or rules of execution that aren't clearly articulated. This collection exists in the background, much like the assumption that gravity exists. These rules are so ingrained in how some people think, certain ideas or positions are just obvious and not questioned.

There is a popular parable that talks of fish not "seeing" the water. The point is that while fish live in water their entire life, they never appreciate it surrounds them. It so encompasses their life that it becomes part of the background. It just fades away and they focus on more obvious things like finding food or escaping from predators. Default Thinking is our product design 'water'. What makes it so dangerous is it's near invisibility to normal argument. It isn't composed of strong opinions that can you can discuss easily, but subtle beliefs that are hard to pin down. I'd like to present four aspects of Default Thinking: Legacy Vision, Consumer Confusion, Design Syntax and Design Semantics.

Legacy Vision

Legacy Vision is the approach we all take when first considering how to use a new technology: it gives us our initial use. This approach is very understandable: we look backwards at what we are doing, our current legacy, and apply the new technology in a manner to make this existing problem better. We see this approach throughout the history of technology. As an example, an early use for movies was to capture stage plays for later viewing. Another was the use of the telephone to listen to opera from a distant city. History has shown repeatedly that most new technologies are initially applied to an existing, backward looking, legacy task. These first uses aren't wrong, only naïve, as they apply the new technology to well known problems. In retrospect, many technologies are disruptive, changing the status quo and often end up being used in far more profound ways. The initial uses are quickly forgotten. Movies clearly evolved into something very different from stage plays and the phone was used for far more than opera. It takes time before the full impact of a new technology is understood and applied in a more significant way.

Legacy Vision applies to mobile phones today. Once mobile phones had wireless data capability, the 'obvious' thing to do was to look backwards and see the web. "The Web is hot, phones are hot, therefore web + phone has got to be hotter!" was the manic belief in the late 1990s. This lunging grasp isn't necessarily bad, only uninspiring. History implies there will most likely be a much stronger and more meaningful use of data enabled phones that goes well beyond the 'web on a phone' concept.

We need to be on guard against Legacy Vision as it implies a value that may not be there. In the case of MMS, the new technologies that presented themselves were color screens and small optical sensors. Digital cameras were a hot growth market so phones + cameras were perceived to be much hotter. The obvious thing to do was to take this cool new raw technology and extend SMS to send photos. The proven value of a previous market implies success in the future concept. This doesn't mean the concept is wrong of course. The point is that the value of the concept appears to be instantly valid; it just has to be sucessful. While indeed, there appears to be an intuitive value to 'sending a photo', additional questions such a "Do people really need this?" and "What are they doing in their lives where this is a large value?" need to be asked. When Legacy Vision is very strong, these questions are often considered trivial or worse, hopelessly academic. Just because something is a better message doesn't mean that it is the right kind of message.

A second problem with Legacy Vision is it's strong negative impact on any explorations of alternative uses of the same technology. The initial use is often seen as so compelling, it short-circuits discussion in the longer-term solutions that will ultimately capture the true use of a disruptive technology. For example, we jumped from the basic technology of color screens and digital cameras straight into MMS. There are other product concepts that are potentially more interesting, such as sending a photo during a voice call. Somehow concepts like this just vanish from the landscape.

The original use of movies to capture stage plays wasn't wrong; it just wasn't ultimately all that exciting. Something much more interesting happened as the use of the technology matured. Most likely the same will happen with photos and phones. Something far more interesting will most likely come. We should be getting used to this pattern and anticipate it.

Implied Consumer

Most companies that target the consumer don't intentionally try to design overly complex products. The difficulty is in truly understanding the actual consumer. Design problems often come using a naïve stereotype of the consumer that is more sophisticated than actually exists. Here is a good example:

This image is shows how easy it is to miss the mark. This is a credit card pay terminal at a gas station. The clear indication there is a problem is the professionally printed sticker imploring you to 'PRESS THIS BUTTON'. This problem had to be so bad and widespread the company had these stickers distributed to all stations and put onto each terminal after the original terminal was deployed.

The strong implication of the "PRESS THIS BUTTON" sticker is that most people, at least initially, just want to pay for gas the old-fashioned way: by going inside to the cashier. The first mistake this design made was not to make the established task obvious to all users. It didn't understand it had to meet consumers' initial needs before introducing them to a new concept such as pay at the pump.

The Implied Consumer, in this case, is someone who wants the use the new pay at the pump feature. This may seem reasonable but it makes a common design mistake: confusing the need to create a design for a new feature, with the needs of the target customers. While paying at the pump is clearly a nice addition, it doesn't appear to be the first concern of the consumer, at least, not initially. While the designers of this terminal had no doubt good intensions, they adopted an Implied Consumer that didn't match the actual one.

Another aspect of the Implied Consumer is that they share all knowledge that the designers possess. Implied Consumers know enough to make decisions that are fairly complex. This is never intentional of course, but it is all too easy to put the consumer in a position to make a decision that seems 'obvious'.

This decision problem of the Implied Consumer is related to a graphic design rule introduced by Edward Tufte, "1 + 1 = 3". When you draw a single line on a page, you have only that. However, drawing a second parallel line actually adds two additional items to the overall graphic: the second line, and the white space in between. The white space acts like a third graphical element. There is a strong correlation of this rule in product design. Adding a second button to a product actually adds two additional aspects to the design: the second button and the requirement to understand the difference between these two buttons. The user must understand enough to intelligently choose which button to use.

The pay terminal has a severe case of 1+1=3. Its second design mistake is to have a completely unneeded keypad on the left. There was most likely some future use for this keypad but as it is completely unused, it just adds visual clutter, giving the consumer 'another line' to understand and process. The third mistake is a series of instructions in the lower left that assumes the consumer wants to pay at the pump. There is nothing about paying inside. When consumers are confused, the only thing for them to read is something that doesn't help.

These last two mistakes together create quite a bit for the consumer to process in order to make the fairly simple decision to 'just pay as I always have'. In a sense, the consumer is put in the position that they must 'understand what they can safely ignore'. This is a central problem of the Implied Consumer. Asking consumers to make decisions unrelated to their primary task often puts them into a stressful situation: they just stare at the device, not knowing what they need to do. At this point, the need for the "PRESS THIS BUTTON" sticker is no longer so far fetched.

Most companies are sincere in trying to create easy to use products. The Implied Consumer tends to sneaks up on designers, becoming stronger the longer they work with a problem. Complex issues become commonplace and even obvious to the designers. It becomes easy to assume the consumer knows enough to make complex decisions. Any interface, no matter how simple in appearance will increase its difficulty if it asks novice users to make decisions. This is most severe when decisions are required that the consumer doesn't consider relevant to their main task. Of course, there is a large trade off to be made as decisions allow for more features to be presented. The point isn't to remove all decisions from a design but rather to acknowledge that decisions, especially extraneous ones, add complexity. The significance of this trade-off is rarely appreciated and can have a profound impact on many consumer-targeted products.

The issues raised by the Implied Consumer go much further than just the initial use of a consumer product. If this were the only issue, we would be in the age-old argument of "Why doesn't the user just read the manual?" Decisions have an impact not only on novice users but also for advanced users as they can be tired or just in a hurry. Interfaces that reduce decisions can be a win for users of all levels. The point here is not that decisions are inherently bad, but that unnecessary decisions have a large impact on both novice and advanced users.

This is the danger of using the Implied Consumer when designing a product. The underlying assumption is that they share the same pc savvy approach the product team had when making the design. This is why user testing is usually such a revelation to so many product teams. The inability for a consumer to make the correct decision using a particular design in a particular place is often stunning. Of course, this does not reflect on the ability of the consumer, but more in the ability of the product to communicate. The Implied Consumer needs to be well understood as a stumbling block and then exorcized from our product discussions so we can properly appreciate the difficulties in using a product in the field.

Design Syntax and Semantics

The term 'User Interface' causes many problems. It has become so broadly used that it is an imprecise term. A common request of most companies is that their next product has an 'easy to use User Interface'. The problem is that it's not clear what this actually means: nice graphics, no hierarchical menus, simplified task structure, better cognitive model, or fewer features? This is one of the key problems with Default Thinking as it considers the User Interface a little piece of code to be tacked onto the end of a product design. The best way out of the problem is to create a richer set of words to break down the vague phrase User Interface into smaller, more precise terms. There are many ways to tackle this imprecise use of "User Interface". One is to break up the larger concept into two pieces: the Syntax and the Semantics of the design. The Syntax is the screen details. Examples of this are the screen layout, the choice of buttons and the task flow of the design. The Semantics are the broader motivational issues. Examples would be the context of use, the consumer's interpretation the design, and the consumer goals in using the product. Syntax is the HOW, Semantics is the WHY.

Design Syntax

Design Syntax issues were most acutely seen in the Mobile Industry during the early days of WAP. There where significant problems ranging from screen legibility, scrolling screens, hidden buttons, complex navigation, and technical reliability. These issues were rarely discussed by most industry insiders yet seem likely to be a major reason for the lack of consumer acceptance.

In the case of SMS and MMS, Default Thinking considers them to be nearly the same. The belief is that they both are just sending a message. This implies their UIs are also quite similar. The diagrams below show the detailed interaction required to send a message using both products.

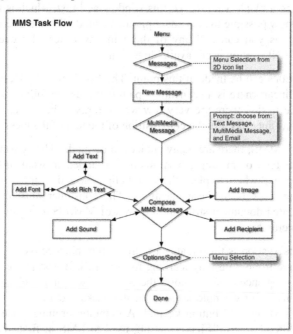

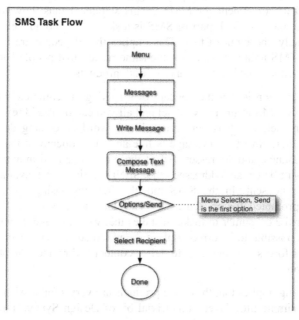

The SMS task flow for the user is fairly trivial. As diagrammed in figure 1, sending a text involves a fairly simple set of steps: chose to send an SMS, compose the message as a long string of text, pick a recipient and then it is gone. MMS, as diagrammed in figure 2, is a bit more complex. First choose to send an MMS over an SMS, leaving a blank window. To this window add text, which is much like an SMS, but it is now possible to also add a photo, a sound clip, and a recipient. There is no sequence as you can add any of these in any order. However, without a recipient, the SEND option is not available to you.

Three observations can be made at this point. The first is that the Design Syntax of SMS is fairly linear: there is a sequential path that must be followed. It is hard to make a mistake in that there are very few wrong turns to be made. The only real freedom the consumer has it in the composition of the text of the message itself.

In contrast with MMS, there are many choices to be made. The consumer is forced to choose what type of message, what should be added in what order, where to place the photo, and where to place the sound clip. These decisions assume that the user knows the answers to these questions. The consumer must understand the fairly sophisticated document structure required of MMS before they can navigate this decision hierarchy.

The second observation is this creates a more mature perspective when discussing why people have trouble initially learning to use SMS. Breaking the SMS process down into this sequence of steps shows the actual "User Interface" can be grouped into two sections: a fairly simple set of sequential tasks and a fairly difficult process of composing text on a 12 button keypad. A common argument used in favor of MMS is that "People had difficulty getting used to SMS at first, there will be a similar period of adjustment for MMS". This statement must now to called into question as the most difficult part of SMS is a skill that is completely transferable to MMS, namely, the input of text. This implies that if people are indeed having trouble with MMS today, it is not for the same reason that people had with SMS. You can't just equate the learning curve of both products.

The final observation is that the concept of a message is completely different for MMS and SMS. SMS is an empty vessel and all you can do is add text. MMS has a more robust model, which is very much like a word processing document on a desktop computer. An MMS message is like an empty document that can contain text, photos, sounds, and addresses. All of these can be added in any order. If the message doesn't have an addressee, the SEND option isn't available and the message can't be sent. In the SMS model, after composing the message, the consumer is prompted for an addressee. The data richness of MMS creates the possibility for the consumer to make mistakes that were impossible with SMS. For example, it is possible to incorrectly place the photo so it is above the text instead of below. This forces the consumer to delete content and replace the photo it in the correct position.

Default Thinking implies that these two products are very similar when we can now see that this 'simple little layer', this trivial bit of Design Syntax, informs several deep observations of these two products. By escaping our Default Thinking it is quite obvious that these products differ not just in menu labels and icons but in a much more profound way at the data level and even the the numbers of mistakes possible in the process.

Analyzing the Design Syntax of a product is a communications tool. It is a technique to break through broad statements and get some detail into the discussion of a product. I find this tool works at two very different levels. The first is as a reductionist tool, breaking up broad statements with specific examples that can be called out, compared, and studied. This is what we've just completed in comparing SMS and MMS.

The second level is as a motivational tool when working on a product design. The more you take apart the Design Syntax of products, the more you appreciate how a complex flow creates unnecessary problems for the consumers. When working on new products, making the Design Syntax clean and simple becomes a much stronger, and more motivated goal.

Design Semantics

Design Semantics examines the motivation and the values the consumer has in using the product. This includes what they are trying to accomplish, how they interpret the design, or why are they using the product at all. Too often the primary focus of a User Interface is the superficial details of the design such as the icons and menus. Addition insights come from looking at the consumer's interpretation of the design and value it may have to them.

At first blush, SMS is perceived as a complex product, primarily as the text input is so difficult. When first introduced, many people felt that the average consumer would not put in the effort to become proficient in inputting text using a keypad. However, the value of sending an SMS was so high that many, many people persevered. The value actually overcame the difficultly of using early SMS handsets.

Most products rarely start with such a large motivational value upfront. Much more likely, the exact opposite is true: the value for a particular product concept doesn't really exist. No matter how good the design of the product, it will not succeed. The reason for analyzing the Design Semantics of a problem is much like doing user testing: the purpose is to look for problems. If there is no apparent value to a product concept, the user interface is irrelevant.

The problem with Default Thinking is that it creates value too quickly, usually through Legacy Vision. This false value often motivates a product too quickly. This doesn't guarantee a product will fail but it does make it significantly more risky. This concern of a false consumer value isn't a new concept. Most mature consumer industries such as automobiles, prepared food, even beer, all do significant consumer trials before rolling out a full product. It isn't an exact science but it attempts to make sure a product will have value before the big money is spent bringing it to market.

The mobile industry is maturing but still has a ways to go in comparison to other industries. There aren't enough studies of users to find out what consumers are doing to understand their communication needs. This is clearly a very difficult problem to answer well. However it has to be attempted so at least some discussion can occur, highlighting, if anything, at least the assumptions that are being made.

Let's consider the value proposition of MMS. It seems almost obvious, the marketing materials showing how fun it is to send photos, how nice it is to receive a "Happy Birthday!" message with a photo and music, or even showing how to send photos while on vacation. This makes for very enticing advertising copy. By examining the Design Semantics a little more, I am attempting to discover the underlying value to the consumer. The best place to start here is to understand the current value of SMS today. Once we have a better understanding of what is driving SMS, we will be in a much stronger position to evaluate the value of MMS.

Summary of existing work

There has been a considerable amount of work on the values that SMS currently provides, as well as some of the misconceptions about those values. For example, it is still a common belief that SMS has succeeded because it is a cheap alternative to voice communications. The basis of this idea appears to be the accounts provided by teenagers explaining their behavior by alluding to the minimal cost entailed. Close examination of their actual behavior shows clearly that cost is a very minimal driver of usage. This is not to say that these same users are without awareness of costs, but that other values provided by text are greater than and supersede these. For example, Kasesniemi (2003) shows convincingly that the ways in which SMS gets undertaken results in an increase of costs when compared to the costs that result from voice only communication: though each individual text costs considerably less than an individual voice call, Kasesniemi shows that texts are rarely if ever solitary, and are more often made up of a series. It is the series of texts that creates cost; and these are often very substantial. In addition, she and many others have shown that these costs are in practice viewed as insignificant to the value that SMS provides.

The most obvious value of SMS is it's low level of intrusion: a recipient is not required to interrupt their activity to deal with the message nor is there any rule of conduct demanding specific speed of reply (Kasesniem, 2003; but see also chapter 3 in this book looking at the moral obligation to reply at some time). SMS also allows both parties to modulate their turn – taking to suit their circumstances (chapters 5 and 6). A related value has to do with the time shifting nature of SMS, whereby it affords a mix of real time and asynchronous messaging (Ling, et al, chapter 4; for the benefits that this provides for minority groups see Bakken, chapter 8).

SMS also affords a degree of privacy that voice (and even MMS) does not, through allowing the user to create and read messages without the activity being excessively conspicuous to those around. One consequence of this is the still largely undocumented practice of using texts to subvert particular contexts such as meetings and TV watching (for exception see Taylor, forthcoming). A more thoroughly researched area is on the use of text to develop relationships that would otherwise be subject to social control, the most clear example of this being Philippino women using text to have emotional and even sexual relationships with men (see chapter 10). Part of these usage patterns have to do with the ability of texts to have gift like properties, binding both sender and receiver into systems of obligation and exchange (chapter 14). Text also has some particular benefits when it comes to the articulation of meaning, with many researchers noting that with text individuals find that they can express themselves more clearly and with greater forethought than with real time talk. This results in the gifting just mentioned and also other shifts in social practices. Riviere & Licoppe for example (chapter 5) note that SMS is used by couples in France to avoid the violence that sometimes attends difficult emotional conversations.

When SMS first arrived, most people felt it was a trivial product. However, it met a deep need to communicate simply, less intensely, and in a time shifted manner, all of which enabled people to communicate in ways they wouldn't have normally done before.

In light of these studies, MMS's value proposition doesn't appear to be as strong. These studies show how SMS is used primarily for social interaction and information coordination. Lots of quick, small messages are going back and forth. People are sending lots of messages, exchanging information over time, and setting up rendezvous. In reading these studies, many ideas come to mind to extend these services, some of which will be discussed below. However, the current interaction style that has been documented with these studies doesn't give the impression that sending photos is the obvious next step.

Of course, these studies do show potential uses for photos. The Fillipino women using SMS to augment the dating ritual has could clearly gain value from being able to send a photo. However just because something can have initial value doesn't mean that it has longer term potential, i.e. it will continue to have value after initial use.

In addition, the gift exchange studies may indeed show a potential value. It is possible to create quite a complex MMS, one that includes not only a picture but sound and text as well. This has value as a gift. There clearly could be a small study in the gift giving groups to see how they would respond to photos as gifts to understand this further. The real issue is not that this could be a gift but more likely, how often it would be used. If used rarely, it has little long term potential.

It must be made perfectly clear that discussing these studies does not prove anything. These studies only point out that there is strong reason to be skeptical. While there are many issues to discuss further, these studies show that the primary uses of SMS do not appear to be reflected in the benefits of MMS. Understanding more of how SMS is used puts us in a stronger position to discuss its strengths.

This doesn't mean that MMS can't eventually succeed; only that is clearly will not replace SMS usage. MMS's market value is hardly a given.

This discussion is not meant to be a proof of MMS's demise. The point here isn't to use Design Semantics to create an "equation of product success", only a topology of analysis. In the case of SMS, the current ethnographic research enables us to debate potential future products with more facts and less opinion. We are at least trying to see the problem from the eyes of the user, raising concerns and discussing options. To be fair, there could easily be a new, as yet undiscovered, social need that will enthusiastically embrace photo messaging. My concern is that at this point, MMS appears to be working more on wishful thinking.

MMS summary

We started off this chapter with the quote, "MMS is an extension of SMS and therefore a natural progression for the industry". Here are the four aspects of Default Thinking in summary applied to MMS:

There is clearly Legacy Vision in that it sees itself as an extension of SMS. This is a warning sign as there is an implied value that may not be justified. The considerable success of digital cameras is interesting but certainly not a guarantee of the future success of MMS.

There is the Implied Consumer as a more experienced user is required to use the more complex document model, one which is more like a PC document than an SMS. This too is a risk and needs to be discussed further.

The Design Syntax of the MMS is also much more complex as it involves a series of branching decisions instead of the SMS model of sequential use. This, and its more complex document model, requires more of the consumer and may create some problems for a potentially broad range of users.

The Design Semantics of MMS assumes its value is based on the value SMS. Current user research implies the true value of SMS is based on a complex series of social and interactive attributes which don't seem to be greatly enhanced by photos. There are many directions that SMS can be improved upon based on the studies cited above, but it isn't clear that photos are an obvious means to accomplish that.

Of course, to definitively state that MMS is a hopeless flawed concept would be rash. My point in this discussion is to show how these four aspects of Default Thinking provide a way to decontruct a concept and to provide a means to discuss a product in greater detail. While I do think this discussion has shown significant weakness in the MMS product concept, the larger purpose is to have a means to discuss any issue in greater detail. This of course can cut both ways as I'm handing critics a set of tools to dispute my claims. I would heartily encourage this. The purpose of this chapter isn't to prove MMS is doomed but rather to show both how we can discuss it in greater detail and also use this discussion to discuss other mobile service concepts.

For example, an improved MMS client that significantly reduces the complexity of its current Design Syntax could far more interesting product to discuss. There might also be other groups whose value of a photo is so high that they will avidly use this service. These are all useful and forward-looking conversations.

Creating future product concepts

Approach

This chapter is only half complete. Going through the Default Thinking of MMS was a useful exercise but to use this analysis only to criticize is a bit of a waste. There are several insights here that imply many future products. A fundamental rule of design is that criticism is easy, creation is hard. However, this type of criticism puts us into a good position to create future concepts that build upon the success of SMS.

Creating new product concepts is a rather complex process. As a professional designer, I often see new ideas that that are very experimental, with no possible means of implementation. Of course, this can be useful as it opens up new ways of thinking. However, products that are too far out into the future tend to be easily forgotten. Sometimes, a more efficacious approach is to use technology as a lens, constraining your designs within a certain technological framework. This is, ironically, often a liberating experience as it focuses your thoughts and concepts. In a sense, it gives you your vocabulary and you have to write the verse. To show how this works, I'd like to use the MMS analysis of this chapter to brainstorm a series of new products, each using a different technology as a starting point: an existing SMS handset, an extension of SMS, and an extension of MMS. Just so I don't become too beholden to technology, I'd like to offer a fourth product with no technological basis at all.

How do we start?

The natural Default Thinking approach of MMS focuses on improving the message. Adding photo and sound capability to SMS implies an inherently a better message. In light of our growing understanding of how and why SMS's are being sent, it seems more useful to focus new technology not on the message, but more the needs motivating the message. Why are people sending messages and how can we make this easier and more useful?

The research cited in this book shows that the use of SMS is inherently social: coordinating meetings, exchanging scraps of information, giving gifts and sharing emotions. Instead of focusing on just the message we should look at the entire social transaction. Here is just one concept of how a typical SMS exchange would take place:

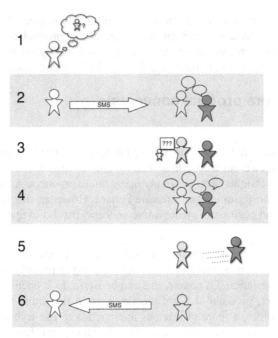

Figure 4

Figure 4 diagrams a more complete social scene. In Step 1, the initial sender is curious about the person on the right. This represents a very broad concern and SMS is only one possible solution to this question. Step 2 is the actual use of SMS to ask a "Where are you?" type of question. Step 3 is the receipt of the SMS. Notice that the receiver is in the middle of a conversation and the SMS interrupts this. However in step 4, the conversation resumes. In Step 5, the conversation concludes and a reply is sent in step 6.

There are many possible directions and observations that come from looking at SMS this particular way. It becomes clear that the actual SMS is just a small part of a larger social motivation and transaction. In light of this, focusing on just improving SMS seems a bit trivial. Seeing this larger context invites several questions:

Step 1: What other ways can the sender answer their question? Is the receiver available at this time? Would they mind an interruption?

Step2: What is the impact of receiving a message? Does this create problems?

Step 3: What are coping mechanisms of receiving SMS or voice calls?

Step 4: How important is it to reply to an SMS immediately? Does this create other tensions?

Step 5: Is the conversation terminated early due to the pending message?

Step 6: What are possible ways to reply to this message? Is it possible to forget to reply?

Another question arises when looking at this process as a negotiation. The tools are fairly blunt with little ability to control the intensity of the interaction. When in physical proximity, there are many choices in interacting, ranging from a wave across the room, a tap on the shoulder, a vocal interruption to even a strong physical shove. None of these choices are available with SMS. This situation becomes even more complex when considering a group interaction.

SMS may be a bit humble to attempt to be a full part of this social dynamic. However, it is an intriguing position from which to ponder and reflect. If anything, it puts me 'in my place' as a designer so I appreciate how difficult it will be for any technology to integrate well within a typical social interaction. On the other hand, I also find this empowering as it implies very profound products, such as SMS, have very simple features. Their complexity comes in the social machinations of use, not from their technological depth. The next great mobile service will most likely be denounced by industry experts as trivially simple.

Technology and business issues

Limiting any new product concepts to SMS or MMS has a large advantage: there will be no need to change the underlying infrastructure of the mobile network. This is important as it means that new products can be immediately used, without waiting for standards bodies or worldwide rollout for these services to begin.

However, nothing is ever easy in the real world. These new concepts will require custom software on the handsets. This raises a common problem in any business level discussion: how can you introduce a new product when initially, very few consumers will have it? The thinking goes that you won't have a viable product until it is widespread. The problem, of course, is how do you initially motivate people to get the new product? This chicken or egg problem was an issue when SMS first appeared, and is still an ongoing problem with MMS today.

I don't wish to dwell on this issue as this chapter is about insight and discussion of new product concepts. However I need to quickly establish that this isn't a hopeless endeavor, even though this point clearly needs a deeper discussion. There is no doubt that any concept we come up with, will have to face this problem of a broader market acceptance. However there are two factors that make this problem less severe. The first is that some new handsets can download applications to be used immediately. This removes the problem of waiting for a new handset each time you want to try a new feature.

The second is that that most communication for consumers is between a small numbers of people. If everyone is this social network has this new feature, the value will most likely be strong enough for it to be used. Example social networks would be a family, a small business, or a group of friends. Push-To-Talk services in the

US succeeded using this very approach by selling contracts into small businesses, giving everyone in the company, effectively a new set of services.

Four product concepts

Existing handsets: gift storage

This first product concept will attempt to use SMS and mobile handsets as they are, without any change. This is particularly challenging as the beautiful simplicity of SMS, by its very nature, doesn't allow much room to add anything new to the mix. SMS does what it does very well, but no more. Attempts at SMS 'applications' have succeeded, but only by forcing the consumer to use keywords or websites to configure a service before using it, making their user interface syntax quite complex.

Any attempt at a new concept must be based on a problem to be solved. The gift exchange work done and reported by Berg et al in chapter 15 and Taylor & Harper, (2003) pointed out a key problem for many teenagers: how to safely store prized messages. It was too easy for them to loose messages through accidental deletion, lack of capacity on the handset or lost phones. Their work suggests some interesting hardware concepts to solve the problem. The attempt here is to stick with exactly what we have today.

One approach would be for a service provider to provide a "SafeStorage" phone number. If a particularly valuable text has just been received, the person just forwards it to this number for safekeeping. Later all forwarded messages could be retrieved through a website, logging into it with the forwarding handset's phone number. As most service providers already have a website suite of services for existing customers, this is a fairly simple addition.

Given the strong value for storage Berg et al and Taylor & harper (2003) have documented, it would make sense to discuss what could be done with the stored messages at the website. In addition to storage, organization and annotation come to mind as having potential value.

This application is rather modest in scope but it seems worth considering as it is fairly easy to implement and motivated by a clear social need.

SMS with new software: Tap

We'll now move up the technology curve and consider an application that works using SMS but requires custom software on the handset. One of the insights covered by the other chapters in this book is that the value from SMS comes not from its rich feature set but what is said using these limited features. Even an empty SMS can have value. Even though no text is sent, the message isn't really empty as it has a sender and an arrival time, both of which can have meaning depending on social context.

By considering an empty text message, the Design Syntax becomes radically simpler. All you have to do is pick a person and the message is gone. This quickness can have significant value itself, encouraging people to send messages when they normally wouldn't.

This content-free message is the social equivalent of a 'tap' that lets the other person know you have contacted them. It could have all sorts of potential meanings, each dictated by the particular social environment in which it was sent. For a family in a theme park, tapping could mean it is time for lunch. It could just mean a lover is thinking of their partner during the day. It could even have a business value, signaling a colleague it is time to come into a meeting.

The Design Syntax would be practically non-existent. Scrolling through the address book, you'd highlight a contact, select the "Tap" option and you'd be done. The receiver would get some type of Tap specific notification and they could look at the screen to verify who sent it. This is backward compatible for standard handsets as the message sent is still an SMS so could be received by anyone. All they would be loosing is the custom notification alert.

This empty message is just a brainstorm but has definite potential. A quick prototype and field study would go a long way in determining the value and potential issues. Notice how this concept design is strengthened on two fronts. First, the social insights of the existing research help us discuss value, or the Design Semantics of the service. Second, the very simple nature of the low-level user interface, or the Design Syntax, is also powerful. We can discuss how quick and easy this service will be and how this affects its appeal. By creating a service that can be evaluated at both levels, the strength of an idea becomes easier to see and discuss.

MMS with new software: VoiceSMS

We'll now move even further up the technology curve and consider an application that works using MMS but requires custom software on the handset. It became clear through the Design Syntax section above that the majority of the 'UI work' in sending an SMS was the text input. When people choose not to send an SMS it is usually due to the frustrations of text entry and not problems with the user interface.

One solution to this problem would be to mimic the simple SMS Design Syntax but replace text input aspect with a voice recording. This VoiceSMS would be sent with just 2 actions, one to start recording and another to select a recipient. Like the original SMS syntax, it would be sequential with no branching. In addition to being simple and fast, it also has the benefit of conveying real emotion through the voice so it might add value by allowing the message to carry more meaning.

On the negative side, the message would be harder to receive in noisy environments. It also isn't as easy to send in crowded situations as you would have to announce to the world your message content. However, given the propensity for people to have conversations in public, is doesn't seem unreasonable to speak messages as well. It seems reasonable that VoiceSMS will not replace SMS but offer an alternative for many people would never bother with just SMS as it currently stands.

What I enjoy about the VoiceSMS concept is that it pulls from our discussion at both the Design Syntax and Semantics levels. We know that increasing the emotive content is important to a message but our Design Syntax work pushes the design to be more like the SMS model with no branching a very few interaction steps. So while one might be tempted to argue that VoiceSMS is just a restricted MMS, the significantly streamlined nature of its Design Syntax puts it into a completely different category. This is one reason why I find exploring mobile services so interesting. It is surprising that something like VoiceSMS, which is so easily dismissed as a derivative MMS is in reality a very different product.

As with Tap above, this is an exploration that clearly needs further study. The purpose here is not to pull a barn burner project out of thin air but to show how concentrating on breaking out of Default Thinking can lead us to more interesting concepts. Clearly some marketing work and certainly a prototype trial would go a long way in identifying any concerns with this product.

No technical grounding: GroupSMS

The problem

The previous three concepts all used existing technologies. This has its place in creating more short-term concepts that can be more easily implemented. At this time, I'd like to ignore technology completely and discuss just an existing problem and try to brainstorm a useful product.

Communicating with a group is a strong use of SMS today. However it involves a complicated clustering of a series of one-to-one messages in order to build up a group consensus. Providing a means to simply this would have very strong value; this isn't a new observation. In the prior chapter Keyani & Farham looked at how to facilitate group behaviours with SMS, for example. However, the industry has taken been pushing Instant Messaging (IM) or even Email as solutions to this problem.

IM ignores all of the lessons we have learned from SMS. It can never work for at least two reasons. The first is that it requires everyone in the group to be "Logged on" at the same time. One of the key values of SMS, and even voice calling, is that the receiver doesn't have to do anything special. SMS and calls always arrive with no effort on the receiver's part. Requiring people to be logged in to a chat server means that that chatting is only possible with some of your friends some of the time. SMS and Voice work for all of your friends all of the time.

The second is that SMS gives the receiver a little breathing room. If they are in a discussion, or getting off of a bus, they can take care of whatever they are doing before replying. SMS in a sense allows a certain amount of time shifting so conversations can take place as the situation allows. You can be getting along with your life and still maintain an SMS conversation over an entire day. Chatting through IM is very different as it is fairly demanding of your attention, intruding into your life. This provides a disincentive to turning on chat during many portions of the day.

Email isn't a solution either as it makes managing the thread of a conversation difficult: not everyone does a 'reply to all". Even if they did, the inbox is littered with messages that don't form a coherent conversation. This is why the group send feature of SMS, which mimics some of this email behavior, is also inadequate.

Concerns

Any solution to group interaction needs to understand the environment in which it will be used. Independent of the technology, any solution should address the following needs:

It should be possible to post a question to a group of people. All should receive it and all replies should be visible to the same group.

There should be no requirement to log into a server throughout the day. Messages should be able to be received with no premeditated effort.

Like SMS, messages could be replied to at a convenient time.

One to one SMS messages will still exist! A completely separate 'Group Message' application is an odd exposure of the consumer to technology. Sending a message to a single person or a group is almost the same act, the only difference is that more people receive the message.

Group messages could get quite busy with replies and replies to replies. A means of grouping them together would be helpful.

Creating groups could be a complex problem and needs to be watched carefully as the Design Syntax of this issue could overwhelm the process.

Discussion

The concerns have given us quite a list! The key insight is that we want a group discussion application integrated with, and based on, the interaction style of SMS. What we are really after is an SMS style bulletin board system where everyone in the group can see all postings. This has the time-shifted value of SMS so replies can happen when the receiver has time. It also has the advantage of growing with the user. They can start off sending one-on-one SMS messages and slowly grow in sophistication and start sending group messages that can turn into conversations.

This also raises a surprising issue. Managing a group thread of SMS messages also has value for one-on-one situations! In fact, there may be very little difference between one-on-one messaging and group messaging, both manage replies into threads to be viewed easily. The only difference is that more people are involved.

This is a very significant observation as it implies there is really no difference between the social uses of SMS and IM. Both are just exchanging small text messages. The point isn't necessarily that SMS must grow to encompass IM but more that the two need to merge into a single application. Forcing consumers to choose between sending an SMS or sending a chat message is exposing too much technical plumbing.

In fact, there is seems likely to a be a major train wreck in the making as the industry will be asking the consumer to use up to 4 types of messaging technologies in the same handset: SMS, MMS, Email, and IM. This feels like the Implied Consumer all over. How will your basic consumer be able to make a decision on which product to use? Breaking out of default thinking propels us to take pity on the deluged consumer and create a product that simplifies this presentation.

A second important point is that we can't just wave our hands and say "SMS needs to add group addressing". Design Syntax should warn us that we have to look at this issue very carefully and not assume it is a trivial problem. Sending a message to a group implies that messages either have to have multiple recipients or that it is possible to create groups. Creating groups isn't terribly hard but it is a very proactive PC centered concept. It implies that users create 'group objects', know where to find them, and know how to edit them. These tasks all seem trivial to us PC savvy users but they, much like MMS, require a certain sophisication that not all consumers will share with us.

The final point is that we really don't even have a strong understanding of what 'groups' mean in the context of mobile phones. Will most messaging be between 2 people, 3, 12? If most group discussions will be small, just adding recipients to a chat and not allow the creation of stored groups might be completely acceptable. I don't have the answer to this question at this time. However, it has to be called out as a key issue. In my experience what most likely will happen is that no one will be able to figure it out for sure. This creates fear in the product team so they choose the most complete solution they can just to be sure that every possible contingency is covered. This of course will most likely create a heavy solution that will spoil the ability for most consumers to ever cope with the design. My gut reaction is that most groups will be fairly small and that making multiple addresses easy is critical to the problem.

Clearly GroupSMS is a complex product and I haven't done it justice in this limited space. However the purpose of this chapter is to show how Default Thinking takes place in mobile service product discussions and how to combat it. There is clearly lots of work left in creating a good GroupSMS product but these discussions have put us in a much stronger position to create a product that will work for most consumers.

Conclusion

This chapter started out with a criticism of MMS, showing how Default Thinking is a common approach used in many product design situations. While MMS has some flaws, the goal was not to prove its design defaults but to show how we can discuss products in a more articulate way, using the components of Default Thinking: Legacy Vision, Implied Consumer, Design Syntax and Design Semantics.

The MMS discussion enabled a broader consideration of the mobile space, creating not absolute truth but a richer landscape to discuss and argue. Doing this put us into a much stronger position to discuss future products. The four examples given are all in need of more work to validate them, but they are at least motivated by user insights that go beyond classic Default Thinking that is currently seen in the Mobile Service space today.

References

Jenson, S. (2003) *The Simplicity Shift,* New York, NY, Cambridge University Press, Cambridge.

Jordan, P. & Jenson, S. (2001) Disorganization and How to Support it. Reflections on the Design of Wireless Information Devices, *Mobile HCI 01.*

Taylor, A. S. (forthcoming) Phone talk, In, Ling, R. & Pedersen, P. (eds) *Mobile Communications: Re-negotiation of the Social Sphere.* Godalming, UK, Springer-Verlag,

Tufte, e. (1983) *The Visual Display of Quantitative Information.* Cheshire, CT, Graphics Press.

Kaseniemi, E. (2001) Mobile Message, Tampere University Press, Tampere, Finland.

Taylor, A. & Harper R. (2003) The Gift of the Gab?: A Design Oriented Sociology of Young People's Use of Mobiles. *Computer Supported Cooperative Work 12(3):* 267-296.

Index

The Kluwer International Series on Computer Supported Cooperative Work

1. G. Fitzpatrick: *The Locales Framework*. Understanding and Designing for Wicked Problems. 2003   ISBN 1-4020-1190-3
2. K. O'Hara, M. Perry, E. Churchill and D. Russell (eds.): *Public and Situated Displays*. Social and Interactional Aspects of Shared Display Technologies. 2003   ISBN 1-4020-1677-8
3. D.V. Frohlich: *Audiophotography*. Bringing photos to life with sounds. 2004   ISBN 1-4020-2209-3
4. R. Harper, L. Palen and A. Taylor (eds.): *The Inside Text*. Social, Cultural and Design Perspectives on SMS. 2005   ISBN 1-4020-3059-2